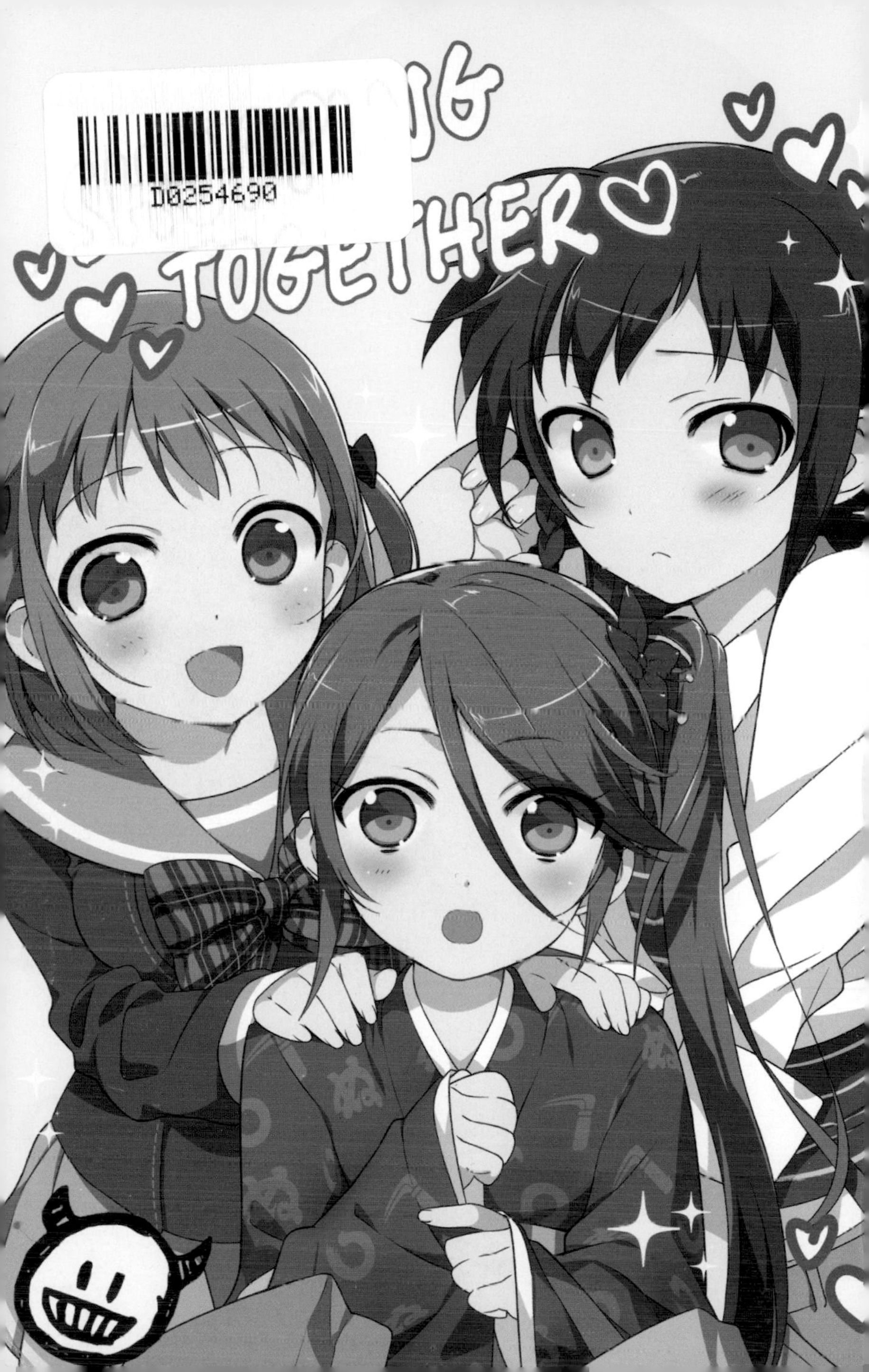
TOGETHER

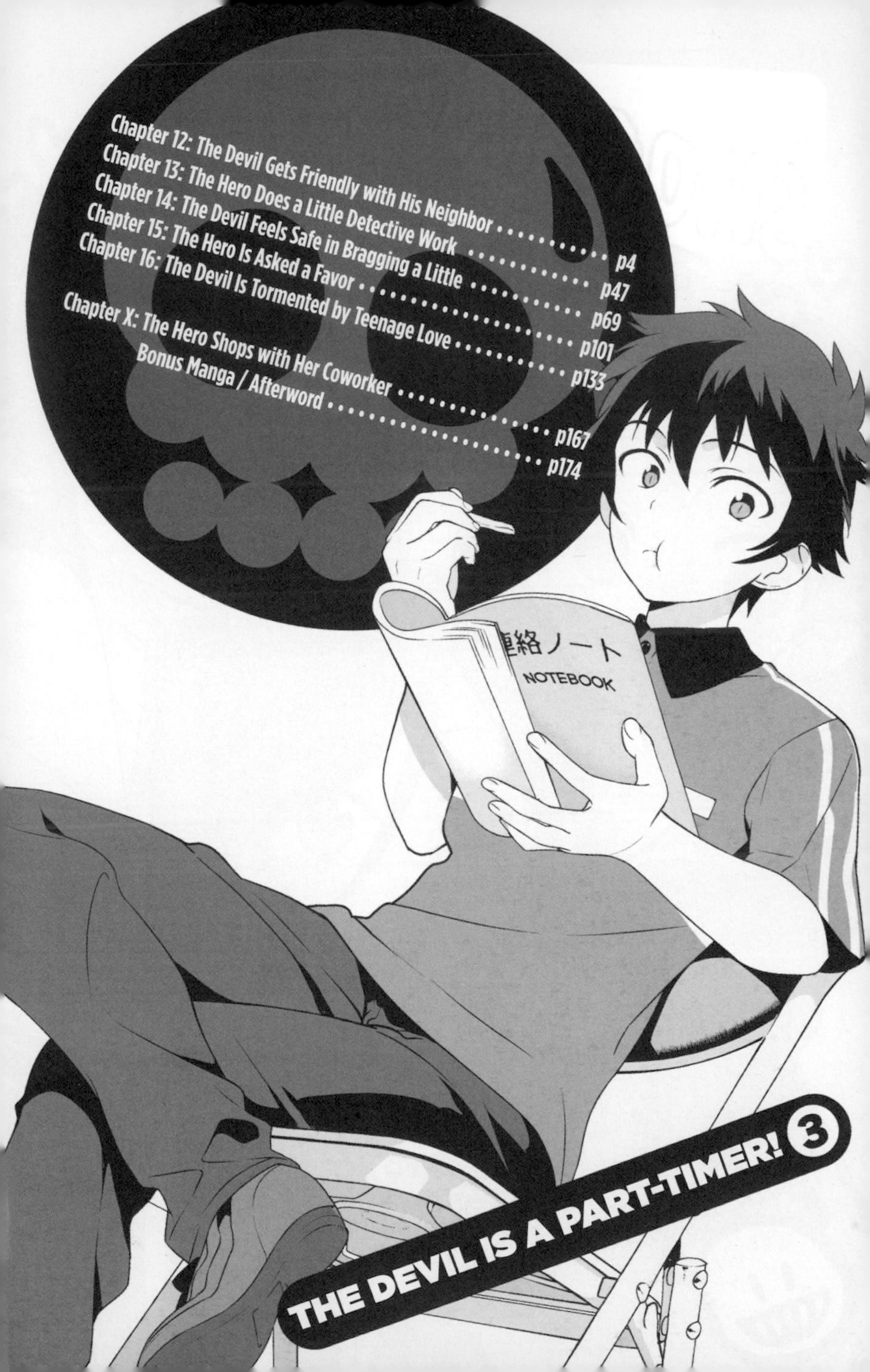

NOTEBOOK
THE DEVIL IS A PART-TIMER! 3

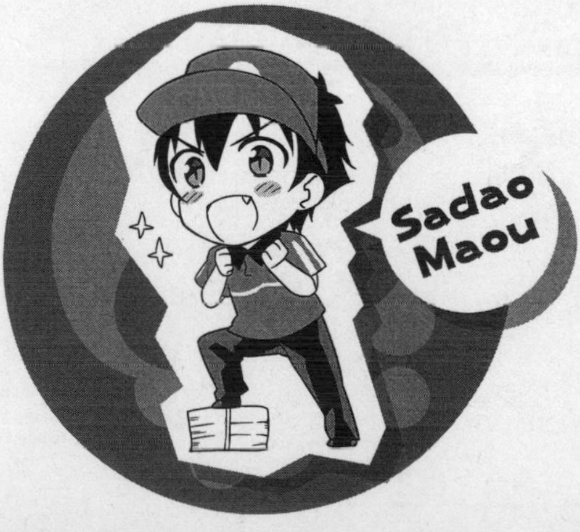
Sadao Maou

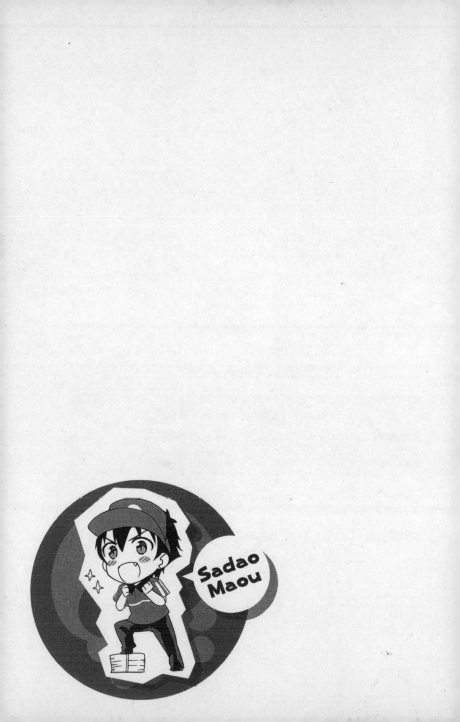

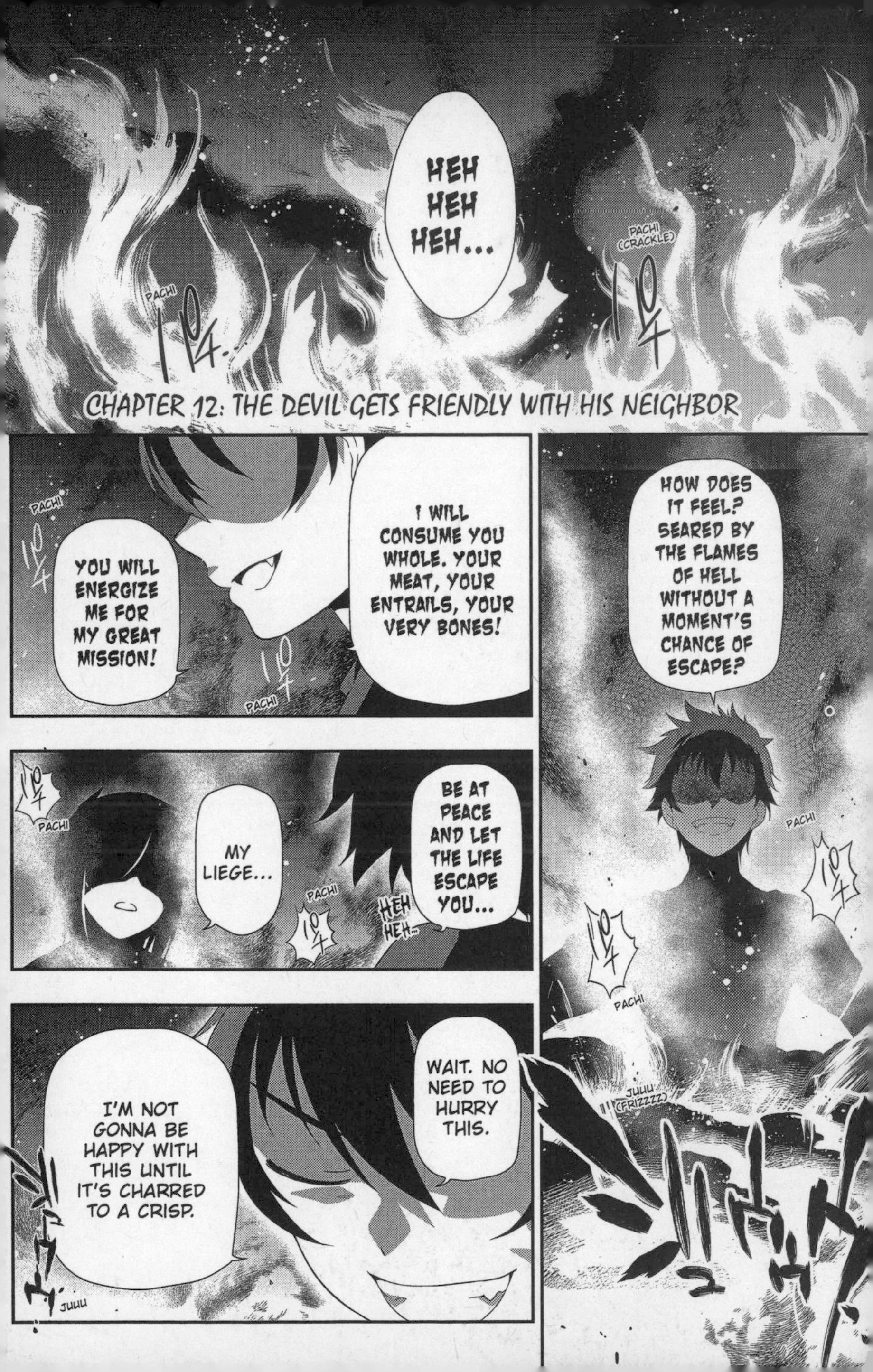
PACHI (CRACKLE)
HEH HEH HEH...
PACHI
CHAPTER 12: THE DEVIL GETS FRIENDLY WITH HIS NEIGHBOR
HOW DOES IT FEEL? SEARED BY THE FLAMES OF HELL WITHOUT A MOMENT'S CHANCE OF ESCAPE?
PACHI
PACHI
JUUU (FRIZZZZ)
I WILL CONSUME YOU WHOLE. YOUR MEAT, YOUR ENTRAILS, YOUR VERY BONES!
PACHI
YOU WILL ENERGIZE ME FOR MY GREAT MISSION!
PACHI
BE AT PEACE AND LET THE LIFE ESCAPE YOU...
HEH HEH..
PACHI
MY LIEGE...
PACHI
WAIT. NO NEED TO HURRY THIS.
I'M NOT GONNA BE HAPPY WITH THIS UNTIL IT'S CHARRED TO A CRISP.
JUUU

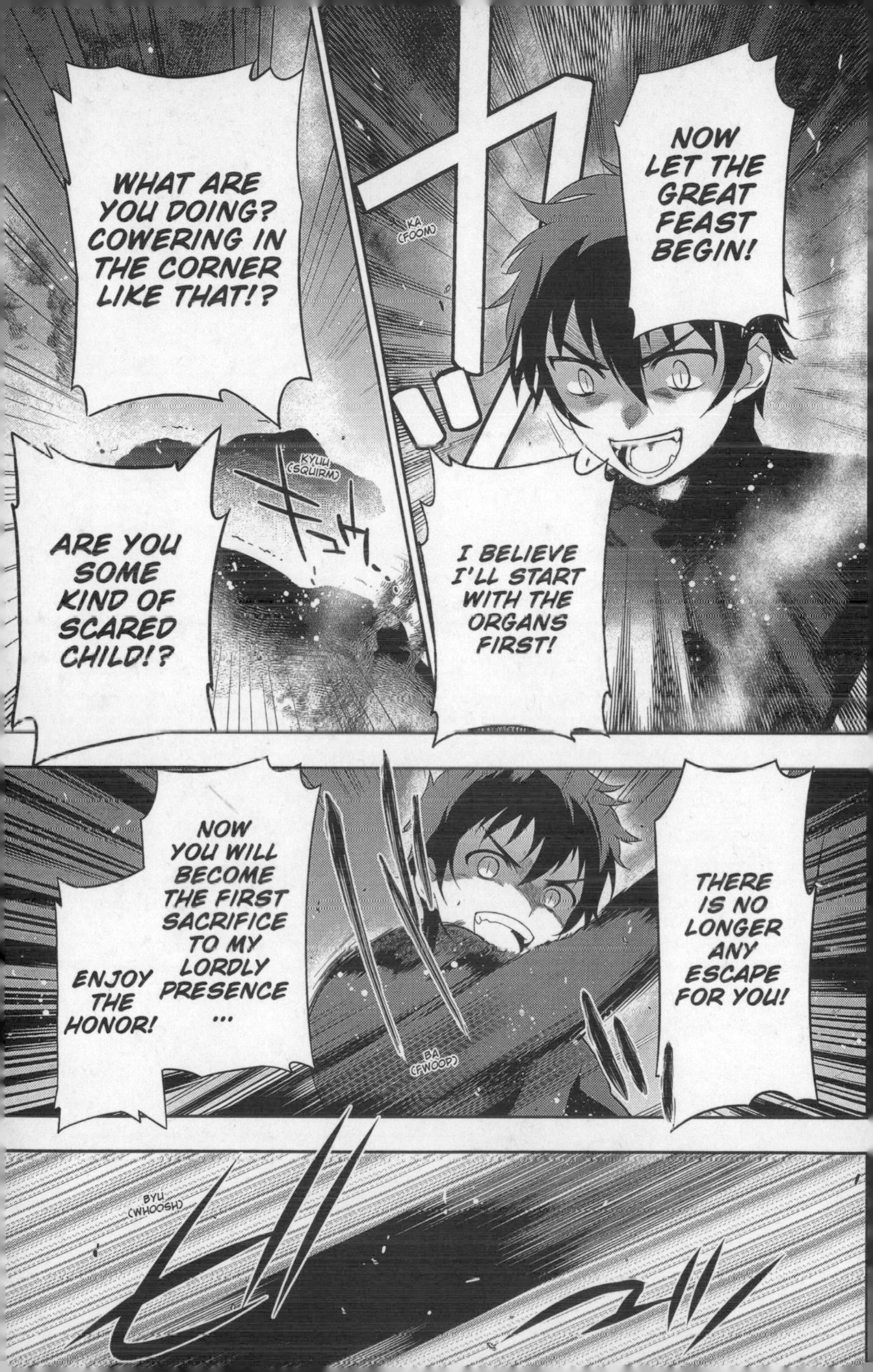
NOW LET THE GREAT FEAST BEGIN!
KA (FOOM)
I BELIEVE I'LL START WITH THE ORGANS FIRST!
WHAT ARE YOU DOING? COWERING IN THE CORNER LIKE THAT!?
KYUU (SQUIRM)
ARE YOU SOME KIND OF SCARED CHILD!?
THERE IS NO LONGER ANY ESCAPE FOR YOU!
NOW YOU WILL BECOME THE FIRST SACRIFICE TO MY LORDLY PRESENCE...
ENJOY THE HONOR!
BA (FWOOP)
BYU (WHOOSH)

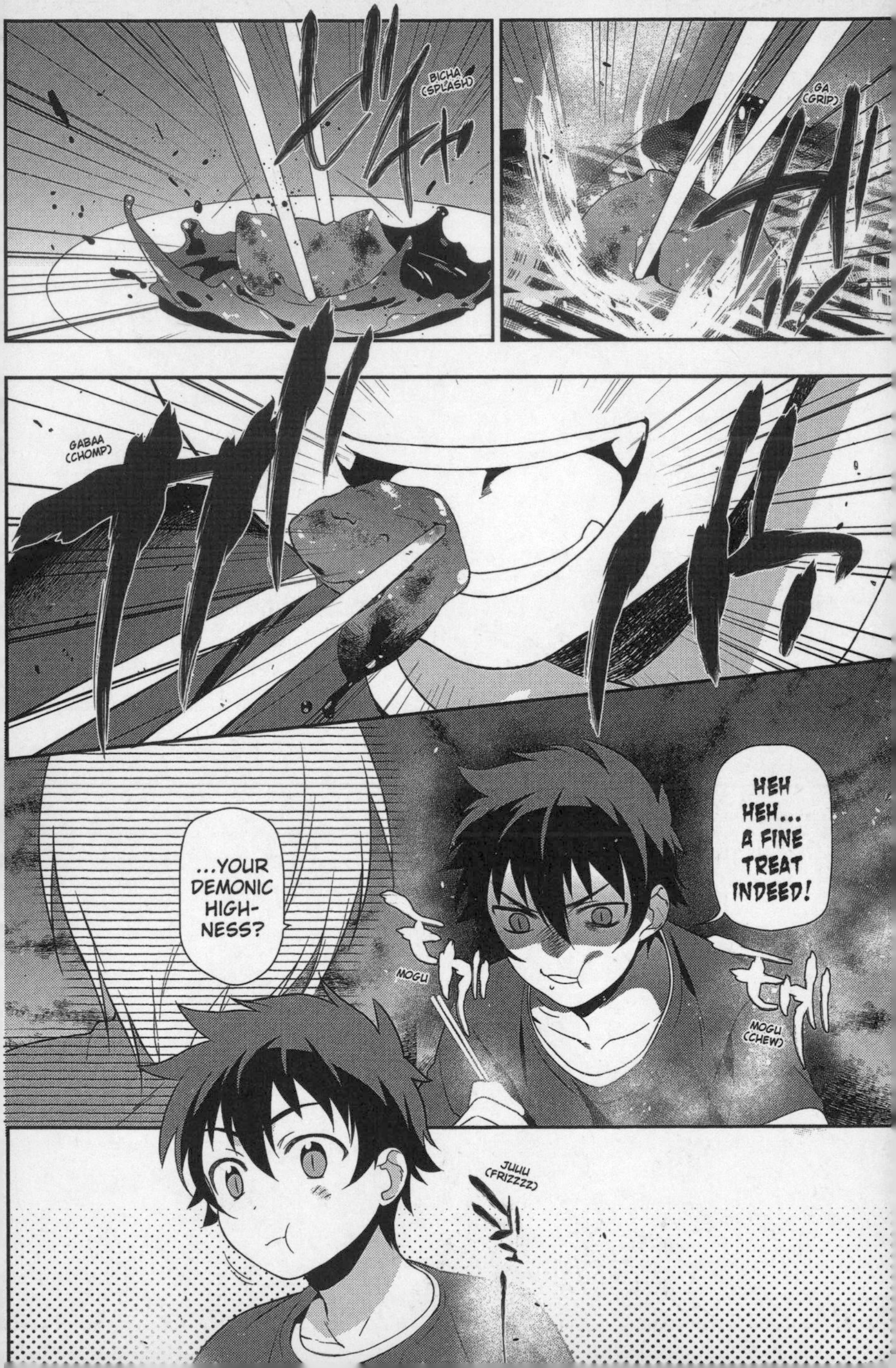
GA
(GRIP)
BICHA
(SPLASH)
GABAA
(CHOMP)
HEH HEH... A FINE TREAT INDEED!
MOGU
(CHEW)
MOGU
...YOUR DEMONIC HIGH-NESS?
JUUU
(FRIZZZZ)

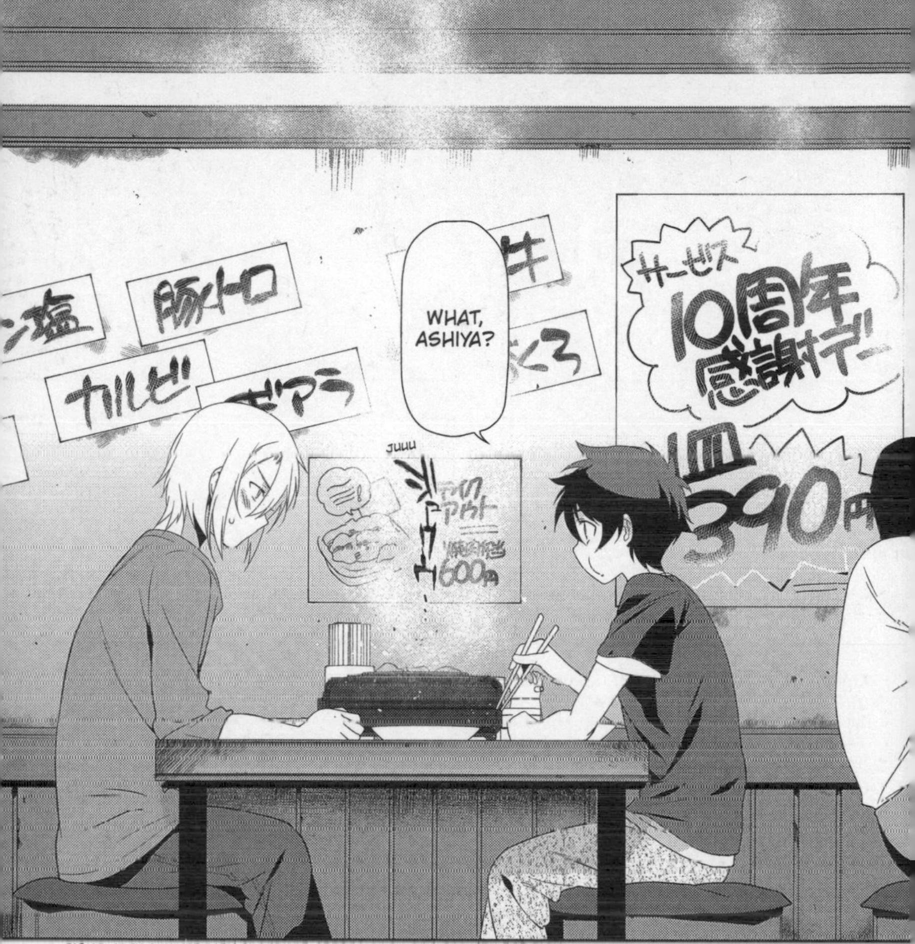

WHAT, ASHIYA?
JUUU
サービス 10周年感謝デー
皿390円
豚トロ
カルビ
600円

SIGNS: 10TH ANNIVERSARY CUSTOMER APPRECIATION DAY, 390 YEN PER DISH, TAKEOUT—YAKINIKU BENTO: 600 YEN, GALBI, TONTORO

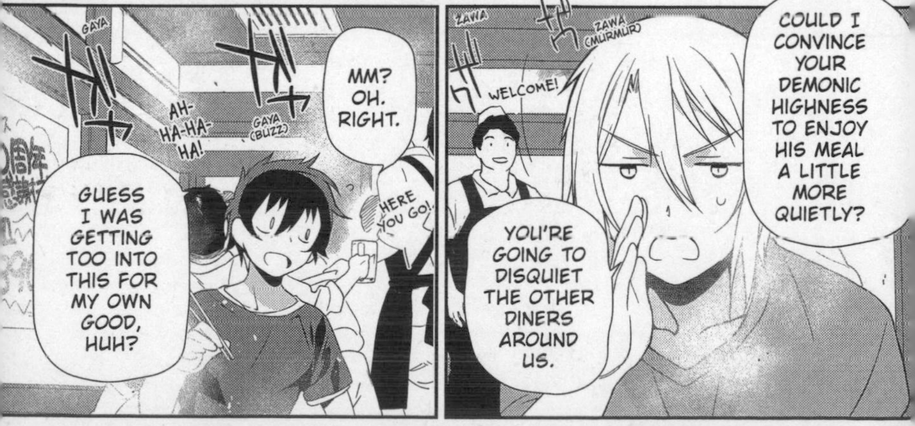

ZAWA
ZAWA (MURMUR)
WELCOME!
COULD I CONVINCE YOUR DEMONIC HIGHNESS TO ENJOY HIS MEAL A LITTLE MORE QUIETLY?
YOU'RE GOING TO DISQUIET THE OTHER DINERS AROUND US.
GAYA
GAYA (BUZZ)
AH-HA-HA-HA!
MM? OH. RIGHT.
HERE YOU GO!
GUESS I WAS GETTING TOO INTO THIS FOR MY OWN GOOD, HUH?

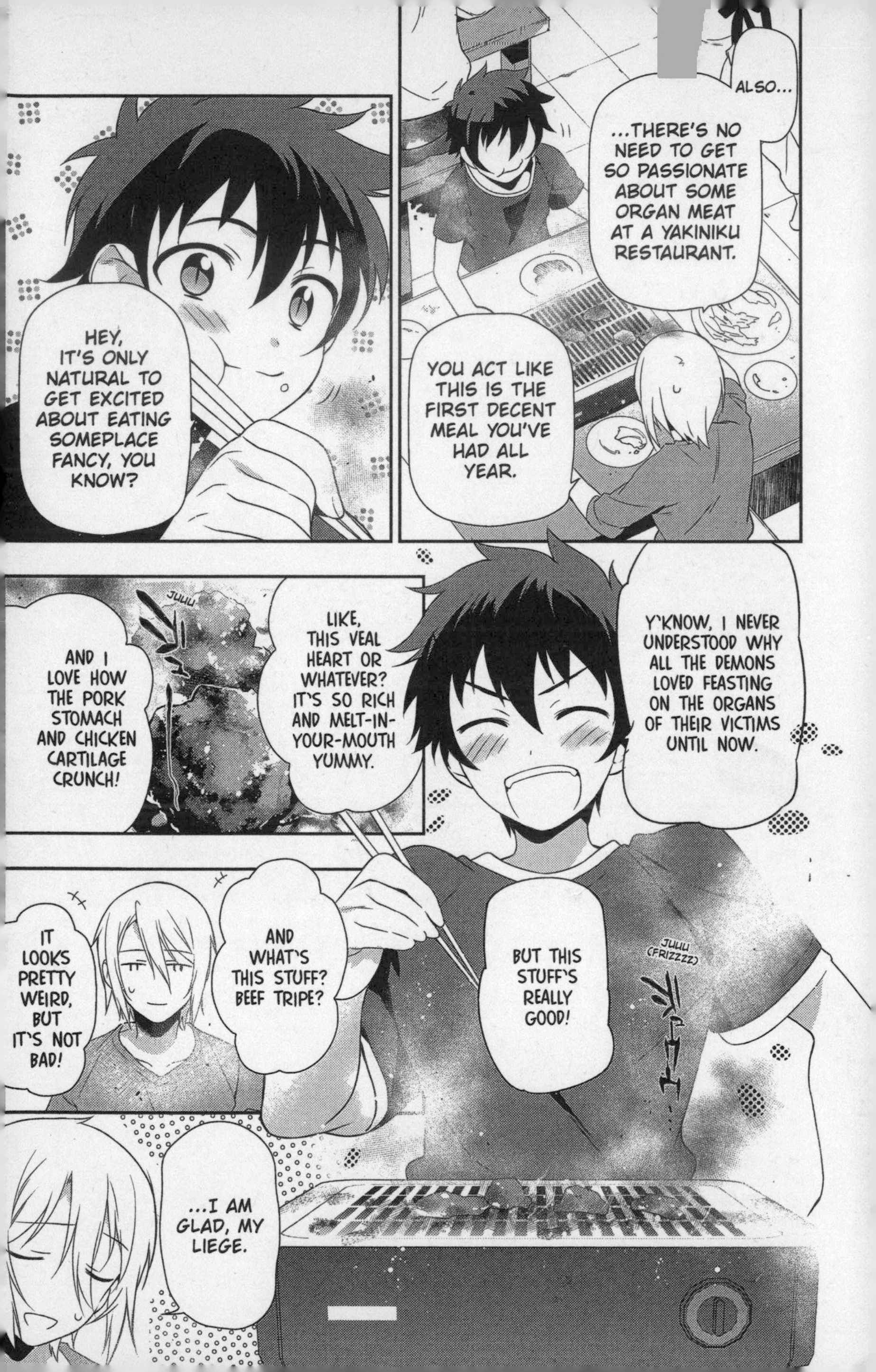
ALSO...
...THERE'S NO NEED TO GET SO PASSIONATE ABOUT SOME ORGAN MEAT AT A YAKINIKU RESTAURANT.
YOU ACT LIKE THIS IS THE FIRST DECENT MEAL YOU'VE HAD ALL YEAR.
HEY, IT'S ONLY NATURAL TO GET EXCITED ABOUT EATING SOMEPLACE FANCY, YOU KNOW?
Y'KNOW, I NEVER UNDERSTOOD WHY ALL THE DEMONS LOVED FEASTING ON THE ORGANS OF THEIR VICTIMS UNTIL NOW.
JUUU
LIKE, THIS VEAL HEART OR WHATEVER? IT'S SO RICH AND MELT-IN-YOUR-MOUTH YUMMY.
AND I LOVE HOW THE PORK STOMACH AND CHICKEN CARTILAGE CRUNCH!
JUUU (FRIZZZZ)
BUT THIS STUFF'S REALLY GOOD!
AND WHAT'S THIS STUFF? BEEF TRIPE?
IT LOOKS PRETTY WEIRD, BUT IT'S NOT BAD!
...I AM GLAD, MY LIEGE.

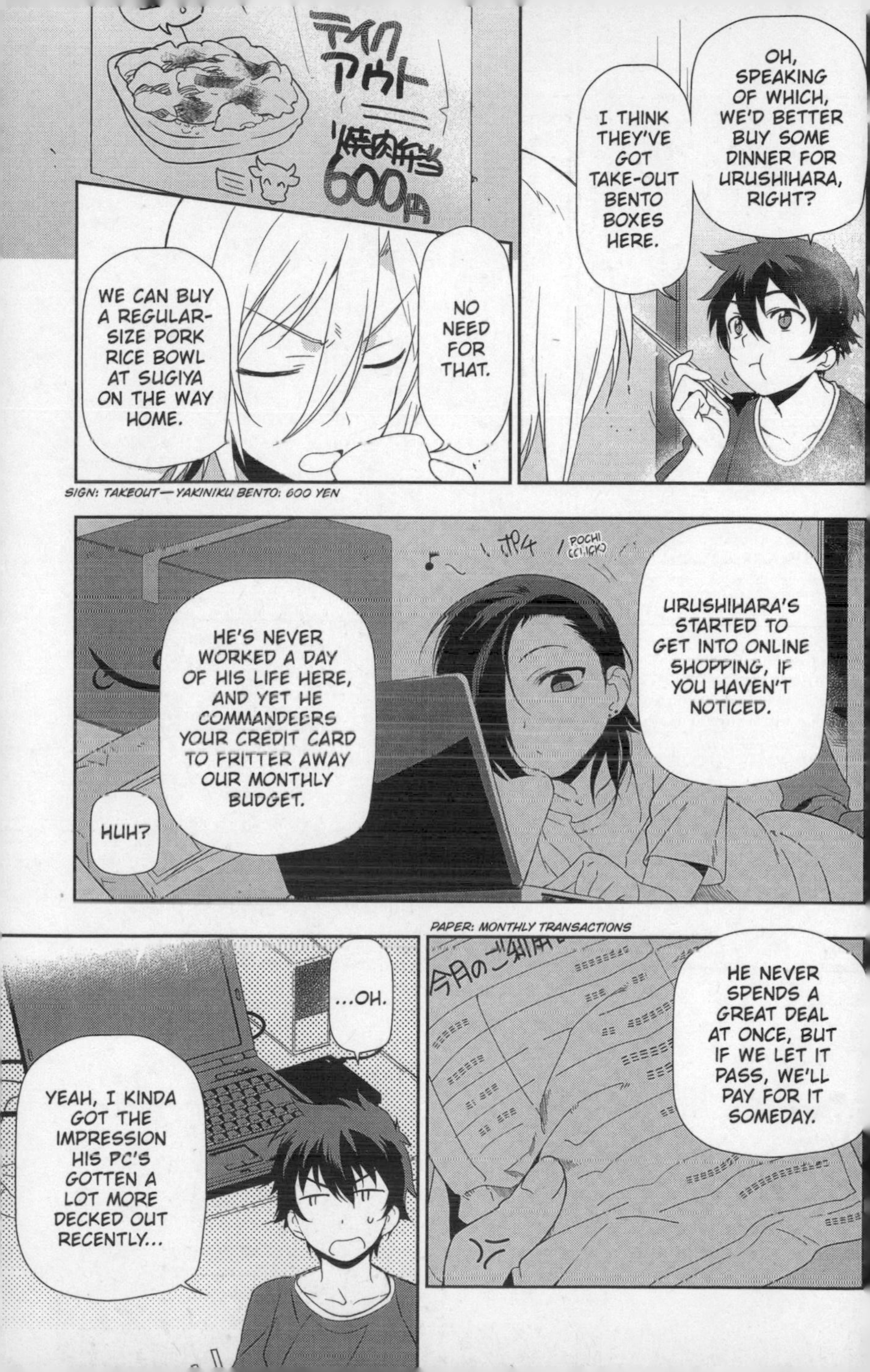

OH, SPEAKING OF WHICH, WE'D BETTER BUY SOME DINNER FOR URUSHIHARA, RIGHT?
I THINK THEY'VE GOT TAKE-OUT BENTO BOXES HERE.
テイクアウト
焼肉弁当 600円
NO NEED FOR THAT.
WE CAN BUY A REGULAR-SIZE PORK RICE BOWL AT SUGIYA ON THE WAY HOME.
SIGN: TAKEOUT—YAKINIKU BENTO: 600 YEN
POCHI (CLICK)
URUSHIHARA'S STARTED TO GET INTO ONLINE SHOPPING, IF YOU HAVEN'T NOTICED.
HE'S NEVER WORKED A DAY OF HIS LIFE HERE, AND YET HE COMMANDEERS YOUR CREDIT CARD TO FRITTER AWAY OUR MONTHLY BUDGET.
HUH?
PAPER: MONTHLY TRANSACTIONS
HE NEVER SPENDS A GREAT DEAL AT ONCE, BUT IF WE LET IT PASS, WE'LL PAY FOR IT SOMEDAY.
...OH.
YEAH, I KINDA GOT THE IMPRESSION HIS PC'S GOTTEN A LOT MORE DECKED OUT RECENTLY...

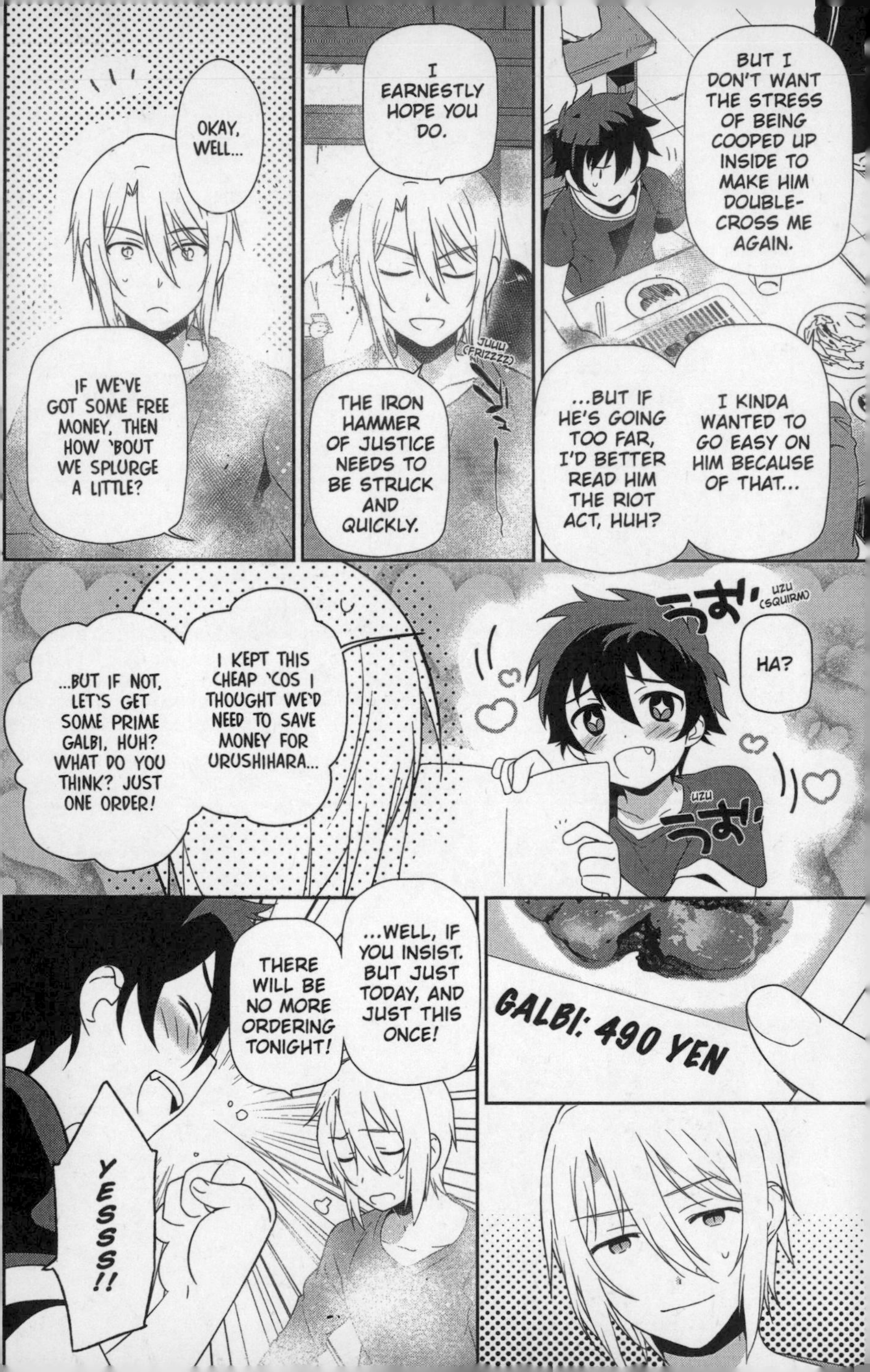
BUT I DON'T WANT THE STRESS OF BEING COOPED UP INSIDE TO MAKE HIM DOUBLE-CROSS ME AGAIN.
I KINDA WANTED TO GO EASY ON HIM BECAUSE OF THAT...
...BUT IF HE'S GOING TOO FAR, I'D BETTER READ HIM THE RIOT ACT, HUH?
I EARNESTLY HOPE YOU DO.
JUUU (FRIZZZZ)
THE IRON HAMMER OF JUSTICE NEEDS TO BE STRUCK AND QUICKLY.
OKAY, WELL...
IF WE'VE GOT SOME FREE MONEY, THEN HOW 'BOUT WE SPLURGE A LITTLE?
UZU (SQUIRM)
HA?
UZU
I KEPT THIS CHEAP 'COS I THOUGHT WE'D NEED TO SAVE MONEY FOR URUSHIHARA...
...BUT IF NOT, LET'S GET SOME PRIME GALBI, HUH? WHAT DO YOU THINK? JUST ONE ORDER!
GALBI: 490 YEN
...WELL, IF YOU INSIST. BUT JUST TODAY, AND JUST THIS ONCE!
THERE WILL BE NO MORE ORDERING TONIGHT!
YESSS!!

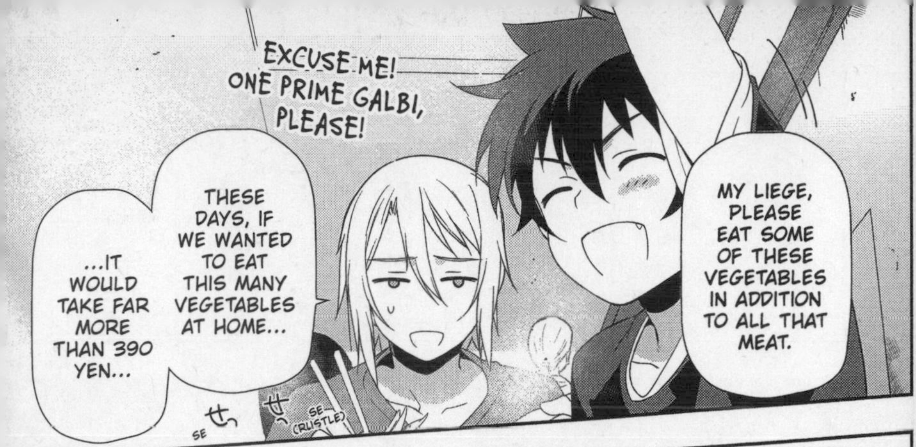
EXCUSE ME! ONE PRIME GALBI, PLEASE!
MY LIEGE, PLEASE EAT SOME OF THESE VEGETABLES IN ADDITION TO ALL THAT MEAT.
THESE DAYS, IF WE WANTED TO EAT THIS MANY VEGETABLES AT HOME...
...IT WOULD TAKE FAR MORE THAN 390 YEN...
SE (RUSTLE)
SE
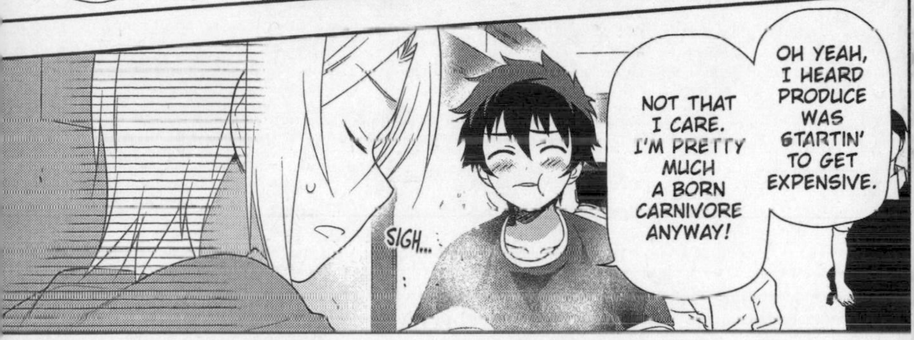
OH YEAH, I HEARD PRODUCE WAS STARTIN' TO GET EXPENSIVE.
NOT THAT I CARE. I'M PRETTY MUCH A BORN CARNIVORE ANYWAY!
SIGH...
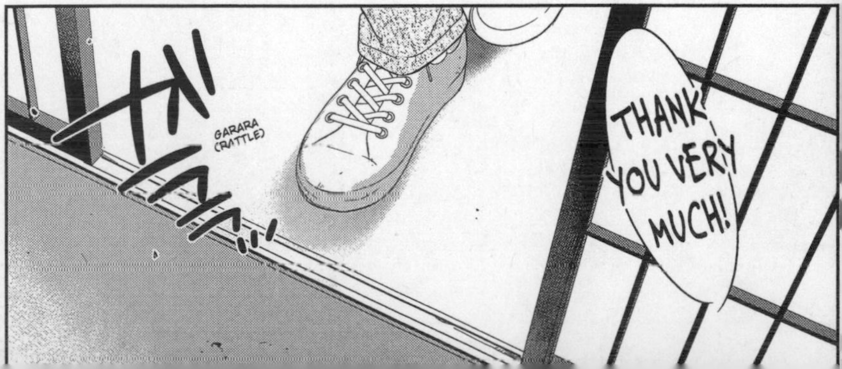
THANK YOU VERY MUCH!
GARARA (RATTLE)

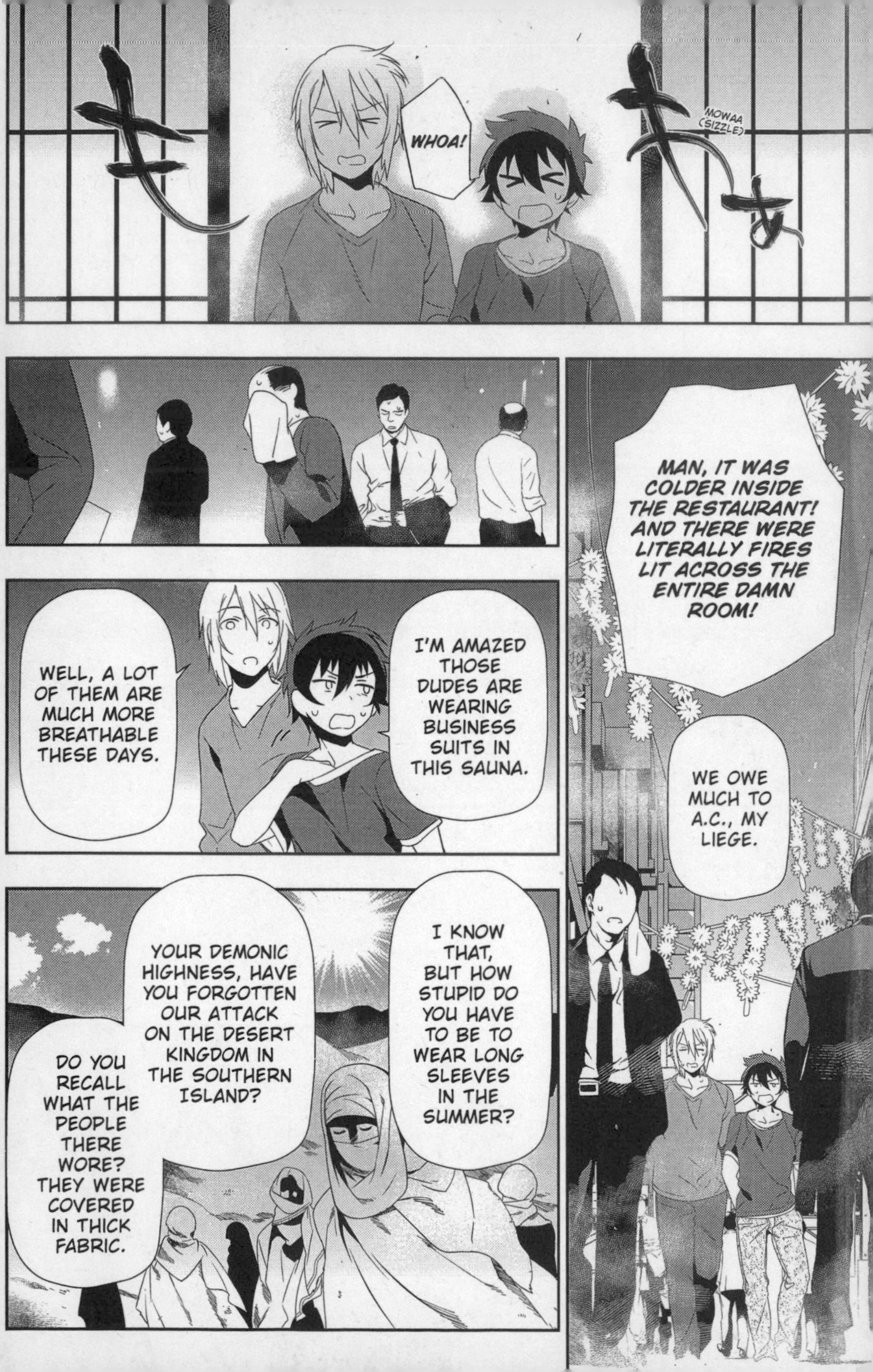
MOWAA (SIZZLE)
WHOA!
MAN, IT WAS COLDER INSIDE THE RESTAURANT! AND THERE WERE LITERALLY FIRES LIT ACROSS THE ENTIRE DAMN ROOM!
WE OWE MUCH TO A.C., MY LIEGE.
I'M AMAZED THOSE DUDES ARE WEARING BUSINESS SUITS IN THIS SAUNA.
WELL, A LOT OF THEM ARE MUCH MORE BREATHABLE THESE DAYS.
I KNOW THAT, BUT HOW STUPID DO YOU HAVE TO BE TO WEAR LONG SLEEVES IN THE SUMMER?
YOUR DEMONIC HIGHNESS, HAVE YOU FORGOTTEN OUR ATTACK ON THE DESERT KINGDOM IN THE SOUTHERN ISLAND?
DO YOU RECALL WHAT THE PEOPLE THERE WORE? THEY WERE COVERED IN THICK FABRIC.

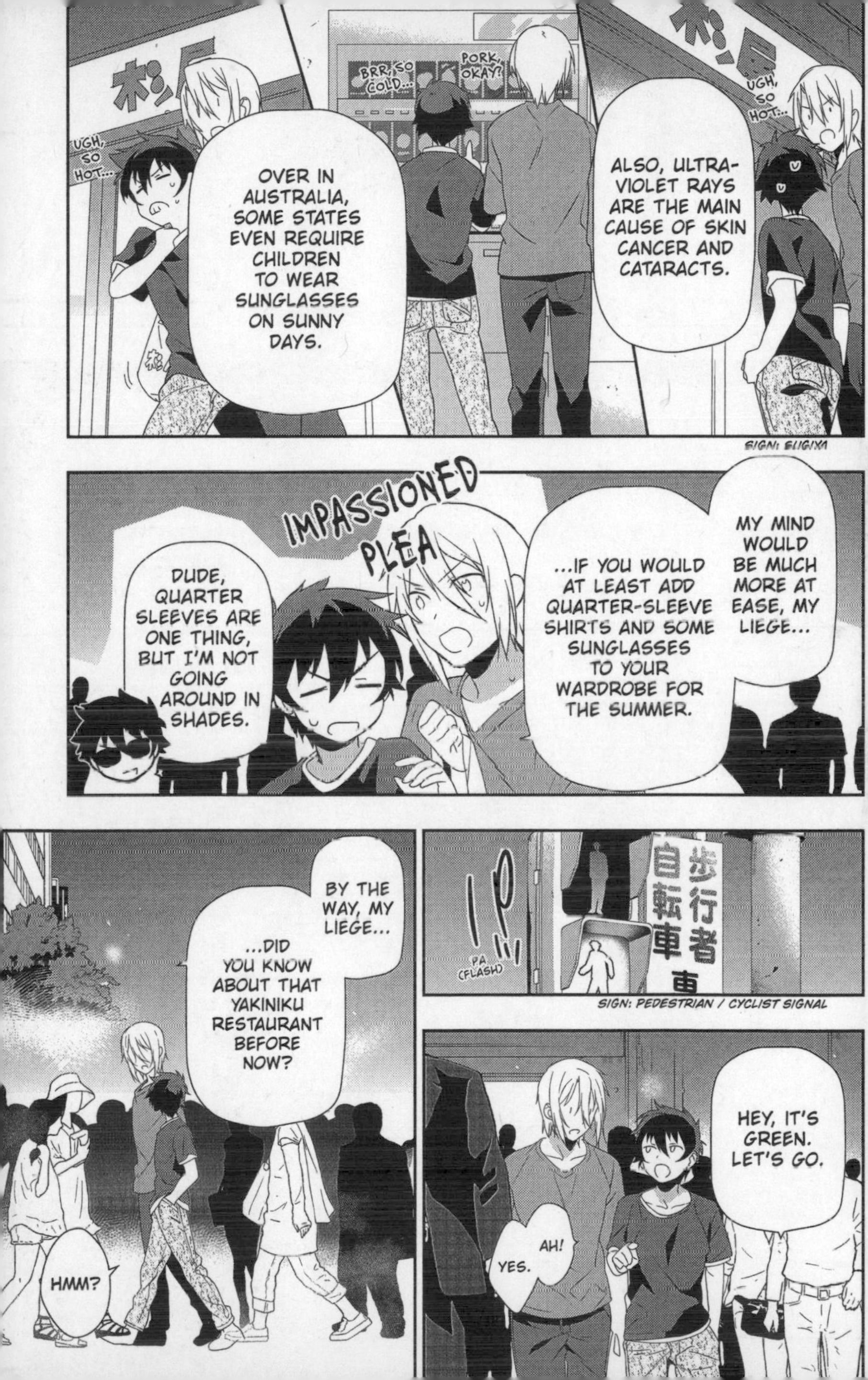
UGH, SO HOT...
OVER IN AUSTRALIA, SOME STATES EVEN REQUIRE CHILDREN TO WEAR SUNGLASSES ON SUNNY DAYS.
BRR, SO COLD...
PORK, OKAY?
ALSO, ULTRA-VIOLET RAYS ARE THE MAIN CAUSE OF SKIN CANCER AND CATARACTS.
UGH, SO HOT...
SIGN: ELIGIXA
MY MIND WOULD BE MUCH MORE AT EASE, MY LIEGE...
...IF YOU WOULD AT LEAST ADD QUARTER-SLEEVE SHIRTS AND SOME SUNGLASSES TO YOUR WARDROBE FOR THE SUMMER.
IMPASSIONED PLEA
DUDE, QUARTER SLEEVES ARE ONE THING, BUT I'M NOT GOING AROUND IN SHADES.
BY THE WAY, MY LIEGE...
...DID YOU KNOW ABOUT THAT YAKINIKU RESTAURANT BEFORE NOW?
HMM?
PA (FLASH)
SIGN: PEDESTRIAN / CYCLIST SIGNAL
HEY, IT'S GREEN. LET'S GO.
AH! YES.

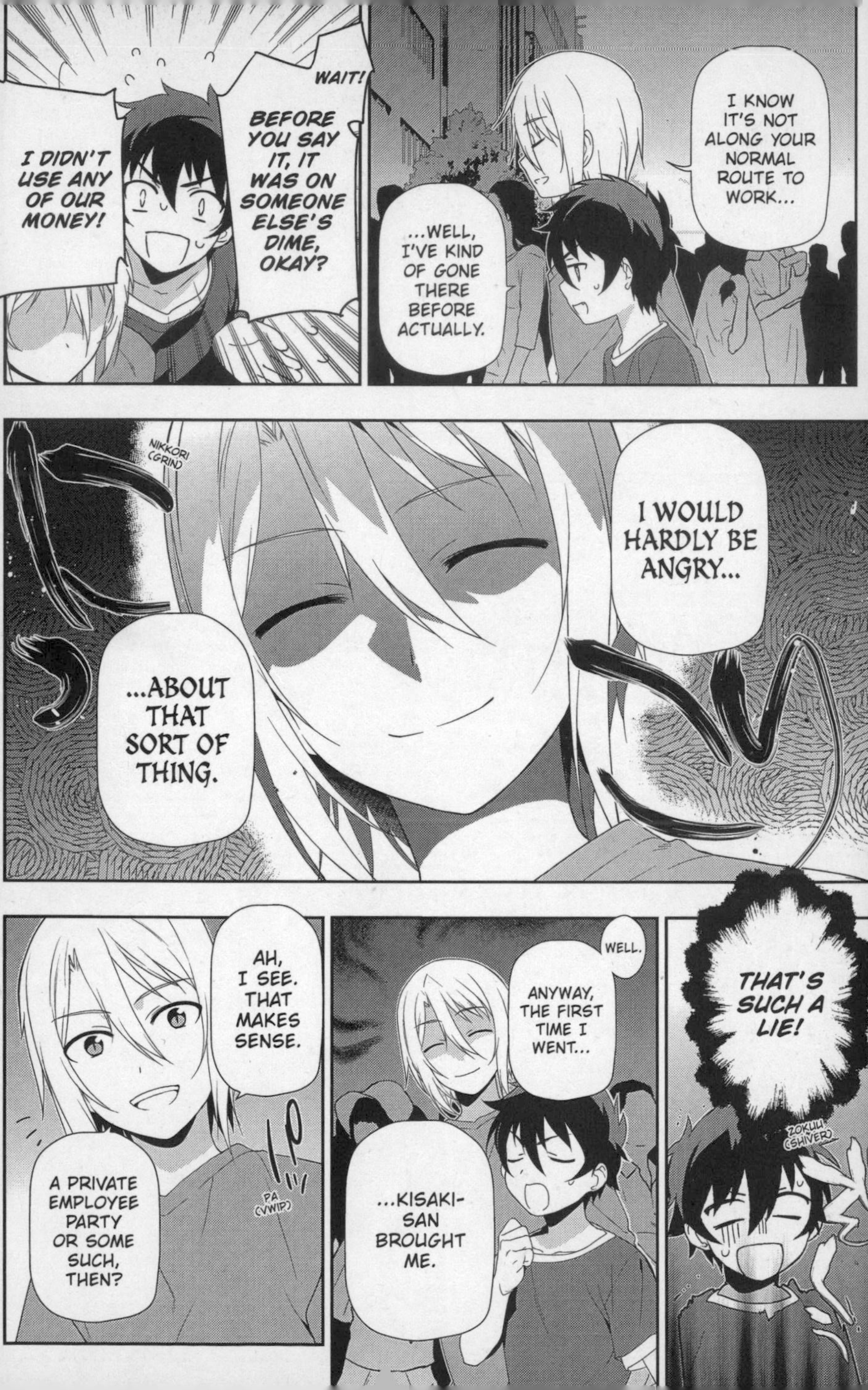
I KNOW IT'S NOT ALONG YOUR NORMAL ROUTE TO WORK...
...WELL, I'VE KIND OF GONE THERE BEFORE ACTUALLY.
WAIT!
BEFORE YOU SAY IT, IT WAS ON SOMEONE ELSE'S DIME, OKAY?
I DIDN'T USE ANY OF OUR MONEY!
I WOULD HARDLY BE ANGRY...
NIKKORI (GRIN)
...ABOUT THAT SORT OF THING.
THAT'S SUCH A LIE!
ZOKUU (SHIVER)
WELL.
ANYWAY, THE FIRST TIME I WENT...
...KISAKI-SAN BROUGHT ME.
AH, I SEE. THAT MAKES SENSE.
PA (VWIP)
A PRIVATE EMPLOYEE PARTY OR SOME SUCH, THEN?

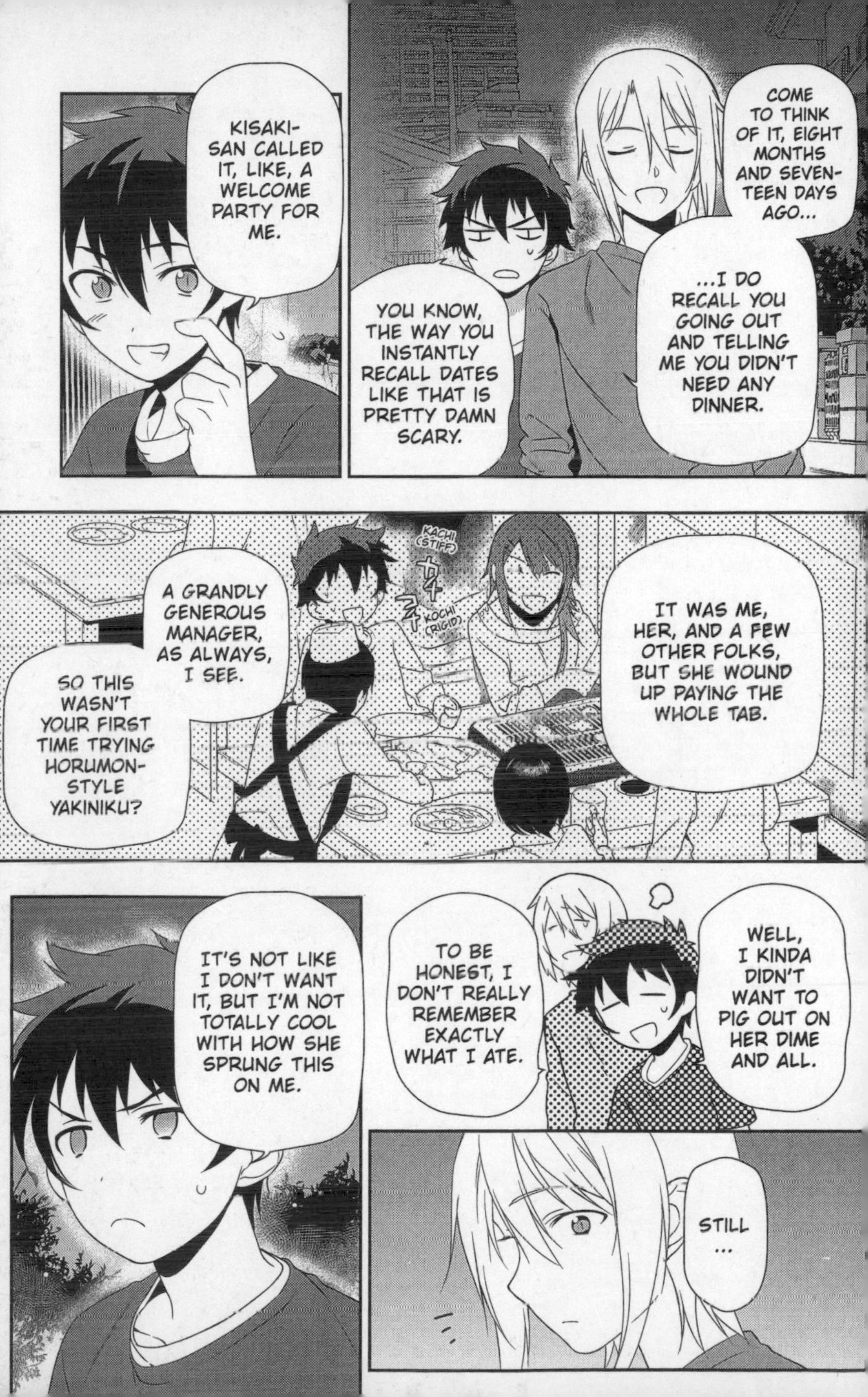
COME TO THINK OF IT, EIGHT MONTHS AND SEVENTEEN DAYS AGO...
...I DO RECALL YOU GOING OUT AND TELLING ME YOU DIDN'T NEED ANY DINNER.
YOU KNOW, THE WAY YOU INSTANTLY RECALL DATES LIKE THAT IS PRETTY DAMN SCARY.
KISAKI-SAN CALLED IT, LIKE, A WELCOME PARTY FOR ME.
IT WAS ME, HER, AND A FEW OTHER FOLKS, BUT SHE WOUND UP PAYING THE WHOLE TAB.
KACHI (STIFF)
KOCHI (RIGID)
A GRANDLY GENEROUS MANAGER, AS ALWAYS, I SEE.
SO THIS WASN'T YOUR FIRST TIME TRYING HORUMON-STYLE YAKINIKU?
WELL, I KINDA DIDN'T WANT TO PIG OUT ON HER DIME AND ALL.
TO BE HONEST, I DON'T REALLY REMEMBER EXACTLY WHAT I ATE.
STILL ...
IT'S NOT LIKE I DON'T WANT IT, BUT I'M NOT TOTALLY COOL WITH HOW SHE SPRUNG THIS ON ME.

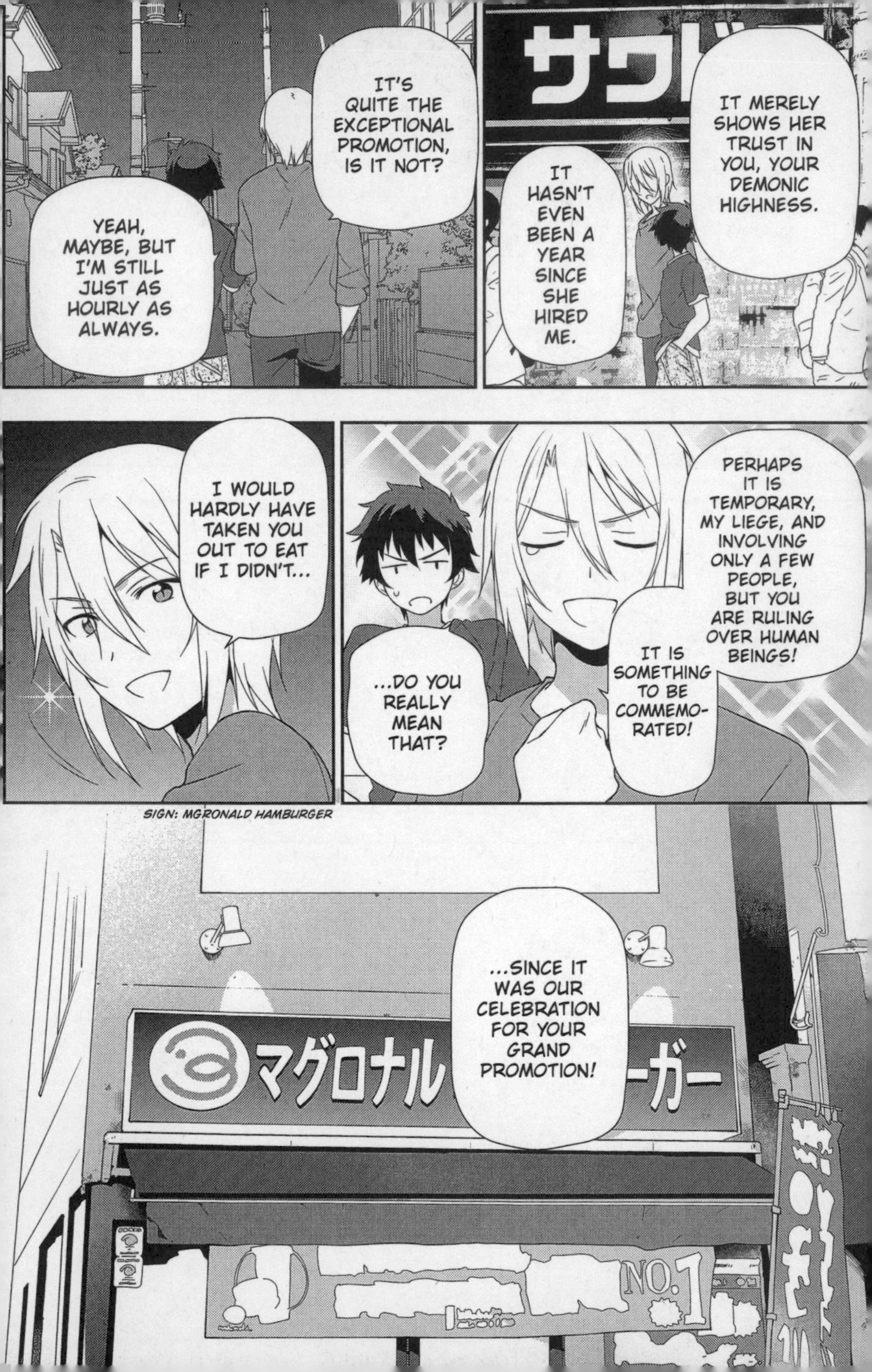
IT MERELY SHOWS HER TRUST IN YOU, YOUR DEMONIC HIGHNESS.
IT HASN'T EVEN BEEN A YEAR SINCE SHE HIRED ME.
IT'S QUITE THE EXCEPTIONAL PROMOTION, IS IT NOT?
YEAH, MAYBE, BUT I'M STILL JUST AS HOURLY AS ALWAYS.
PERHAPS IT IS TEMPORARY, MY LIEGE, AND INVOLVING ONLY A FEW PEOPLE, BUT YOU ARE RULING OVER HUMAN BEINGS!
IT IS SOMETHING TO BE COMMEMORATED!
...DO YOU REALLY MEAN THAT?
I WOULD HARDLY HAVE TAKEN YOU OUT TO EAT IF I DIDN'T...
SIGN: MGRONALD HAMBURGER
マグロナル
ーガー
...SINCE IT WAS OUR CELEBRATION FOR YOUR GRAND PROMOTION!
NO.1

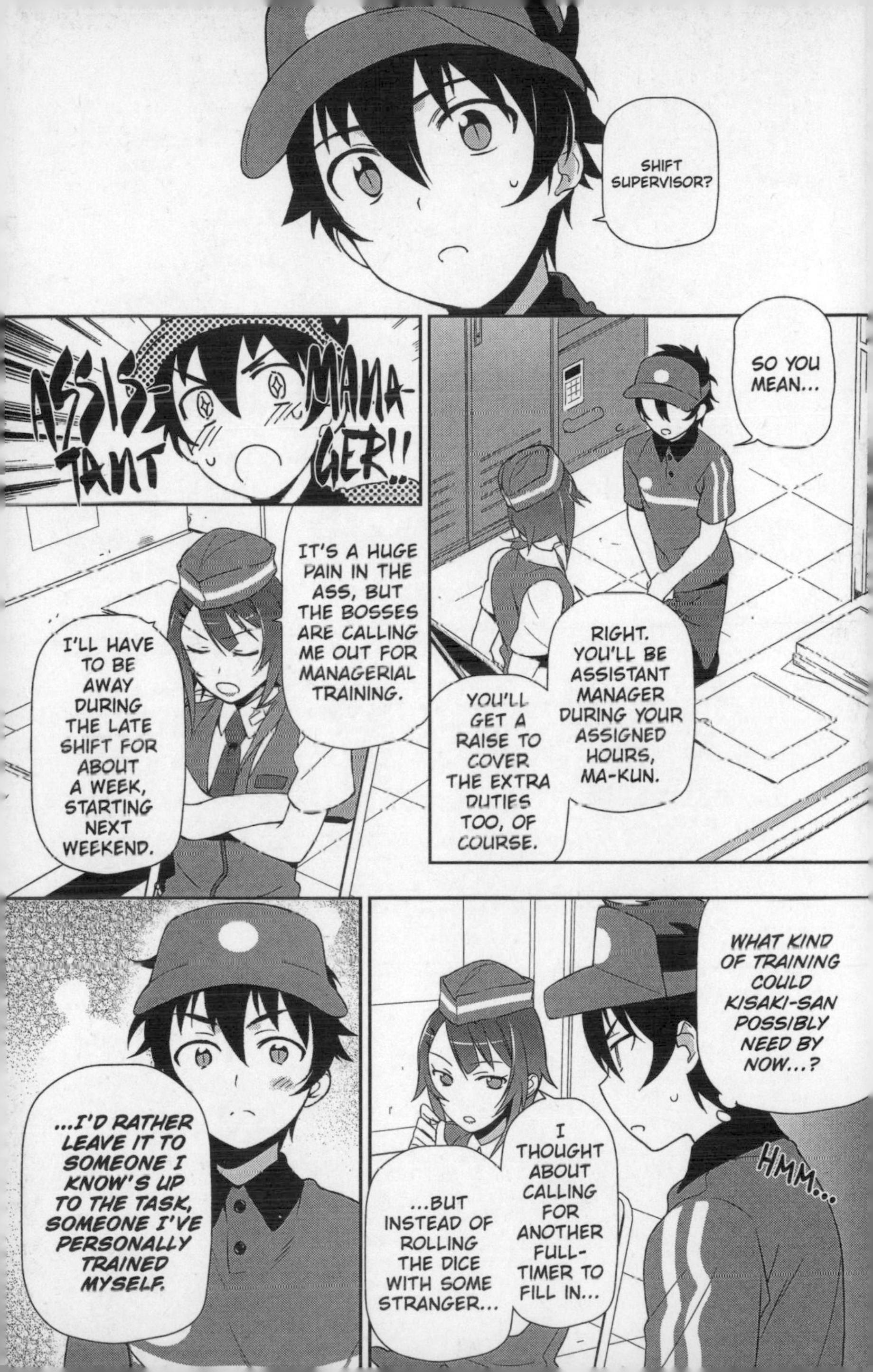
SHIFT SUPERVISOR?
SO YOU MEAN...
RIGHT. YOU'LL BE ASSISTANT MANAGER DURING YOUR ASSIGNED HOURS, MA-KUN.
YOU'LL GET A RAISE TO COVER THE EXTRA DUTIES TOO, OF COURSE.
ASSIS-TANT MANA-GER!!
IT'S A HUGE PAIN IN THE ASS, BUT THE BOSSES ARE CALLING ME OUT FOR MANAGERIAL TRAINING.
I'LL HAVE TO BE AWAY DURING THE LATE SHIFT FOR ABOUT A WEEK, STARTING NEXT WEEKEND.
WHAT KIND OF TRAINING COULD KISAKI-SAN POSSIBLY NEED BY NOW...?
HMM...
I THOUGHT ABOUT CALLING FOR ANOTHER FULL-TIMER TO FILL IN...
...BUT INSTEAD OF ROLLING THE DICE WITH SOME STRANGER...
...I'D RATHER LEAVE IT TO SOMEONE I KNOW'S UP TO THE TASK, SOMEONE I'VE PERSONALLY TRAINED MYSELF.

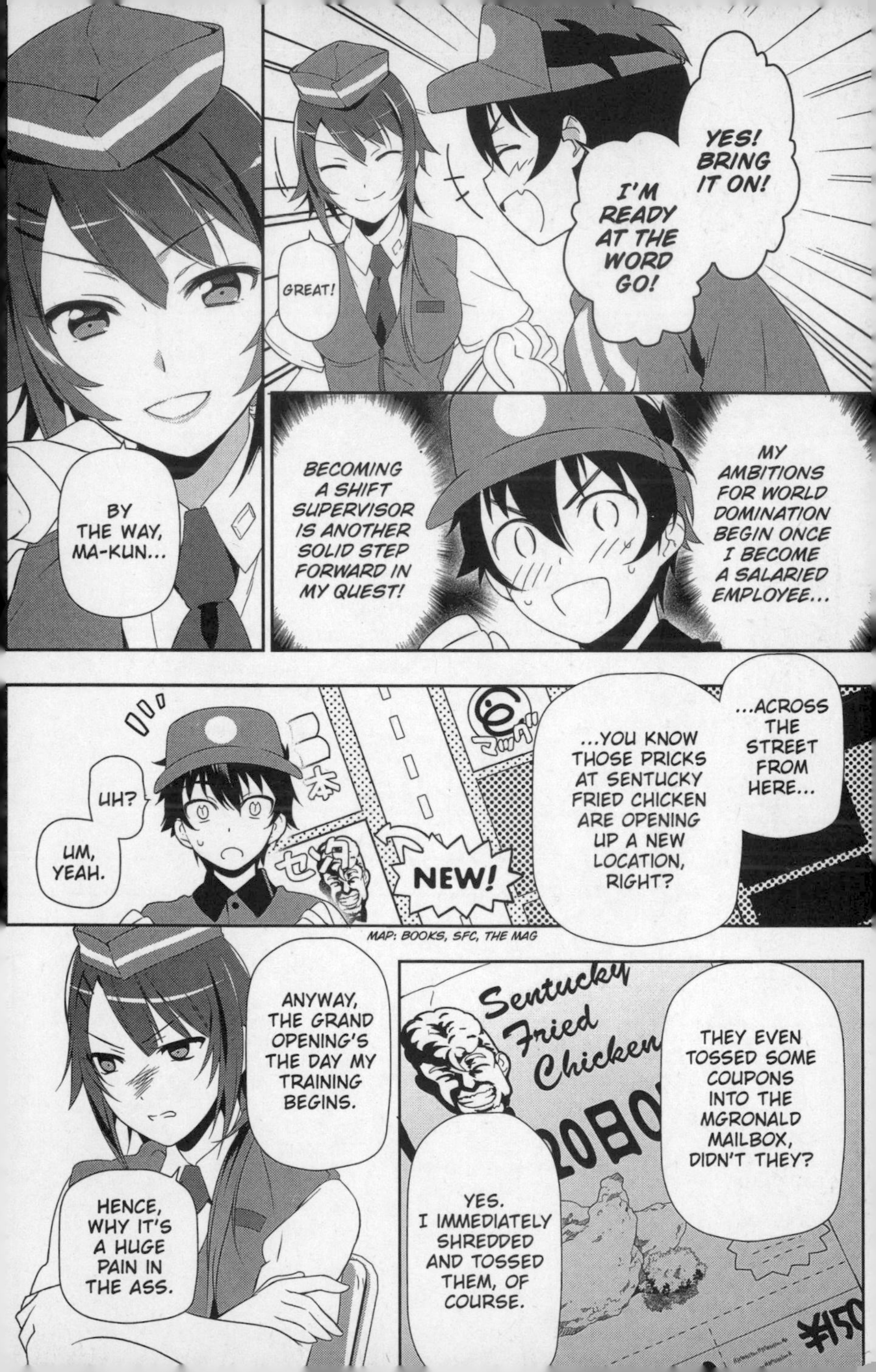
YES! BRING IT ON!
I'M READY AT THE WORD GO!
GREAT!
MY AMBITIONS FOR WORLD DOMINATION BEGIN ONCE I BECOME A SALARIED EMPLOYEE...
BECOMING A SHIFT SUPERVISOR IS ANOTHER SOLID STEP FORWARD IN MY QUEST!
BY THE WAY, MA-KUN...
...ACROSS THE STREET FROM HERE...
...YOU KNOW THOSE PRICKS AT SENTUCKY FRIED CHICKEN ARE OPENING UP A NEW LOCATION, RIGHT?
NEW!
UH?
UM, YEAH.
MAP: BOOKS, SFC, THE MAG
Sentucky Fried Chicken
THEY EVEN TOSSED SOME COUPONS INTO THE MGRONALD MAILBOX, DIDN'T THEY?
YES. I IMMEDIATELY SHREDDED AND TOSSED THEM, OF COURSE.
¥150
ANYWAY, THE GRAND OPENING'S THE DAY MY TRAINING BEGINS.
HENCE, WHY IT'S A HUGE PAIN IN THE ASS.

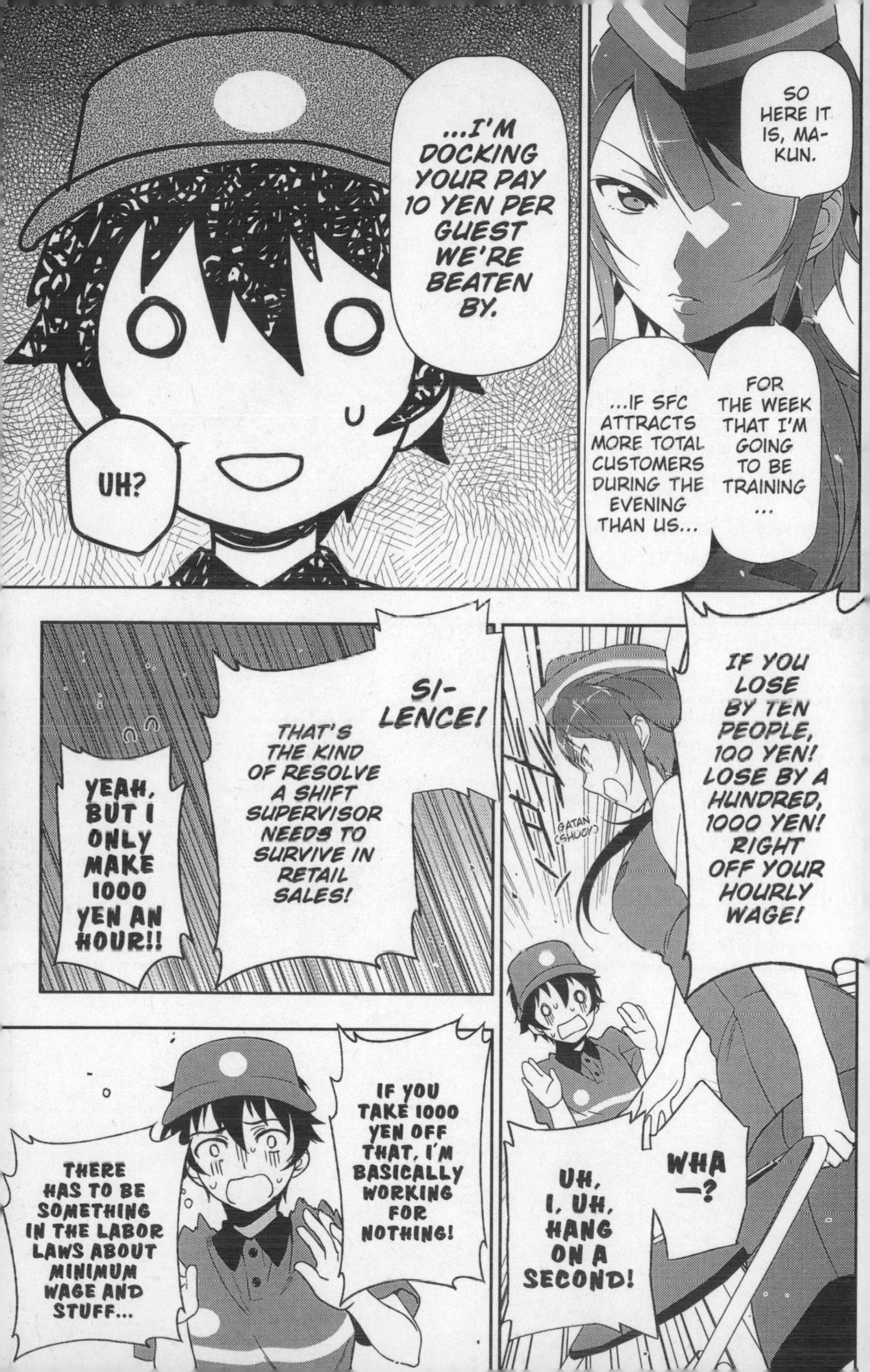
SO HERE IT IS, MA-KUN.
FOR THE WEEK THAT I'M GOING TO BE TRAINING...
...IF SFC ATTRACTS MORE TOTAL CUSTOMERS DURING THE EVENING THAN US...
...I'M DOCKING YOUR PAY 10 YEN PER GUEST WE'RE BEATEN BY.
UH?
IF YOU LOSE BY TEN PEOPLE, 100 YEN! LOSE BY A HUNDRED, 1000 YEN! RIGHT OFF YOUR HOURLY WAGE!
GATAN (SHUCK)
WHA—?
UH, I, UH, HANG ON A SECOND!
SI-LENCE!
THAT'S THE KIND OF RESOLVE A SHIFT SUPERVISOR NEEDS TO SURVIVE IN RETAIL SALES!
YEAH, BUT I ONLY MAKE 1000 YEN AN HOUR!!
IF YOU TAKE 1000 YEN OFF THAT, I'M BASICALLY WORKING FOR NOTHING!
THERE HAS TO BE SOMETHING IN THE LABOR LAWS ABOUT MINIMUM WAGE AND STUFF...

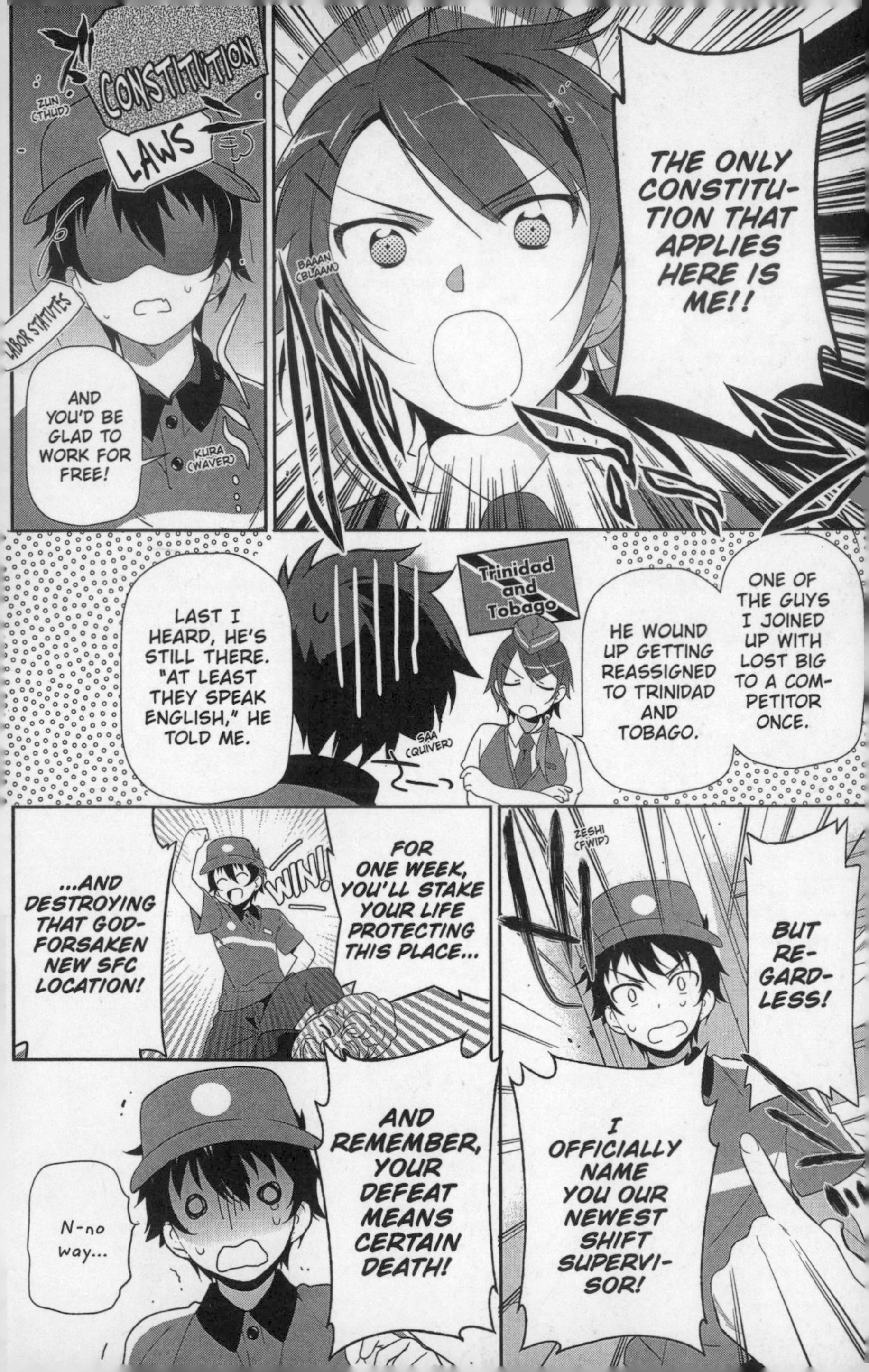
BAAAN (BLAAM)
THE ONLY CONSTITUTION THAT APPLIES HERE IS ME!!
ZUN (THUD)
CONSTITUTION
LAWS
LABOR STATUTES
AND YOU'D BE GLAD TO WORK FOR FREE!
KURA (WAVER)
ONE OF THE GUYS I JOINED UP WITH LOST BIG TO A COMPETITOR ONCE.
HE WOUND UP GETTING REASSIGNED TO TRINIDAD AND TOBAGO.
Trinidad and Tobago
SAA (QUIVER)
LAST I HEARD, HE'S STILL THERE. "AT LEAST THEY SPEAK ENGLISH," HE TOLD ME.
ZESHI (FWIP)
BUT REGARDLESS!
I OFFICIALLY NAME YOU OUR NEWEST SHIFT SUPERVISOR!
FOR ONE WEEK, YOU'LL STAKE YOUR LIFE PROTECTING THIS PLACE...
WIN!
...AND DESTROYING THAT GOD-FORSAKEN NEW SFC LOCATION!
AND REMEMBER, YOUR DEFEAT MEANS CERTAIN DEATH!
N-no way...

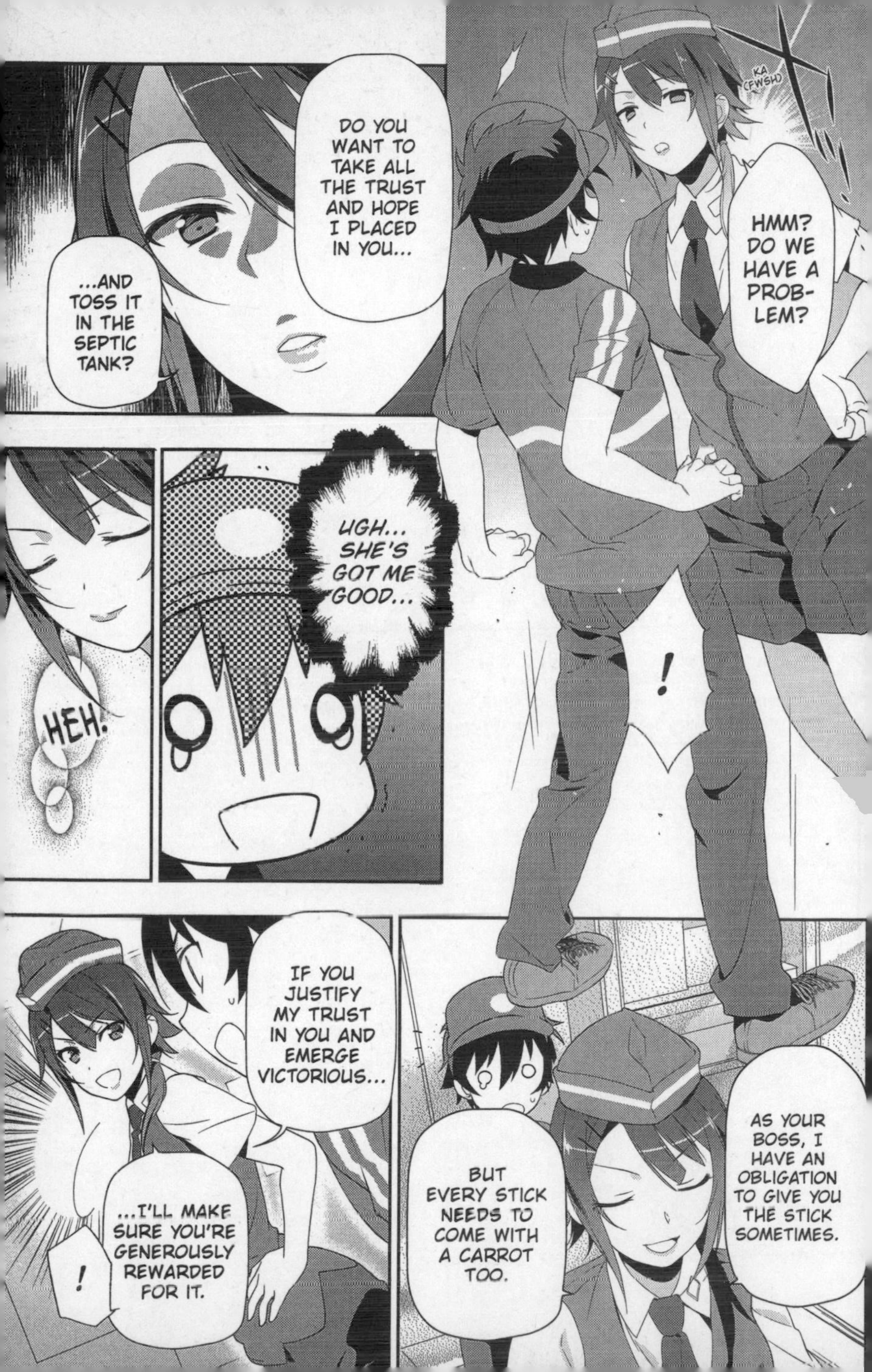
KA (FWSH)
HMM? DO WE HAVE A PROB-LEM?
!
DO YOU WANT TO TAKE ALL THE TRUST AND HOPE I PLACED IN YOU...
...AND TOSS IT IN THE SEPTIC TANK?
UGH... SHE'S GOT ME GOOD...
HEH!
AS YOUR BOSS, I HAVE AN OBLIGATION TO GIVE YOU THE STICK SOMETIMES.
BUT EVERY STICK NEEDS TO COME WITH A CARROT TOO.
IF YOU JUSTIFY MY TRUST IN YOU AND EMERGE VICTORIOUS...
...I'LL MAKE SURE YOU'RE GENEROUSLY REWARDED FOR IT.
!

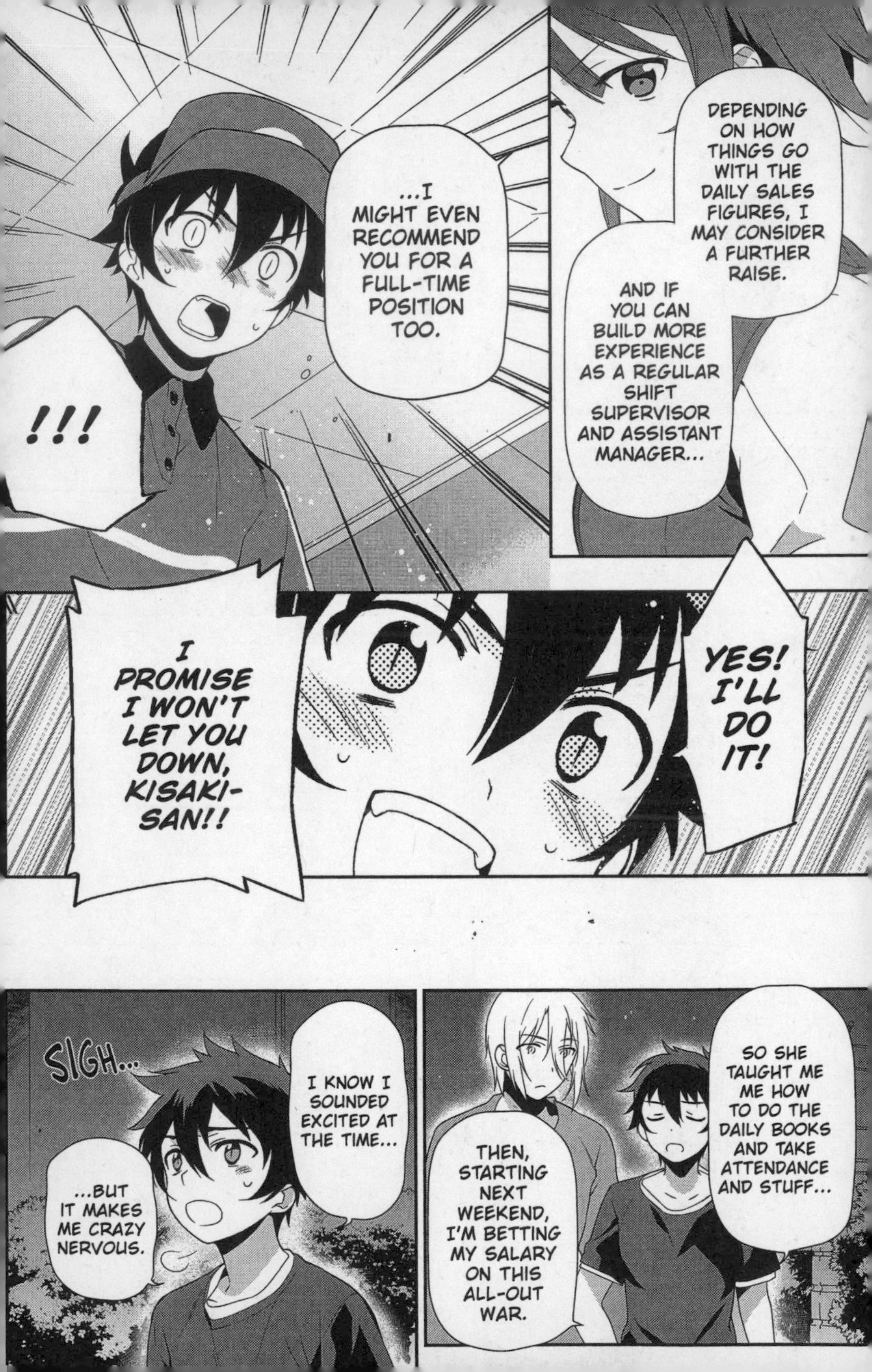
DEPENDING ON HOW THINGS GO WITH THE DAILY SALES FIGURES, I MAY CONSIDER A FURTHER RAISE.
AND IF YOU CAN BUILD MORE EXPERIENCE AS A REGULAR SHIFT SUPERVISOR AND ASSISTANT MANAGER...
...I MIGHT EVEN RECOMMEND YOU FOR A FULL-TIME POSITION TOO.
!!!
YES! I'LL DO IT!
I PROMISE I WON'T LET YOU DOWN, KISAKI-SAN!!
SO SHE TAUGHT ME ME HOW TO DO THE DAILY BOOKS AND TAKE ATTENDANCE AND STUFF...
THEN, STARTING NEXT WEEKEND, I'M BETTING MY SALARY ON THIS ALL-OUT WAR.
SIGH...
I KNOW I SOUNDED EXCITED AT THE TIME...
...BUT IT MAKES ME CRAZY NERVOUS.

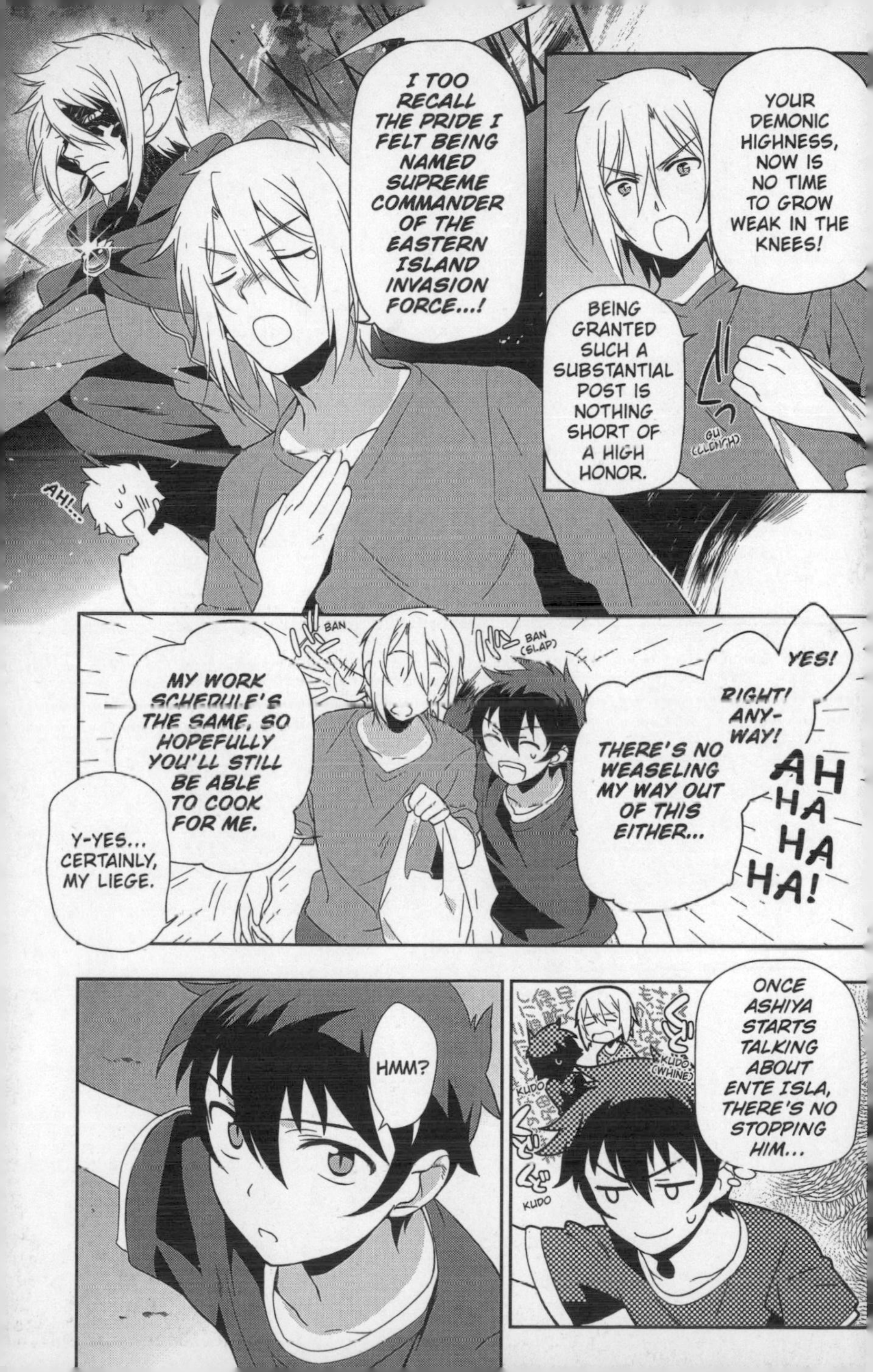
YOUR DEMONIC HIGHNESS, NOW IS NO TIME TO GROW WEAK IN THE KNEES!
BEING GRANTED SUCH A SUBSTANTIAL POST IS NOTHING SHORT OF A HIGH HONOR.
GU (CLENCH)
I TOO RECALL THE PRIDE I FELT BEING NAMED SUPREME COMMANDER OF THE EASTERN ISLAND INVASION FORCE...!
AH!...
YES!
RIGHT! ANYWAY!
AH HA HA HA HA!
THERE'S NO WEASELING MY WAY OUT OF THIS EITHER...
BAN (SLAP)
BAN
MY WORK SCHEDULE'S THE SAME, SO HOPEFULLY YOU'LL STILL BE ABLE TO COOK FOR ME.
Y-YES... CERTAINLY, MY LIEGE.
ONCE ASHIYA STARTS TALKING ABOUT ENTE ISLA, THERE'S NO STOPPING HIM...
KUDO (WHINE)
KUDO
KUDO
HMM?

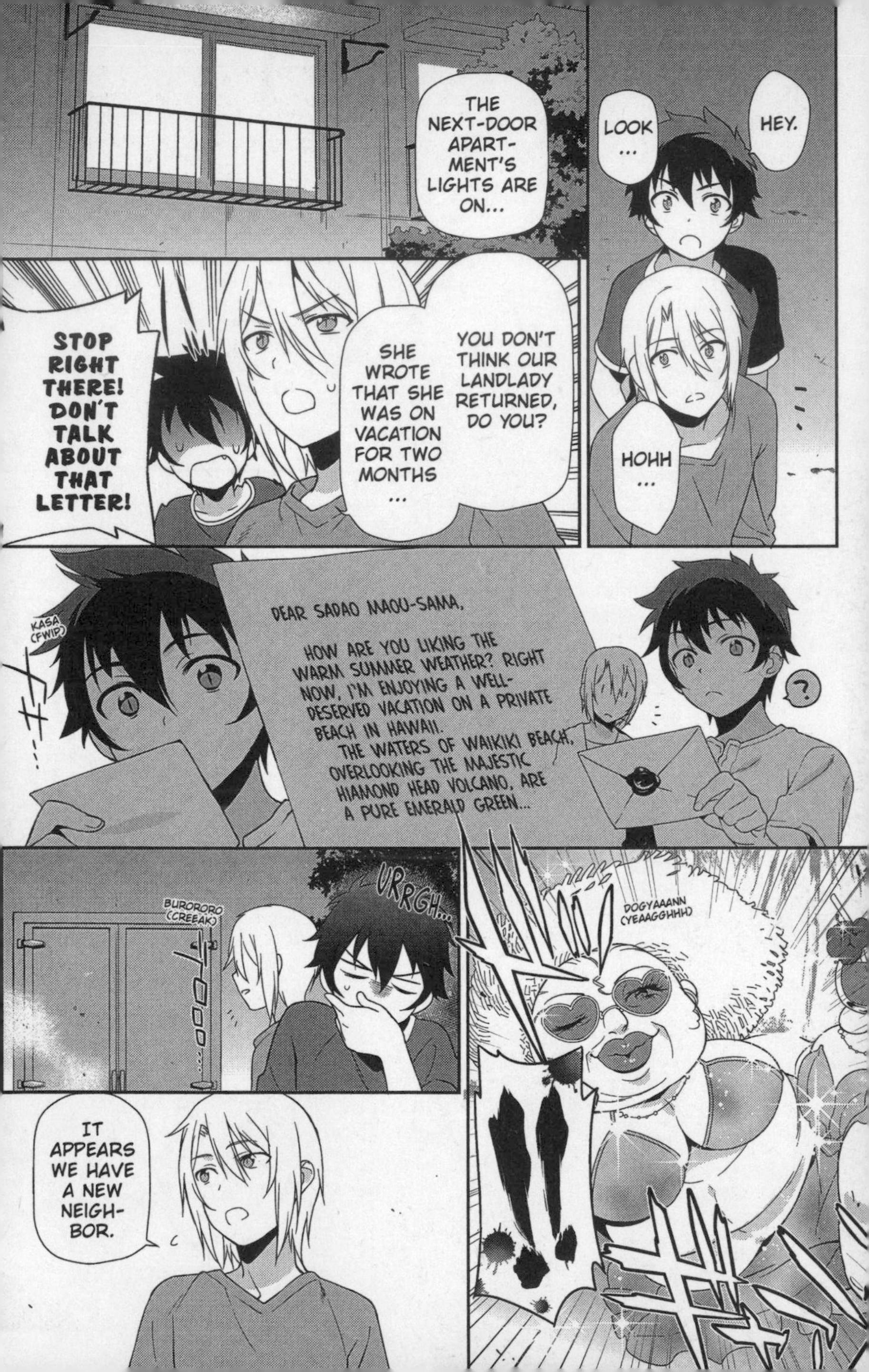
HEY.
LOOK...
HOHH...
THE NEXT-DOOR APARTMENT'S LIGHTS ARE ON...
YOU DON'T THINK OUR LANDLADY RETURNED, DO YOU?
SHE WROTE THAT SHE WAS ON VACATION FOR TWO MONTHS...
STOP RIGHT THERE! DON'T TALK ABOUT THAT LETTER!
KASA (FWIP)
DEAR SADAO MAOU-SAMA,
HOW ARE YOU LIKING THE WARM SUMMER WEATHER? RIGHT NOW, I'M ENJOYING A WELL-DESERVED VACATION ON A PRIVATE BEACH IN HAWAII.
THE WATERS OF WAIKIKI BEACH, OVERLOOKING THE MAJESTIC HIAMOND HEAD VOLCANO, ARE A PURE EMERALD GREEN...
DOGYAAANN (YEAAGGHHH)
URRGH...
BURORORO (CREEAK)
IT APPEARS WE HAVE A NEW NEIGHBOR.

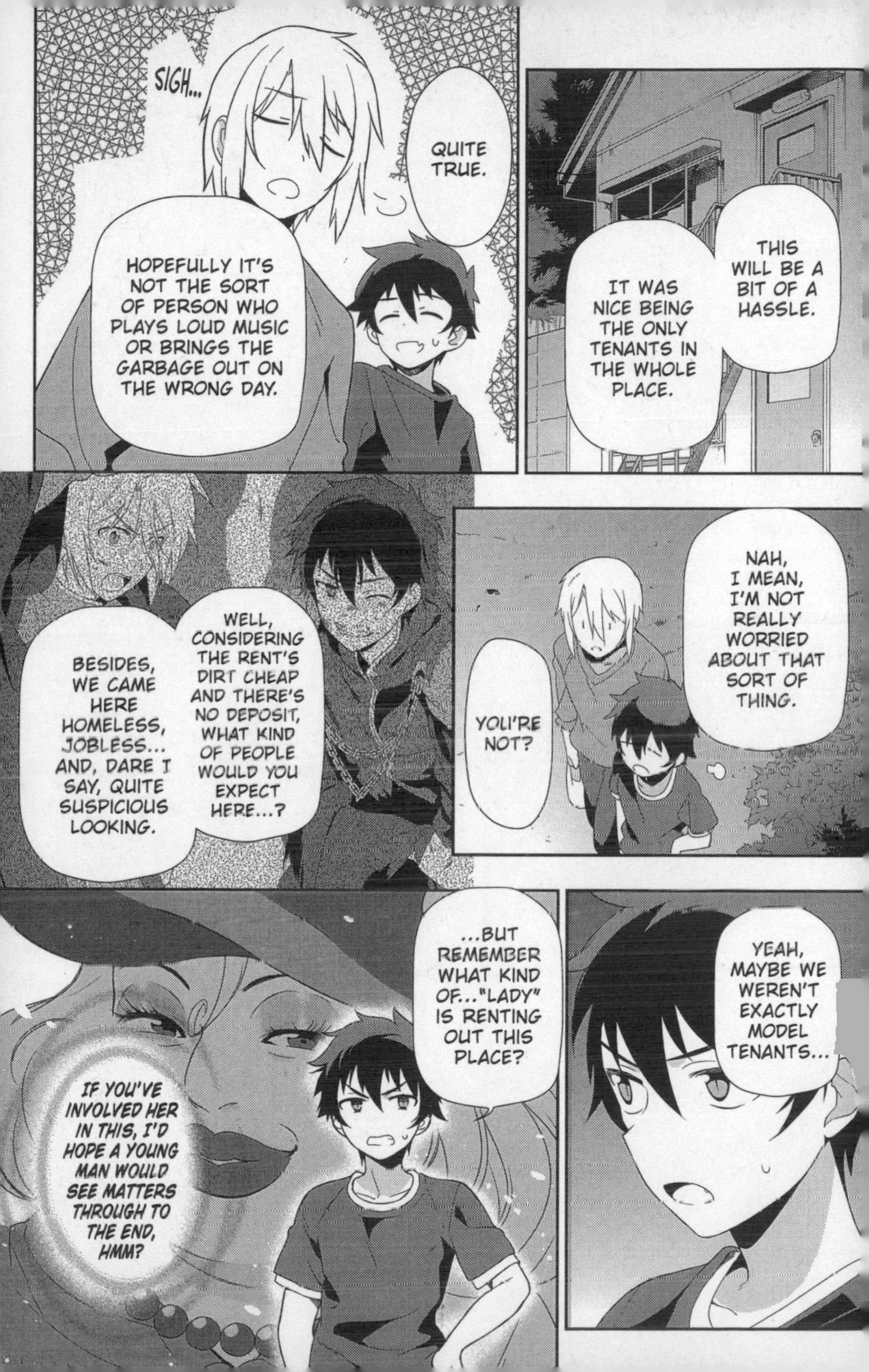
THIS WILL BE A BIT OF A HASSLE.
IT WAS NICE BEING THE ONLY TENANTS IN THE WHOLE PLACE.
QUITE TRUE.
SIGH...
HOPEFULLY IT'S NOT THE SORT OF PERSON WHO PLAYS LOUD MUSIC OR BRINGS THE GARBAGE OUT ON THE WRONG DAY.
NAH, I MEAN, I'M NOT REALLY WORRIED ABOUT THAT SORT OF THING.
YOU'RE NOT?
WELL, CONSIDERING THE RENT'S DIRT CHEAP AND THERE'S NO DEPOSIT, WHAT KIND OF PEOPLE WOULD YOU EXPECT HERE...?
BESIDES, WE CAME HERE HOMELESS, JOBLESS... AND, DARE I SAY, QUITE SUSPICIOUS LOOKING.
YEAH, MAYBE WE WEREN'T EXACTLY MODEL TENANTS...
...BUT REMEMBER WHAT KIND OF..."LADY" IS RENTING OUT THIS PLACE?
IF YOU'VE INVOLVED HER IN THIS, I'D HOPE A YOUNG MAN WOULD SEE MATTERS THROUGH TO THE END, HMM?

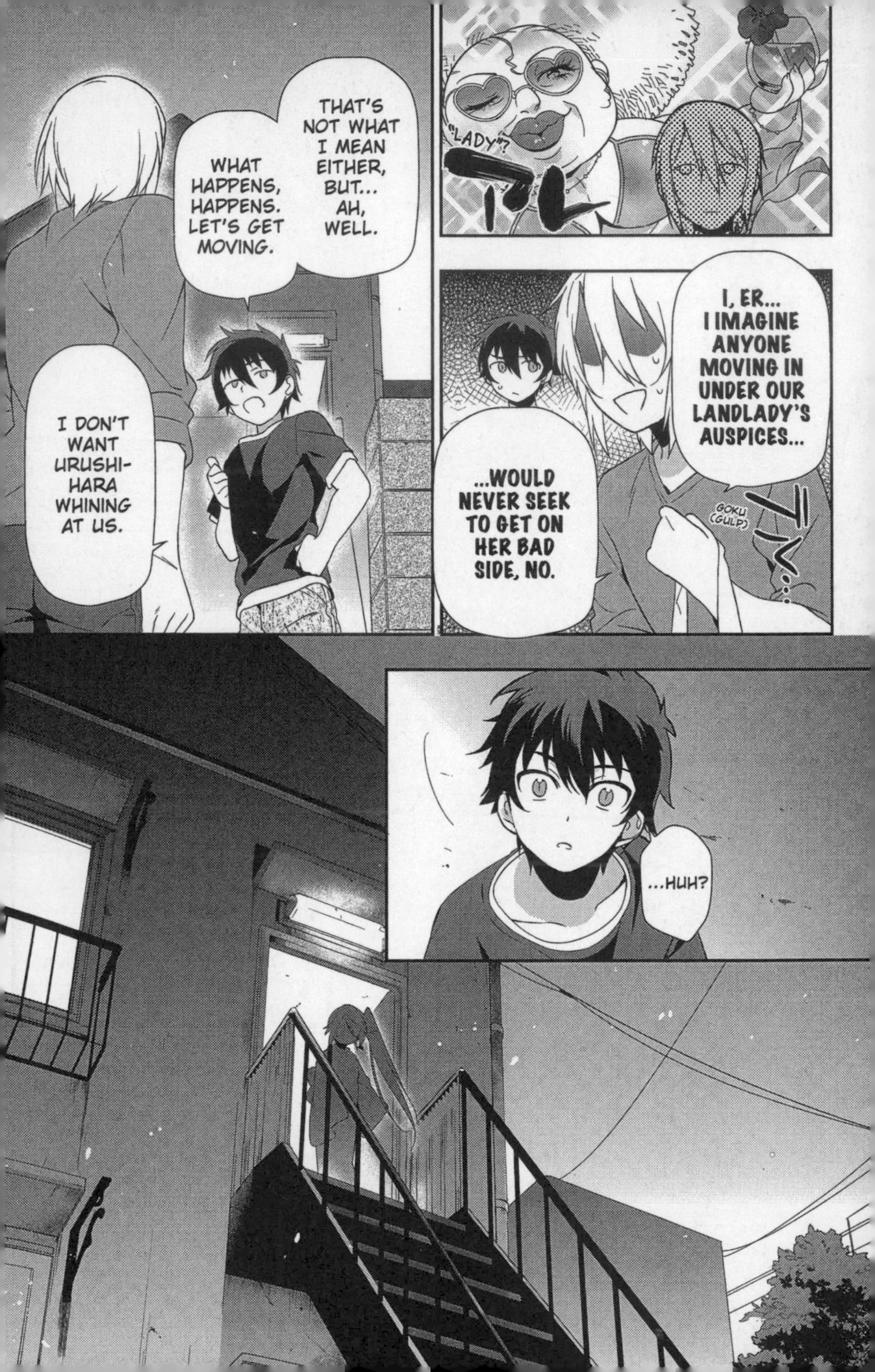
"LADY"?
I, ER... I IMAGINE ANYONE MOVING IN UNDER OUR LANDLADY'S AUSPICES...
GOKU (GULP)
...WOULD NEVER SEEK TO GET ON HER BAD SIDE, NO.
THAT'S NOT WHAT I MEAN EITHER, BUT... AH, WELL.
WHAT HAPPENS, HAPPENS. LET'S GET MOVING.
I DON'T WANT URUSHI-HARA WHINING AT US.
...HUH?

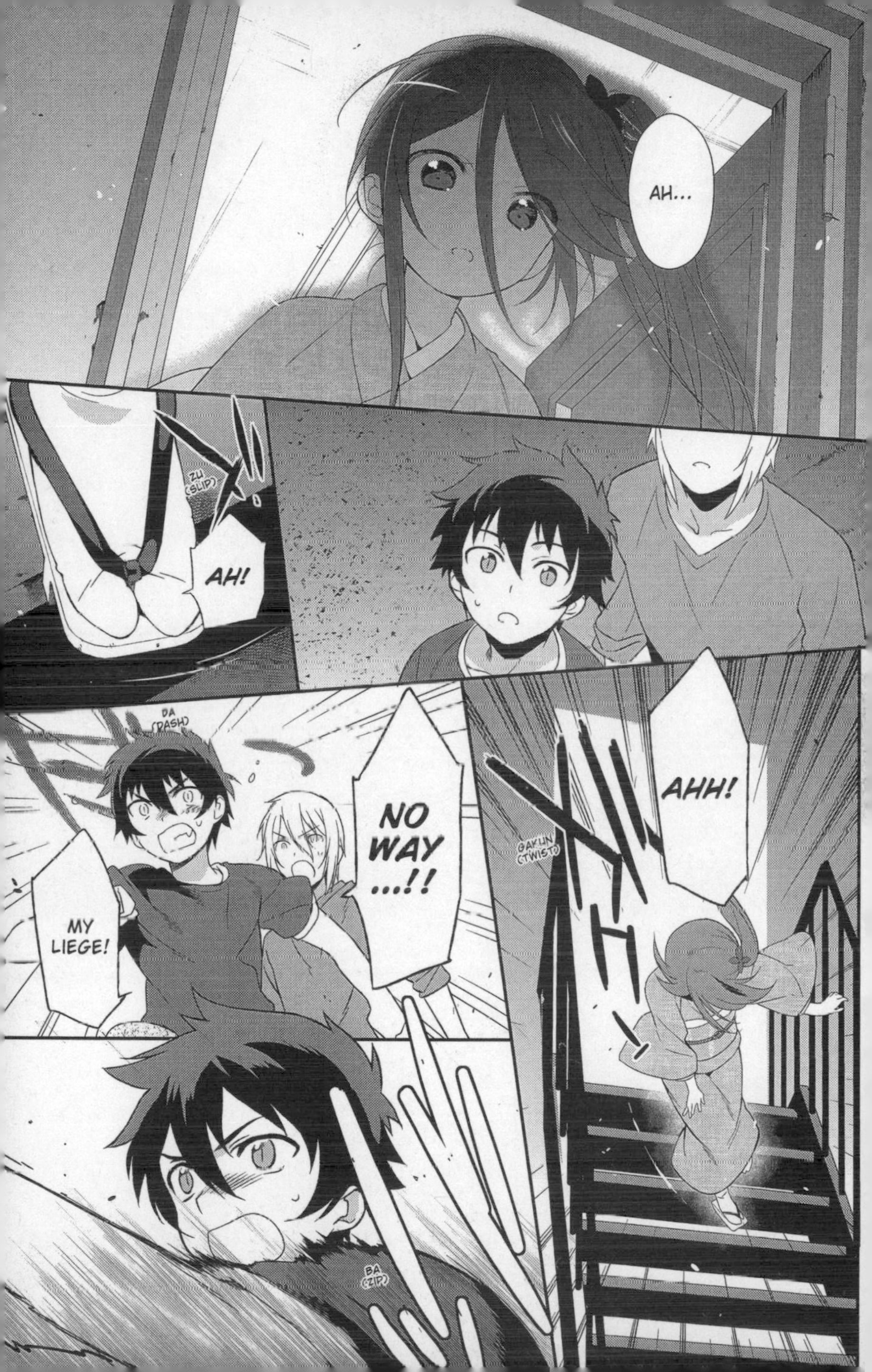
AH...
ZU (SLIP)
AH!
AHH!
GAKUN (TWIST)
NO WAY ...!!
BA (DASH)
MY LIEGE!
BA (ZIP)

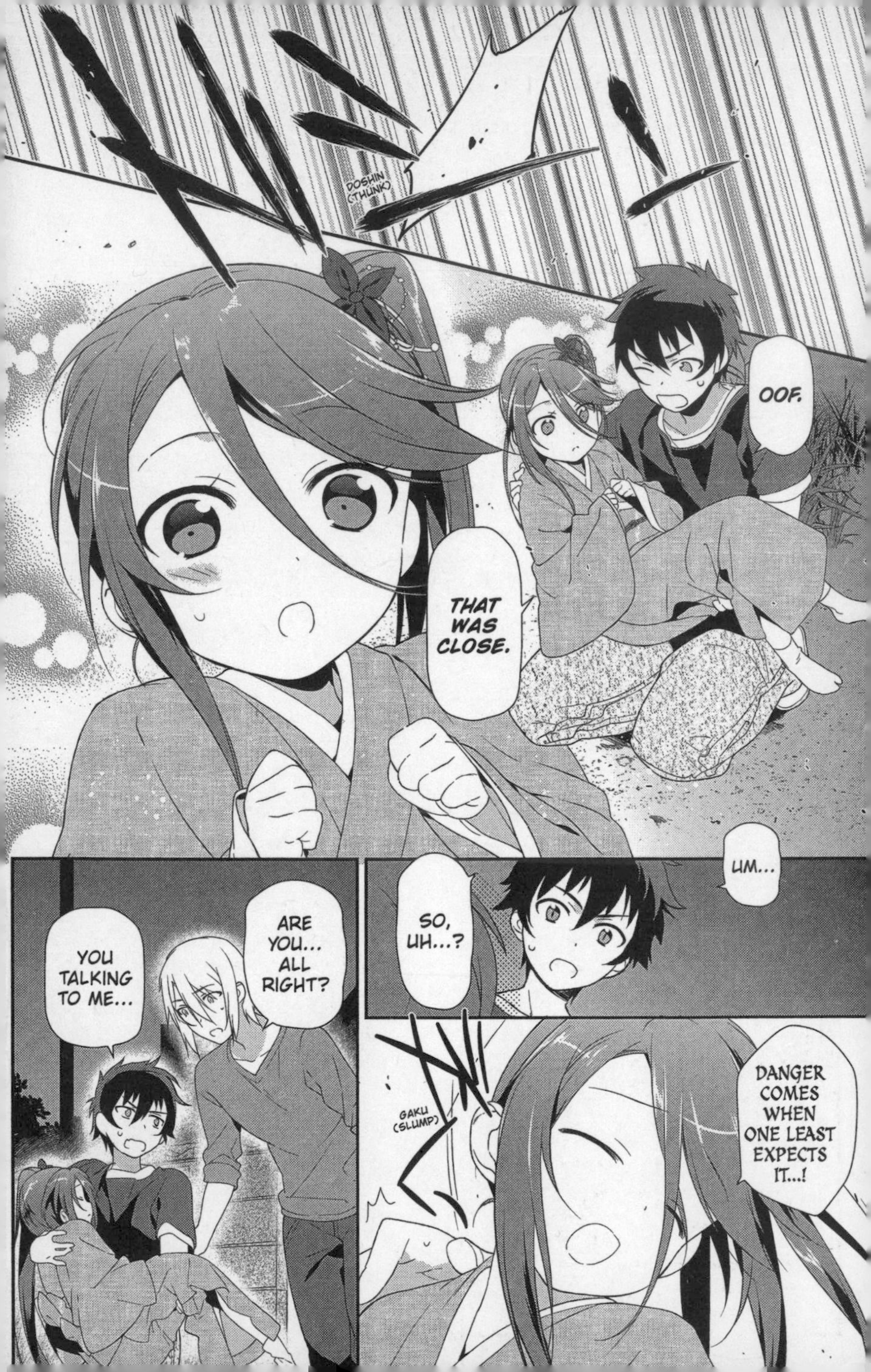
DOSHIN (THUNK)
OOF.
THAT WAS CLOSE.
UM...
SO, UH...?
DANGER COMES WHEN ONE LEAST EXPECTS IT...!
GAKU (SLUMP)
ARE YOU... ALL RIGHT?
YOU TALKING TO ME...

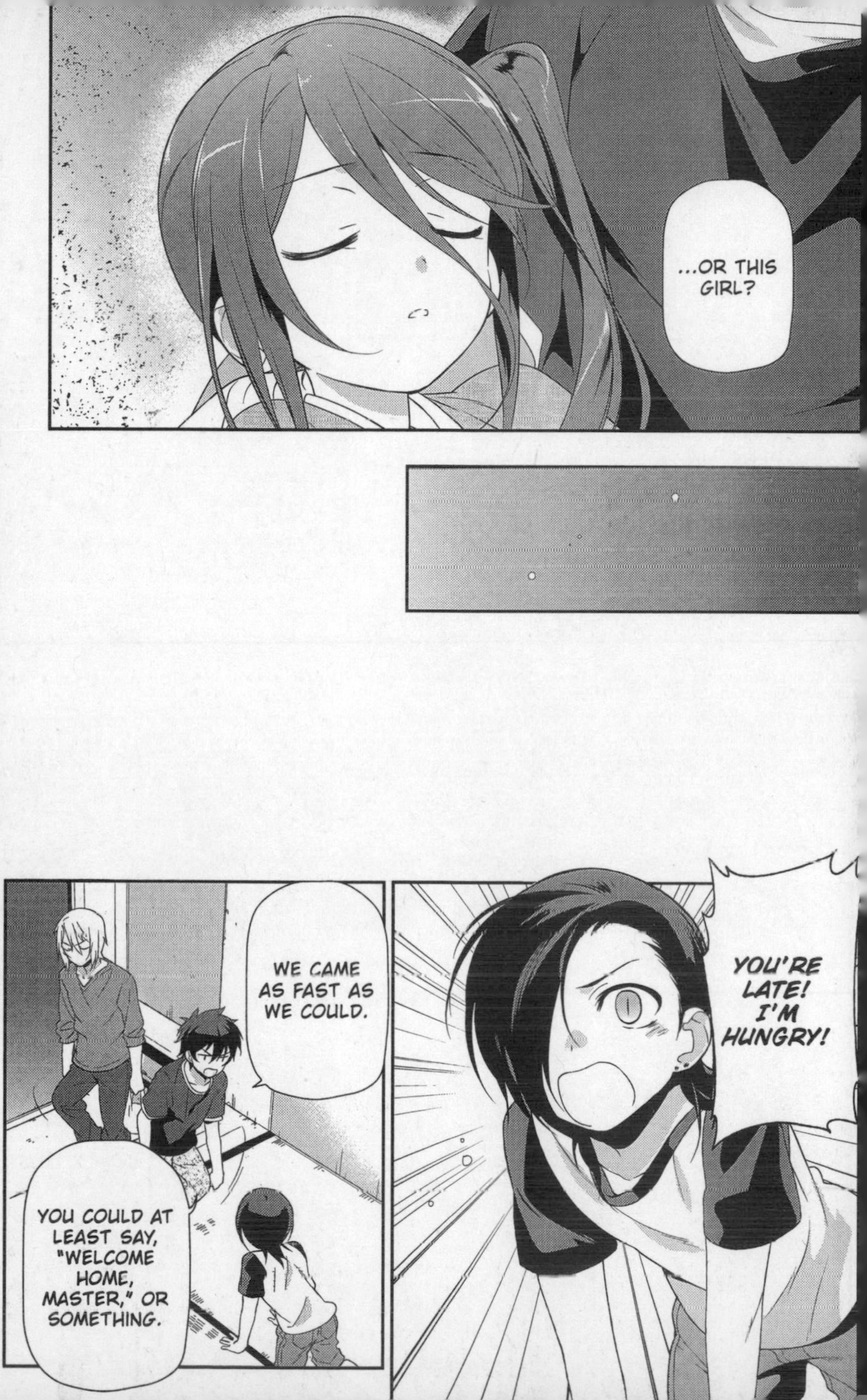
...OR THIS GIRL?
YOU'RE LATE! I'M HUNGRY!
WE CAME AS FAST AS WE COULD.
YOU COULD AT LEAST SAY, "WELCOME HOME, MASTER," OR SOMETHING.

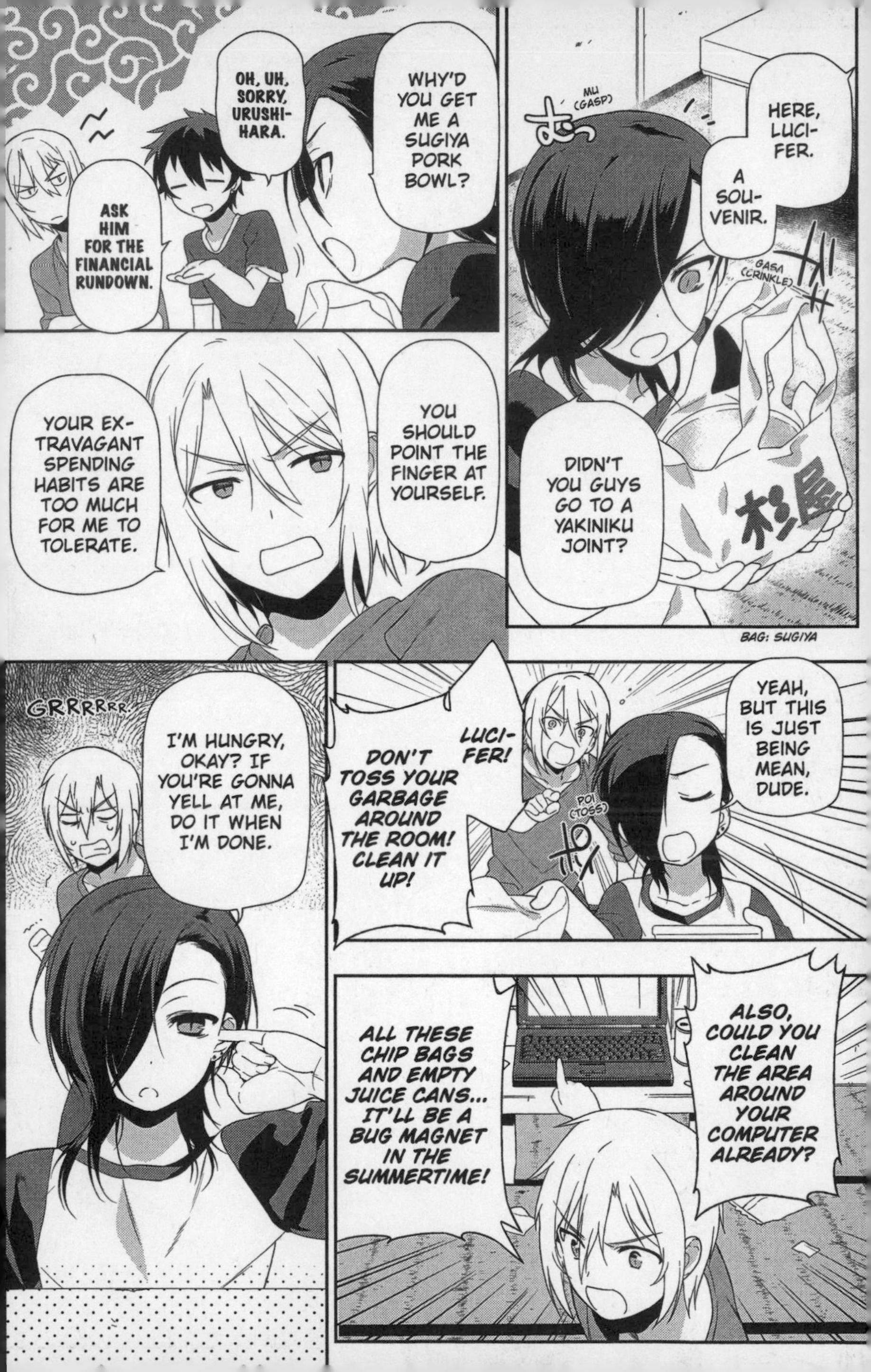
HERE, LUCIFER.
A SOUVENIR.
MU (GASP)
GASA (CRINKLE)
DIDN'T YOU GUYS GO TO A YAKINIKU JOINT?
BAG: SUGIYA
WHY'D YOU GET ME A SUGIYA PORK BOWL?
OH, UH, SORRY, URUSHIHARA.
ASK HIM FOR THE FINANCIAL RUNDOWN.
YOU SHOULD POINT THE FINGER AT YOURSELF.
YOUR EXTRAVAGANT SPENDING HABITS ARE TOO MUCH FOR ME TO TOLERATE.
YEAH, BUT THIS IS JUST BEING MEAN, DUDE.
POI (TOSS)
LUCIFER!
DON'T TOSS YOUR GARBAGE AROUND THE ROOM! CLEAN IT UP!
ALSO, COULD YOU CLEAN THE AREA AROUND YOUR COMPUTER ALREADY?
ALL THESE CHIP BAGS AND EMPTY JUICE CANS... IT'LL BE A BUG MAGNET IN THE SUMMERTIME!
GRRRRRR
I'M HUNGRY, OKAY? IF YOU'RE GONNA YELL AT ME, DO IT WHEN I'M DONE.

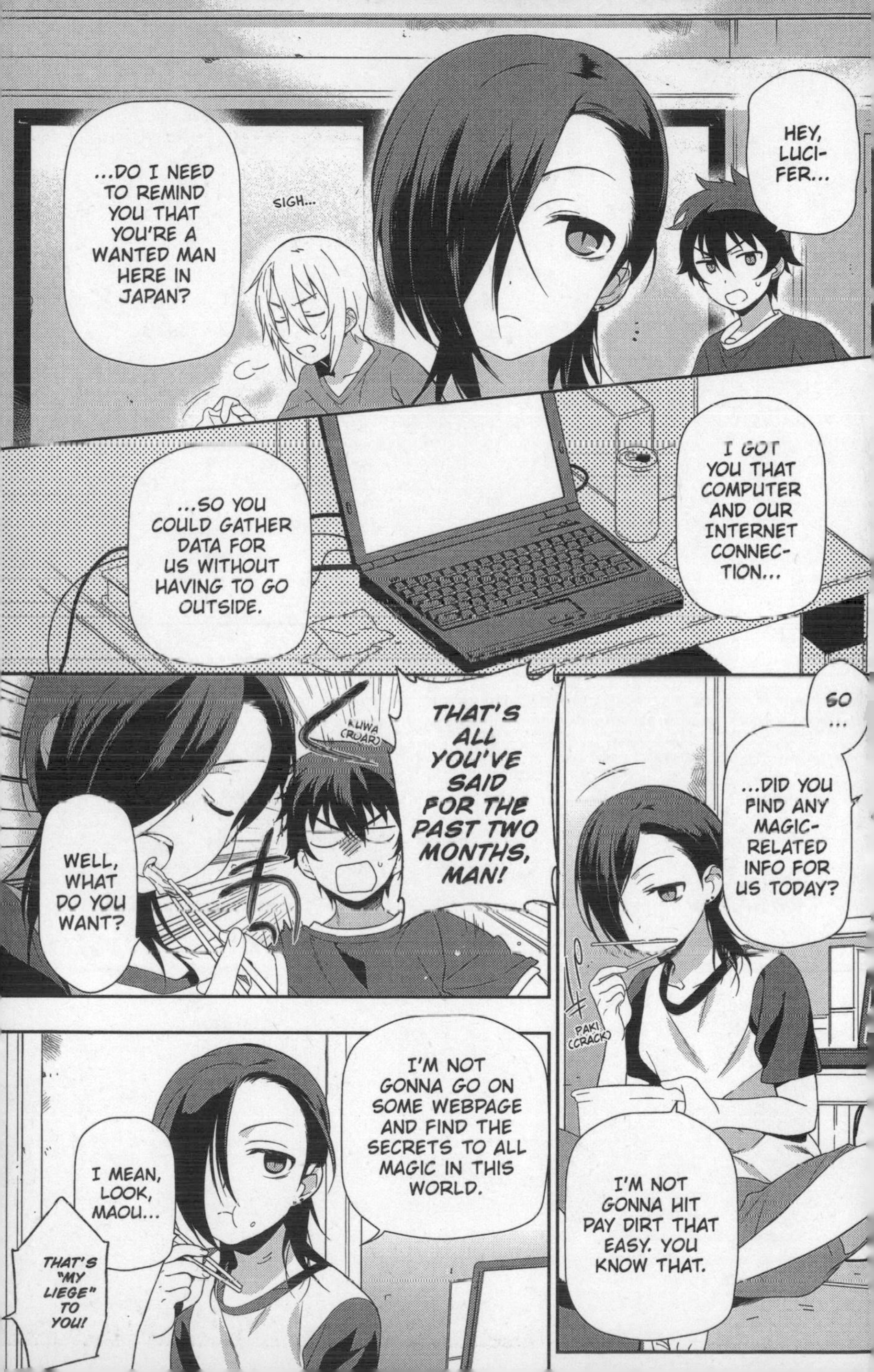
HEY, LUCIFER...
SIGH...
...DO I NEED TO REMIND YOU THAT YOU'RE A WANTED MAN HERE IN JAPAN?
I GOT YOU THAT COMPUTER AND OUR INTERNET CONNECTION...
...SO YOU COULD GATHER DATA FOR US WITHOUT HAVING TO GO OUTSIDE.
SO ...
...DID YOU FIND ANY MAGIC-RELATED INFO FOR US TODAY?
PAKI (CRACK)
I'M NOT GONNA HIT PAY DIRT THAT EASY. YOU KNOW THAT.
THAT'S ALL YOU'VE SAID FOR THE PAST TWO MONTHS, MAN!
KUWA (ROAR)
WELL, WHAT DO YOU WANT?
I'M NOT GONNA GO ON SOME WEBPAGE AND FIND THE SECRETS TO ALL MAGIC IN THIS WORLD.
I MEAN, LOOK, MAOU...
THAT'S "MY LIEGE" TO YOU!

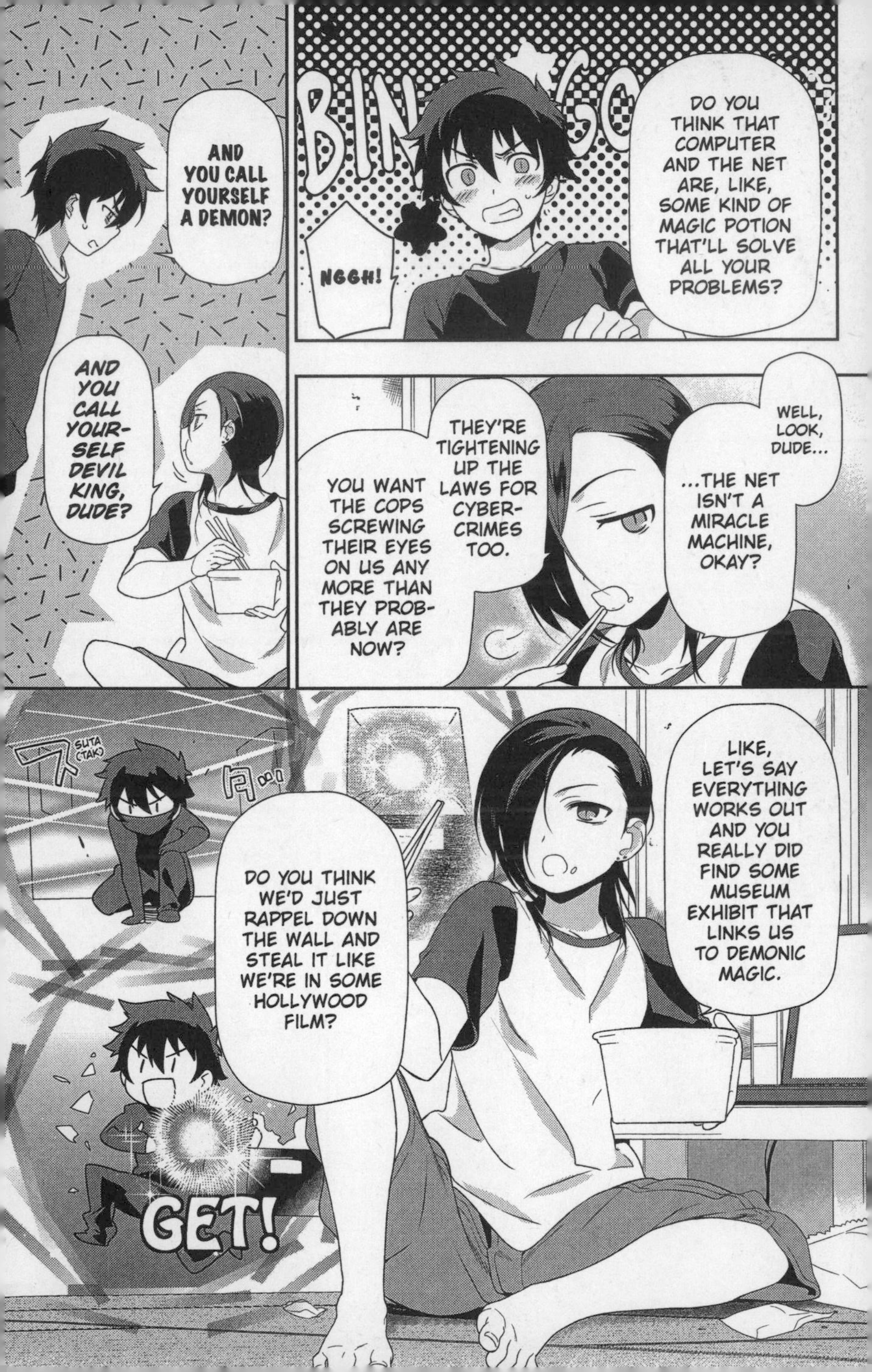
BINGO
DO YOU THINK THAT COMPUTER AND THE NET ARE, LIKE, SOME KIND OF MAGIC POTION THAT'LL SOLVE ALL YOUR PROBLEMS?
NGGH!
WELL, LOOK, DUDE...
...THE NET ISN'T A MIRACLE MACHINE, OKAY?
THEY'RE TIGHTENING UP THE LAWS FOR CYBER-CRIMES TOO.
YOU WANT THE COPS SCREWING THEIR EYES ON US ANY MORE THAN THEY PROBABLY ARE NOW?
AND YOU CALL YOURSELF A DEMON?
AND YOU CALL YOURSELF DEVIL KING, DUDE?
LIKE, LET'S SAY EVERYTHING WORKS OUT AND YOU REALLY DID FIND SOME MUSEUM EXHIBIT THAT LINKS US TO DEMONIC MAGIC.
DO YOU THINK WE'D JUST RAPPEL DOWN THE WALL AND STEAL IT LIKE WE'RE IN SOME HOLLYWOOD FILM?
SUTA (TAK)
GET!

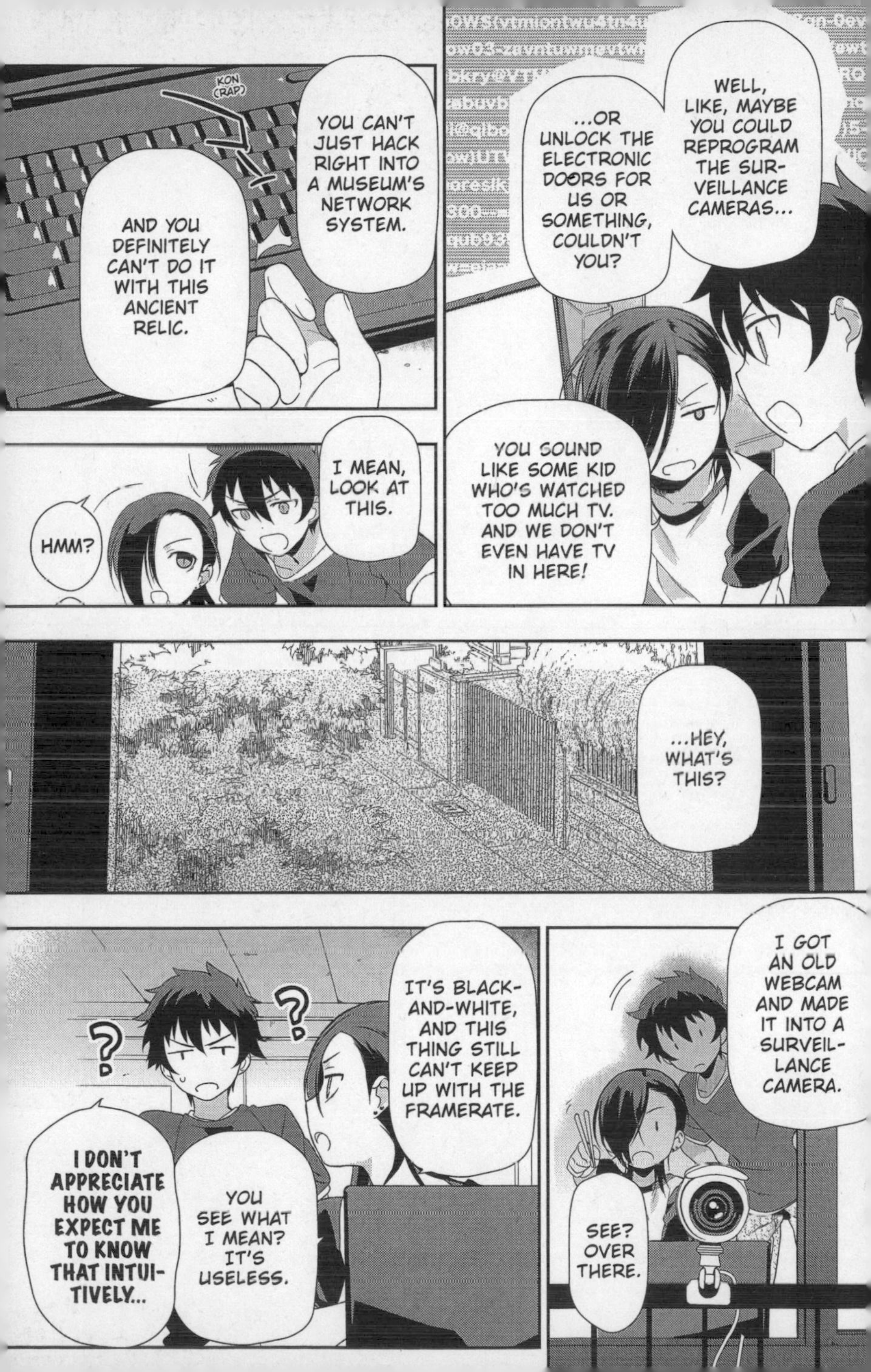
WELL, LIKE, MAYBE YOU COULD REPROGRAM THE SUR-VEILLANCE CAMERAS...
...OR UNLOCK THE ELECTRONIC DOORS FOR US OR SOMETHING, COULDN'T YOU?
YOU SOUND LIKE SOME KID WHO'S WATCHED TOO MUCH TV. AND WE DON'T EVEN HAVE TV IN HERE!
KON (RAP)
YOU CAN'T JUST HACK RIGHT INTO A MUSEUM'S NETWORK SYSTEM.
AND YOU DEFINITELY CAN'T DO IT WITH THIS ANCIENT RELIC.
I MEAN, LOOK AT THIS.
HMM?
...HEY, WHAT'S THIS?
I GOT AN OLD WEBCAM AND MADE IT INTO A SURVEIL-LANCE CAMERA.
SEE? OVER THERE.
IT'S BLACK-AND-WHITE, AND THIS THING STILL CAN'T KEEP UP WITH THE FRAMERATE.
YOU SEE WHAT I MEAN? IT'S USELESS.
I DON'T APPRECIATE HOW YOU EXPECT ME TO KNOW THAT INTUI-TIVELY...

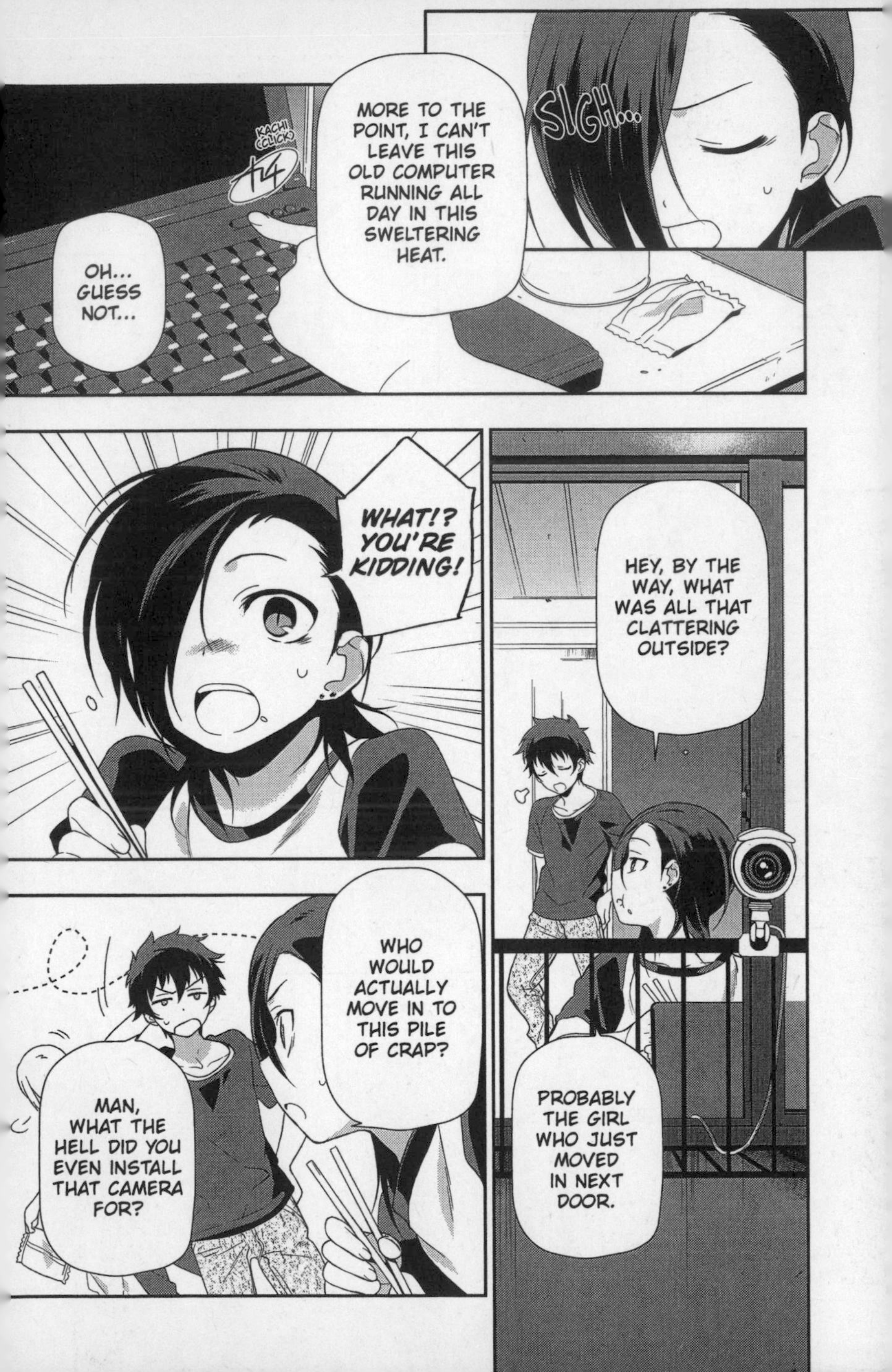
SIGH...
MORE TO THE POINT, I CAN'T LEAVE THIS OLD COMPUTER RUNNING ALL DAY IN THIS SWELTERING HEAT.
KACHI (CLICK)
OH... GUESS NOT...
HEY, BY THE WAY, WHAT WAS ALL THAT CLATTERING OUTSIDE?
PROBABLY THE GIRL WHO JUST MOVED IN NEXT DOOR.
WHAT!? YOU'RE KIDDING!
WHO WOULD ACTUALLY MOVE IN TO THIS PILE OF CRAP?
MAN, WHAT THE HELL DID YOU EVEN INSTALL THAT CAMERA FOR?

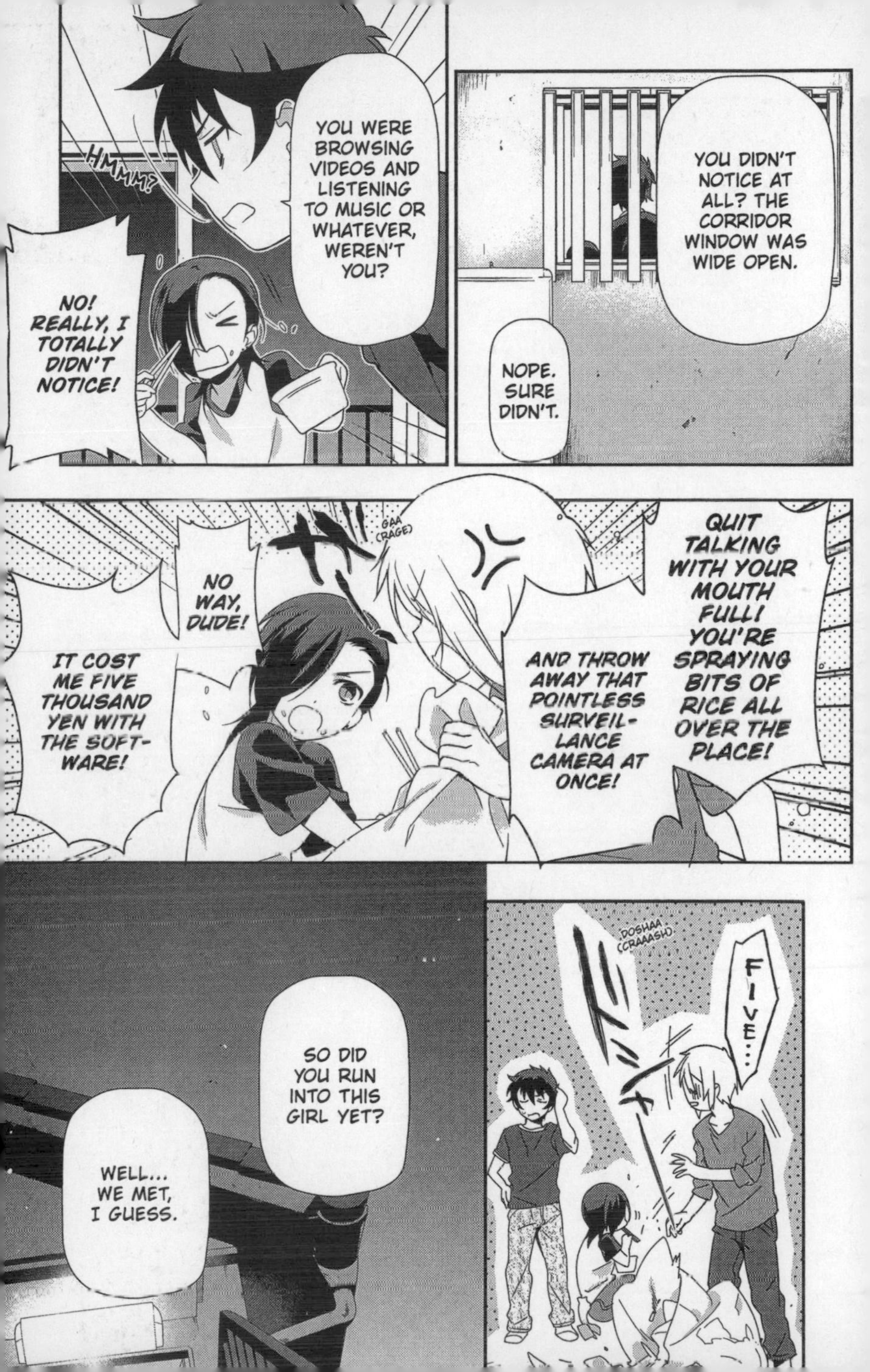
YOU DIDN'T NOTICE AT ALL? THE CORRIDOR WINDOW WAS WIDE OPEN.
NOPE. SURE DIDN'T.
YOU WERE BROWSING VIDEOS AND LISTENING TO MUSIC OR WHATEVER, WEREN'T YOU?
HMMM?
NO! REALLY, I TOTALLY DIDN'T NOTICE!
QUIT TALKING WITH YOUR MOUTH FULL! YOU'RE SPRAYING BITS OF RICE ALL OVER THE PLACE!
AND THROW AWAY THAT POINTLESS SURVEIL-LANCE CAMERA AT ONCE!
GAA (RAGE)
NO WAY, DUDE!
IT COST ME FIVE THOUSAND YEN WITH THE SOFT-WARE!
DOSHAA (CRAAASH)
FIVE...
SO DID YOU RUN INTO THIS GIRL YET?
WELL... WE MET, I GUESS.

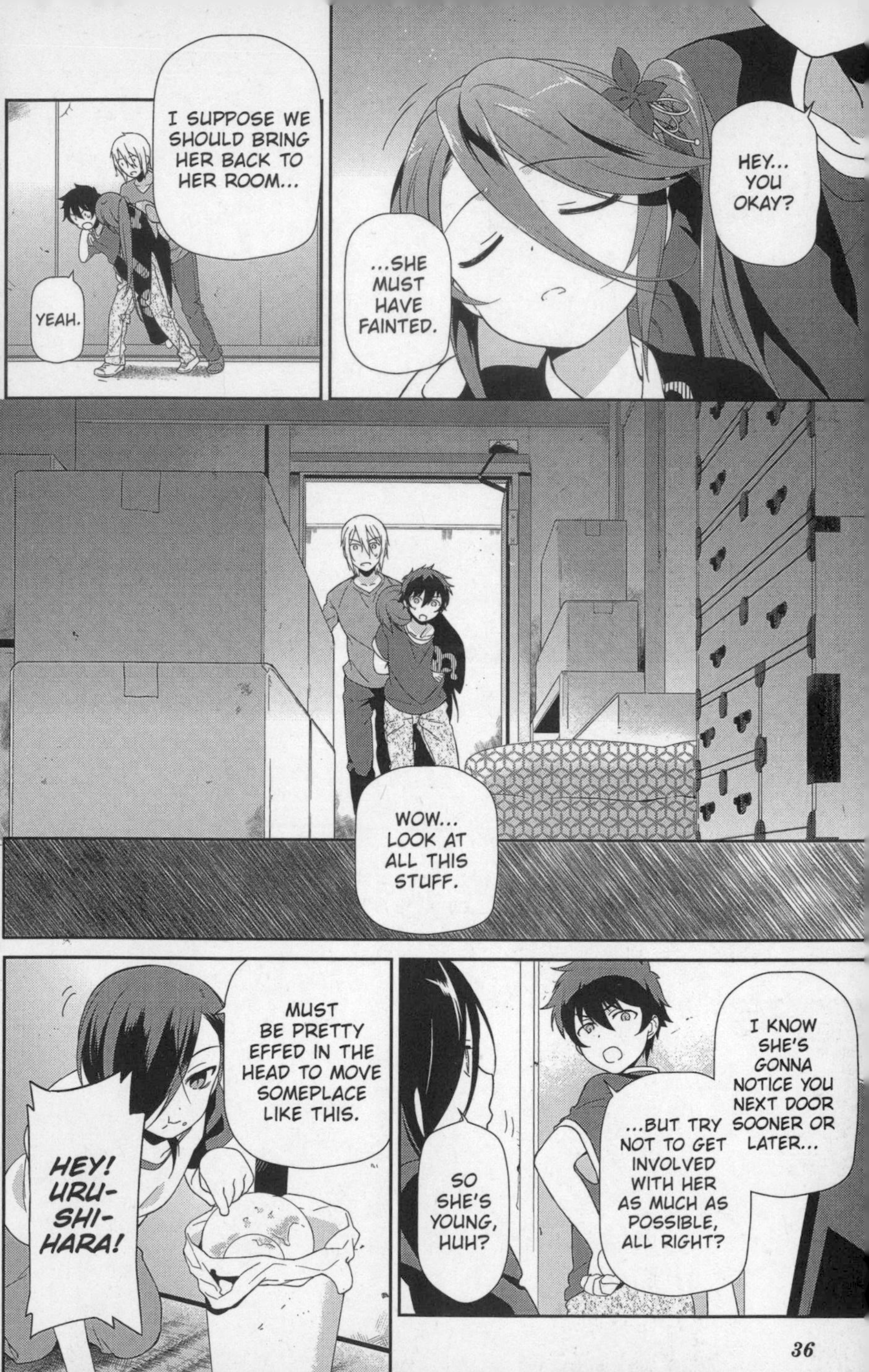
HEY... YOU OKAY?
...SHE MUST HAVE FAINTED.
I SUPPOSE WE SHOULD BRING HER BACK TO HER ROOM...
YEAH.
WOW... LOOK AT ALL THIS STUFF.
I KNOW SHE'S GONNA NOTICE YOU NEXT DOOR SOONER OR LATER...
...BUT TRY NOT TO GET INVOLVED WITH HER AS MUCH AS POSSIBLE, ALL RIGHT?
SO SHE'S YOUNG, HUH?
MUST BE PRETTY EFFED IN THE HEAD TO MOVE SOMEPLACE LIKE THIS.
HEY! URU-SHI-HARA!

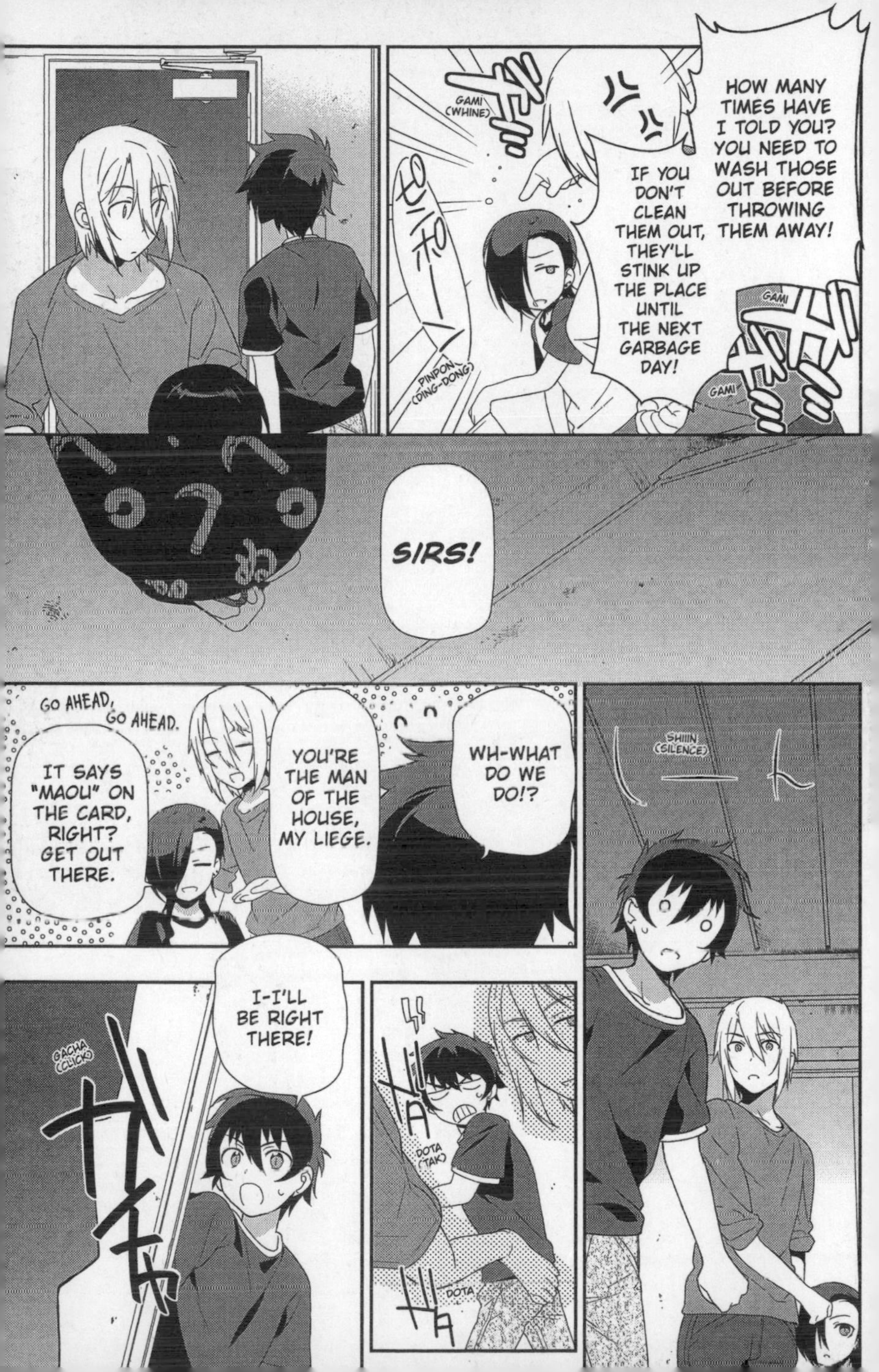
HOW MANY TIMES HAVE I TOLD YOU? YOU NEED TO WASH THOSE OUT BEFORE THROWING THEM AWAY!
IF YOU DON'T CLEAN THEM OUT, THEY'LL STINK UP THE PLACE UNTIL THE NEXT GARBAGE DAY!
GAMI (WHINE)
GAMI
GAMI
PINPON (DING-DONG)
SIRS!
SHIIN (SILENCE)
WH-WHAT DO WE DO!?
YOU'RE THE MAN OF THE HOUSE, MY LIEGE.
IT SAYS "MAOU" ON THE CARD, RIGHT? GET OUT THERE.
GO AHEAD, GO AHEAD.
DOTA (TAK)
DOTA
I-I'LL BE RIGHT THERE!
GACHA (CLICK)

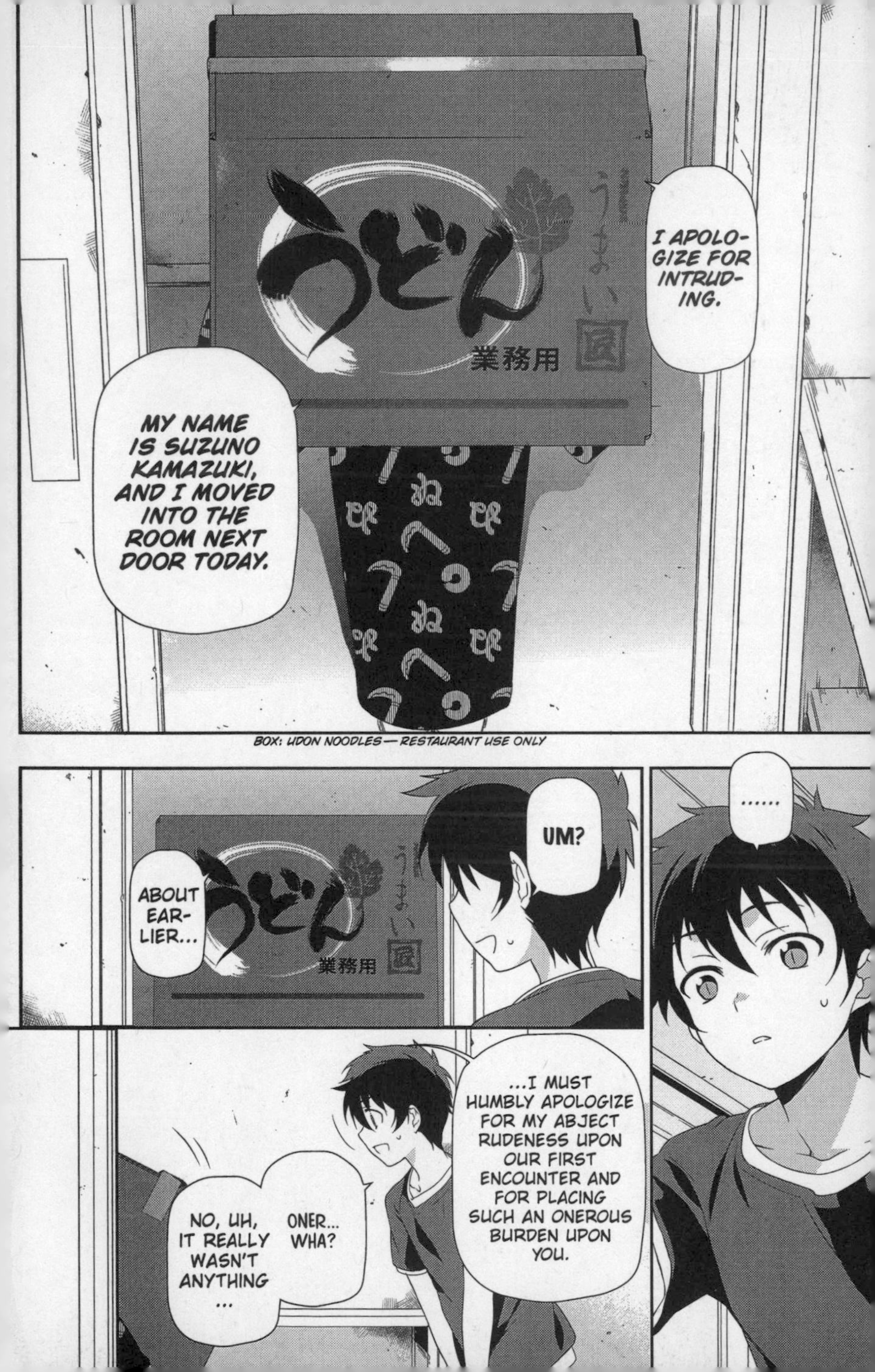
I APOLOGIZE FOR INTRUDING.
うどん
うまい
業務用
MY NAME IS SUZUNO KAMAZUKI, AND I MOVED INTO THE ROOM NEXT DOOR TODAY.
BOX: UDON NOODLES— RESTAURANT USE ONLY
......
UM?
ABOUT EARLIER...
うどん
業務用
...I MUST HUMBLY APOLOGIZE FOR MY ABJECT RUDENESS UPON OUR FIRST ENCOUNTER AND FOR PLACING SUCH AN ONEROUS BURDEN UPON YOU.
ONER... WHA?
NO, UH, IT REALLY WASN'T ANYTHING ...

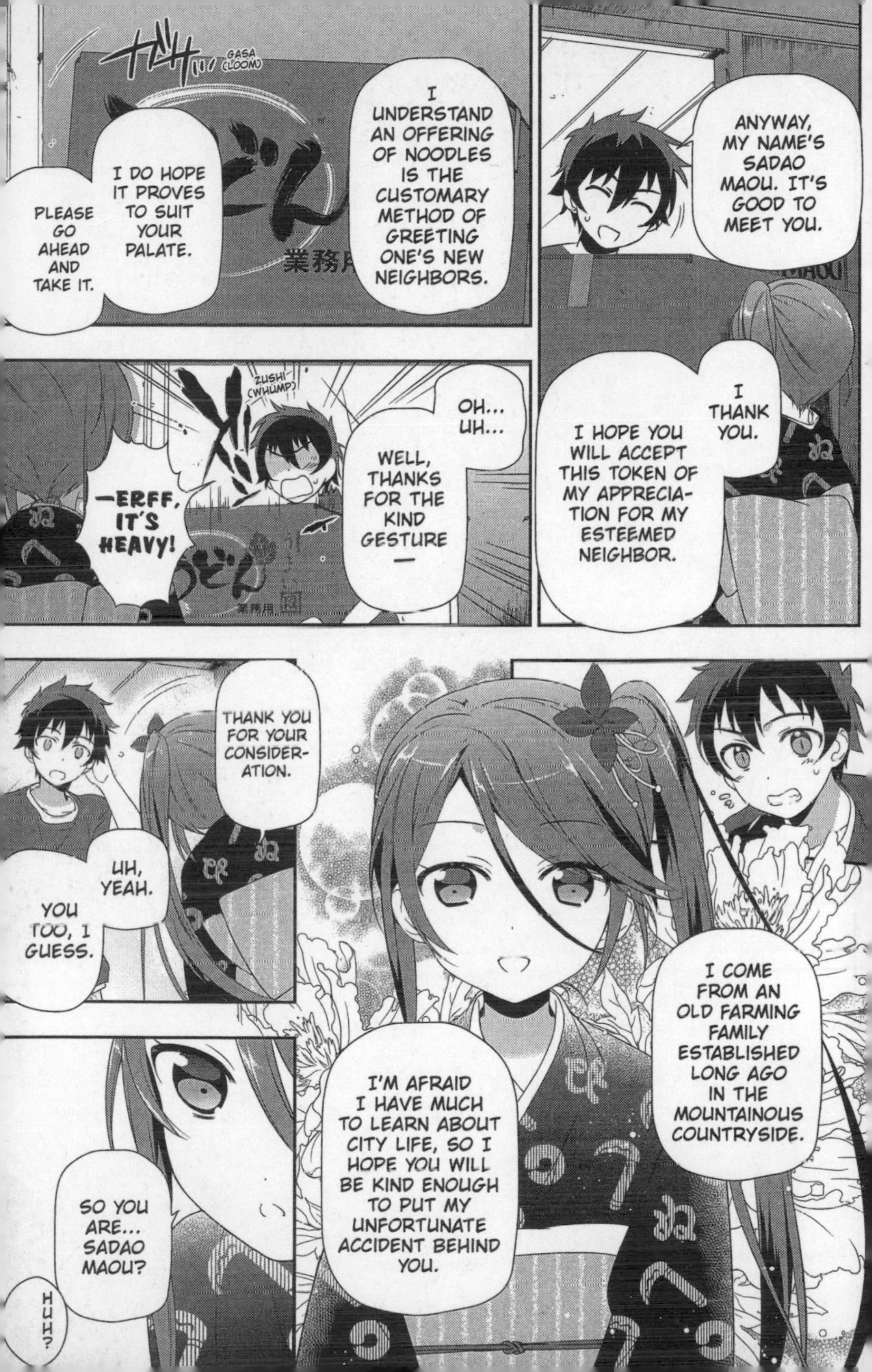
ANYWAY, MY NAME'S SADAO MAOU. IT'S GOOD TO MEET YOU.
I UNDERSTAND AN OFFERING OF NOODLES IS THE CUSTOMARY METHOD OF GREETING ONE'S NEW NEIGHBORS.
GASA (LOOM)
I DO HOPE IT PROVES TO SUIT YOUR PALATE.
PLEASE GO AHEAD AND TAKE IT.
I THANK YOU.
I HOPE YOU WILL ACCEPT THIS TOKEN OF MY APPRECIATION FOR MY ESTEEMED NEIGHBOR.
OH... UH...
WELL, THANKS FOR THE KIND GESTURE—
ZUSHI (WHUMP)
—ERFF, IT'S HEAVY!
I COME FROM AN OLD FARMING FAMILY ESTABLISHED LONG AGO IN THE MOUNTAINOUS COUNTRYSIDE.
I'M AFRAID I HAVE MUCH TO LEARN ABOUT CITY LIFE, SO I HOPE YOU WILL BE KIND ENOUGH TO PUT MY UNFORTUNATE ACCIDENT BEHIND YOU.
THANK YOU FOR YOUR CONSIDERATION.
UH, YEAH.
YOU TOO, I GUESS.
SO YOU ARE... SADAO MAOU?
HUH?

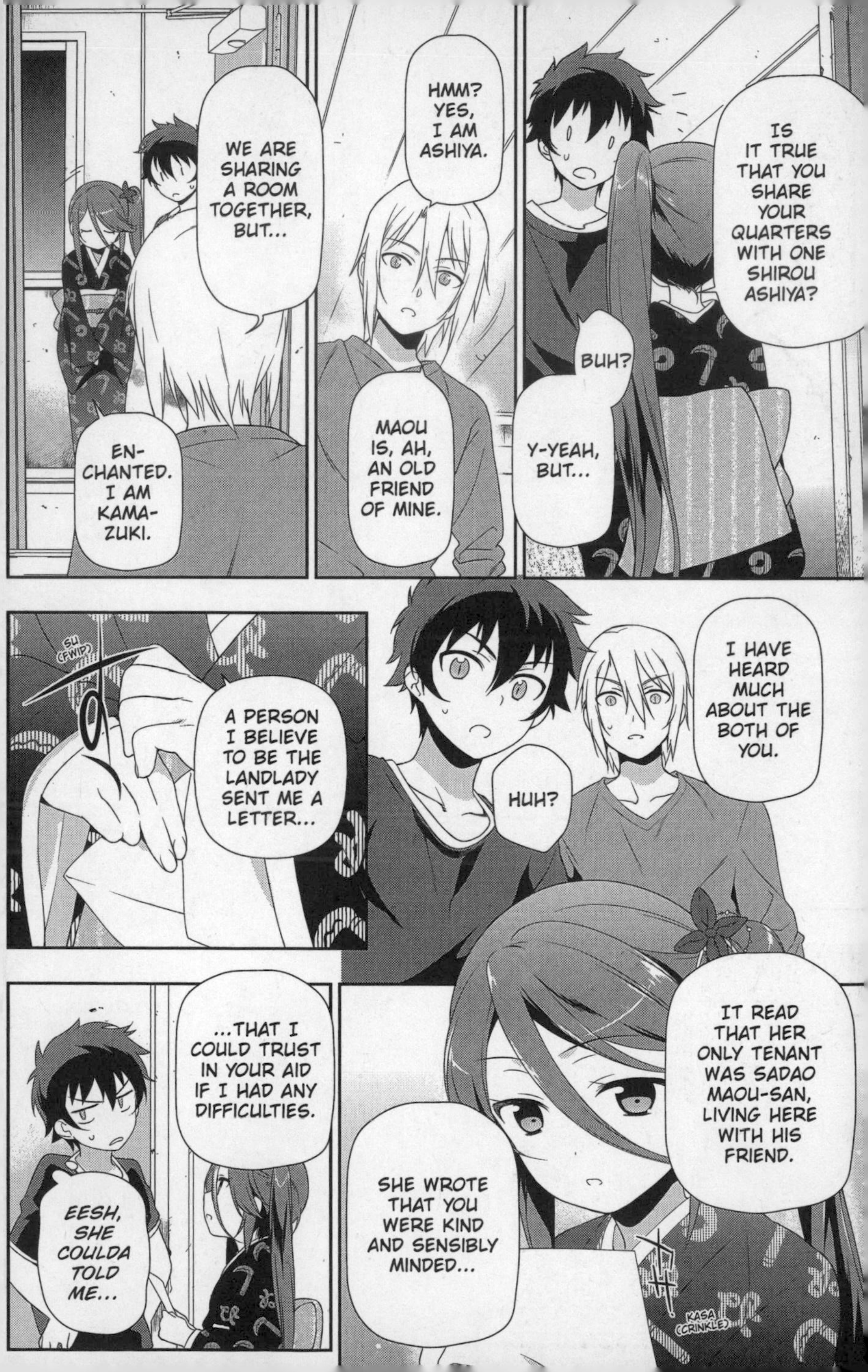
IS IT TRUE THAT YOU SHARE YOUR QUARTERS WITH ONE SHIROU ASHIYA?
BUH?
Y-YEAH, BUT...
HMM? YES, I AM ASHIYA.
MAOU IS, AH, AN OLD FRIEND OF MINE.
WE ARE SHARING A ROOM TOGETHER, BUT...
EN-CHANTED. I AM KAMA-ZUKI.
I HAVE HEARD MUCH ABOUT THE BOTH OF YOU.
HUH?
SU (FWIP)
A PERSON I BELIEVE TO BE THE LANDLADY SENT ME A LETTER...
IT READ THAT HER ONLY TENANT WAS SADAO MAOU-SAN, LIVING HERE WITH HIS FRIEND.
SHE WROTE THAT YOU WERE KIND AND SENSIBLY MINDED...
KASA (CRINKLE)
...THAT I COULD TRUST IN YOUR AID IF I HAD ANY DIFFICULTIES.
EESH, SHE COULDA TOLD ME...

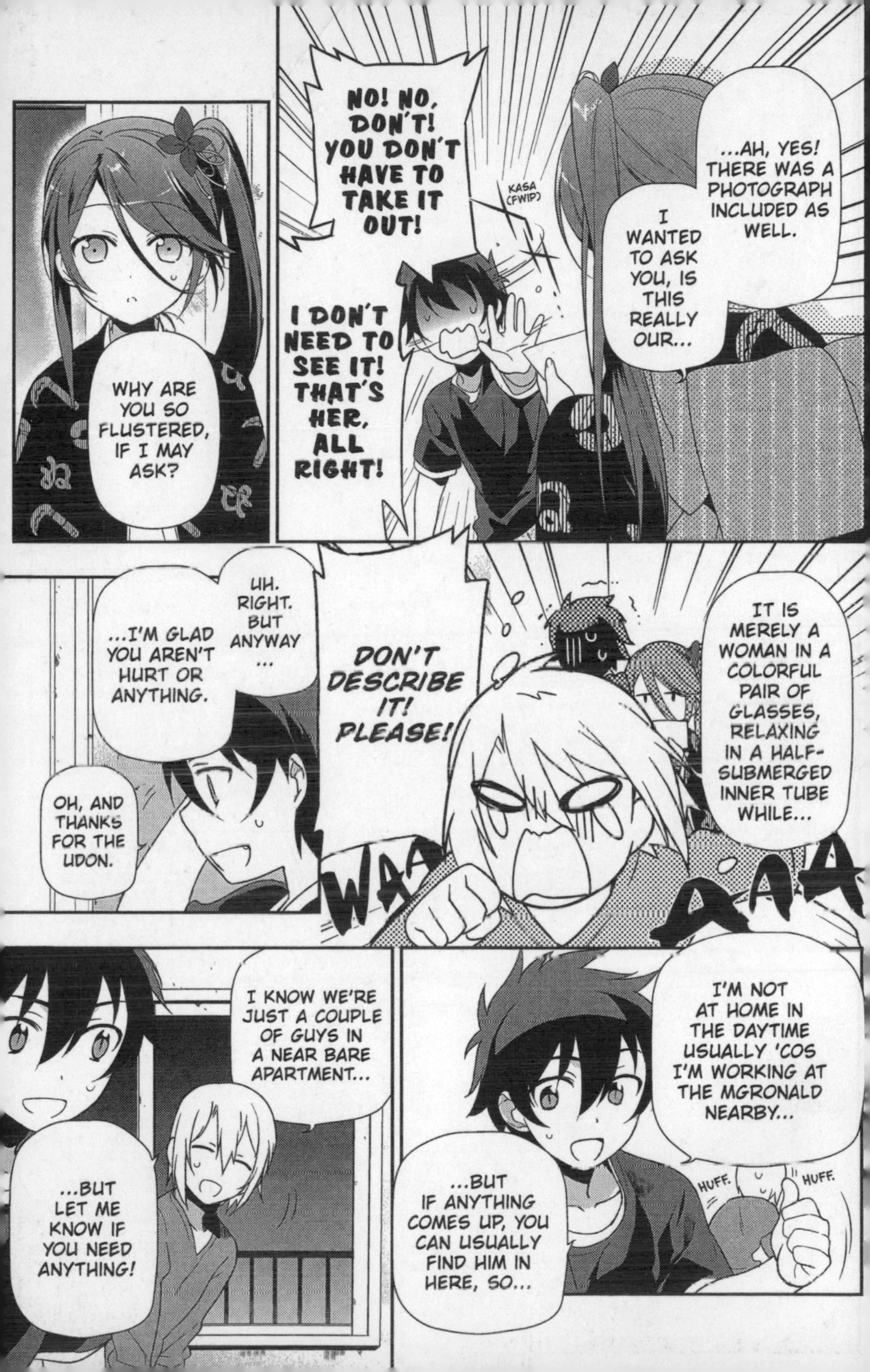
...AH, YES! THERE WAS A PHOTOGRAPH INCLUDED AS WELL.
I WANTED TO ASK YOU, IS THIS REALLY OUR...
NO! NO, DON'T! YOU DON'T HAVE TO TAKE IT OUT!
KASA (FWIP)
I DON'T NEED TO SEE IT! THAT'S HER, ALL RIGHT!
WHY ARE YOU SO FLUSTERED, IF I MAY ASK?
IT IS MERELY A WOMAN IN A COLORFUL PAIR OF GLASSES, RELAXING IN A HALF-SUBMERGED INNER TUBE WHILE...
DON'T DESCRIBE IT! PLEASE!
WAAAAA
UH. RIGHT. BUT ANYWAY ...
...I'M GLAD YOU AREN'T HURT OR ANYTHING.
OH, AND THANKS FOR THE UDON.
I'M NOT AT HOME IN THE DAYTIME USUALLY 'COS I'M WORKING AT THE MGRONALD NEARBY...
...BUT IF ANYTHING COMES UP, YOU CAN USUALLY FIND HIM IN HERE, SO...
HUFF.
HUFF.
I KNOW WE'RE JUST A COUPLE OF GUYS IN A NEAR BARE APARTMENT...
...BUT LET ME KNOW IF YOU NEED ANYTHING!

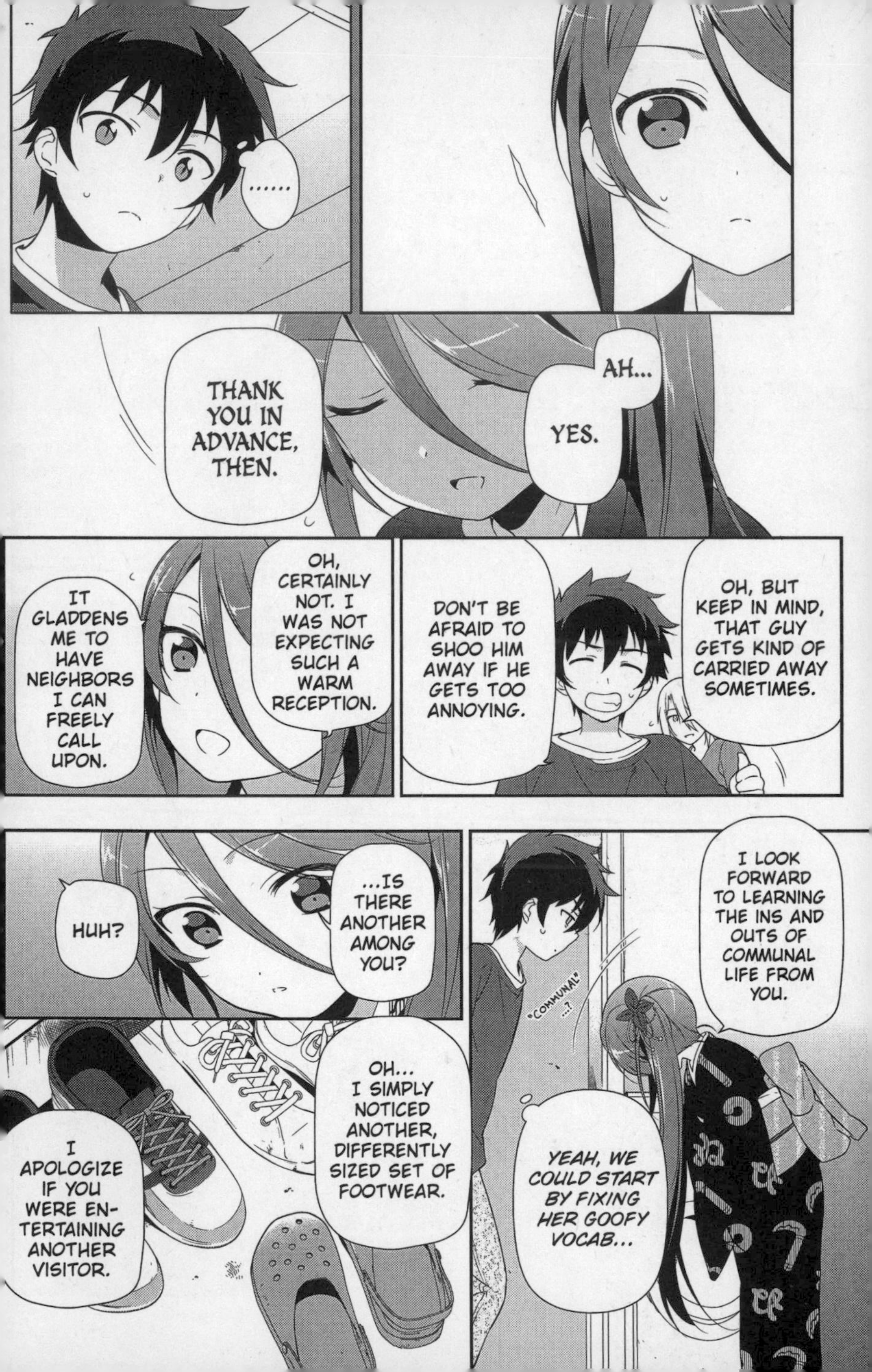
......
AH... YES.
THANK YOU IN ADVANCE, THEN.
OH, BUT KEEP IN MIND, THAT GUY GETS KIND OF CARRIED AWAY SOMETIMES.
DON'T BE AFRAID TO SHOO HIM AWAY IF HE GETS TOO ANNOYING.
OH, CERTAINLY NOT. I WAS NOT EXPECTING SUCH A WARM RECEPTION.
IT GLADDENS ME TO HAVE NEIGHBORS I CAN FREELY CALL UPON.
I LOOK FORWARD TO LEARNING THE INS AND OUTS OF COMMUNAL LIFE FROM YOU.
"COMMUNAL" ...?
YEAH, WE COULD START BY FIXING HER GOOFY VOCAB...
...IS THERE ANOTHER AMONG YOU?
HUH?
OH... I SIMPLY NOTICED ANOTHER, DIFFERENTLY SIZED SET OF FOOTWEAR.
I APOLOGIZE IF YOU WERE EN-TERTAINING ANOTHER VISITOR.

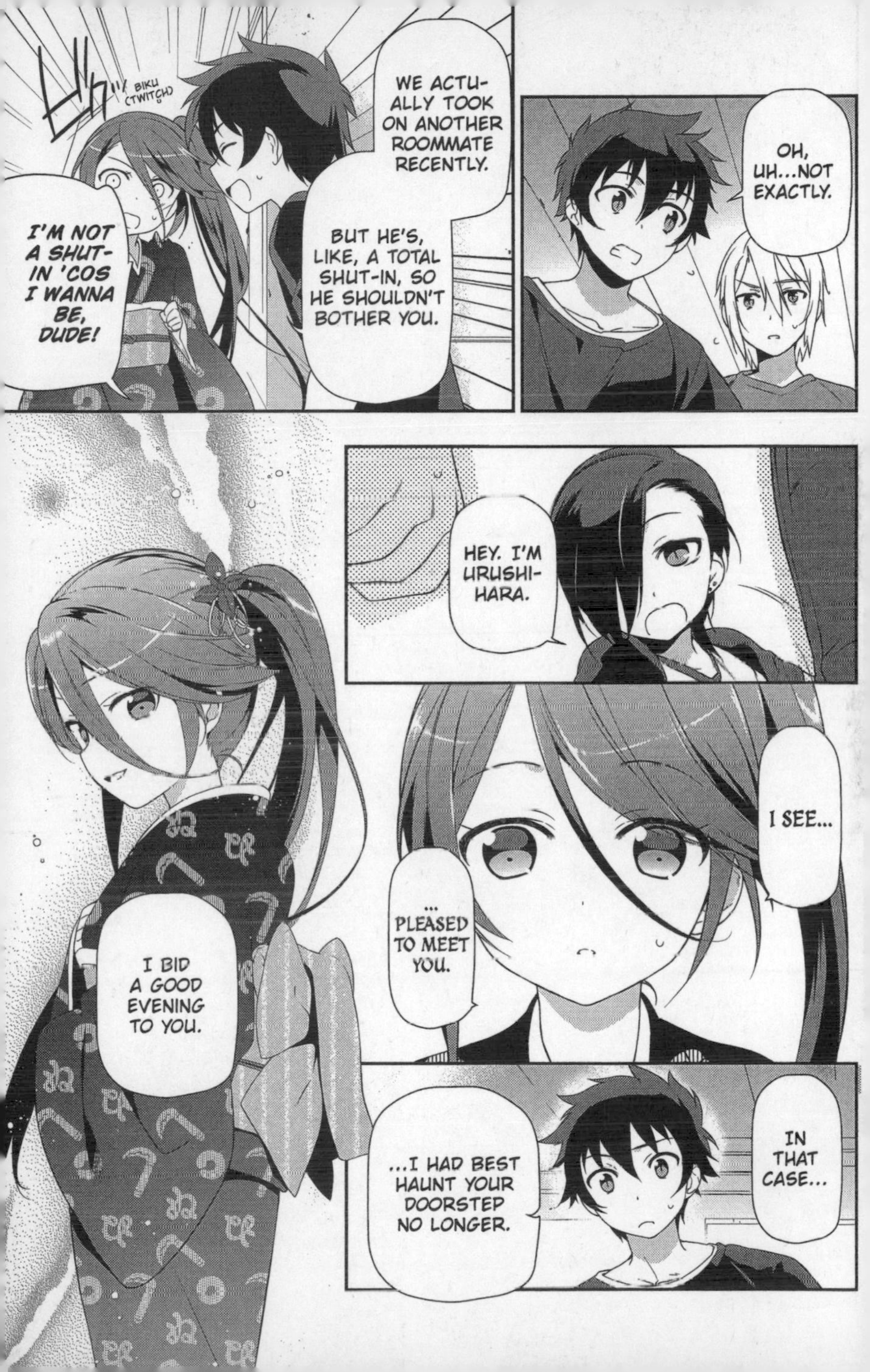
OH, UH...NOT EXACTLY.
WE ACTUALLY TOOK ON ANOTHER ROOMMATE RECENTLY.
BUT HE'S, LIKE, A TOTAL SHUT-IN, SO HE SHOULDN'T BOTHER YOU.
BIKU (TWITCH)
I'M NOT A SHUT-IN 'COS I WANNA BE, DUDE!
HEY. I'M URUSHIHARA.
I SEE...
...PLEASED TO MEET YOU.
IN THAT CASE...
...I HAD BEST HAUNT YOUR DOORSTEP NO LONGER.
I BID A GOOD EVENING TO YOU.

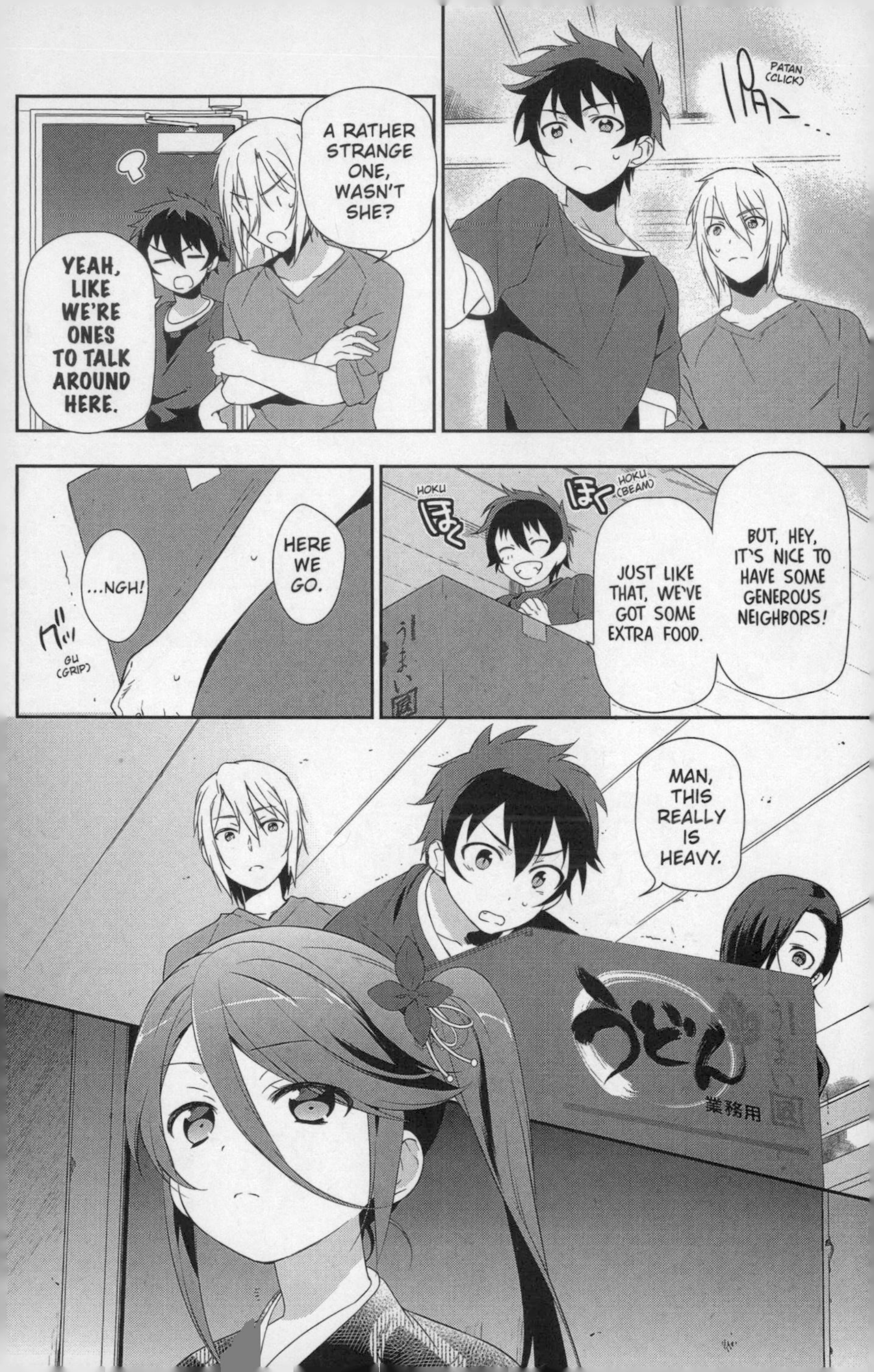
PATAN (CLICK)
A RATHER STRANGE ONE, WASN'T SHE?
YEAH, LIKE WE'RE ONES TO TALK AROUND HERE.
BUT, HEY, IT'S NICE TO HAVE SOME GENEROUS NEIGHBORS!
JUST LIKE THAT, WE'VE GOT SOME EXTRA FOOD.
HOKU (BEAM)
ほく
HOKU
ほく
HERE WE GO.
...NGH!
GU (GRIP)
MAN, THIS REALLY IS HEAVY.
うどん
業務用

Suzuno
Kamazuki

THE DEVIL IS A PART-TIMER!

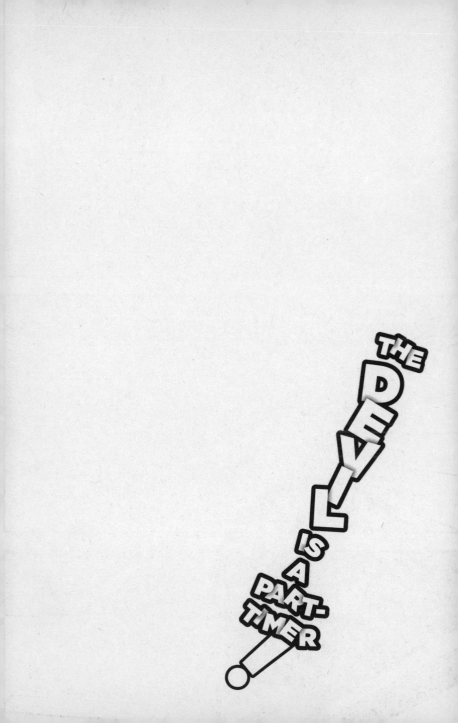

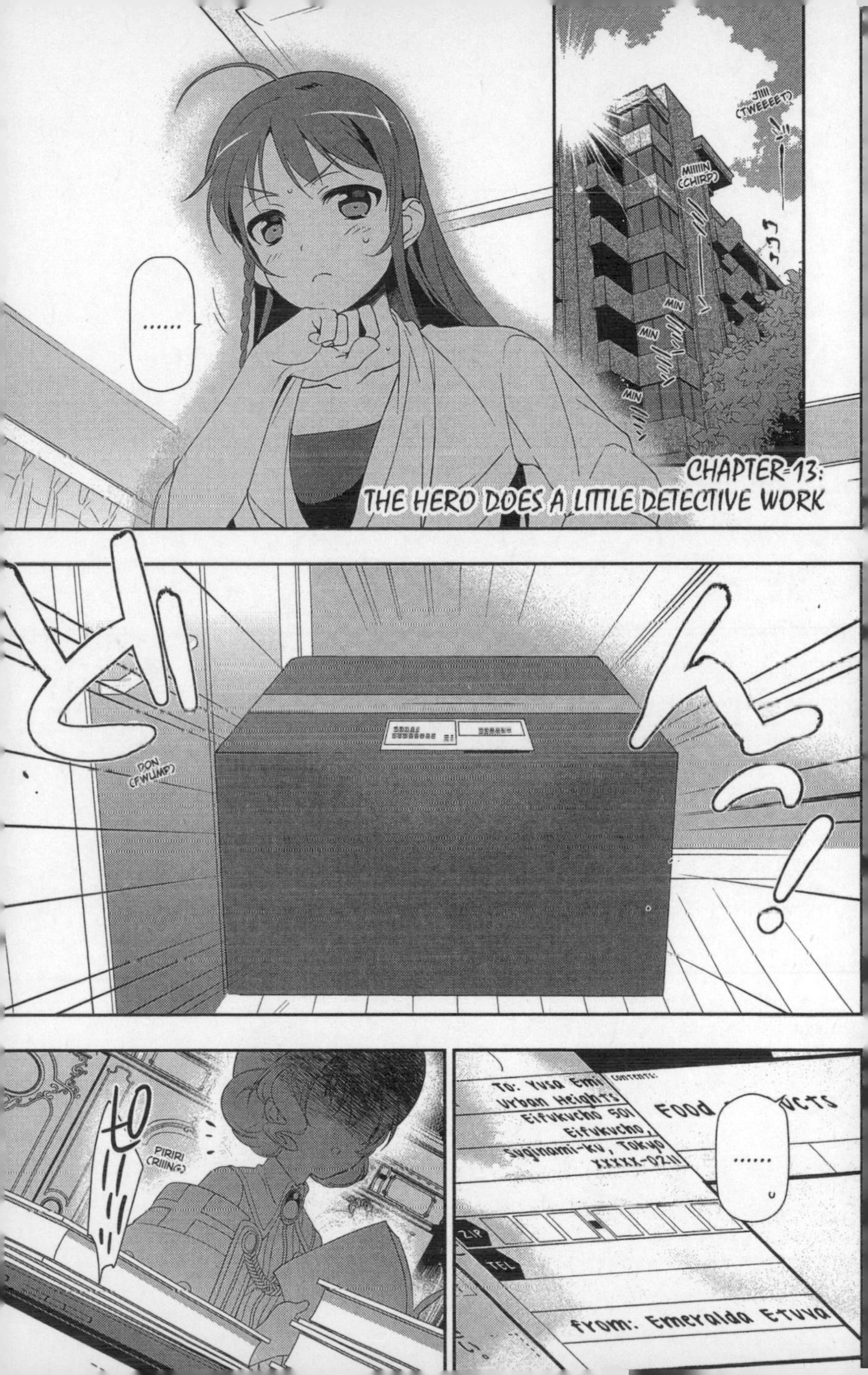
JIIII (TWEEEET)
MIIIIIN (CHIRP)
MIN
MIN
MIN
......
CHAPTER 13: THE HERO DOES A LITTLE DETECTIVE WORK
DON (FWUMP)
To: Yusa Emi
Urban Heights
Eifukucho 501
Eifukucho,
Suginami-ku, Tokyo
xxxxx-0211
CONTENTS:
Food
......
ZIP
TEL
from: Emeralda Etuva
PIRIRI (RIIING)

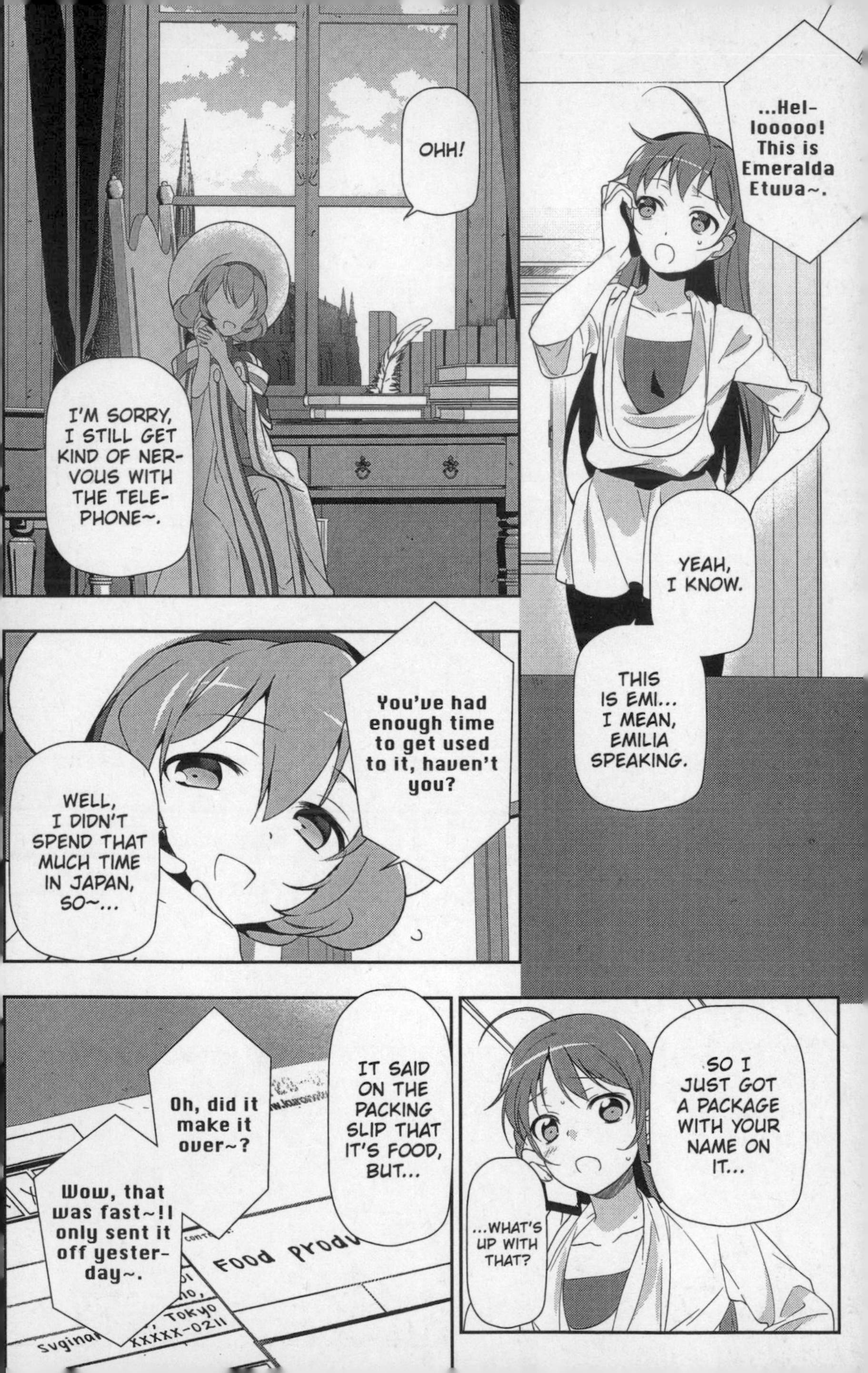
...Hel-looooo! This is Emeralda Etuva~.
YEAH, I KNOW.
THIS IS EMI... I MEAN, EMILIA SPEAKING.
OHH!
I'M SORRY, I STILL GET KIND OF NER-VOUS WITH THE TELE-PHONE~.
You've had enough time to get used to it, haven't you?
WELL, I DIDN'T SPEND THAT MUCH TIME IN JAPAN, SO~...
SO I JUST GOT A PACKAGE WITH YOUR NAME ON IT...
...WHAT'S UP WITH THAT?
IT SAID ON THE PACKING SLIP THAT IT'S FOOD, BUT...
Oh, did it make it over~?
Wow, that was fast~!I only sent it off yester-day~.

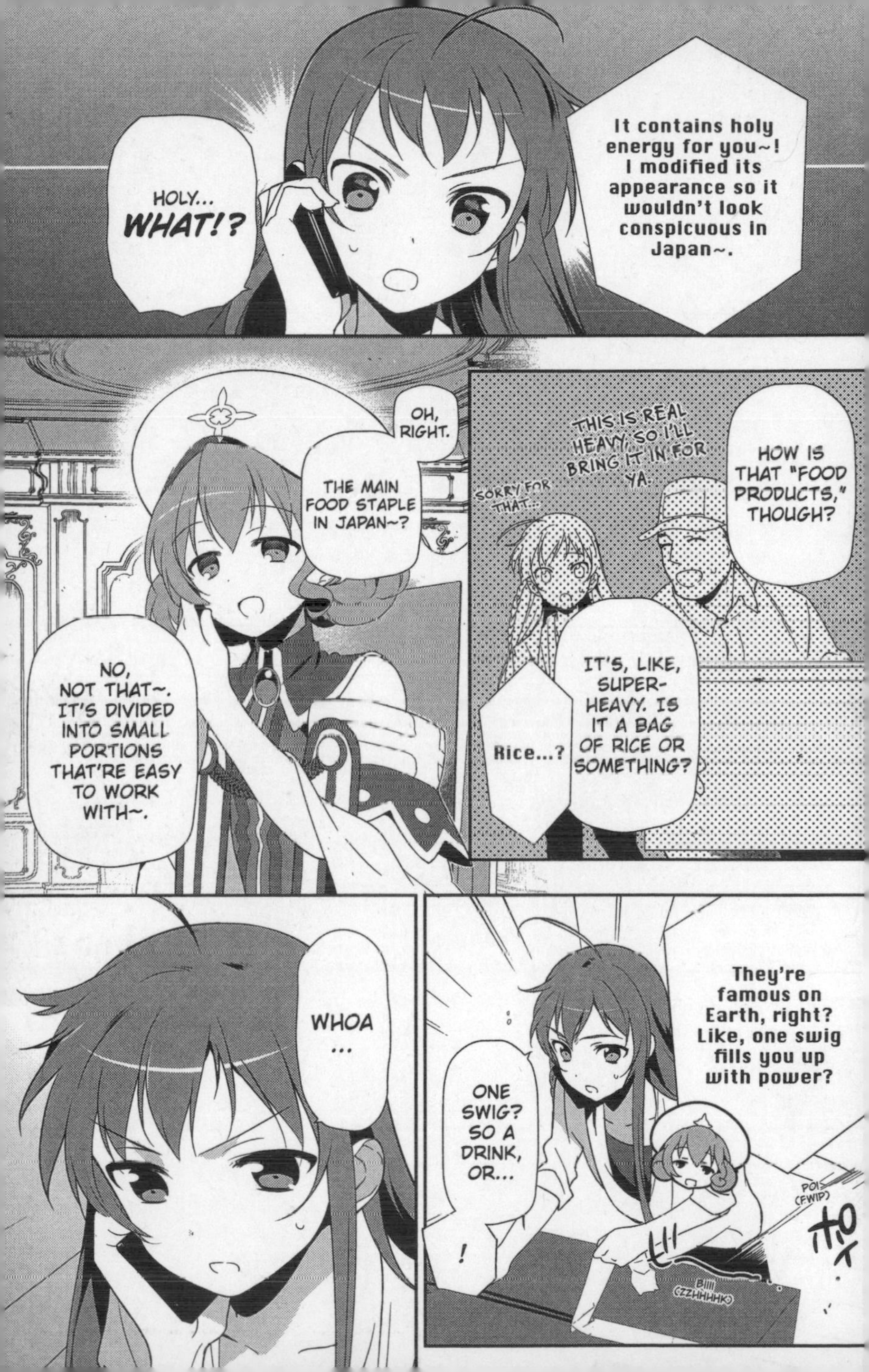
It contains holy energy for you~! I modified its appearance so it wouldn't look conspicuous in Japan~.
HOLY... WHAT!?
HOW IS THAT "FOOD PRODUCTS," THOUGH?
THIS IS REAL HEAVY, SO I'LL BRING IT IN FOR YA.
SORRY FOR THAT...
IT'S, LIKE, SUPER-HEAVY. IS IT A BAG OF RICE OR SOMETHING?
Rice...?
OH, RIGHT.
THE MAIN FOOD STAPLE IN JAPAN~?
NO, NOT THAT~. IT'S DIVIDED INTO SMALL PORTIONS THAT'RE EASY TO WORK WITH~.
They're famous on Earth, right? Like, one swig fills you up with power?
ONE SWIG? SO A DRINK, OR...
!
POI (FWIP)
BIIII (ZZHHHHK)
WHOA ...

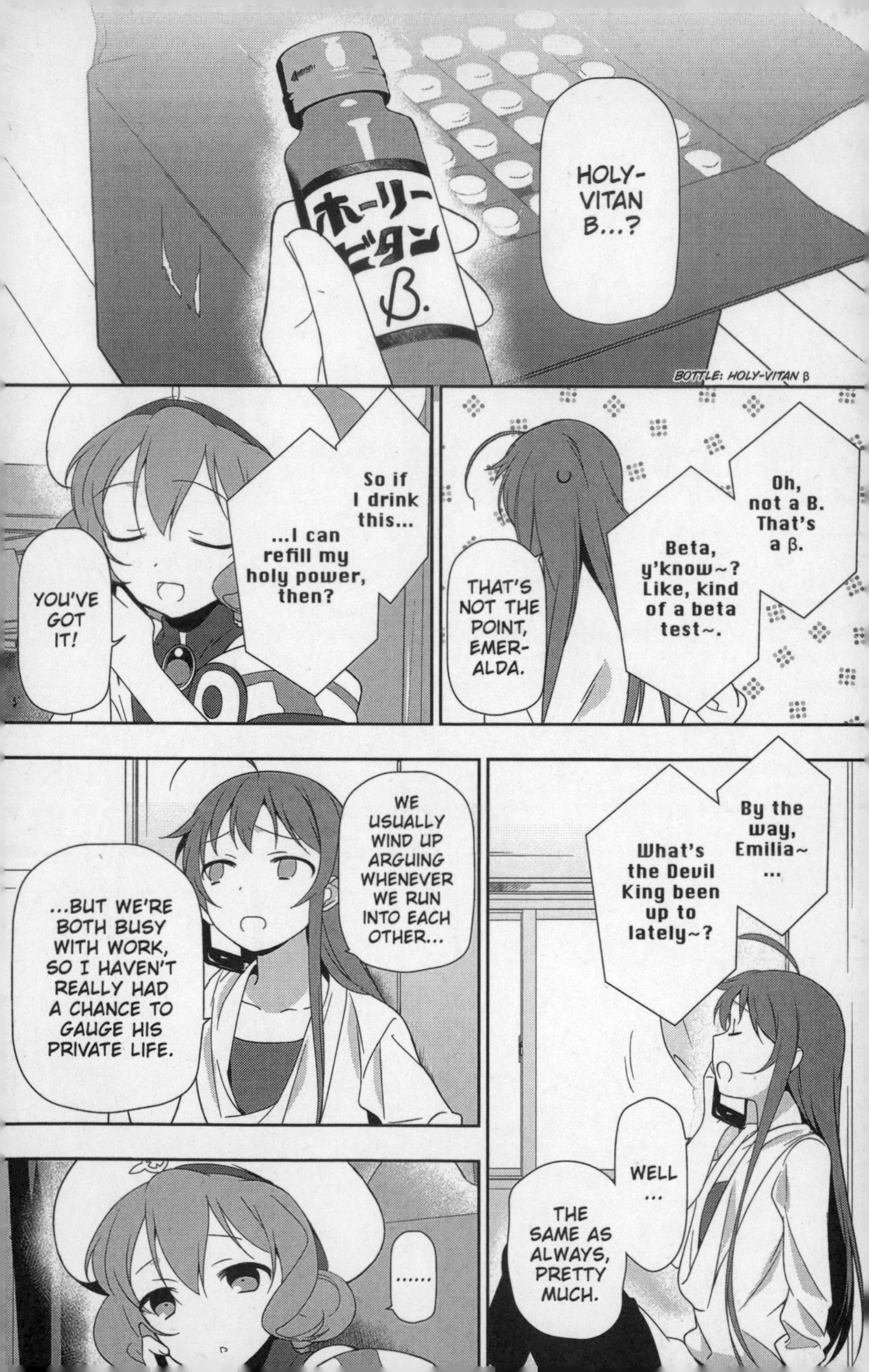
ホーリービタン β.
HOLY-VITAN B...?
BOTTLE: HOLY-VITAN β
Oh, not a B. That's a β.
Beta, y'know~? Like, kind of a beta test~.
THAT'S NOT THE POINT, EMERALDA.
So if I drink this...
...I can refill my holy power, then?
YOU'VE GOT IT!
By the way, Emilia~...
What's the Devil King been up to lately~?
WELL...
THE SAME AS ALWAYS, PRETTY MUCH.
WE USUALLY WIND UP ARGUING WHENEVER WE RUN INTO EACH OTHER...
...BUT WE'RE BOTH BUSY WITH WORK, SO I HAVEN'T REALLY HAD A CHANCE TO GAUGE HIS PRIVATE LIFE.
......

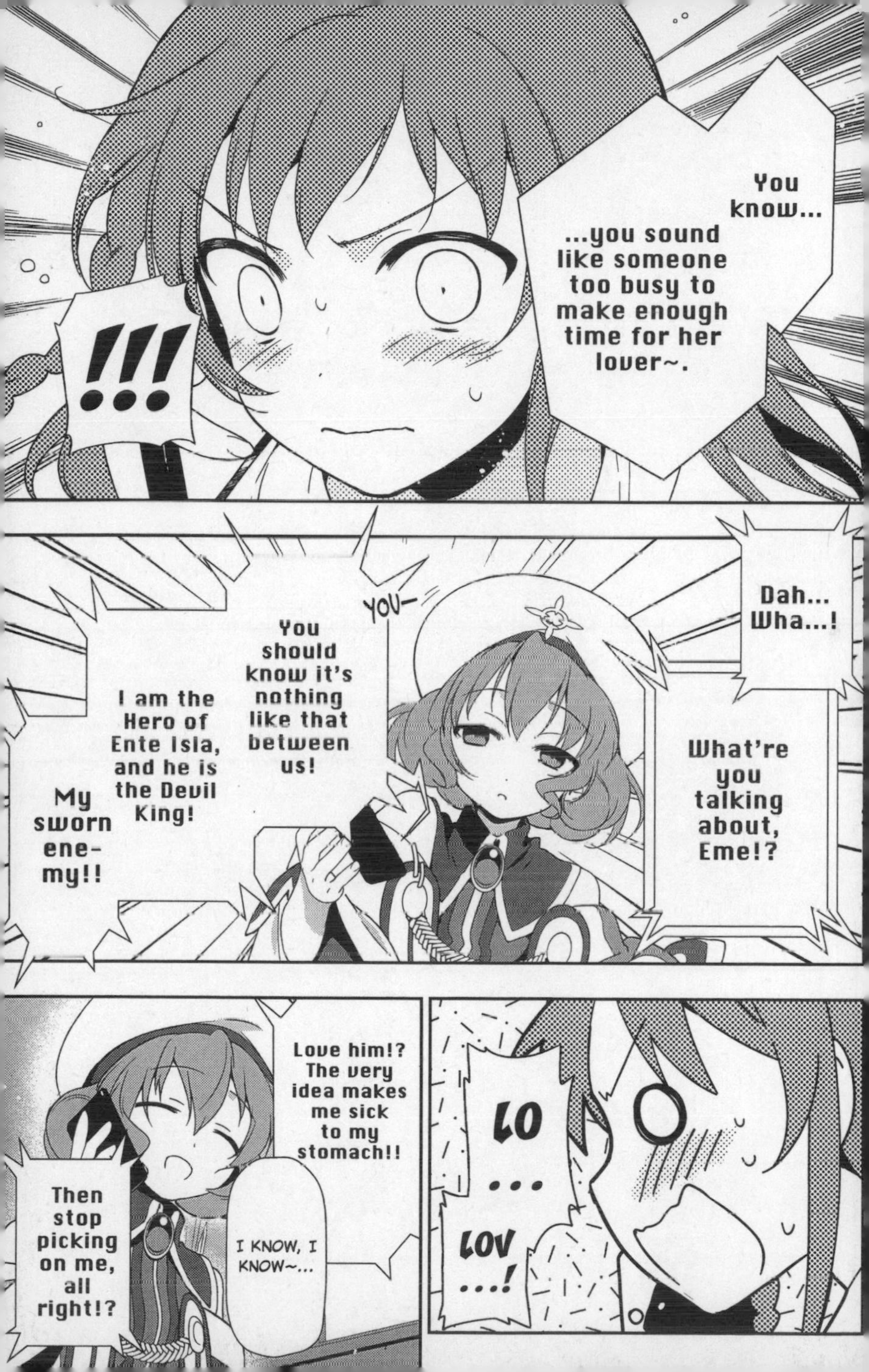
You know...
...you sound like someone too busy to make enough time for her lover~.
!!!
Dah... Wha...!
What're you talking about, Eme!?
YOU—
You should know it's nothing like that between us!
I am the Hero of Ente Isla, and he is the Devil King!
My sworn ene-my!!
LO...
LOV...!
Love him!? The very idea makes me sick to my stomach!!
I KNOW, I KNOW~...
Then stop picking on me, all right!?

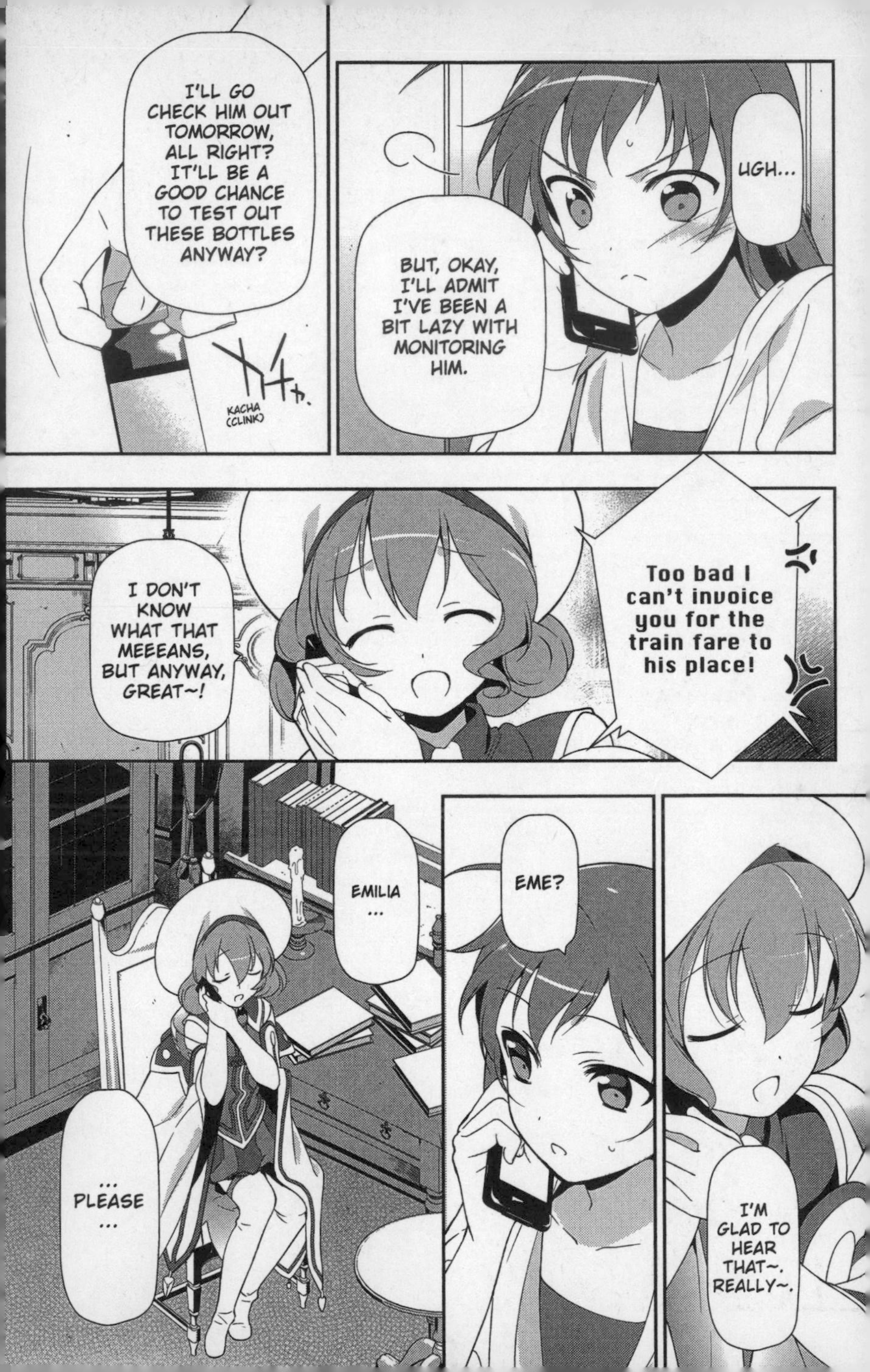
UGH...
BUT, OKAY, I'LL ADMIT I'VE BEEN A BIT LAZY WITH MONITORING HIM.
I'LL GO CHECK HIM OUT TOMORROW, ALL RIGHT? IT'LL BE A GOOD CHANCE TO TEST OUT THESE BOTTLES ANYWAY?
KACHA (CLINK)
Too bad I can't invoice you for the train fare to his place!
I DON'T KNOW WHAT THAT MEEEANS, BUT ANYWAY, GREAT~!
I'M GLAD TO HEAR THAT~. REALLY~.
EME?
EMILIA ...
... PLEASE ...

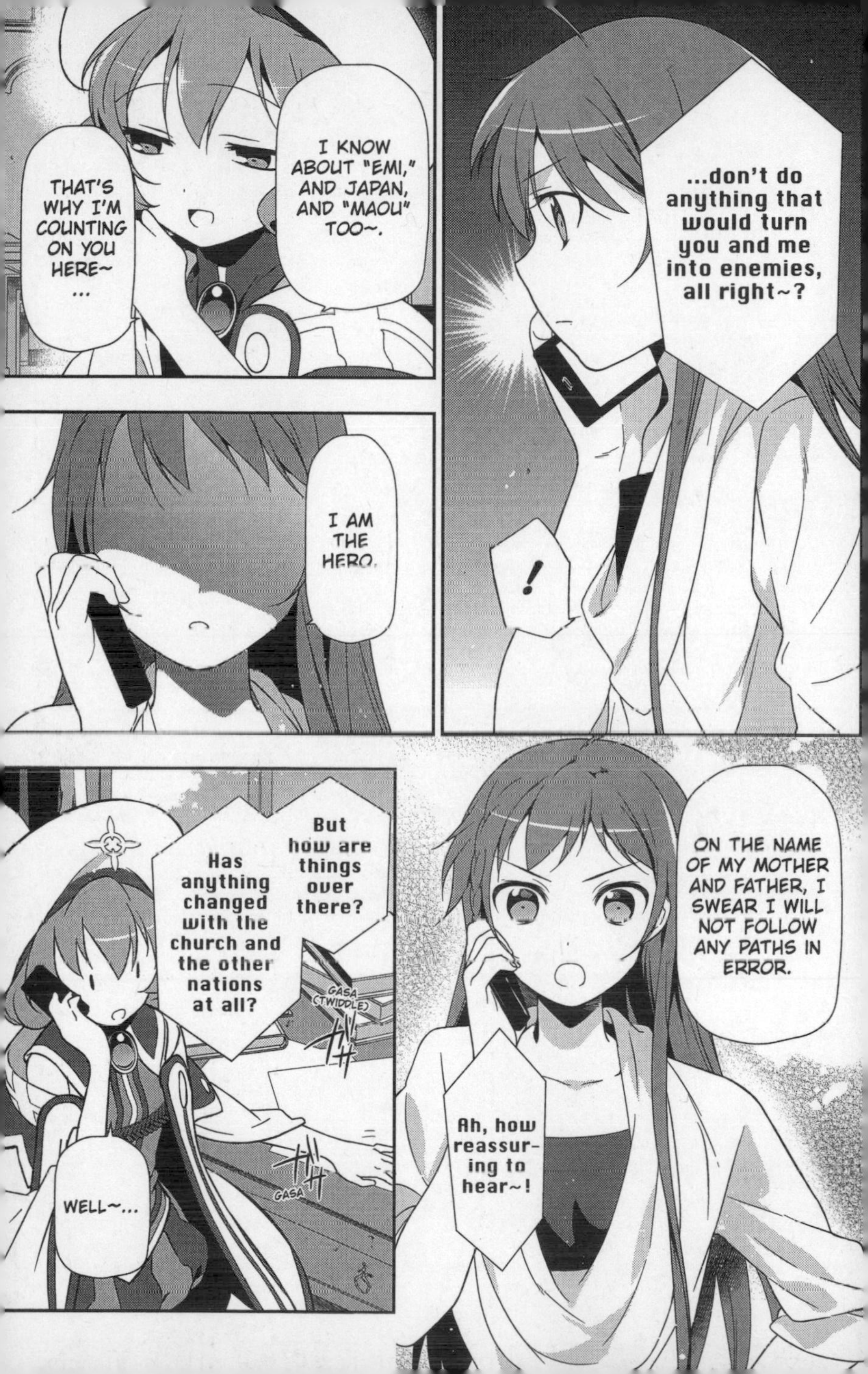
...don't do anything that would turn you and me into enemies, all right~?
!
I KNOW ABOUT "EMI," AND JAPAN, AND "MAOU" TOO~.
THAT'S WHY I'M COUNTING ON YOU HERE~ ...
I AM THE HERO.
ON THE NAME OF MY MOTHER AND FATHER, I SWEAR I WILL NOT FOLLOW ANY PATHS IN ERROR.
Ah, how reassur-ing to hear~!
But how are things over there?
Has anything changed with the church and the other nations at all?
GASA (TWIDDLE)
GASA
WELL~...

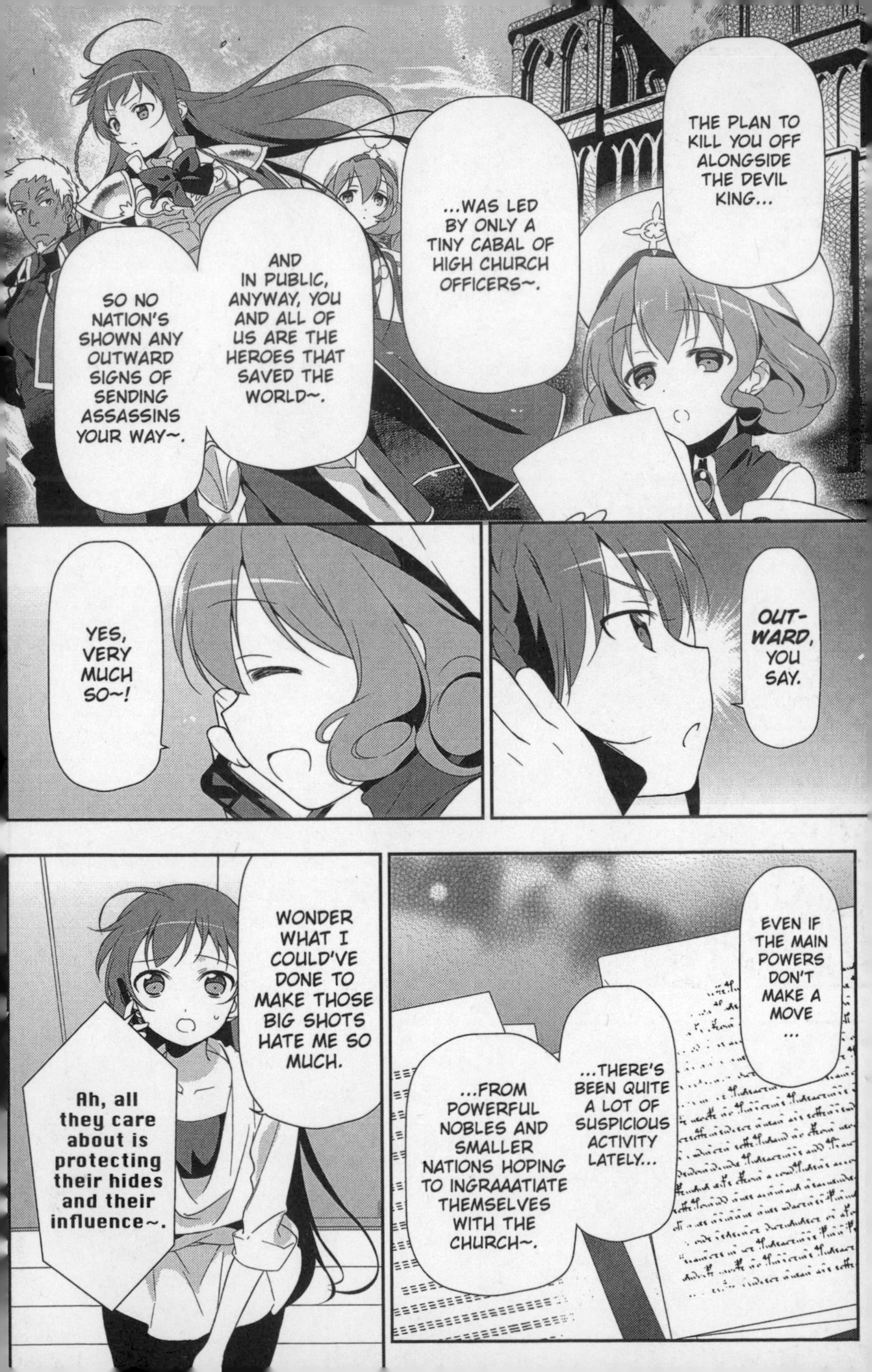
THE PLAN TO KILL YOU OFF ALONGSIDE THE DEVIL KING...
...WAS LED BY ONLY A TINY CABAL OF HIGH CHURCH OFFICERS~.
AND IN PUBLIC, ANYWAY, YOU AND ALL OF US ARE THE HEROES THAT SAVED THE WORLD~.
SO NO NATION'S SHOWN ANY OUTWARD SIGNS OF SENDING ASSASSINS YOUR WAY~.
OUTWARD, YOU SAY.
YES, VERY MUCH SO~!
EVEN IF THE MAIN POWERS DON'T MAKE A MOVE ...
...THERE'S BEEN QUITE A LOT OF SUSPICIOUS ACTIVITY LATELY...
...FROM POWERFUL NOBLES AND SMALLER NATIONS HOPING TO INGRAAATIATE THEMSELVES WITH THE CHURCH~.
WONDER WHAT I COULD'VE DONE TO MAKE THOSE BIG SHOTS HATE ME SO MUCH.
Ah, all they care about is protecting their hides and their influence~.

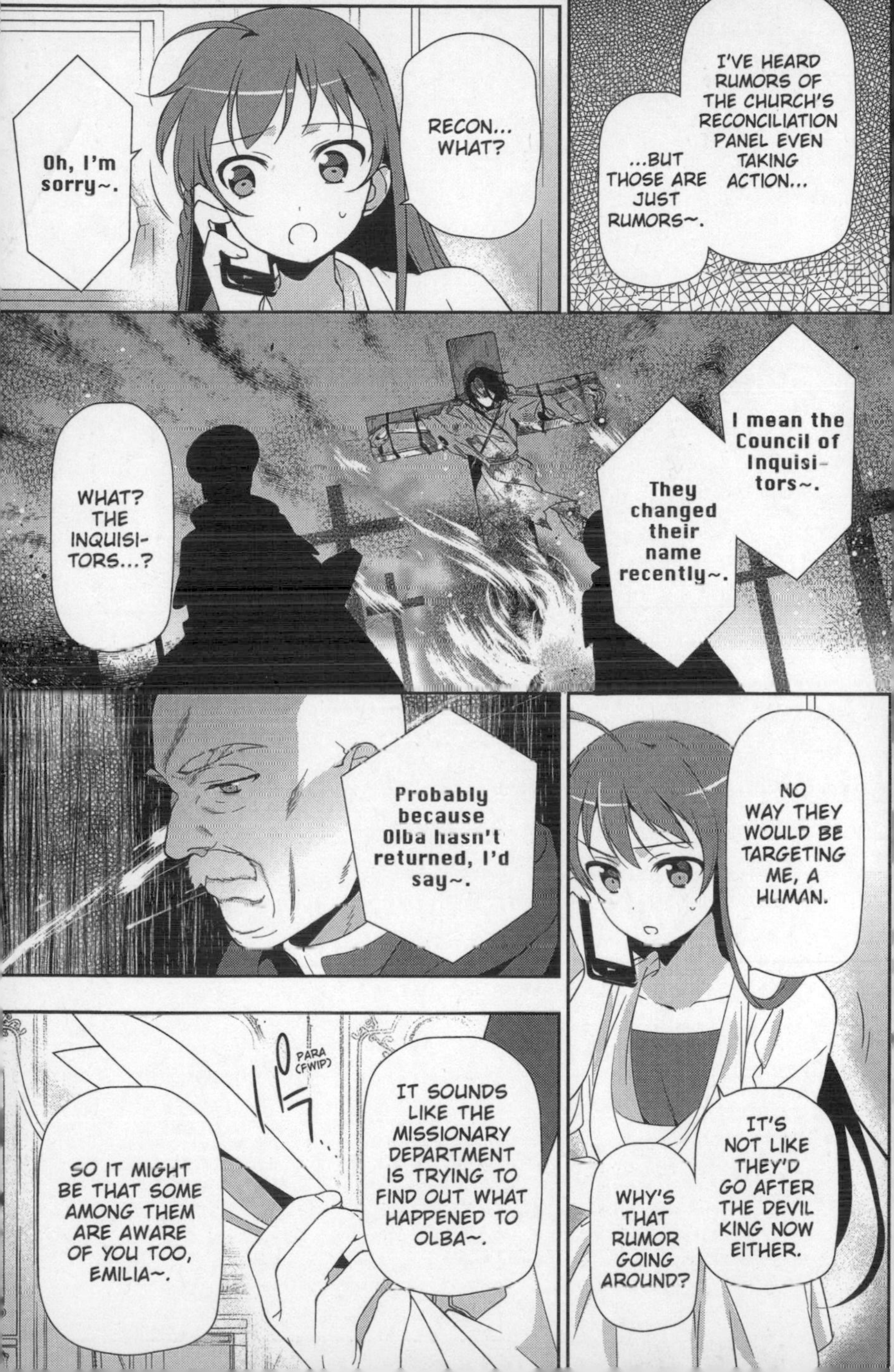
I'VE HEARD RUMORS OF THE CHURCH'S RECONCILIATION PANEL EVEN TAKING ACTION...
...BUT THOSE ARE JUST RUMORS~.
RECON... WHAT?
Oh, I'm sorry~.
I mean the Council of Inquisitors~.
They changed their name recently~.
WHAT? THE INQUISITORS...?
NO WAY THEY WOULD BE TARGETING ME, A HUMAN.
IT'S NOT LIKE THEY'D GO AFTER THE DEVIL KING NOW EITHER.
WHY'S THAT RUMOR GOING AROUND?
Probably because Olba hasn't returned, I'd say~.
PARA (FWIP)
IT SOUNDS LIKE THE MISSIONARY DEPARTMENT IS TRYING TO FIND OUT WHAT HAPPENED TO OLBA~.
SO IT MIGHT BE THAT SOME AMONG THEM ARE AWARE OF YOU TOO, EMILIA~.

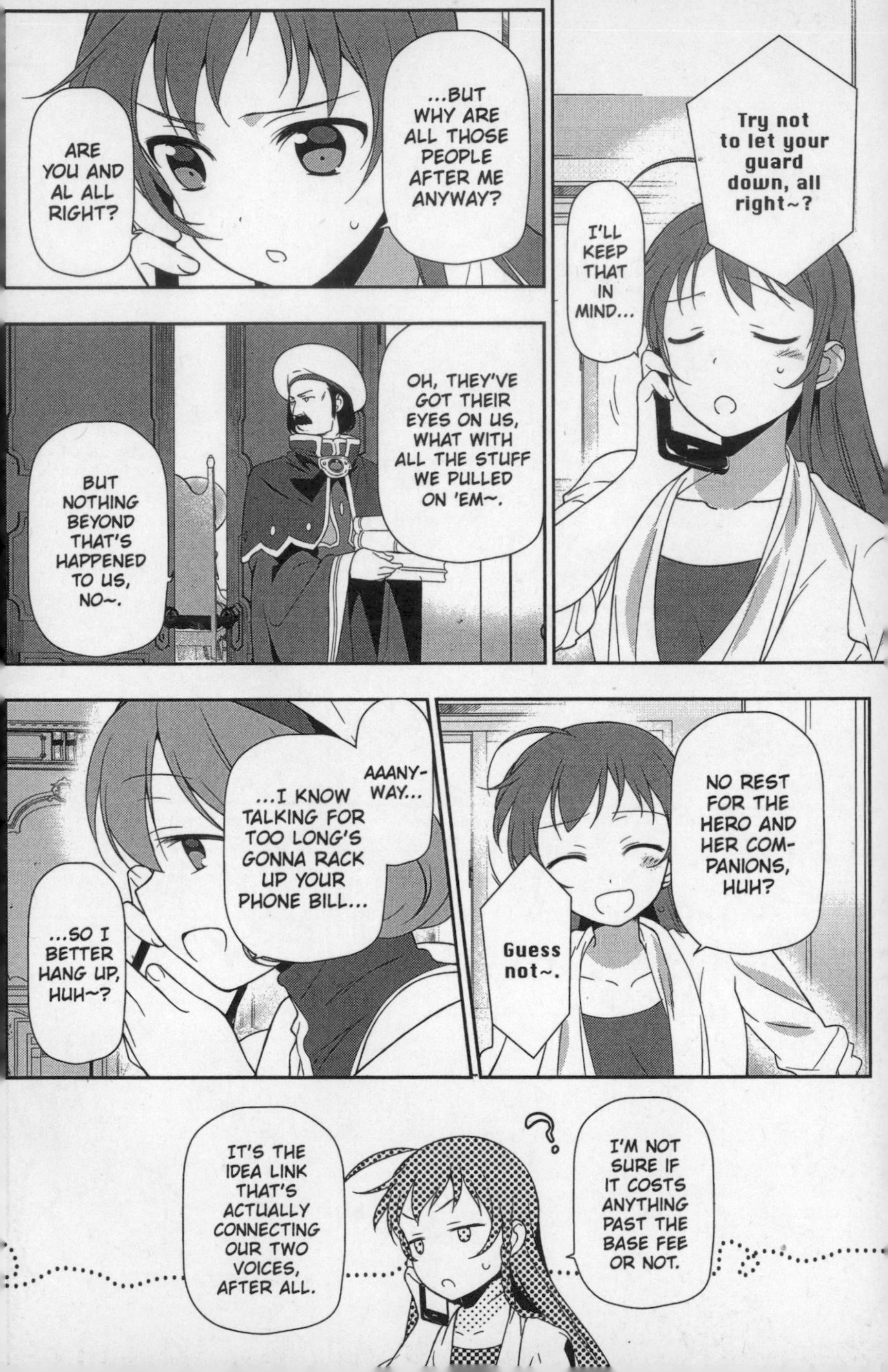
Try not to let your guard down, all right~?
I'LL KEEP THAT IN MIND...
...BUT WHY ARE ALL THOSE PEOPLE AFTER ME ANYWAY?
ARE YOU AND AL ALL RIGHT?
OH, THEY'VE GOT THEIR EYES ON US, WHAT WITH ALL THE STUFF WE PULLED ON 'EM~.
BUT NOTHING BEYOND THAT'S HAPPENED TO US, NO~.
NO REST FOR THE HERO AND HER COM-PANIONS, HUH?
Guess not~.
AAANY-WAY...
...I KNOW TALKING FOR TOO LONG'S GONNA RACK UP YOUR PHONE BILL...
...SO I BETTER HANG UP, HUH~?
I'M NOT SURE IF IT COSTS ANYTHING PAST THE BASE FEE OR NOT.
IT'S THE IDEA LINK THAT'S ACTUALLY CONNECTING OUR TWO VOICES, AFTER ALL.

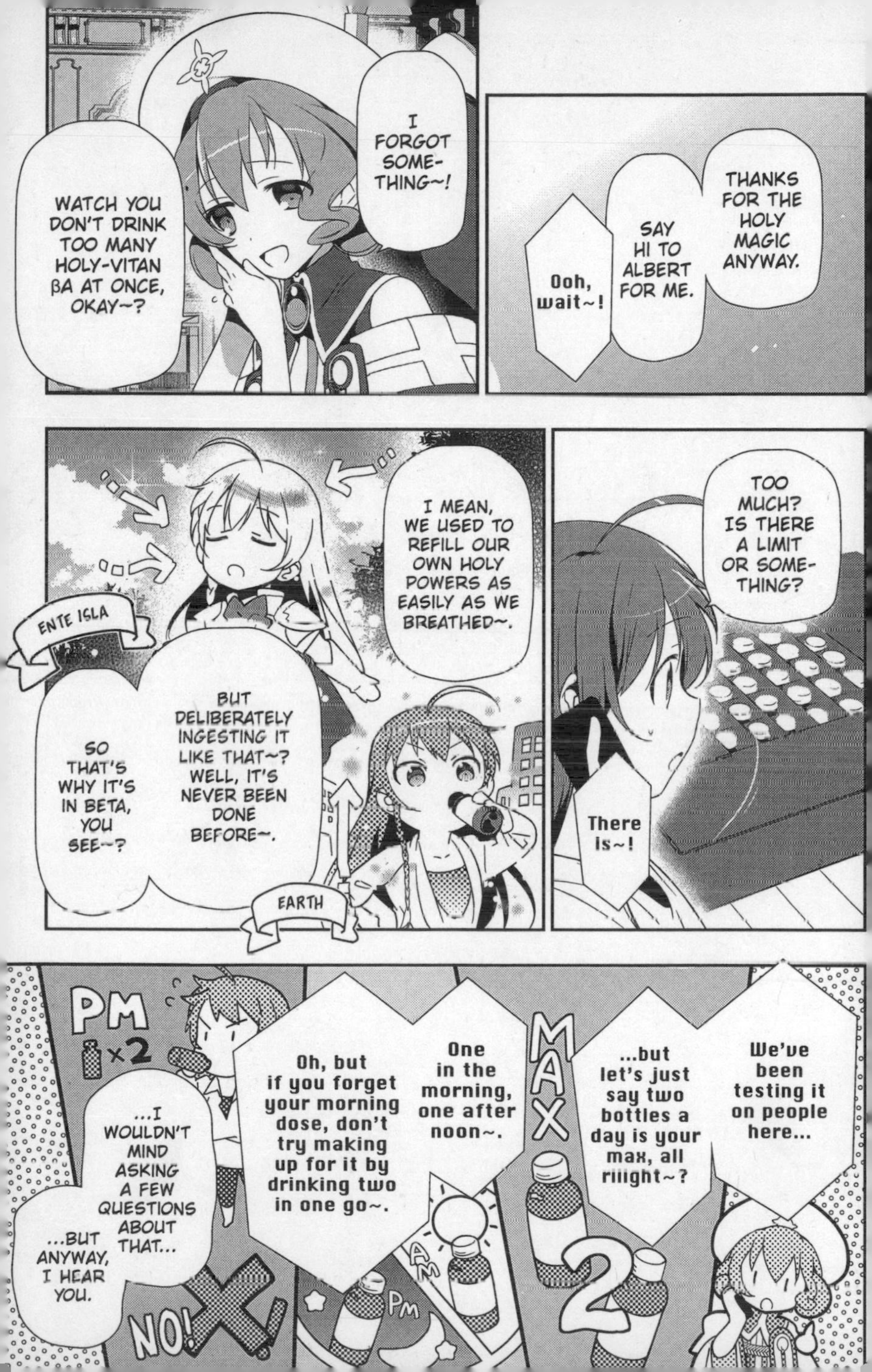
THANKS FOR THE HOLY MAGIC ANYWAY.
SAY HI TO ALBERT FOR ME.
Ooh, wait~!
I FORGOT SOME-THING~!
WATCH YOU DON'T DRINK TOO MANY HOLY-VITAN βA AT ONCE, OKAY~?
TOO MUCH? IS THERE A LIMIT OR SOME-THING?
There is~!
I MEAN, WE USED TO REFILL OUR OWN HOLY POWERS AS EASILY AS WE BREATHED~.
ENTE ISLA
BUT DELIBERATELY INGESTING IT LIKE THAT~? WELL, IT'S NEVER BEEN DONE BEFORE~.
SO THAT'S WHY IT'S IN BETA, YOU SEE~?
EARTH
We've been testing it on people here...
...but let's just say two bottles a day is your max, all riiight~?
MAX
2
One in the morning, one after noon~.
AM
PM
Oh, but if you forget your morning dose, don't try making up for it by drinking two in one go~.
NO!
PM
×2
...I WOULDN'T MIND ASKING A FEW QUESTIONS ABOUT THAT...
...BUT ANYWAY, I HEAR YOU.

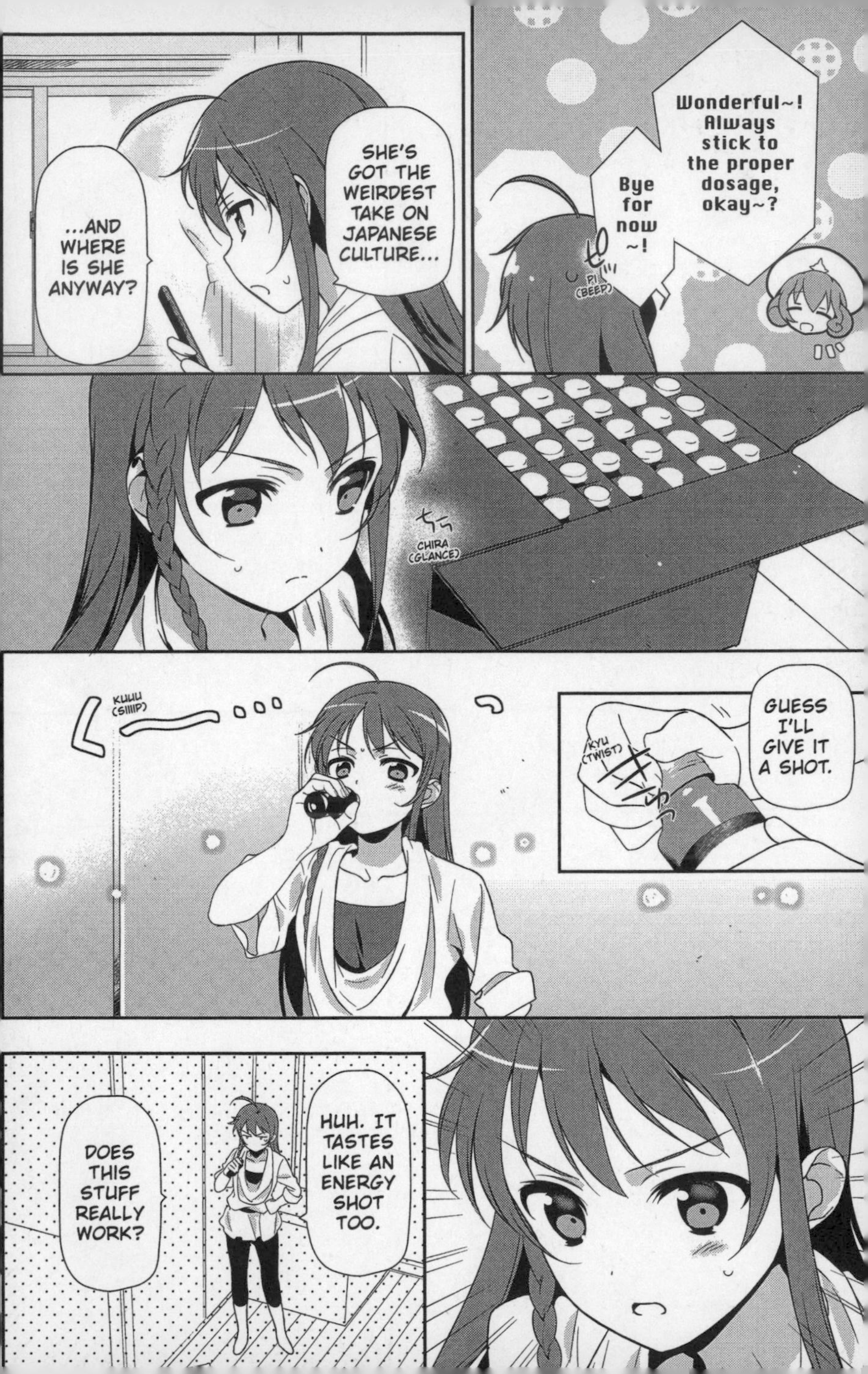
Wonderful~! Always stick to the proper dosage, okay~?
Bye for now ~!
PI (BEEP)
SHE'S GOT THE WEIRDEST TAKE ON JAPANESE CULTURE...
...AND WHERE IS SHE ANYWAY?
CHIRA (GLANCE)
GUESS I'LL GIVE IT A SHOT.
KYU (TWIST)
KUUU (SIIIIP)
HUH. IT TASTES LIKE AN ENERGY SHOT TOO.
DOES THIS STUFF REALLY WORK?

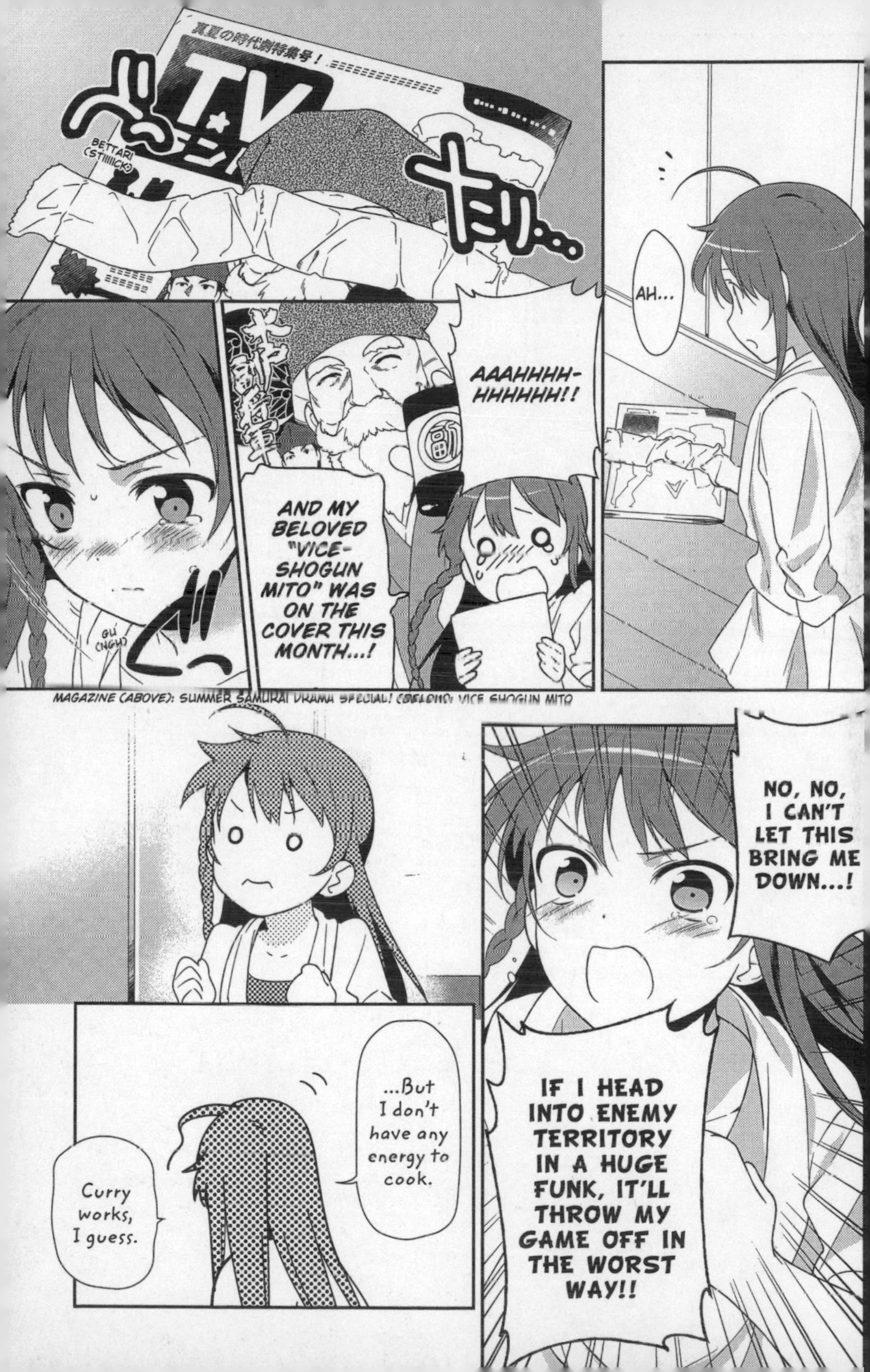
AH...
真夏の時代劇特集号！
TV
BETTARI (STIIIICK)
AAAHHHH-HHHHHH!!
AND MY BELOVED "VICE-SHOGUN MITO" WAS ON THE COVER THIS MONTH...!
GU (NGH)
MAGAZINE (ABOVE): SUMMER SAMURAI DRAMA SPECIAL! (BELOW): VICE SHOGUN MITO
NO, NO, I CAN'T LET THIS BRING ME DOWN...!
IF I HEAD INTO ENEMY TERRITORY IN A HUGE FUNK, IT'LL THROW MY GAME OFF IN THE WORST WAY!!
...But I don't have any energy to cook.
Curry works, I guess.

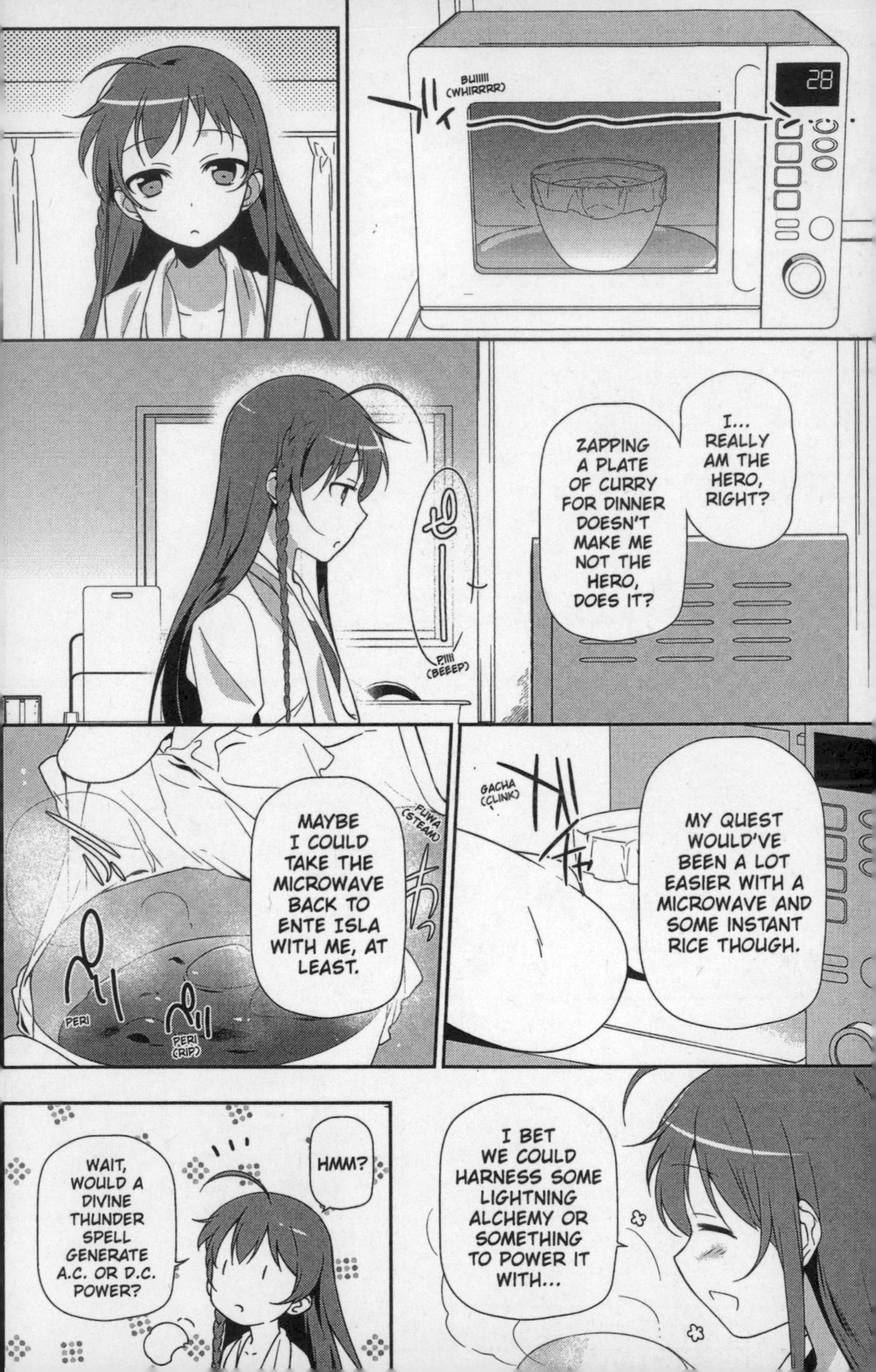
28
BUIIIII (WHIRRRR)
I... REALLY AM THE HERO, RIGHT?
ZAPPING A PLATE OF CURRY FOR DINNER DOESN'T MAKE ME NOT THE HERO, DOES IT?
PIIII (BEEEP)
GACHA (CLINK)
MY QUEST WOULD'VE BEEN A LOT EASIER WITH A MICROWAVE AND SOME INSTANT RICE THOUGH.
FUWA (STEAM)
MAYBE I COULD TAKE THE MICROWAVE BACK TO ENTE ISLA WITH ME, AT LEAST.
PERI
PERI (RIP)
I BET WE COULD HARNESS SOME LIGHTNING ALCHEMY OR SOMETHING TO POWER IT WITH...
HMM?
WAIT, WOULD A DIVINE THUNDER SPELL GENERATE A.C. OR D.C. POWER?

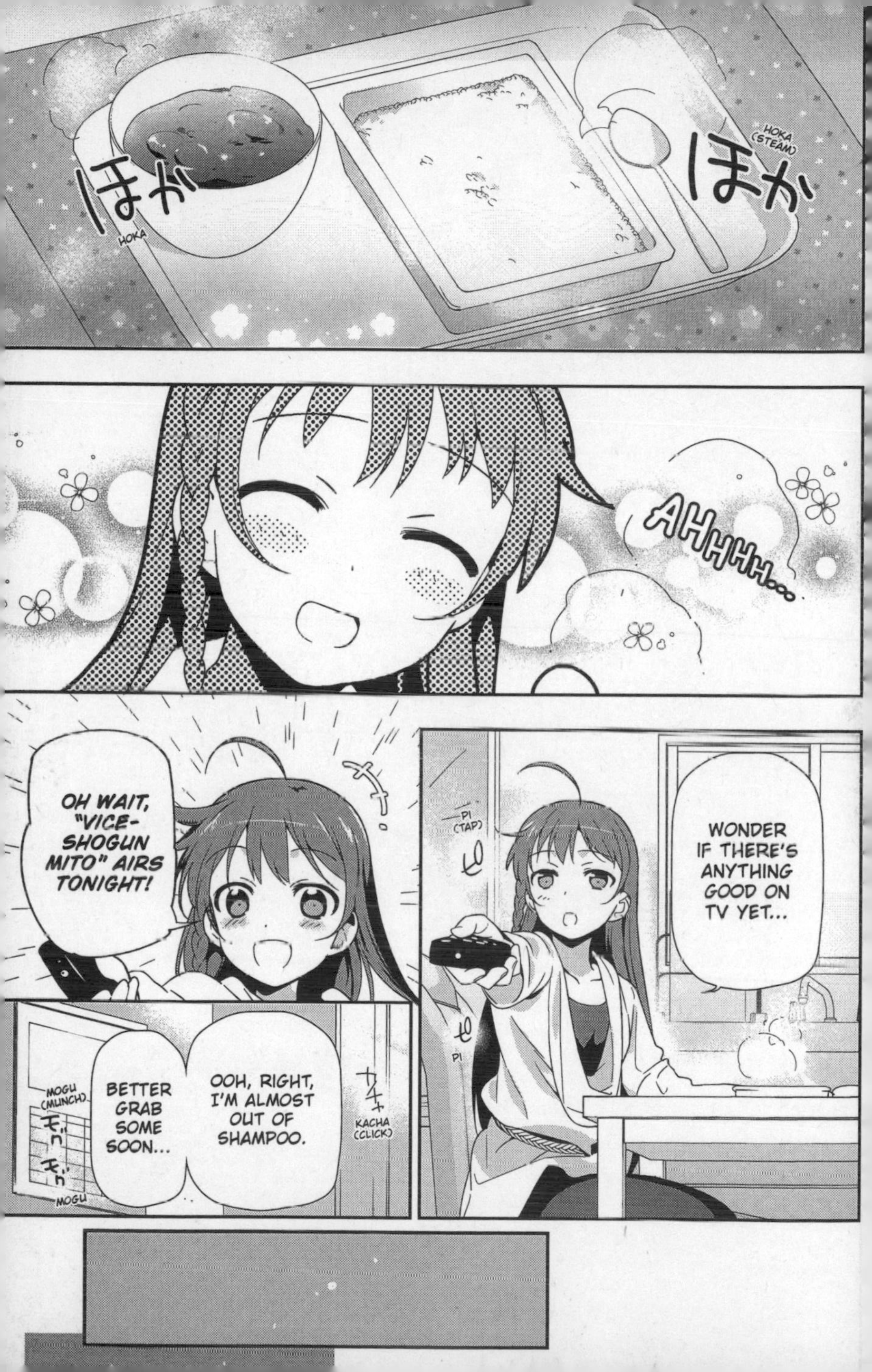
ほか
HOKA (STEAM)
ほか
HOKA
AHHHH...
PI (TAP)
ピ
WONDER IF THERE'S ANYTHING GOOD ON TV YET...
ピ
PI
OH WAIT, "VICE-SHOGUN MITO" AIRS TONIGHT!
カチャ
KACHA (CLICK)
OOH, RIGHT, I'M ALMOST OUT OF SHAMPOO.
BETTER GRAB SOME SOON...
MOGU (MUNCH)
モグ
モグ
MOGU

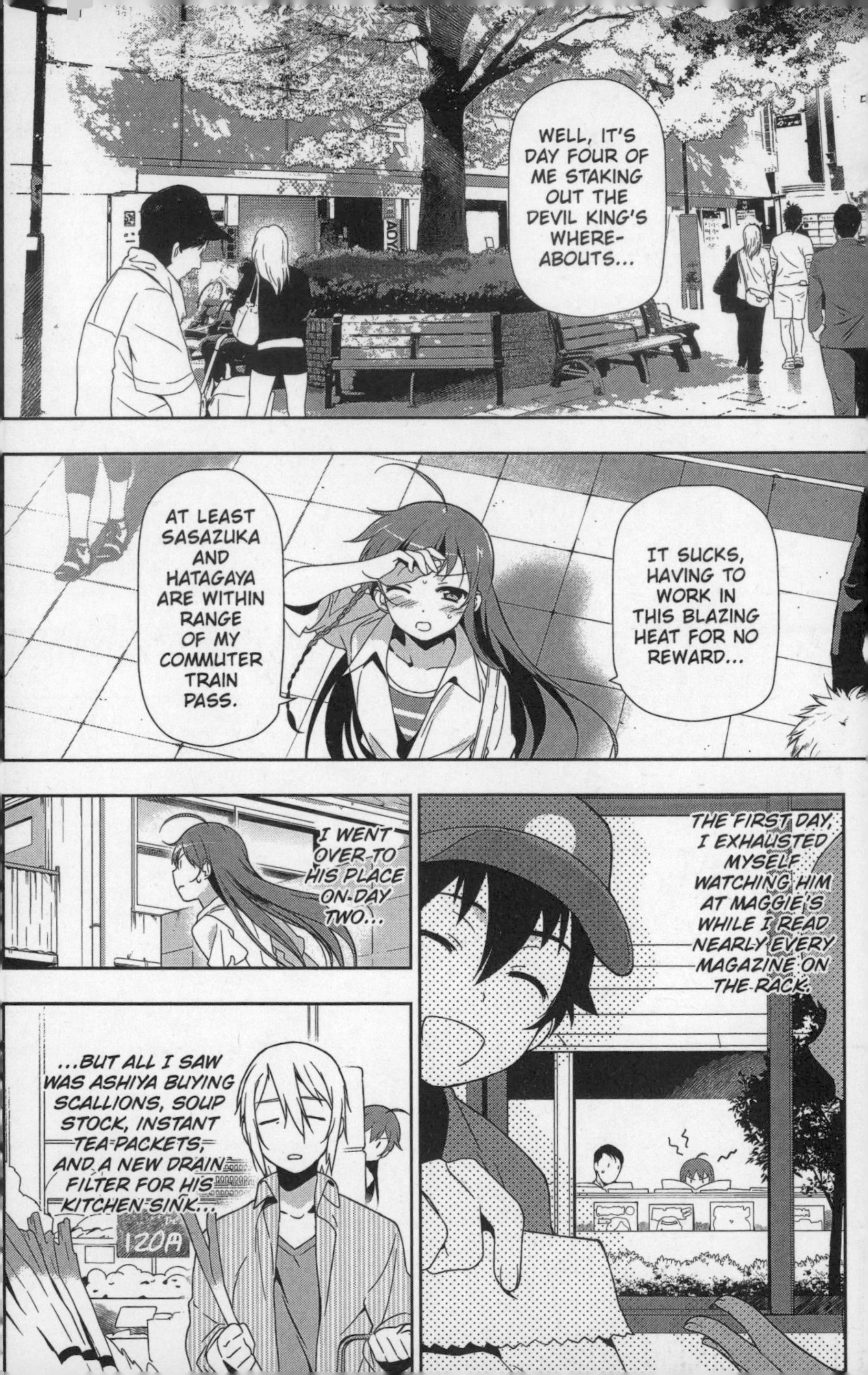
WELL, IT'S DAY FOUR OF ME STAKING OUT THE DEVIL KING'S WHERE-ABOUTS...
IT SUCKS, HAVING TO WORK IN THIS BLAZING HEAT FOR NO REWARD...
AT LEAST SASAZUKA AND HATAGAYA ARE WITHIN RANGE OF MY COMMUTER TRAIN PASS.
THE FIRST DAY, I EXHAUSTED MYSELF WATCHING HIM AT MAGGIE'S WHILE I READ NEARLY EVERY MAGAZINE ON THE RACK.
I WENT OVER TO HIS PLACE ON DAY TWO...
...BUT ALL I SAW WAS ASHIYA BUYING SCALLIONS, SOUP STOCK, INSTANT TEA PACKETS, AND A NEW DRAIN FILTER FOR HIS KITCHEN SINK...
120円

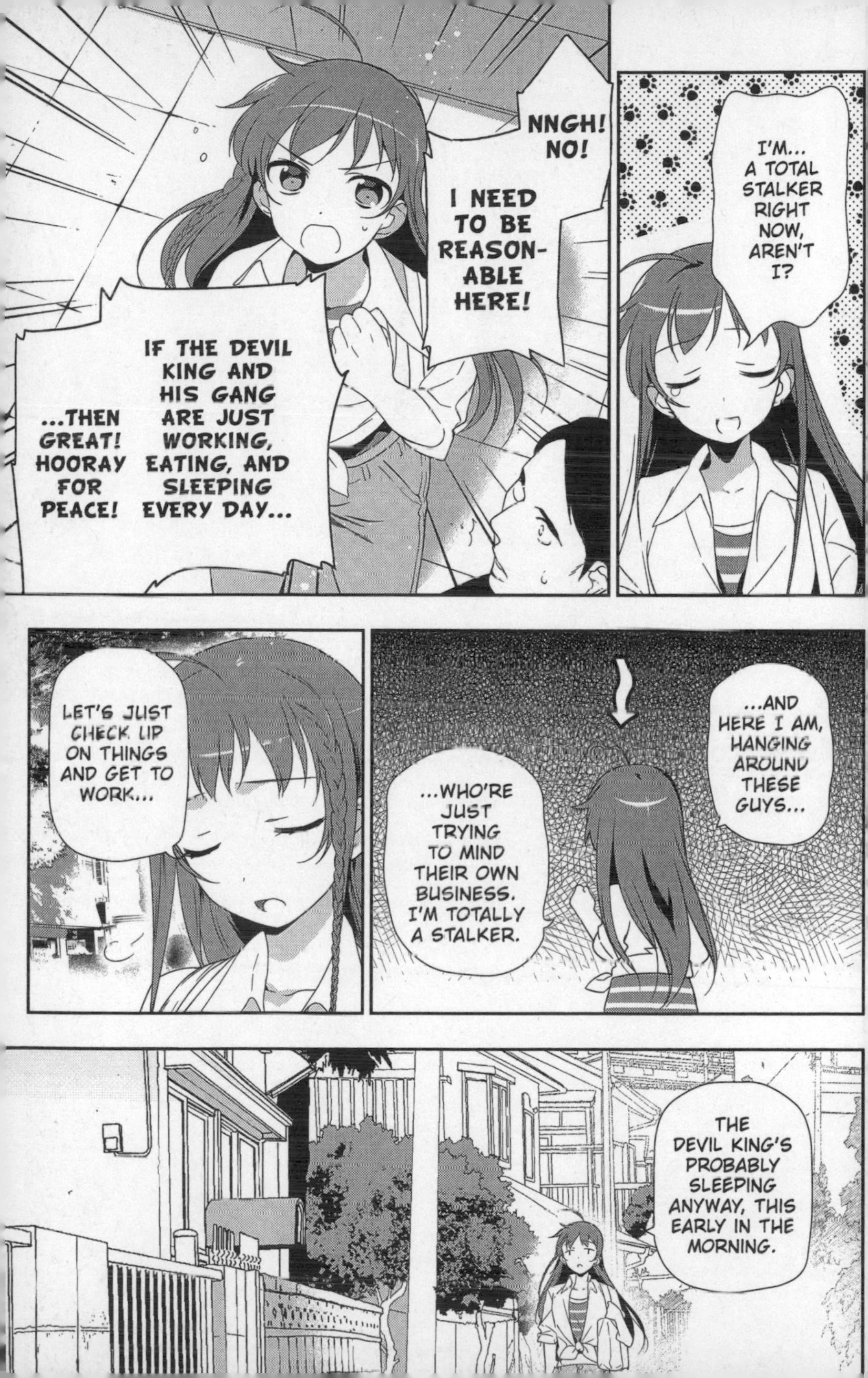
I'M... A TOTAL STALKER RIGHT NOW, AREN'T I?
NNGH! NO!
I NEED TO BE REASON-ABLE HERE!
IF THE DEVIL KING AND HIS GANG ARE JUST WORKING, EATING, AND SLEEPING EVERY DAY...
...THEN GREAT! HOORAY FOR PEACE!
...AND HERE I AM, HANGING AROUND THESE GUYS...
...WHO'RE JUST TRYING TO MIND THEIR OWN BUSINESS. I'M TOTALLY A STALKER.
LET'S JUST CHECK UP ON THINGS AND GET TO WORK...
THE DEVIL KING'S PROBABLY SLEEPING ANYWAY, THIS EARLY IN THE MORNING.

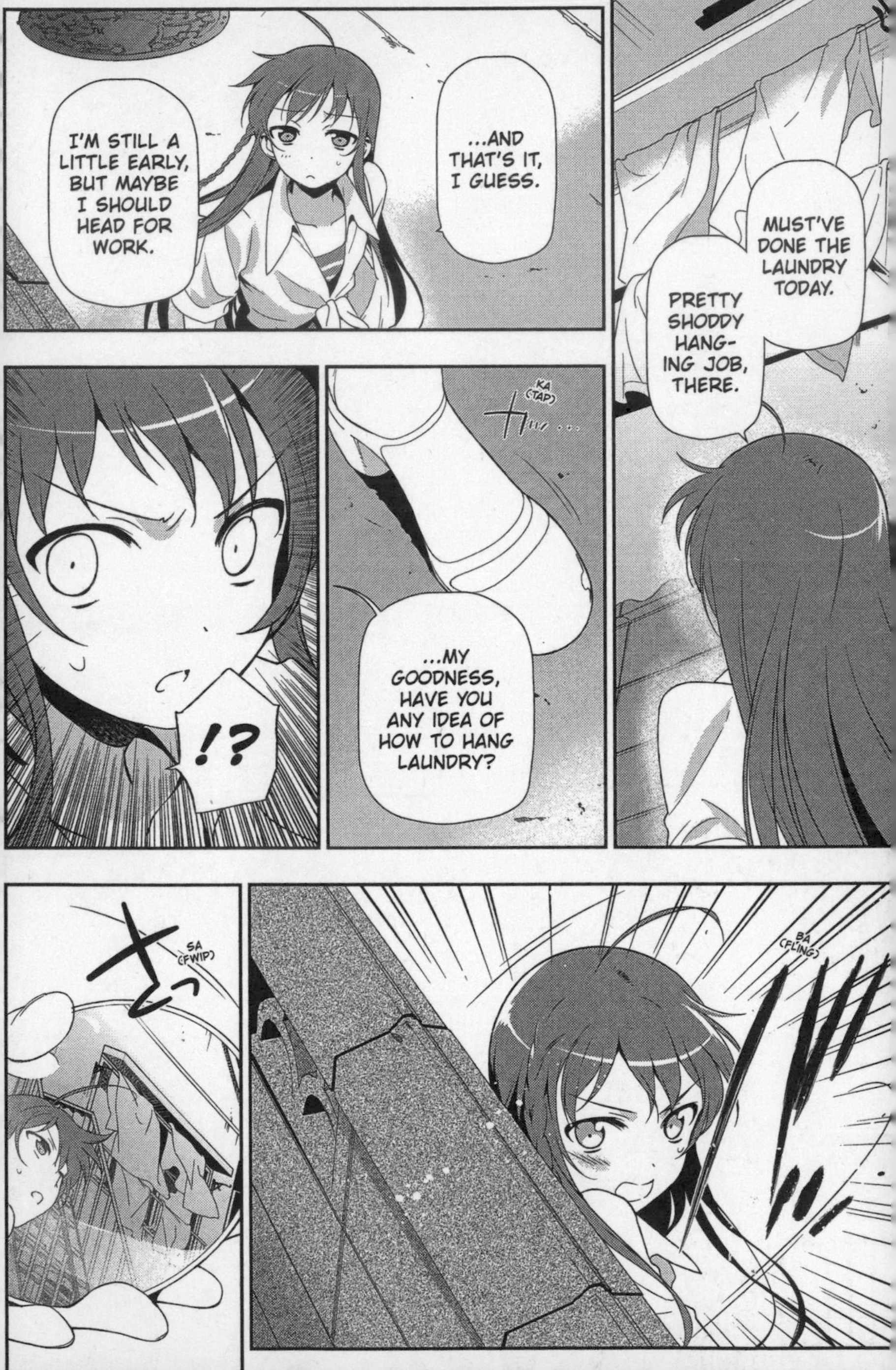
MUST'VE DONE THE LAUNDRY TODAY.
PRETTY SHODDY HANG-ING JOB, THERE.
...AND THAT'S IT, I GUESS.
I'M STILL A LITTLE EARLY, BUT MAYBE I SHOULD HEAD FOR WORK.
KA (TAP)
...MY GOODNESS, HAVE YOU ANY IDEA OF HOW TO HANG LAUNDRY?
!?
BA (FLING)
SA (FWIP)

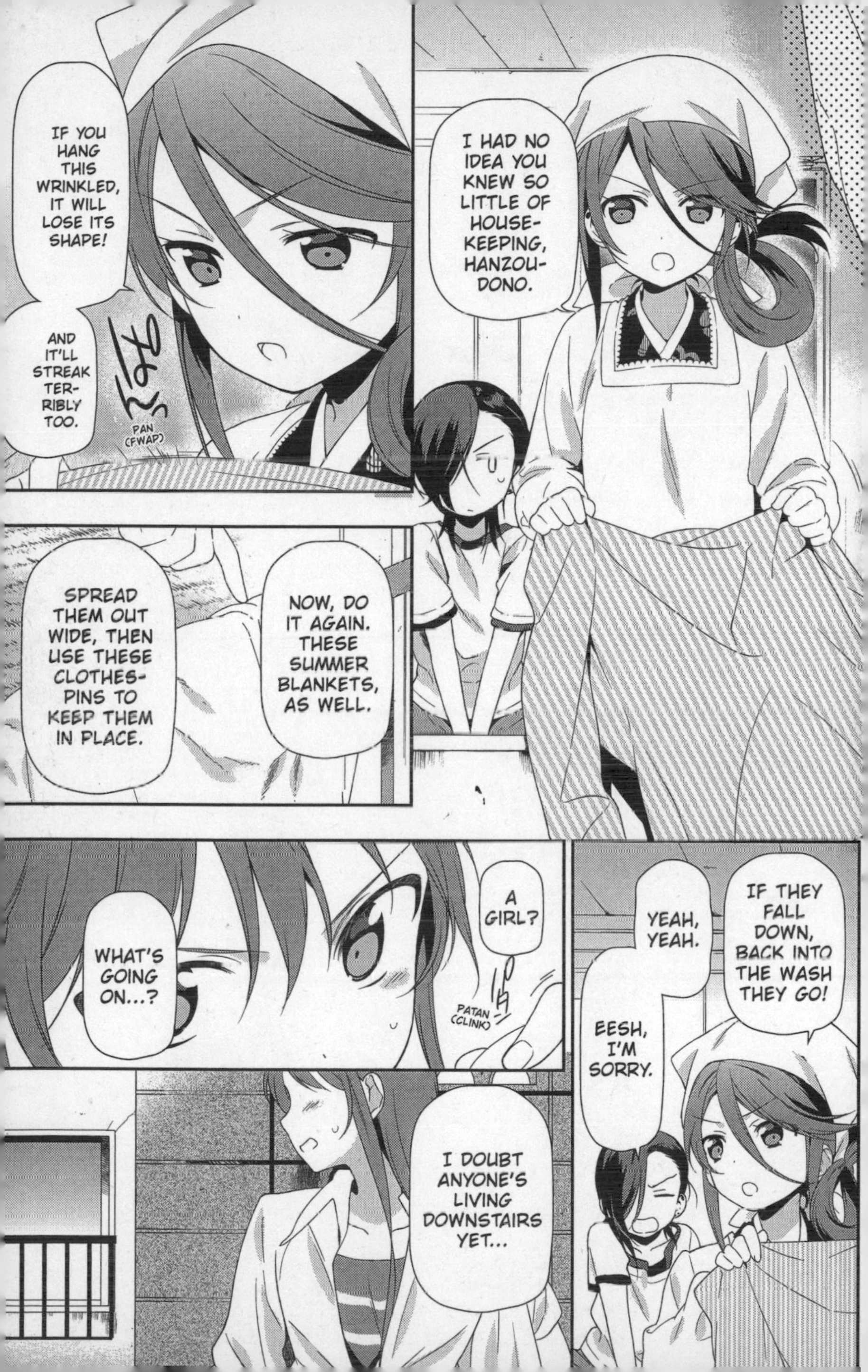
I HAD NO IDEA YOU KNEW SO LITTLE OF HOUSE-KEEPING, HANZOU-DONO.
IF YOU HANG THIS WRINKLED, IT WILL LOSE ITS SHAPE!
AND IT'LL STREAK TER-RIBLY TOO.
PAN (FWAP)
NOW, DO IT AGAIN. THESE SUMMER BLANKETS, AS WELL.
SPREAD THEM OUT WIDE, THEN USE THESE CLOTHES-PINS TO KEEP THEM IN PLACE.
IF THEY FALL DOWN, BACK INTO THE WASH THEY GO!
YEAH, YEAH.
EESH, I'M SORRY.
A GIRL?
PATAN (CLINK)
WHAT'S GOING ON...?
I DOUBT ANYONE'S LIVING DOWNSTAIRS YET...

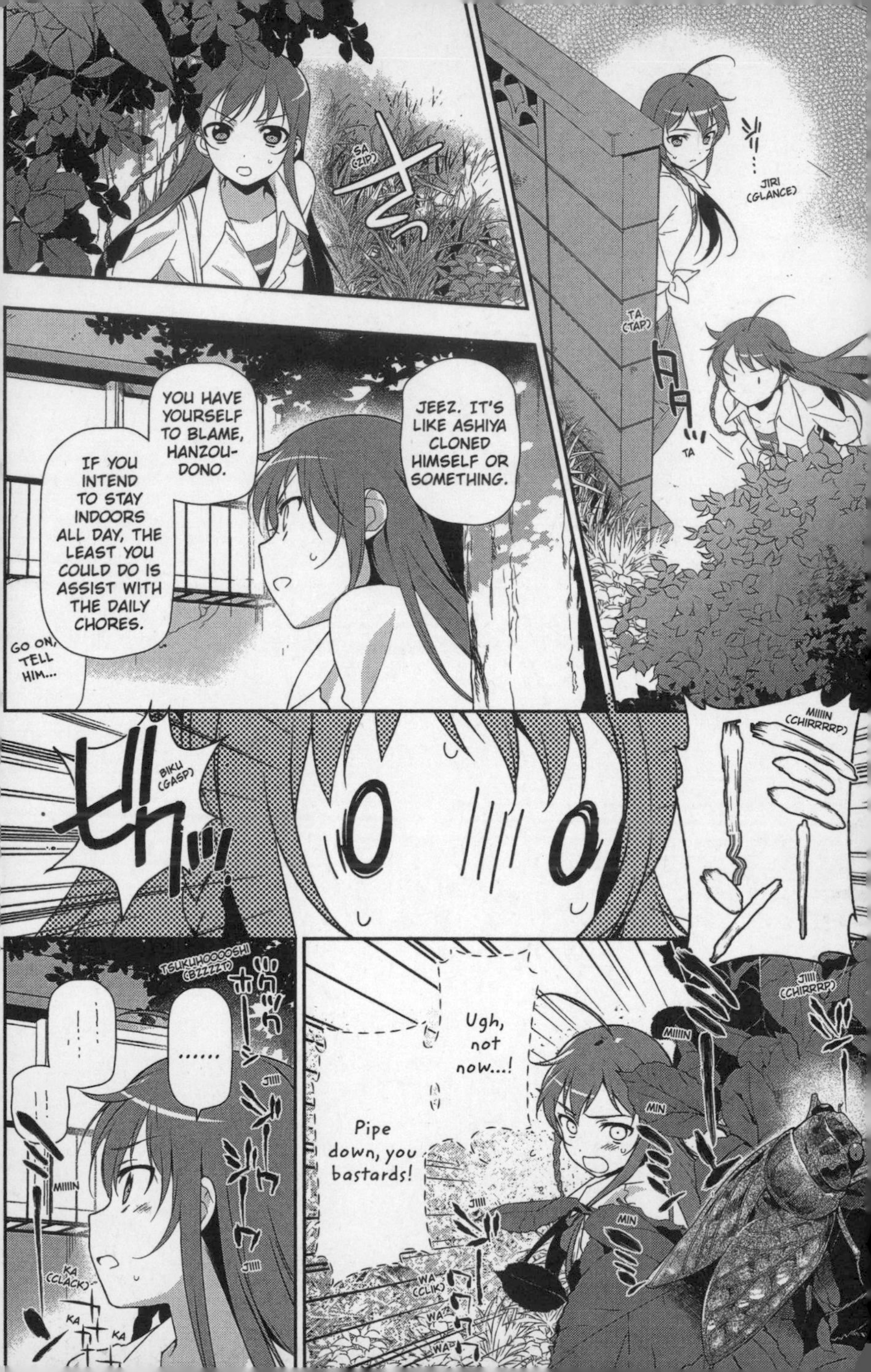
JIRI (GLANCE)
TA (TAP)
TA
SA (ZIP)
JEEZ. IT'S LIKE ASHIYA CLONED HIMSELF OR SOMETHING.
YOU HAVE YOURSELF TO BLAME, HANZOU-DONO.
IF YOU INTEND TO STAY INDOORS ALL DAY, THE LEAST YOU COULD DO IS ASSIST WITH THE DAILY CHORES.
GO ON, TELL HIM...
MIIIN (CHIRRRRP)
BIKU (GASP)
JIIII (CHIRRRP)
MIIIN
Ugh, not now...!
Pipe down, you bastards!
MIN
MIN
JIIII
WA (CLIK)
WA
WA
TSUKUHOOOOSHI (BZZZZT)
......
JIIII
JIIII
MIIIN
KA (CLACK)
KA
KA

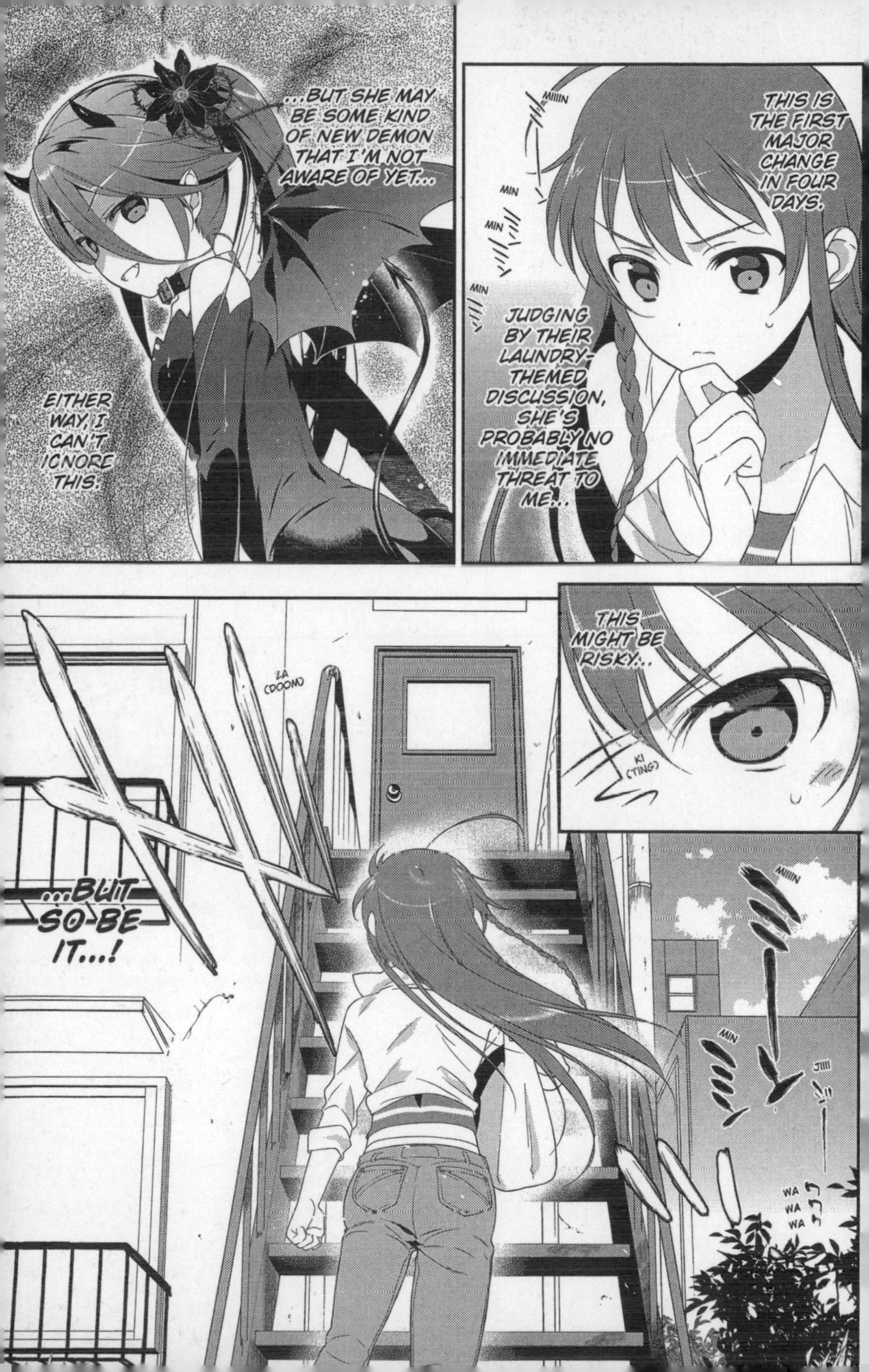
MIIIN
MIN
MIN
MIN
THIS IS THE FIRST MAJOR CHANGE IN FOUR DAYS.
JUDGING BY THEIR LAUNDRY-THEMED DISCUSSION, SHE'S PROBABLY NO IMMEDIATE THREAT TO ME...
...BUT SHE MAY BE SOME KIND OF NEW DEMON THAT I'M NOT AWARE OF YET...
EITHER WAY, I CAN'T IGNORE THIS.
THIS MIGHT BE RISKY...
KI (TING)
MIIIN
MIN
JIIII
WA
WA
WA
ZA (DOOM)
...BUT SO BE IT...!

THE DEVIL IS A PART-TIMER!

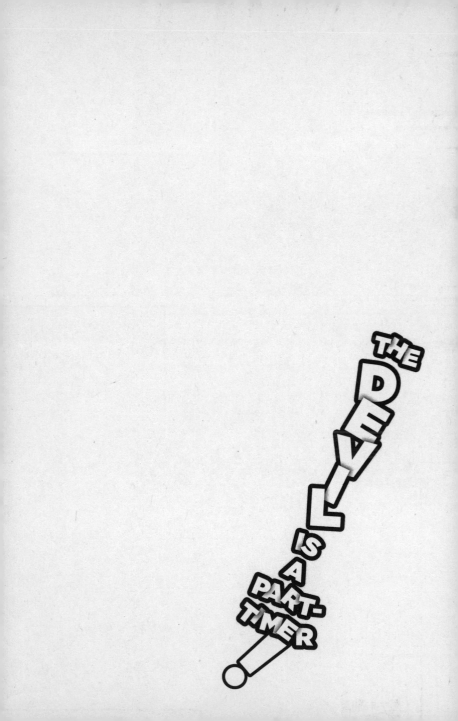

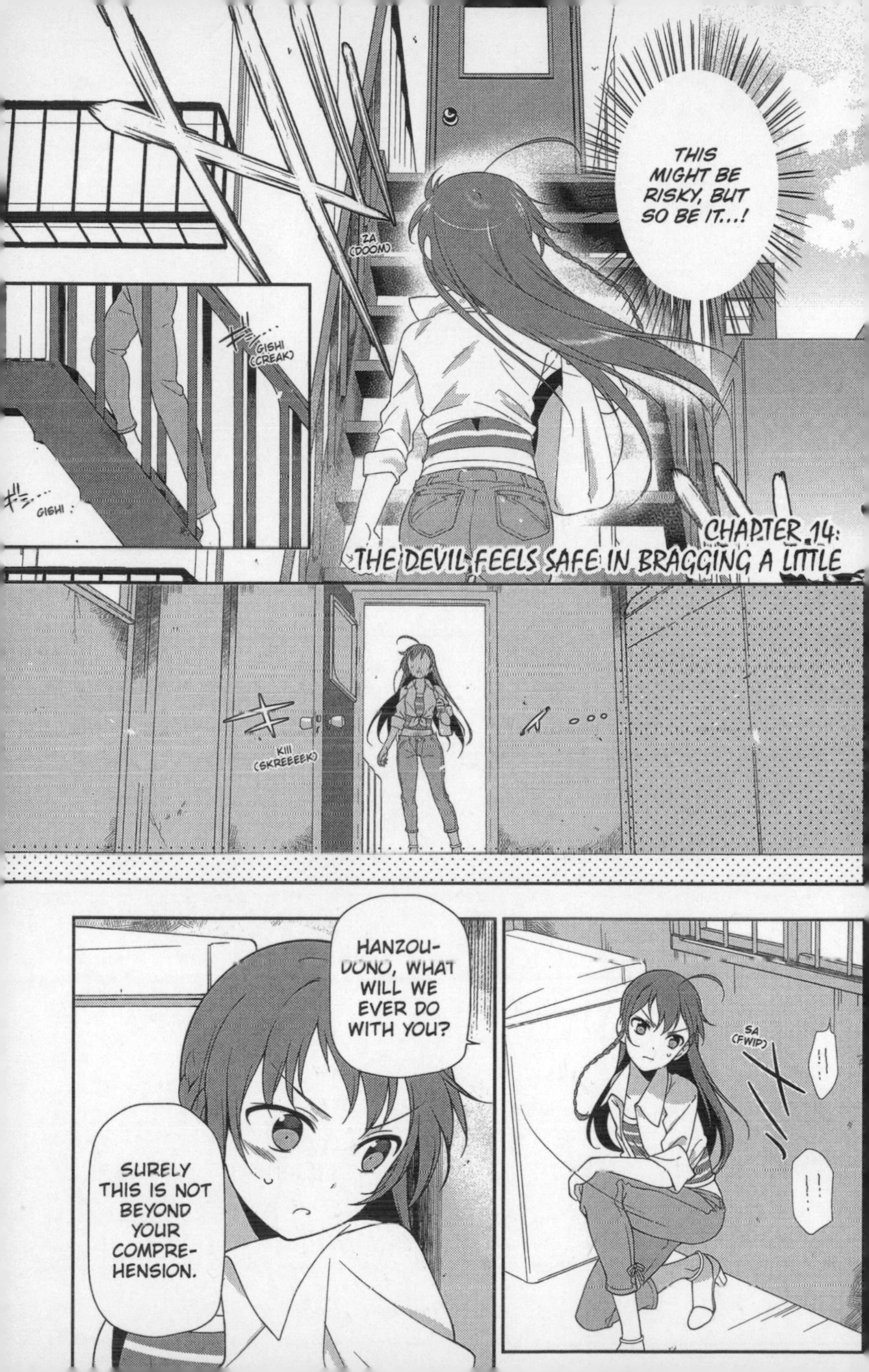
THIS MIGHT BE RISKY, BUT SO BE IT...!
ZA (DOOM)
GISHI (CREAK)
GISHI
CHAPTER 14: THE DEVIL FEELS SAFE IN BRAGGING A LITTLE
KIII (SKREEEEK)
...
SA (FWIP)
!!
!!
HANZOU-DONO, WHAT WILL WE EVER DO WITH YOU?
SURELY THIS IS NOT BEYOND YOUR COMPRE-HENSION.

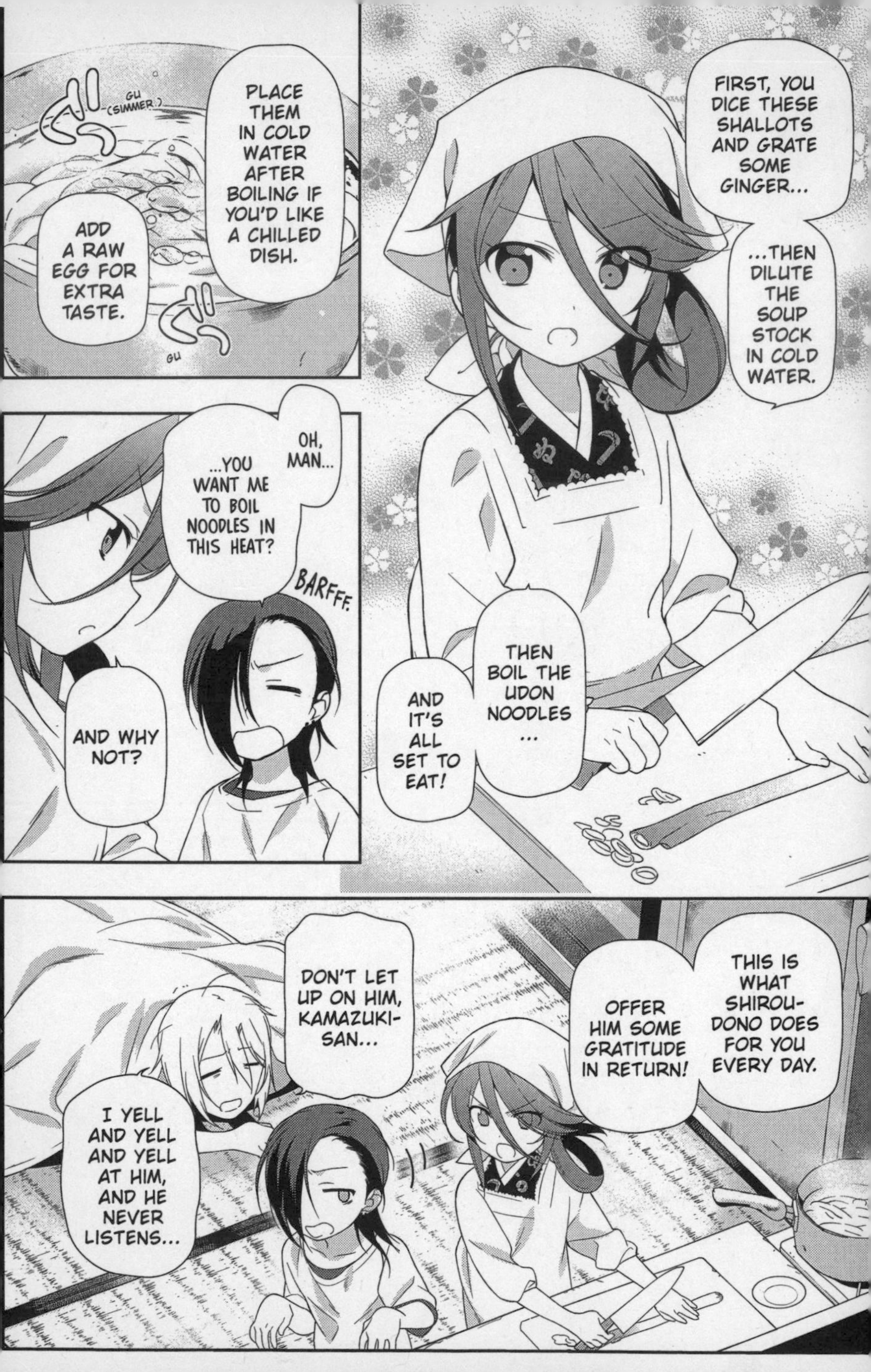
FIRST, YOU DICE THESE SHALLOTS AND GRATE SOME GINGER...
...THEN DILUTE THE SOUP STOCK IN COLD WATER.
THEN BOIL THE UDON NOODLES ...
AND IT'S ALL SET TO EAT!
PLACE THEM IN COLD WATER AFTER BOILING IF YOU'D LIKE A CHILLED DISH.
GU (SIMMER)
ADD A RAW EGG FOR EXTRA TASTE.
GU
OH, MAN...
...YOU WANT ME TO BOIL NOODLES IN THIS HEAT?
BARFFF.
AND WHY NOT?
THIS IS WHAT SHIROU-DONO DOES FOR YOU EVERY DAY.
OFFER HIM SOME GRATITUDE IN RETURN!
DON'T LET UP ON HIM, KAMAZUKI-SAN...
I YELL AND YELL AND YELL AT HIM, AND HE NEVER LISTENS...

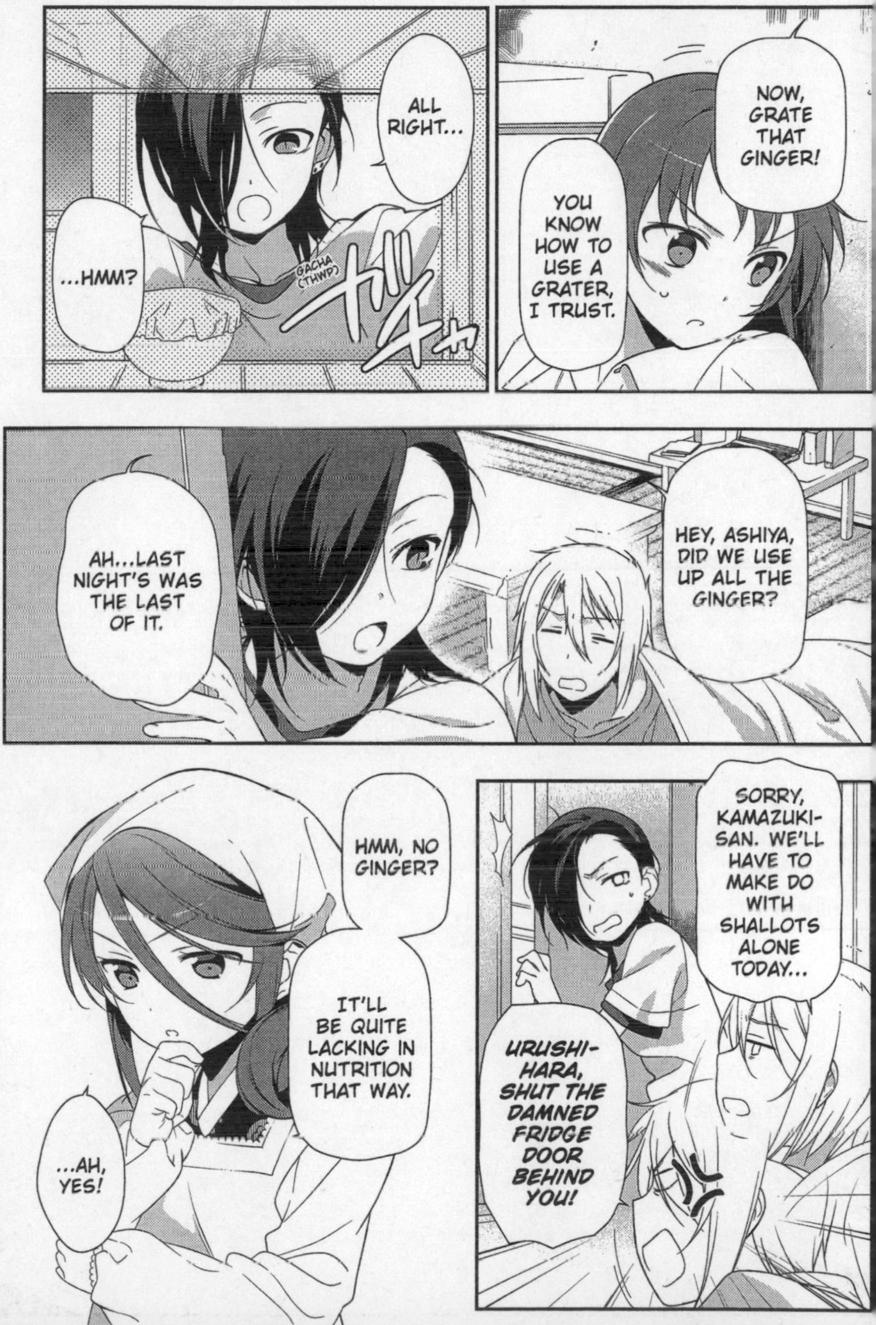
NOW, GRATE THAT GINGER!
YOU KNOW HOW TO USE A GRATER, I TRUST.
ALL RIGHT...
GACHA (THWP)
...HMM?
HEY, ASHIYA, DID WE USE UP ALL THE GINGER?
AH...LAST NIGHT'S WAS THE LAST OF IT.
SORRY, KAMAZUKI-SAN. WE'LL HAVE TO MAKE DO WITH SHALLOTS ALONE TODAY...
URUSHI-HARA, SHUT THE DAMNED FRIDGE DOOR BEHIND YOU!
HMM, NO GINGER?
IT'LL BE QUITE LACKING IN NUTRITION THAT WAY.
...AH, YES!

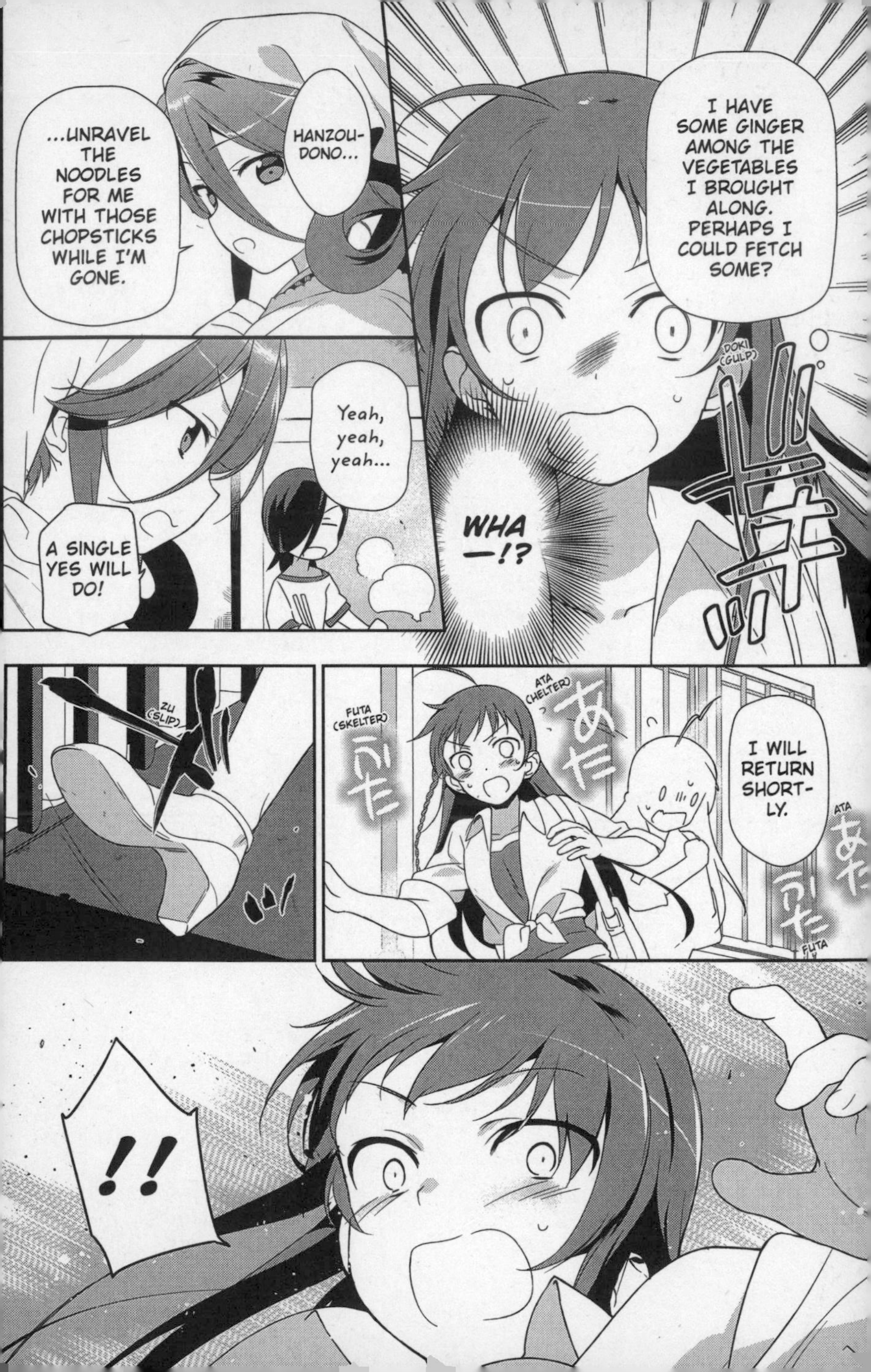
I HAVE SOME GINGER AMONG THE VEGETABLES I BROUGHT ALONG. PERHAPS I COULD FETCH SOME?
DOKI (GULP)
WHA—!?
HANZOU-DONO...
...UNRAVEL THE NOODLES FOR ME WITH THOSE CHOPSTICKS WHILE I'M GONE.
Yeah, yeah, yeah...
A SINGLE YES WILL DO!
I WILL RETURN SHORTLY.
ATA
あた
ふた
FUTA
ATA (HELTER)
あた
FUTA (SKELTER)
ふた
ZU (SLIP)
!!

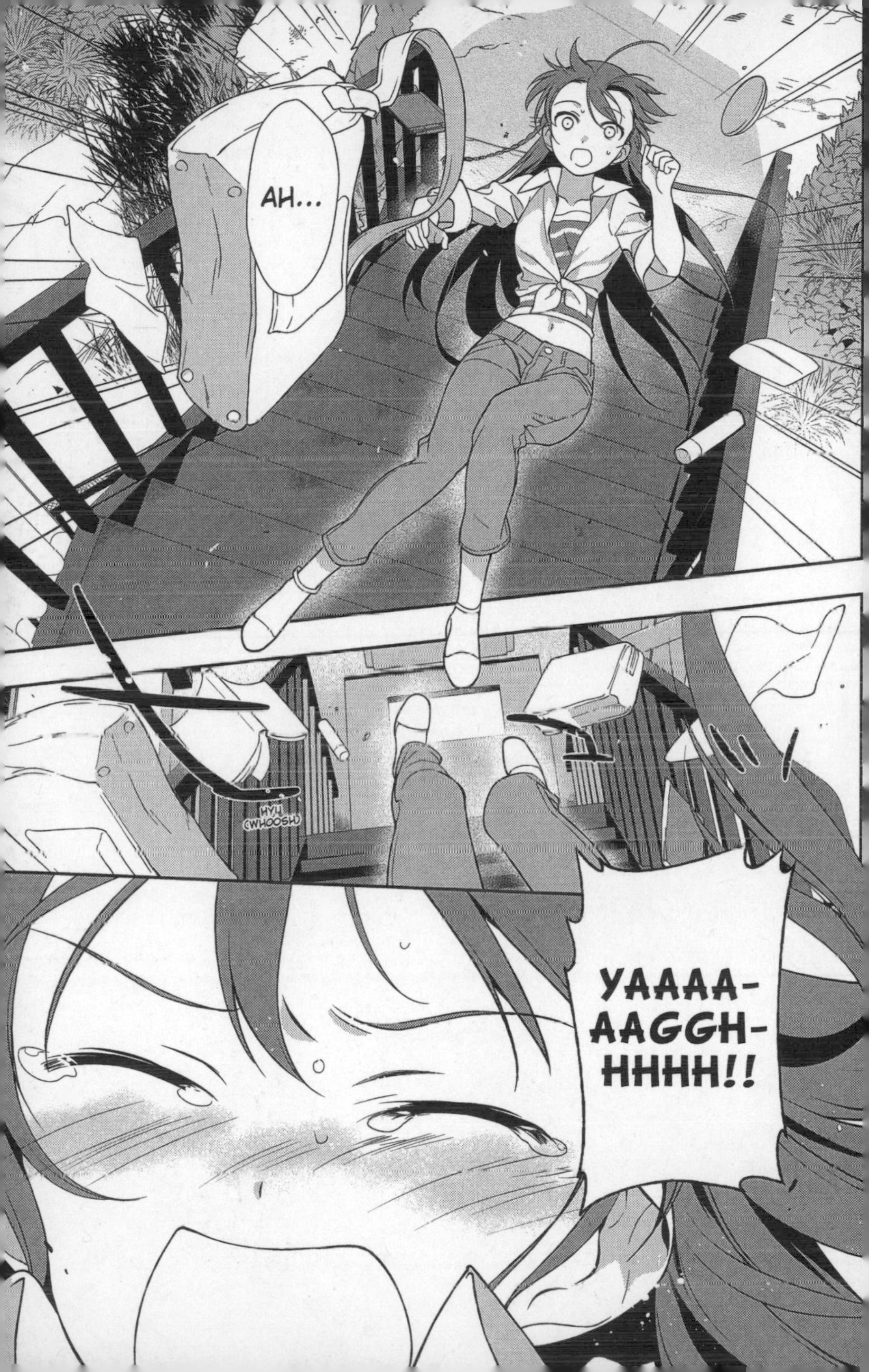
AH...
HYU (WHOOSH)
YAAAA-
AAGGH-
HHHH!!

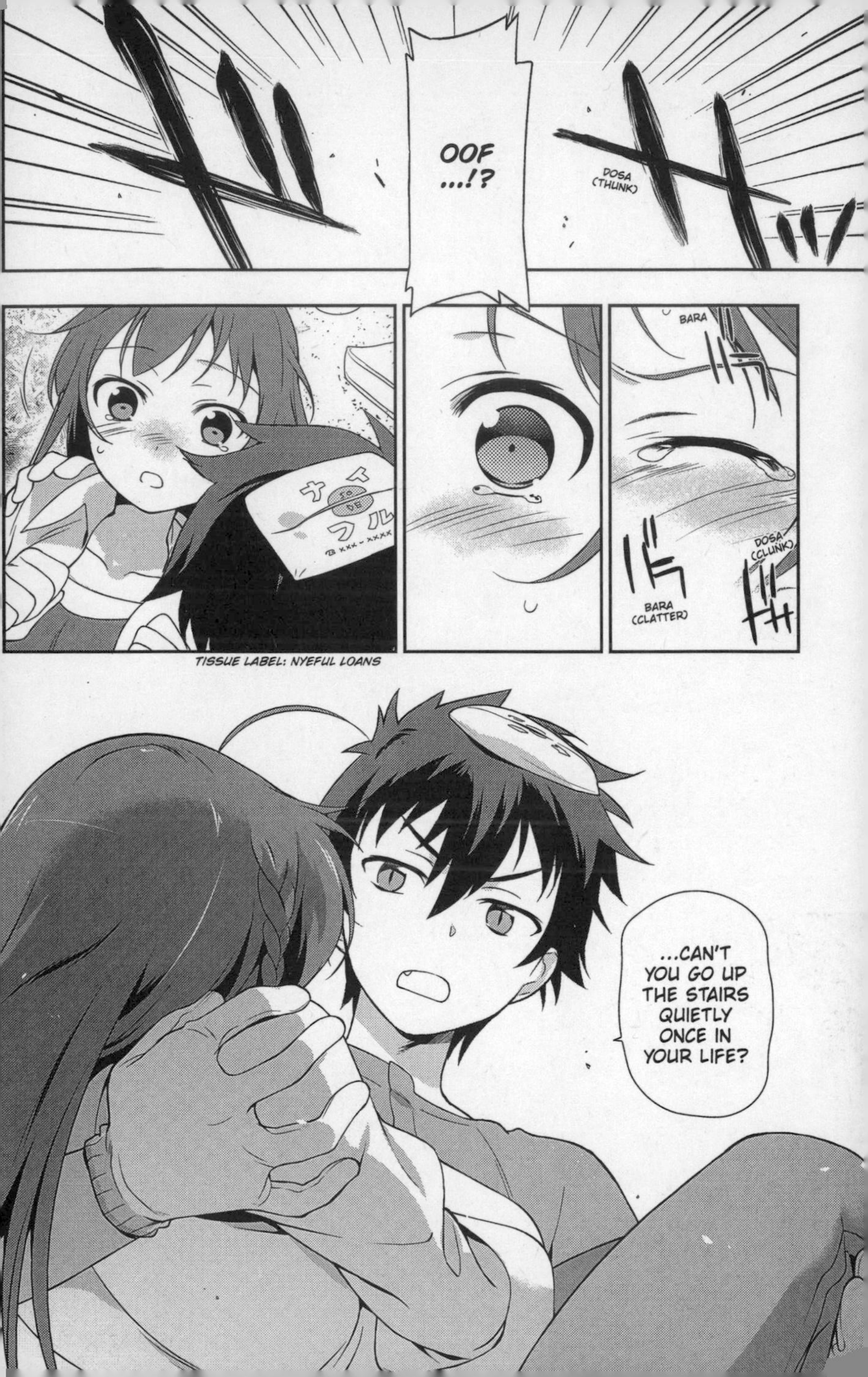
DOSA (THUNK)
OOF ...!?
BARA
DOSA (CLUNK)
BARA (CLATTER)
TISSUE LABEL: NYEFUL LOANS
...CAN'T YOU GO UP THE STAIRS QUIETLY ONCE IN YOUR LIFE?

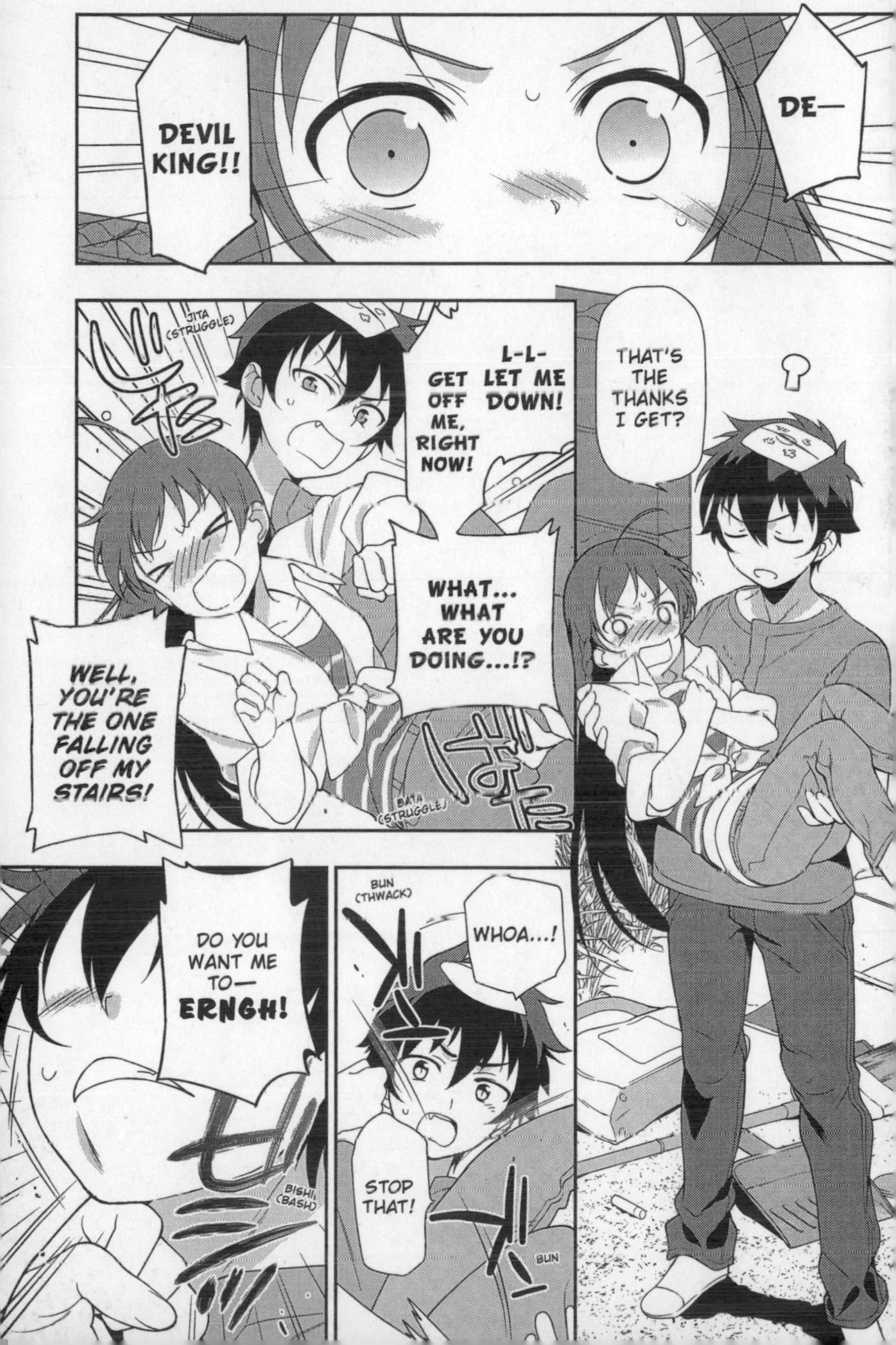
DE—
DEVIL KING!!
THAT'S THE THANKS I GET?
WHAT... WHAT ARE YOU DOING...!?
L-L-LET ME DOWN!
GET OFF ME, RIGHT NOW!
JITA (STRUGGLE)
BATA (STRUGGLE)
WELL, YOU'RE THE ONE FALLING OFF MY STAIRS!
BUN (THWACK)
WHOA...!
STOP THAT!
BUN
DO YOU WANT ME TO— ERNGH!
BISHI (BASH)

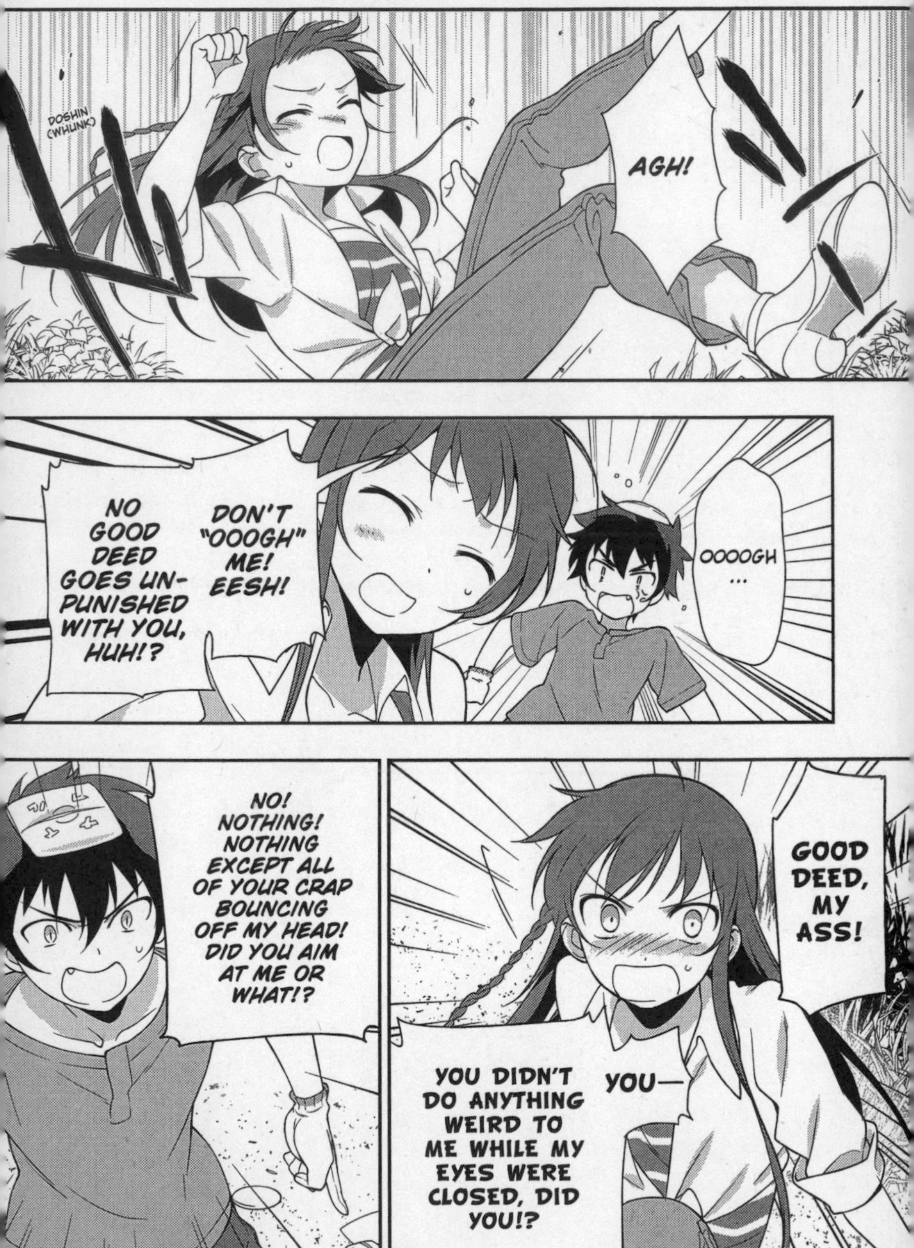
AGH!
DOSHIN (WHUNK)
OOOOGH ...
DON'T "OOOGH" ME! EESH!
NO GOOD DEED GOES UN-PUNISHED WITH YOU, HUH!?
GOOD DEED, MY ASS!
YOU—
YOU DIDN'T DO ANYTHING WEIRD TO ME WHILE MY EYES WERE CLOSED, DID YOU!?
NO! NOTHING! NOTHING EXCEPT ALL OF YOUR CRAP BOUNCING OFF MY HEAD! DID YOU AIM AT ME OR WHAT!?

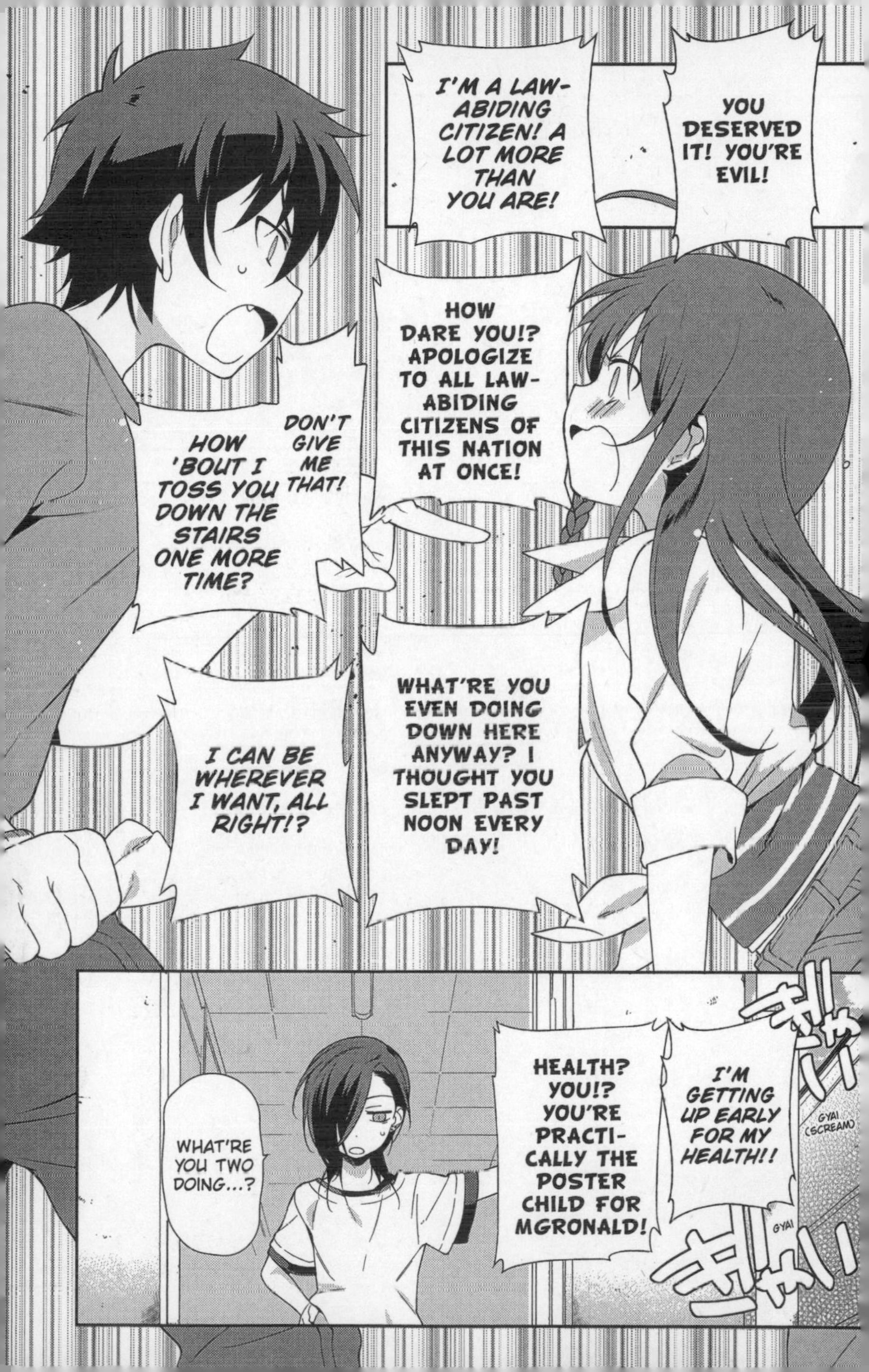
YOU DESERVED IT! YOU'RE EVIL!
I'M A LAW-ABIDING CITIZEN! A LOT MORE THAN YOU ARE!
HOW DARE YOU!? APOLOGIZE TO ALL LAW-ABIDING CITIZENS OF THIS NATION AT ONCE!
DON'T GIVE ME THAT!
HOW 'BOUT I TOSS YOU DOWN THE STAIRS ONE MORE TIME?
WHAT'RE YOU EVEN DOING DOWN HERE ANYWAY? I THOUGHT YOU SLEPT PAST NOON EVERY DAY!
I CAN BE WHEREVER I WANT, ALL RIGHT!?
GYAI (SCREAM)
GYAI
I'M GETTING UP EARLY FOR MY HEALTH!!
HEALTH? YOU!? YOU'RE PRACTI-CALLY THE POSTER CHILD FOR MGRONALD!
WHAT'RE YOU TWO DOING...?

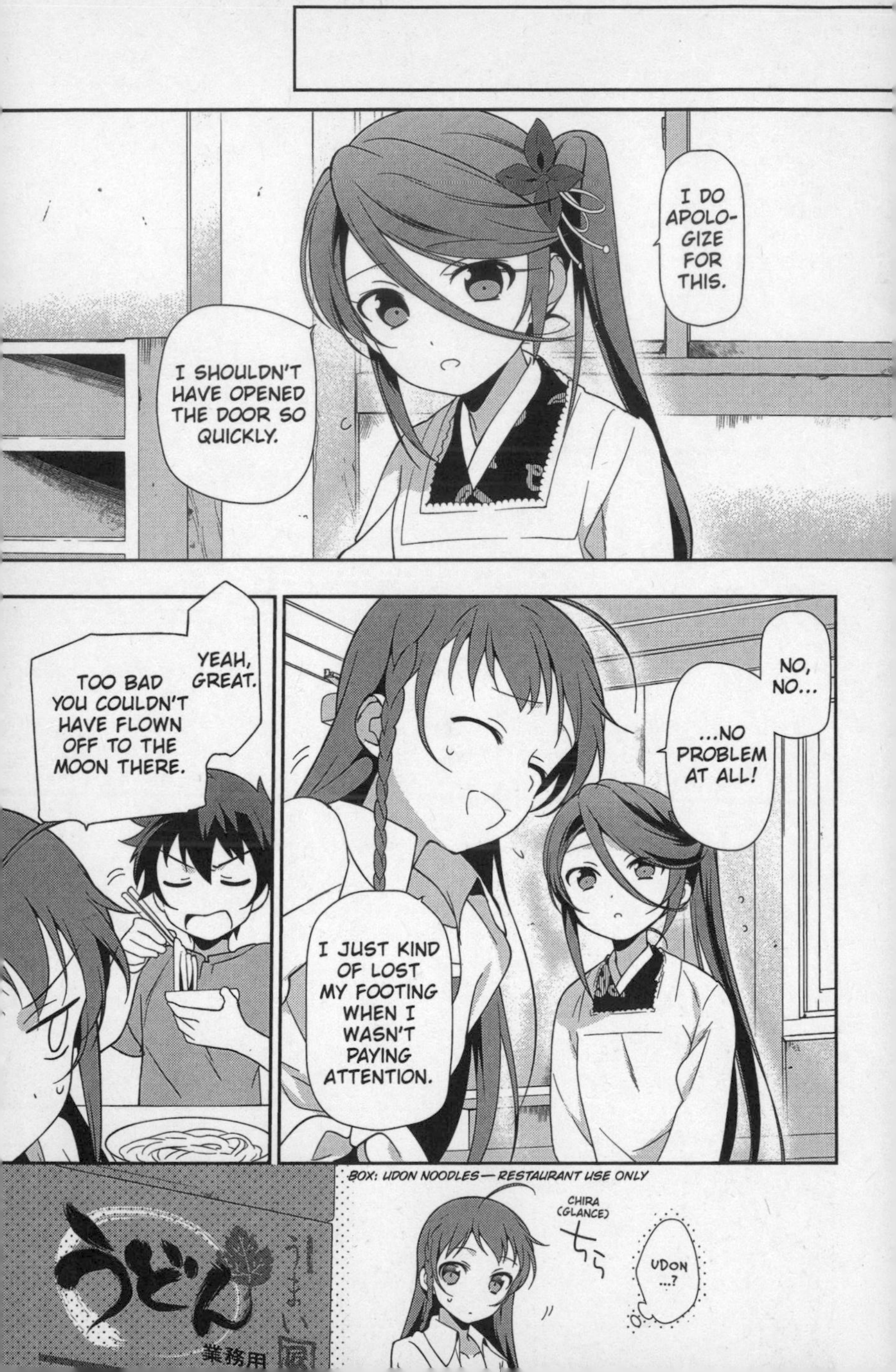

I DO APOLOGIZE FOR THIS.
I SHOULDN'T HAVE OPENED THE DOOR SO QUICKLY.
NO, NO...
...NO PROBLEM AT ALL!
I JUST KIND OF LOST MY FOOTING WHEN I WASN'T PAYING ATTENTION.
YEAH, GREAT.
TOO BAD YOU COULDN'T HAVE FLOWN OFF TO THE MOON THERE.
BOX: UDON NOODLES— RESTAURANT USE ONLY
CHIRA (GLANCE)
ちら
UDON ...?
うどん
業務用

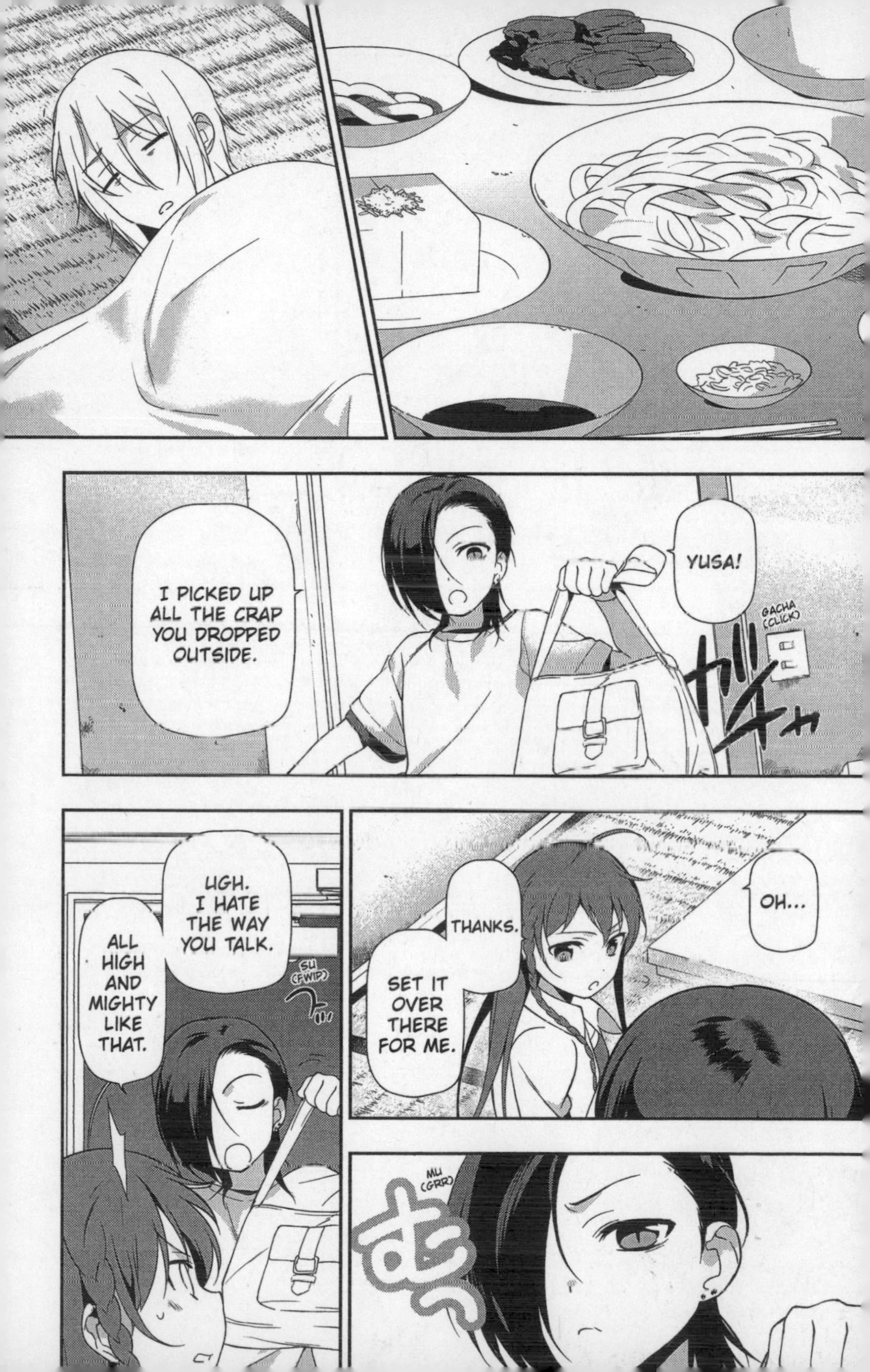
YUSA!
GACHA (CLICK)
I PICKED UP ALL THE CRAP YOU DROPPED OUTSIDE.
OH...
THANKS.
SET IT OVER THERE FOR ME.
MU (GRR)
UGH. I HATE THE WAY YOU TALK.
ALL HIGH AND MIGHTY LIKE THAT.
SU (FWIP)

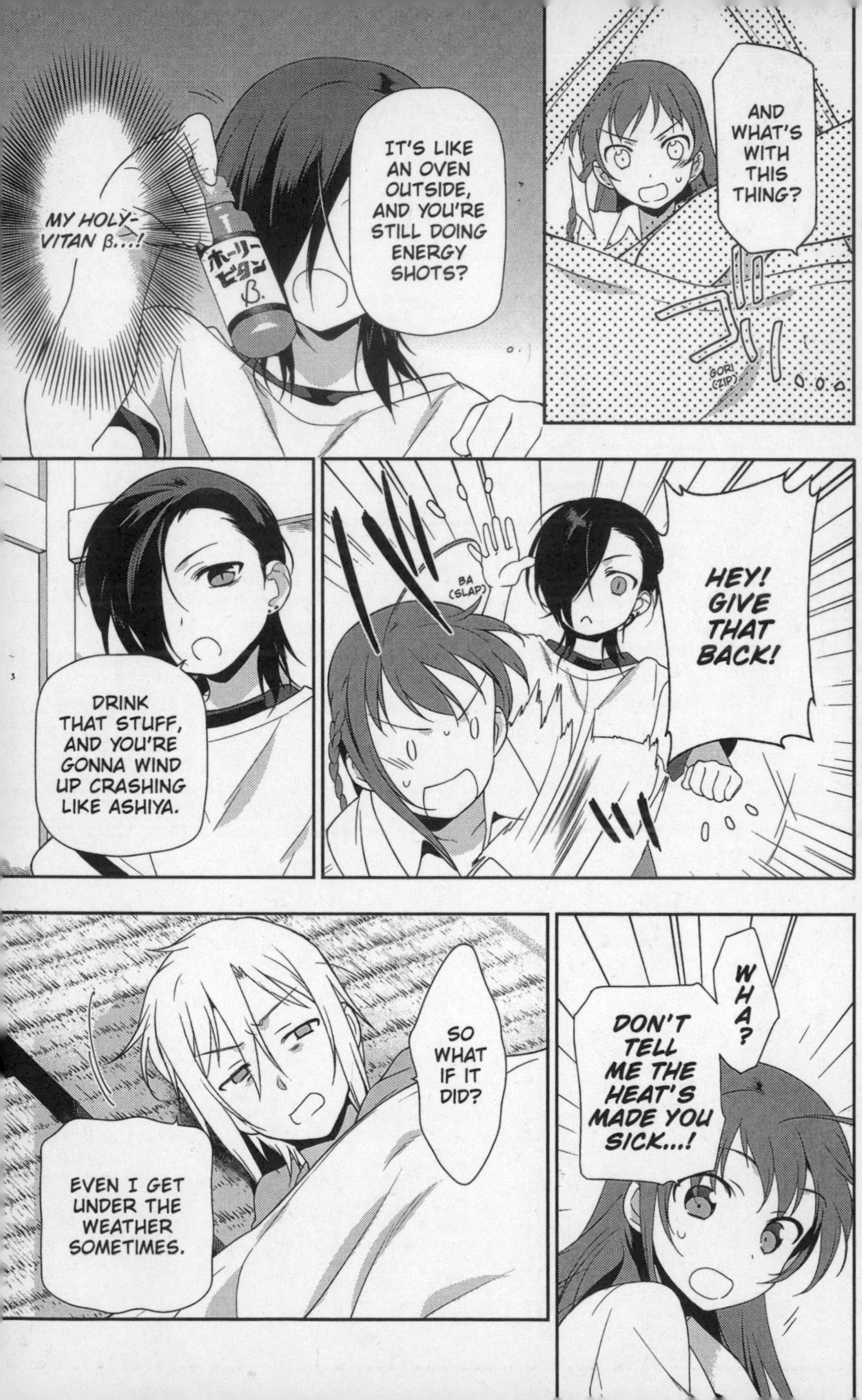
AND WHAT'S WITH THIS THING?
GORI (ZIP)
IT'S LIKE AN OVEN OUTSIDE, AND YOU'RE STILL DOING ENERGY SHOTS?
ホーリービタン β.
MY HOLY-VITAN β...!
HEY! GIVE THAT BACK!
BA (SLAP)
DRINK THAT STUFF, AND YOU'RE GONNA WIND UP CRASHING LIKE ASHIYA.
WHA?
DON'T TELL ME THE HEAT'S MADE YOU SICK...!
SO WHAT IF IT DID?
EVEN I GET UNDER THE WEATHER SOMETIMES.

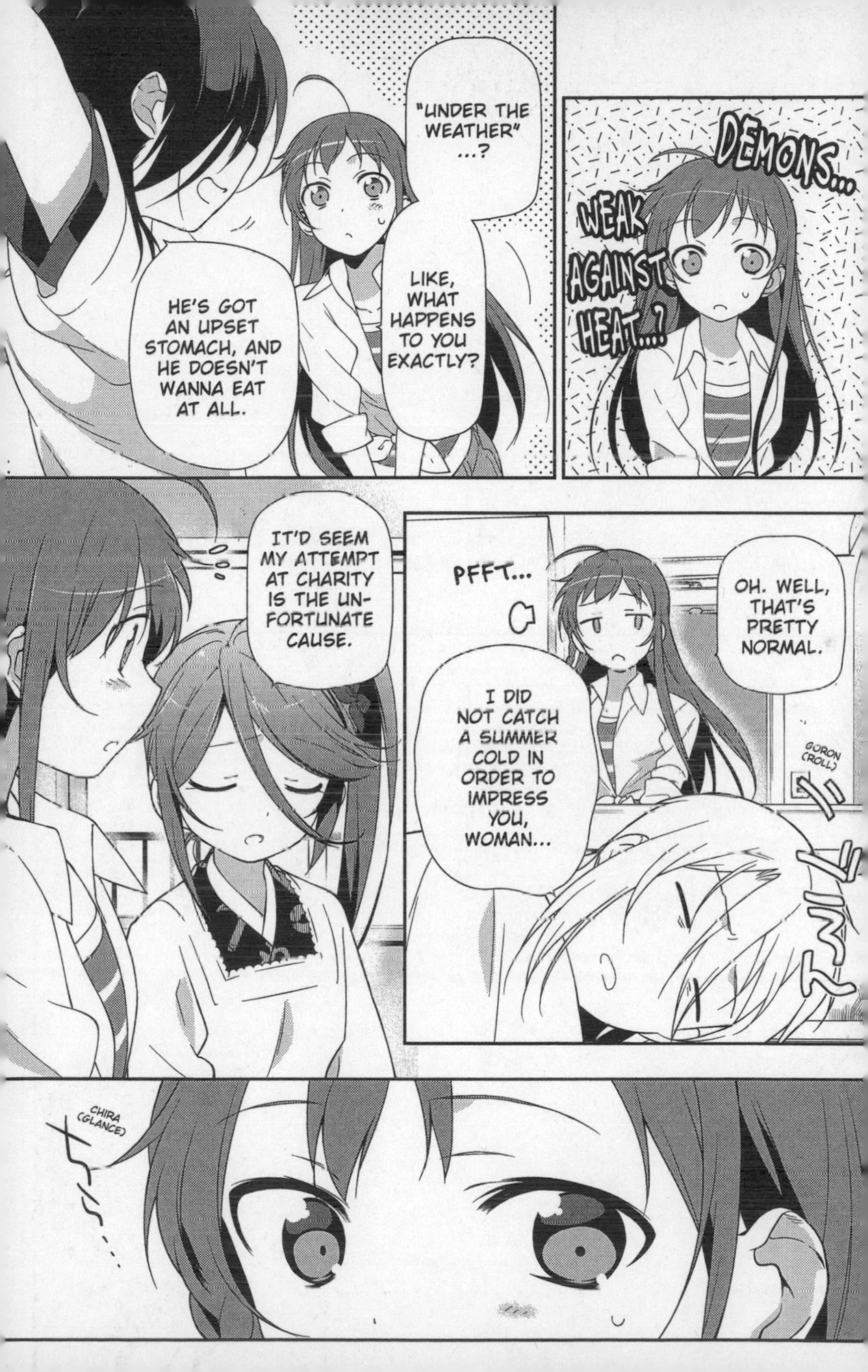
DEMONS...
WEAK AGAINST HEAT...?
"UNDER THE WEATHER" ...?
LIKE, WHAT HAPPENS TO YOU EXACTLY?
HE'S GOT AN UPSET STOMACH, AND HE DOESN'T WANNA EAT AT ALL.
OH. WELL, THAT'S PRETTY NORMAL.
GORON (ROLL)
PFFT...
I DID NOT CATCH A SUMMER COLD IN ORDER TO IMPRESS YOU, WOMAN...
IT'D SEEM MY ATTEMPT AT CHARITY IS THE UN-FORTUNATE CAUSE.
CHIRA (GLANCE)

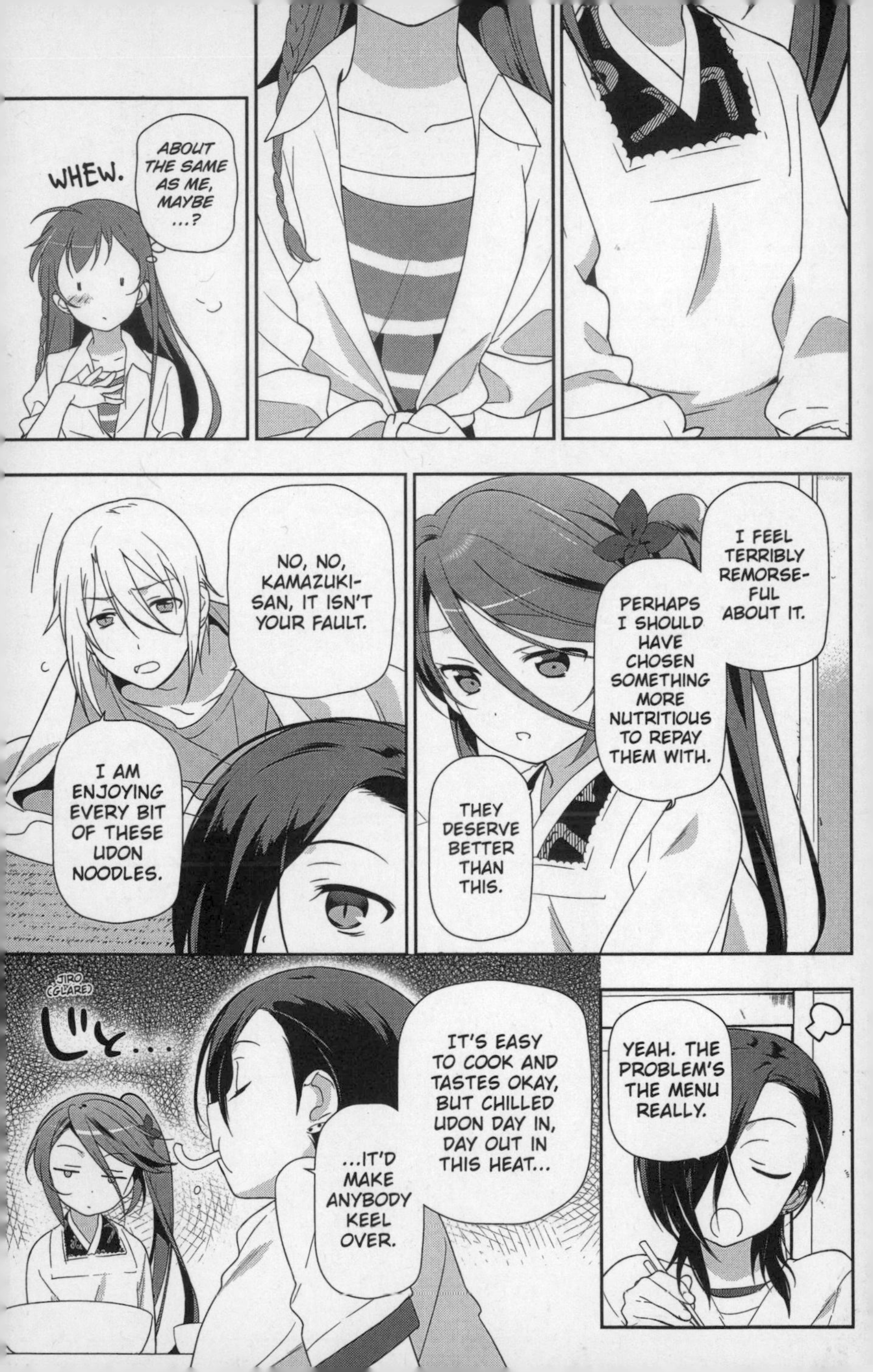
WHEW.
ABOUT THE SAME AS ME, MAYBE ...?
I FEEL TERRIBLY REMORSE-FUL ABOUT IT.
PERHAPS I SHOULD HAVE CHOSEN SOMETHING MORE NUTRITIOUS TO REPAY THEM WITH.
THEY DESERVE BETTER THAN THIS.
NO, NO, KAMAZUKI-SAN, IT ISN'T YOUR FAULT.
I AM ENJOYING EVERY BIT OF THESE UDON NOODLES.
YEAH. THE PROBLEM'S THE MENU REALLY.
IT'S EASY TO COOK AND TASTES OKAY, BUT CHILLED UDON DAY IN, DAY OUT IN THIS HEAT...
...IT'D MAKE ANYBODY KEEL OVER.
JIRO (GLARE)

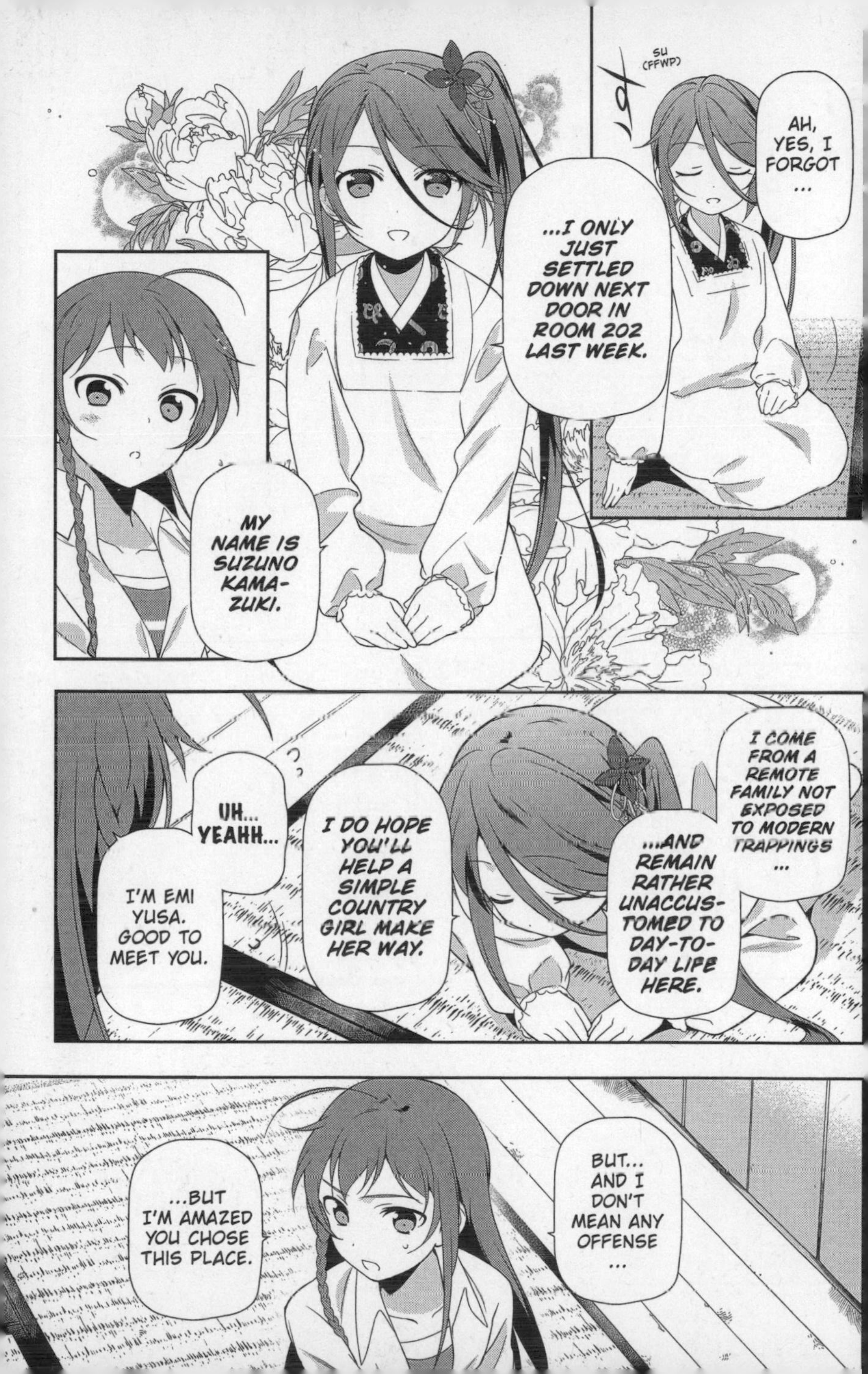
SU
(FFWP)
AH, YES, I FORGOT ...
...I ONLY JUST SETTLED DOWN NEXT DOOR IN ROOM 202 LAST WEEK.
MY NAME IS SUZUNO KAMA-ZUKI.
I COME FROM A REMOTE FAMILY NOT EXPOSED TO MODERN TRAPPINGS ...
...AND REMAIN RATHER UNACCUS-TOMED TO DAY-TO-DAY LIFE HERE.
I DO HOPE YOU'LL HELP A SIMPLE COUNTRY GIRL MAKE HER WAY.
UH... YEAHH...
I'M EMI YUSA. GOOD TO MEET YOU.
BUT... AND I DON'T MEAN ANY OFFENSE ...
...BUT I'M AMAZED YOU CHOSE THIS PLACE.

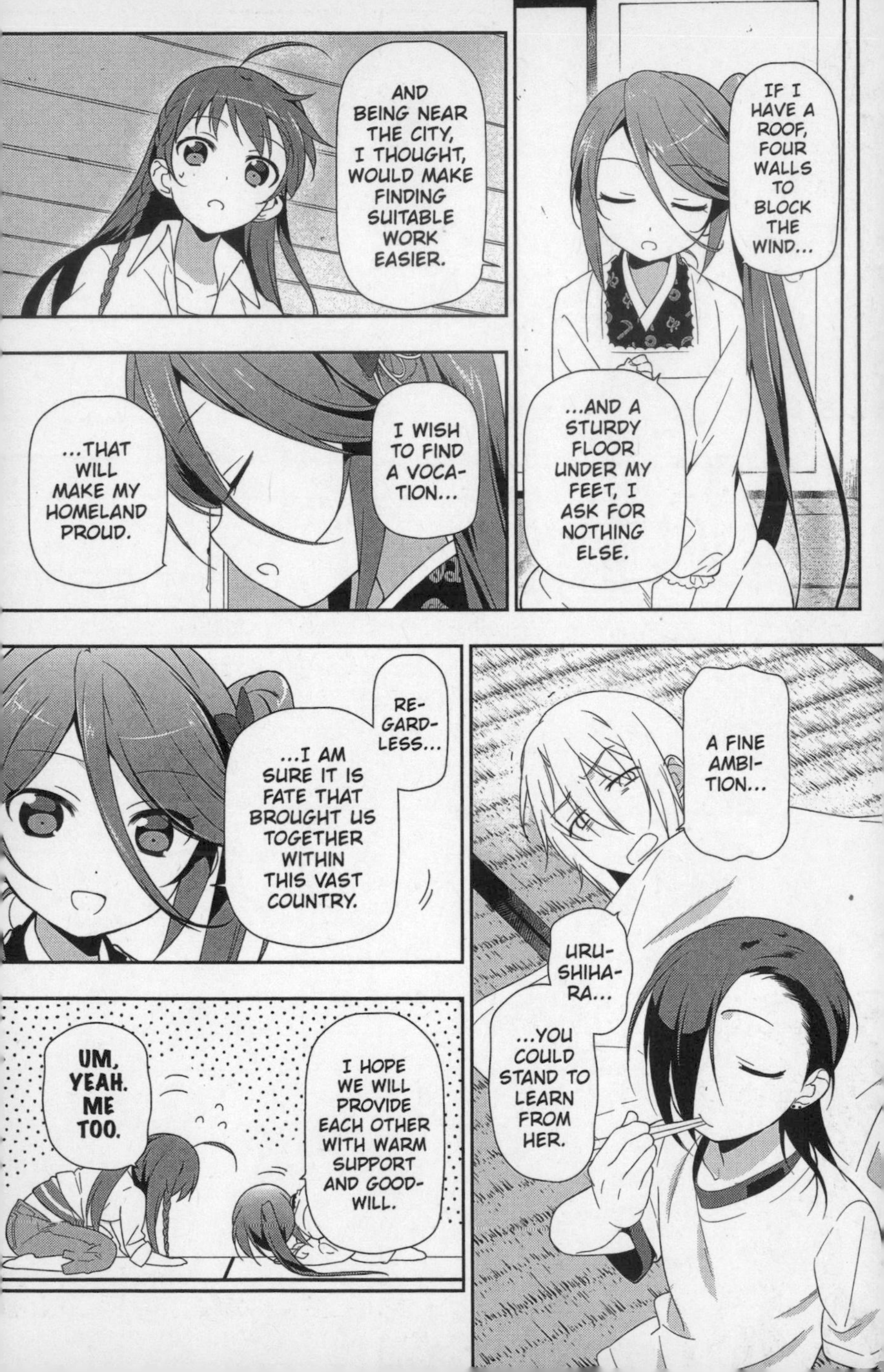
IF I HAVE A ROOF, FOUR WALLS TO BLOCK THE WIND...
...AND A STURDY FLOOR UNDER MY FEET, I ASK FOR NOTHING ELSE.
AND BEING NEAR THE CITY, I THOUGHT, WOULD MAKE FINDING SUITABLE WORK EASIER.
I WISH TO FIND A VOCA-TION...
...THAT WILL MAKE MY HOMELAND PROUD.
A FINE AMBI-TION...
URU-SHIHA-RA...
...YOU COULD STAND TO LEARN FROM HER.
RE-GARD-LESS...
...I AM SURE IT IS FATE THAT BROUGHT US TOGETHER WITHIN THIS VAST COUNTRY.
I HOPE WE WILL PROVIDE EACH OTHER WITH WARM SUPPORT AND GOOD-WILL.
UM, YEAH. ME TOO.

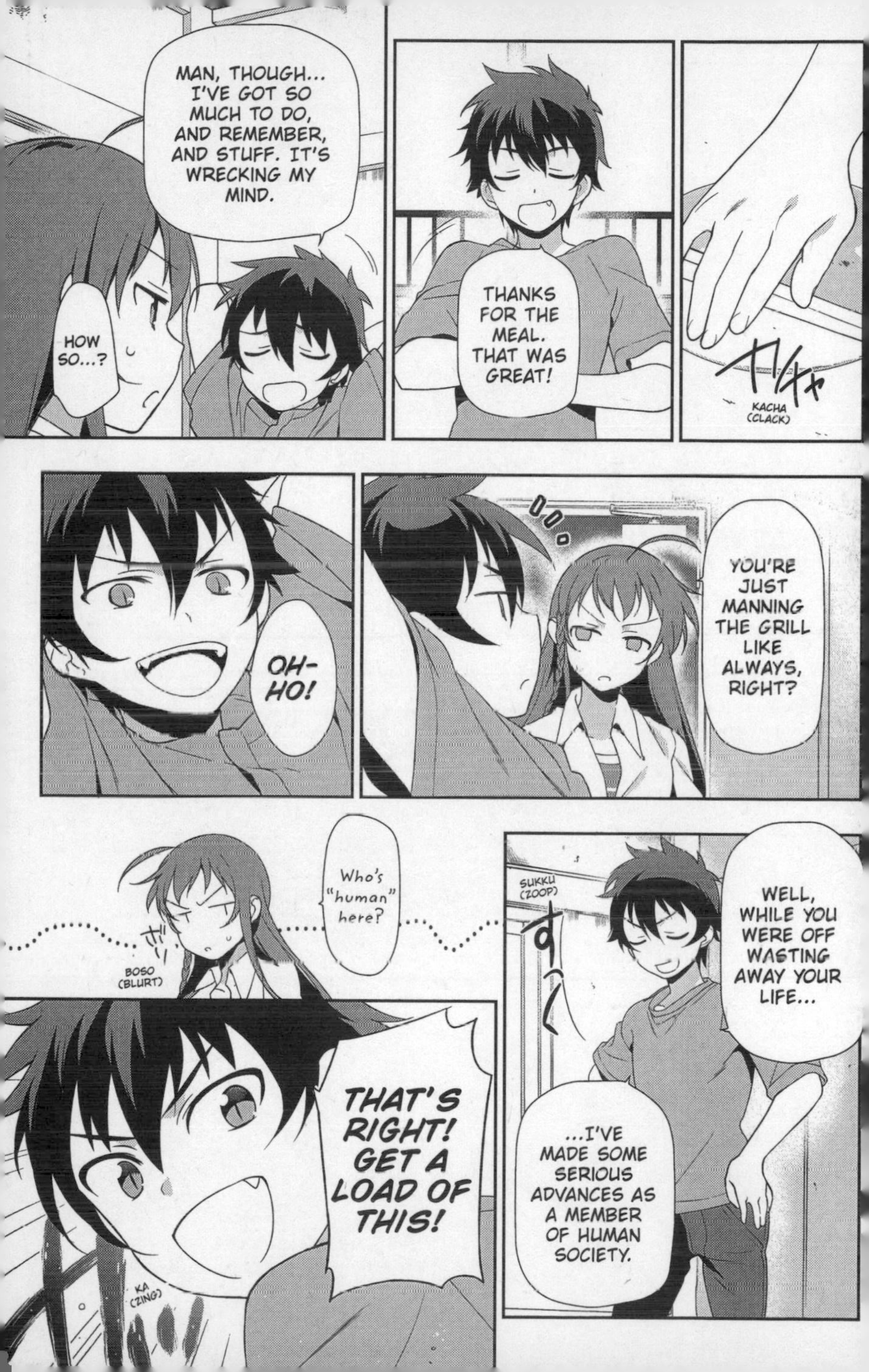
KACHA (CLACK)
THANKS FOR THE MEAL. THAT WAS GREAT!
MAN, THOUGH... I'VE GOT SO MUCH TO DO, AND REMEMBER, AND STUFF. IT'S WRECKING MY MIND.
HOW SO...?
YOU'RE JUST MANNING THE GRILL LIKE ALWAYS, RIGHT?
OH-HO!
WELL, WHILE YOU WERE OFF WASTING AWAY YOUR LIFE...
SUKKU (ZOOP)
...I'VE MADE SOME SERIOUS ADVANCES AS A MEMBER OF HUMAN SOCIETY.
Who's "human" here?
BOSO (BLURT)
THAT'S RIGHT! GET A LOAD OF THIS!
KA (ZING)

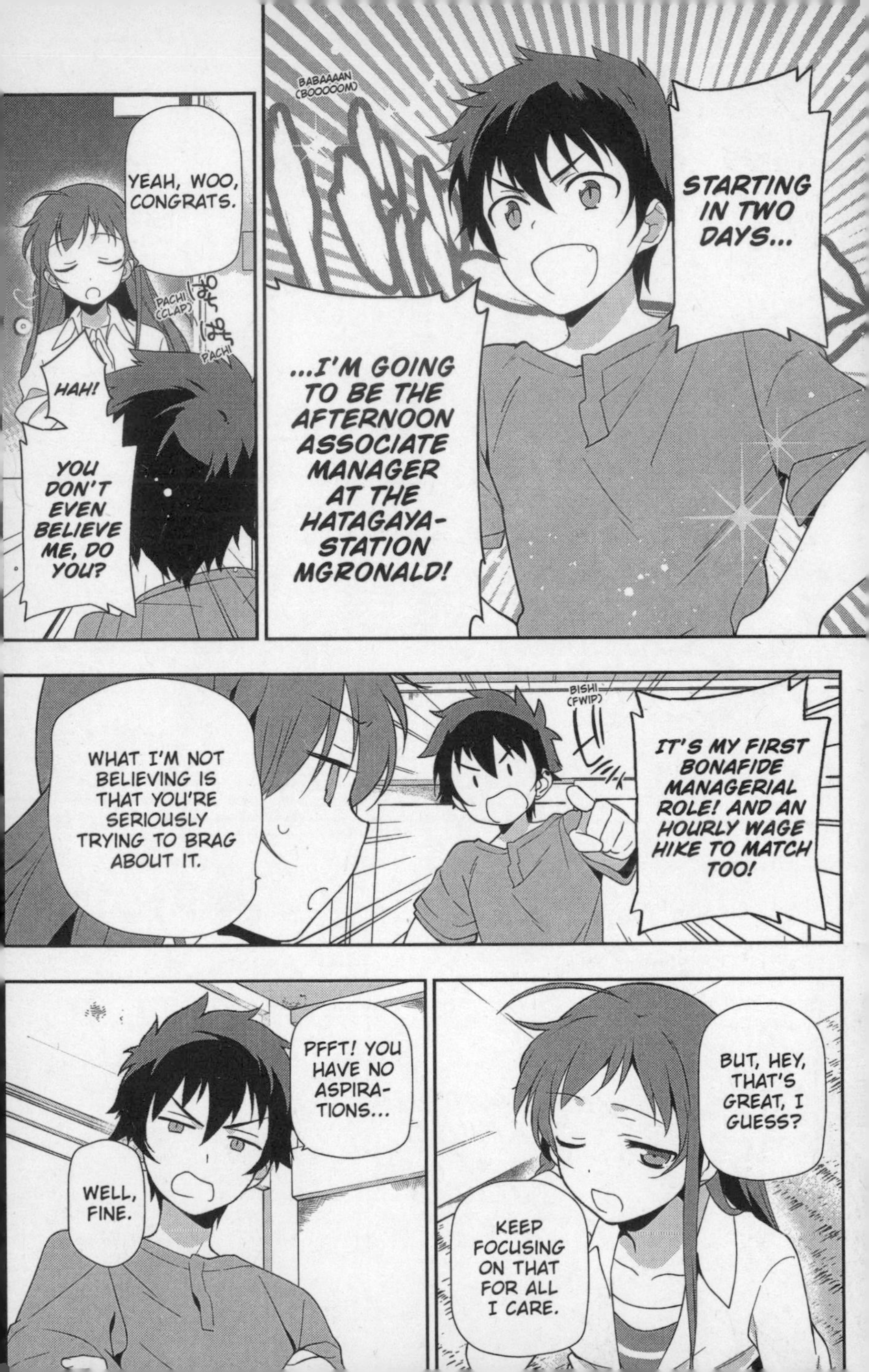
BABAAAAN (BOOOOOM)
STARTING IN TWO DAYS...
...I'M GOING TO BE THE AFTERNOON ASSOCIATE MANAGER AT THE HATAGAYA-STATION MGRONALD!
YEAH, WOO, CONGRATS.
PACHI (CLAP)
PACHI
HAH!
YOU DON'T EVEN BELIEVE ME, DO YOU?
BISHI (FWIP)
IT'S MY FIRST BONAFIDE MANAGERIAL ROLE! AND AN HOURLY WAGE HIKE TO MATCH TOO!
WHAT I'M NOT BELIEVING IS THAT YOU'RE SERIOUSLY TRYING TO BRAG ABOUT IT.
BUT, HEY, THAT'S GREAT, I GUESS?
KEEP FOCUSING ON THAT FOR ALL I CARE.
PFFT! YOU HAVE NO ASPIRA-TIONS...
WELL, FINE.

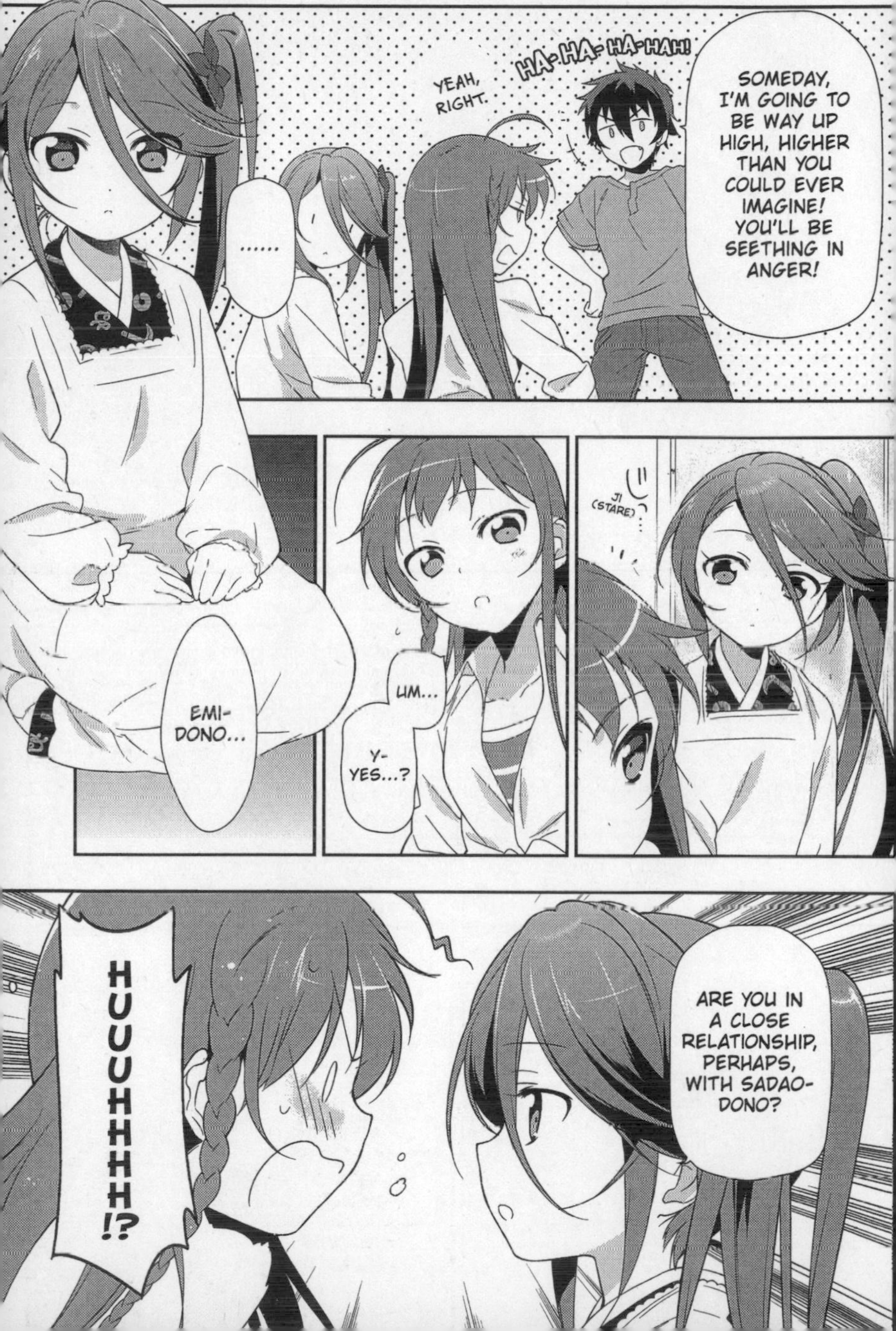
SOMEDAY, I'M GOING TO BE WAY UP HIGH, HIGHER THAN YOU COULD EVER IMAGINE! YOU'LL BE SEETHING IN ANGER!
HA-HA-HA-HAH!
YEAH, RIGHT.
......
JI (STARE)
UM...
Y-YES...?
EMI-DONO...
ARE YOU IN A CLOSE RELATIONSHIP, PERHAPS, WITH SADAO-DONO?
HUUUHHHHH!?

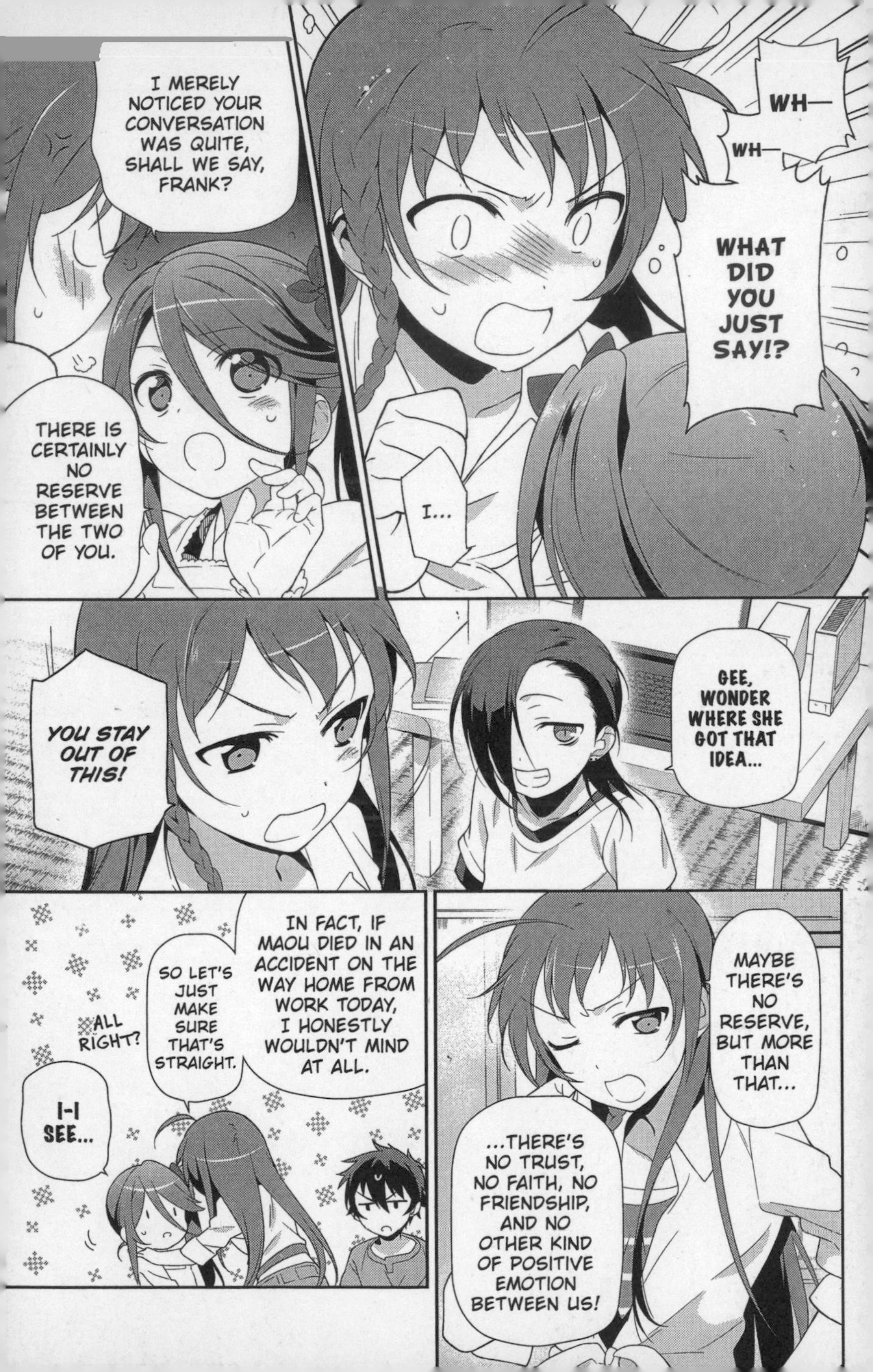
WH—
WH—
WHAT DID YOU JUST SAY!?
I...
I MERELY NOTICED YOUR CONVERSATION WAS QUITE, SHALL WE SAY, FRANK?
THERE IS CERTAINLY NO RESERVE BETWEEN THE TWO OF YOU.
GEE, WONDER WHERE SHE GOT THAT IDEA...
YOU STAY OUT OF THIS!
MAYBE THERE'S NO RESERVE, BUT MORE THAN THAT...
...THERE'S NO TRUST, NO FAITH, NO FRIENDSHIP, AND NO OTHER KIND OF POSITIVE EMOTION BETWEEN US!
IN FACT, IF MAOU DIED IN AN ACCIDENT ON THE WAY HOME FROM WORK TODAY, I HONESTLY WOULDN'T MIND AT ALL.
SO LET'S JUST MAKE SURE THAT'S STRAIGHT.
ALL RIGHT?
I-I SEE...

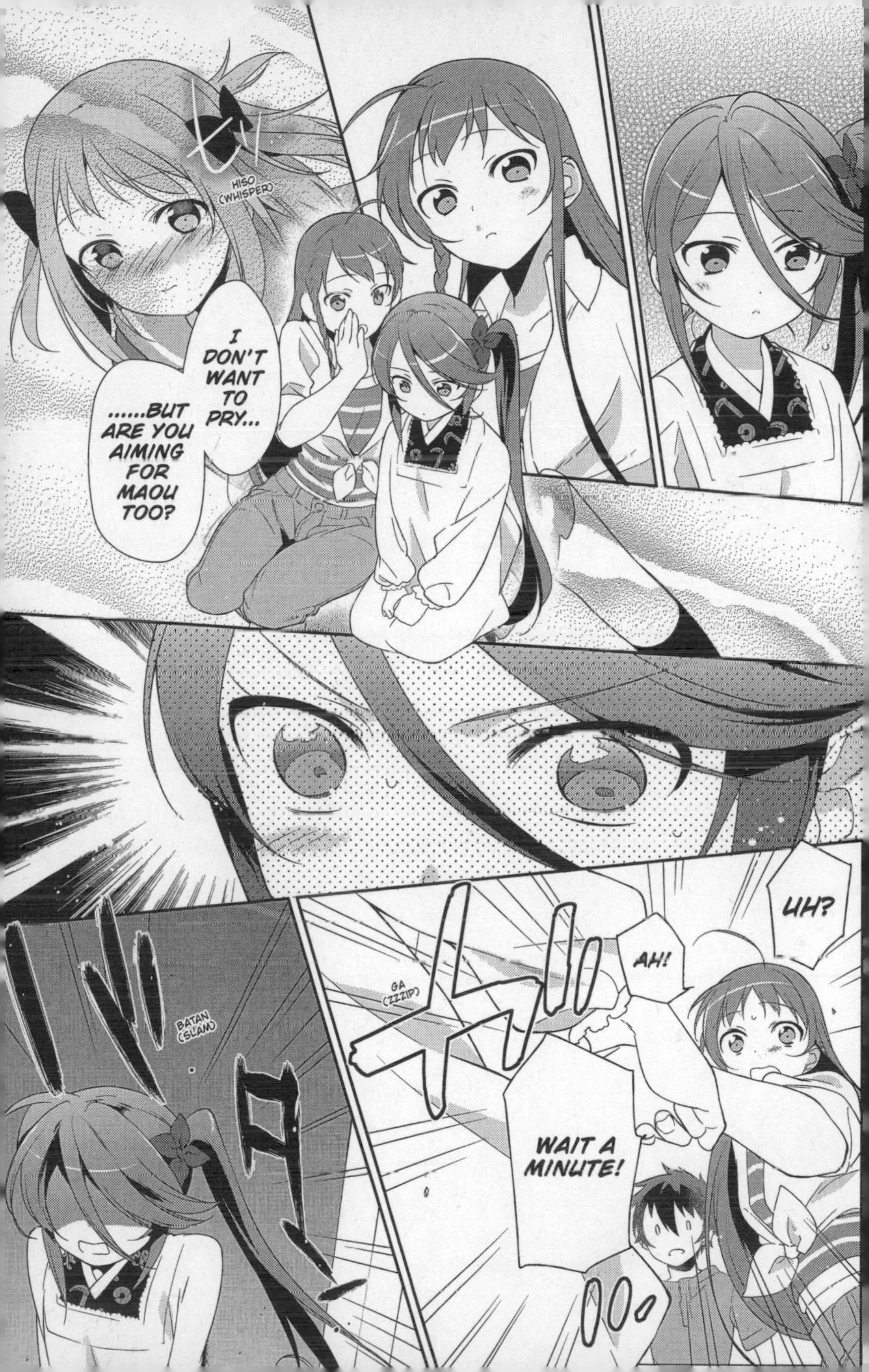
HISO (WHISPER)
I DON'T WANT TO PRY...
......BUT ARE YOU AIMING FOR MAOU TOO?
UH?
AH!
GA (ZZZIP)
WAIT A MINUTE!
BATAN (SLAM)

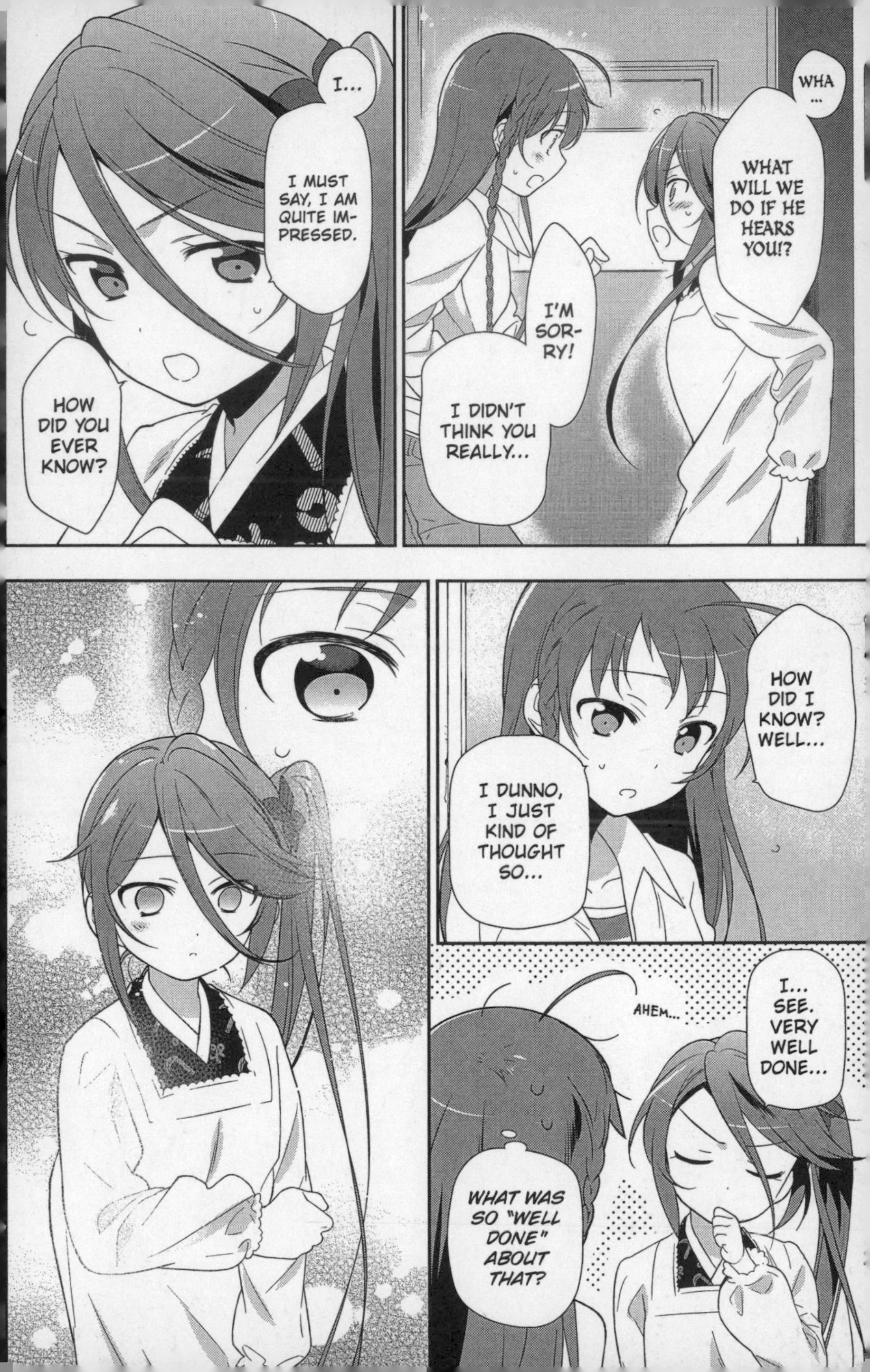
WHA...
WHAT WILL WE DO IF HE HEARS YOU!?
I'M SORRY!
I DIDN'T THINK YOU REALLY...
I...
I MUST SAY, I AM QUITE IMPRESSED.
HOW DID YOU EVER KNOW?
HOW DID I KNOW? WELL...
I DUNNO, I JUST KIND OF THOUGHT SO...
I... SEE. VERY WELL DONE...
AHEM...
WHAT WAS SO "WELL DONE" ABOUT THAT?

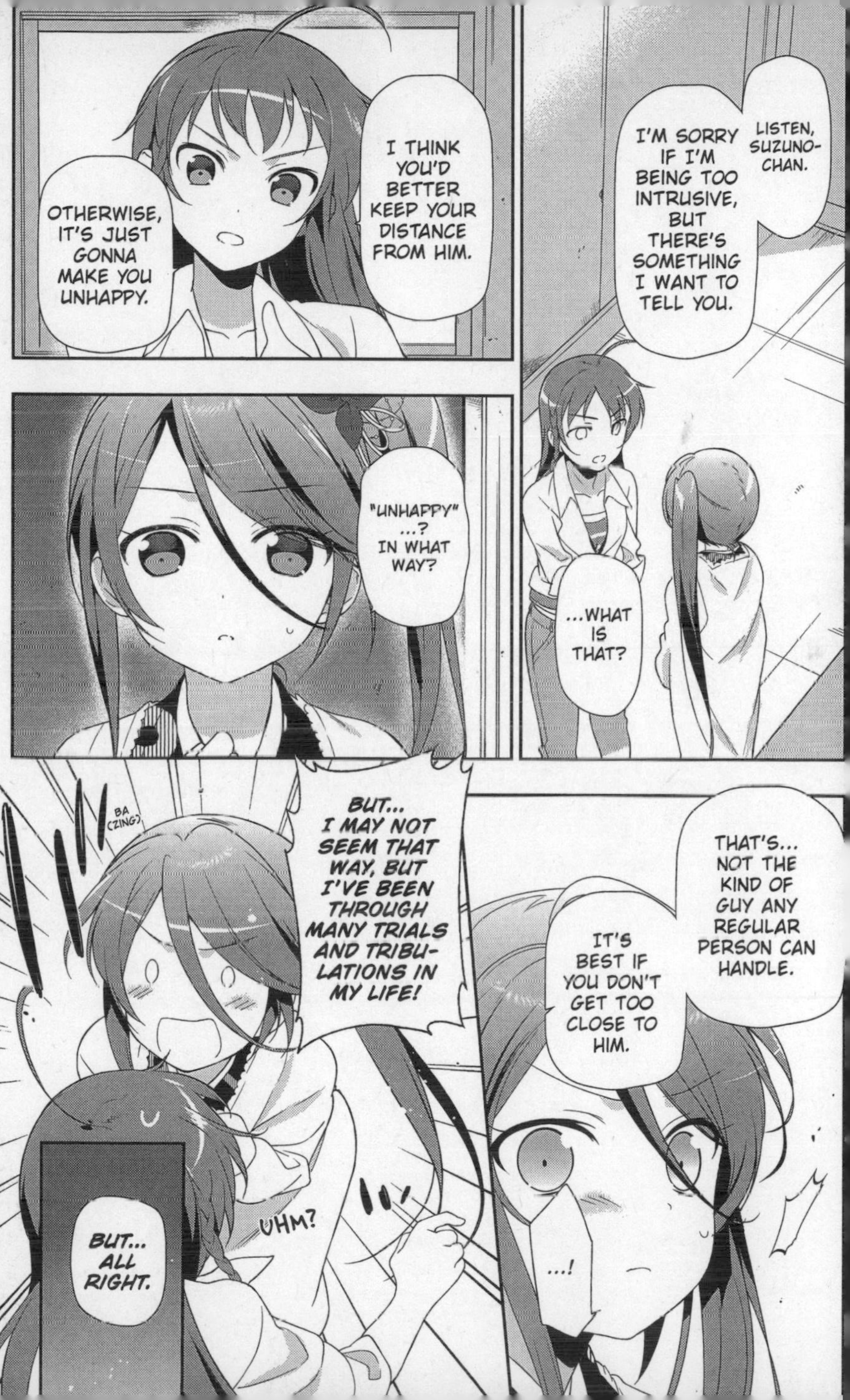
LISTEN, SUZUNO-CHAN.
I'M SORRY IF I'M BEING TOO INTRUSIVE, BUT THERE'S SOMETHING I WANT TO TELL YOU.
...WHAT IS THAT?
I THINK YOU'D BETTER KEEP YOUR DISTANCE FROM HIM.
OTHERWISE, IT'S JUST GONNA MAKE YOU UNHAPPY.
"UNHAPPY" ...? IN WHAT WAY?
THAT'S... NOT THE KIND OF GUY ANY REGULAR PERSON CAN HANDLE.
IT'S BEST IF YOU DON'T GET TOO CLOSE TO HIM.
...!
BUT... I MAY NOT SEEM THAT WAY, BUT I'VE BEEN THROUGH MANY TRIALS AND TRIBU-LATIONS IN MY LIFE!
BA (ZING)
UHM?
BUT... ALL RIGHT.

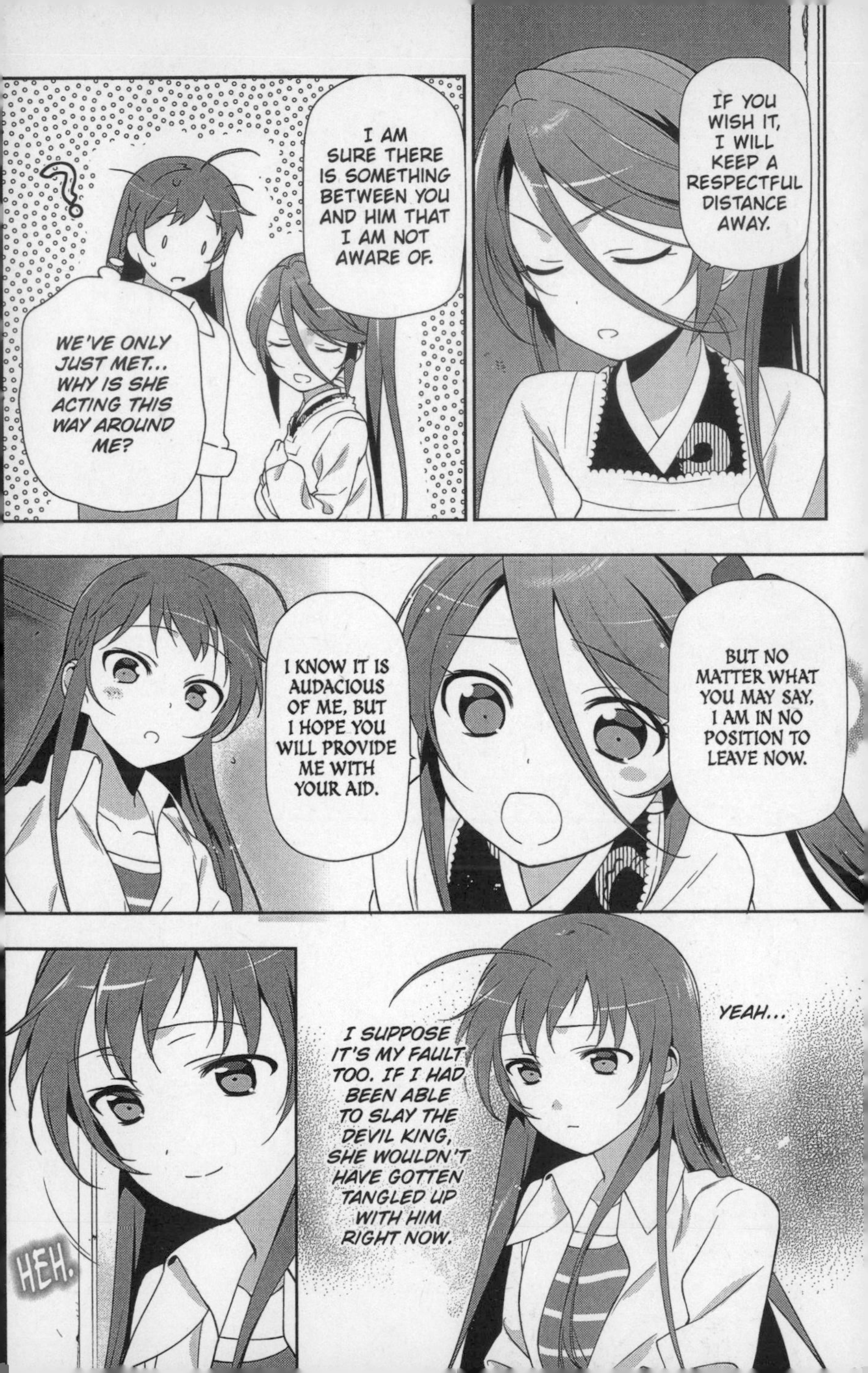
IF YOU WISH IT, I WILL KEEP A RESPECTFUL DISTANCE AWAY.
I AM SURE THERE IS SOMETHING BETWEEN YOU AND HIM THAT I AM NOT AWARE OF.
WE'VE ONLY JUST MET... WHY IS SHE ACTING THIS WAY AROUND ME?
BUT NO MATTER WHAT YOU MAY SAY, I AM IN NO POSITION TO LEAVE NOW.
I KNOW IT IS AUDACIOUS OF ME, BUT I HOPE YOU WILL PROVIDE ME WITH YOUR AID.
YEAH...
I SUPPOSE IT'S MY FAULT TOO. IF I HAD BEEN ABLE TO SLAY THE DEVIL KING, SHE WOULDN'T HAVE GOTTEN TANGLED UP WITH HIM RIGHT NOW.
HEH.

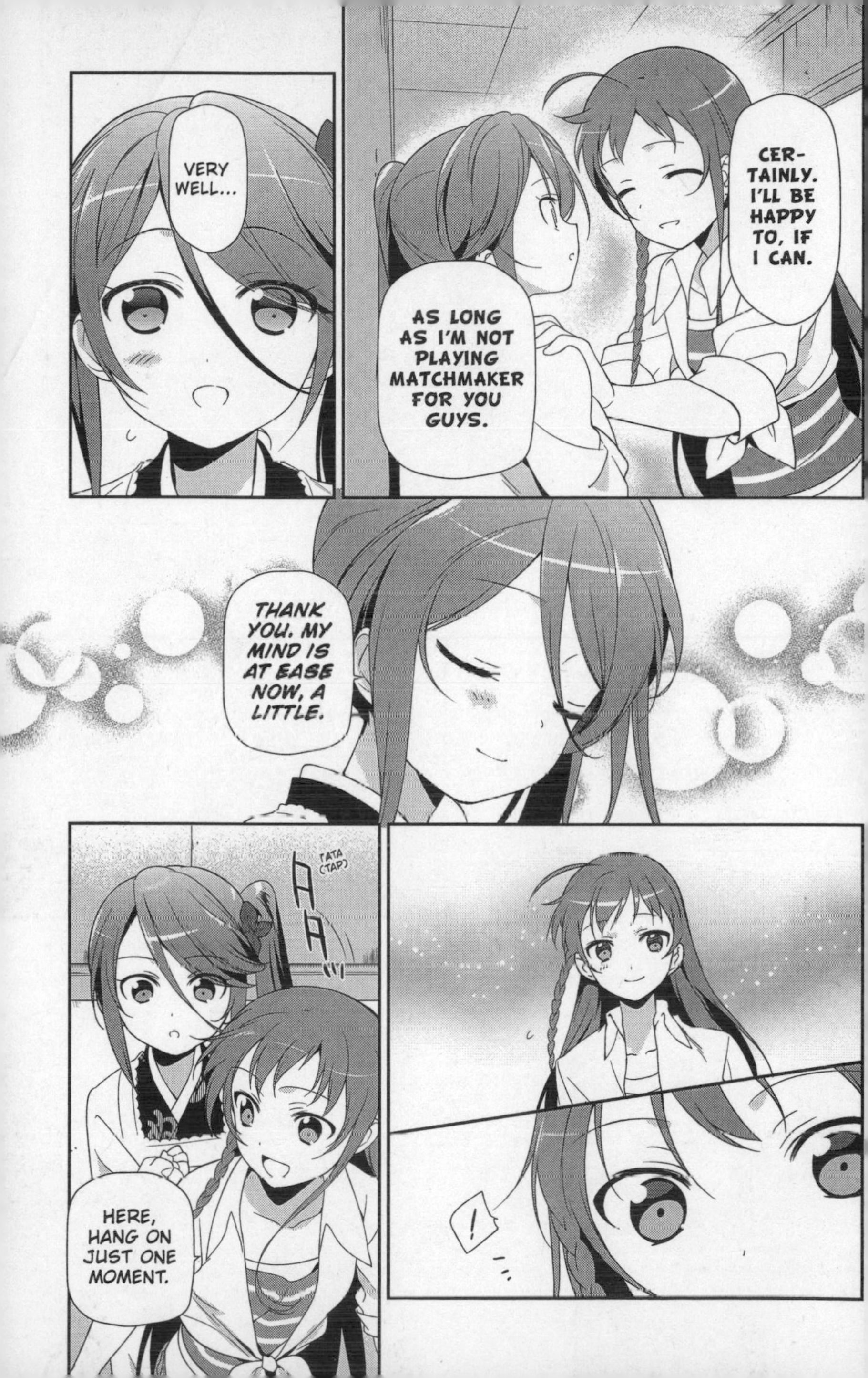
CER-TAINLY. I'LL BE HAPPY TO, IF I CAN.
AS LONG AS I'M NOT PLAYING MATCHMAKER FOR YOU GUYS.
VERY WELL...
THANK YOU. MY MIND IS AT EASE NOW, A LITTLE.
!
TATA (TAP)
HERE, HANG ON JUST ONE MOMENT.

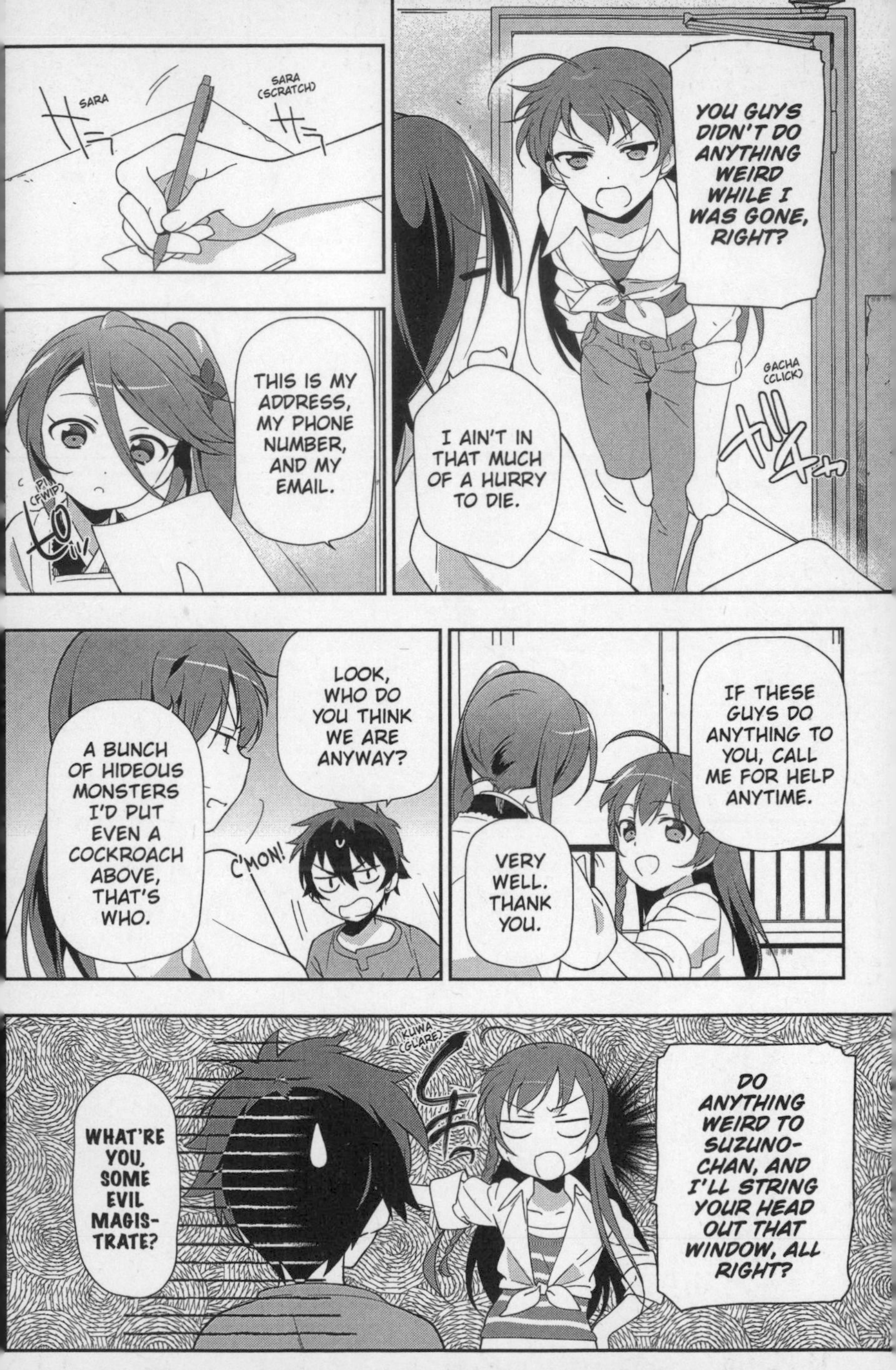
YOU GUYS DIDN'T DO ANYTHING WEIRD WHILE I WAS GONE, RIGHT?
GACHA (CLICK)
I AIN'T IN THAT MUCH OF A HURRY TO DIE.
SARA (SCRATCH)
SARA
THIS IS MY ADDRESS, MY PHONE NUMBER, AND MY EMAIL.
PI (FWIP)
IF THESE GUYS DO ANYTHING TO YOU, CALL ME FOR HELP ANYTIME.
VERY WELL. THANK YOU.
LOOK, WHO DO YOU THINK WE ARE ANYWAY?
C'MON!
A BUNCH OF HIDEOUS MONSTERS I'D PUT EVEN A COCKROACH ABOVE, THAT'S WHO.
DO ANYTHING WEIRD TO SUZUNO-CHAN, AND I'LL STRING YOUR HEAD OUT THAT WINDOW, ALL RIGHT?
KUWA (GLARE)
WHAT'RE YOU, SOME EVIL MAGIS-TRATE?

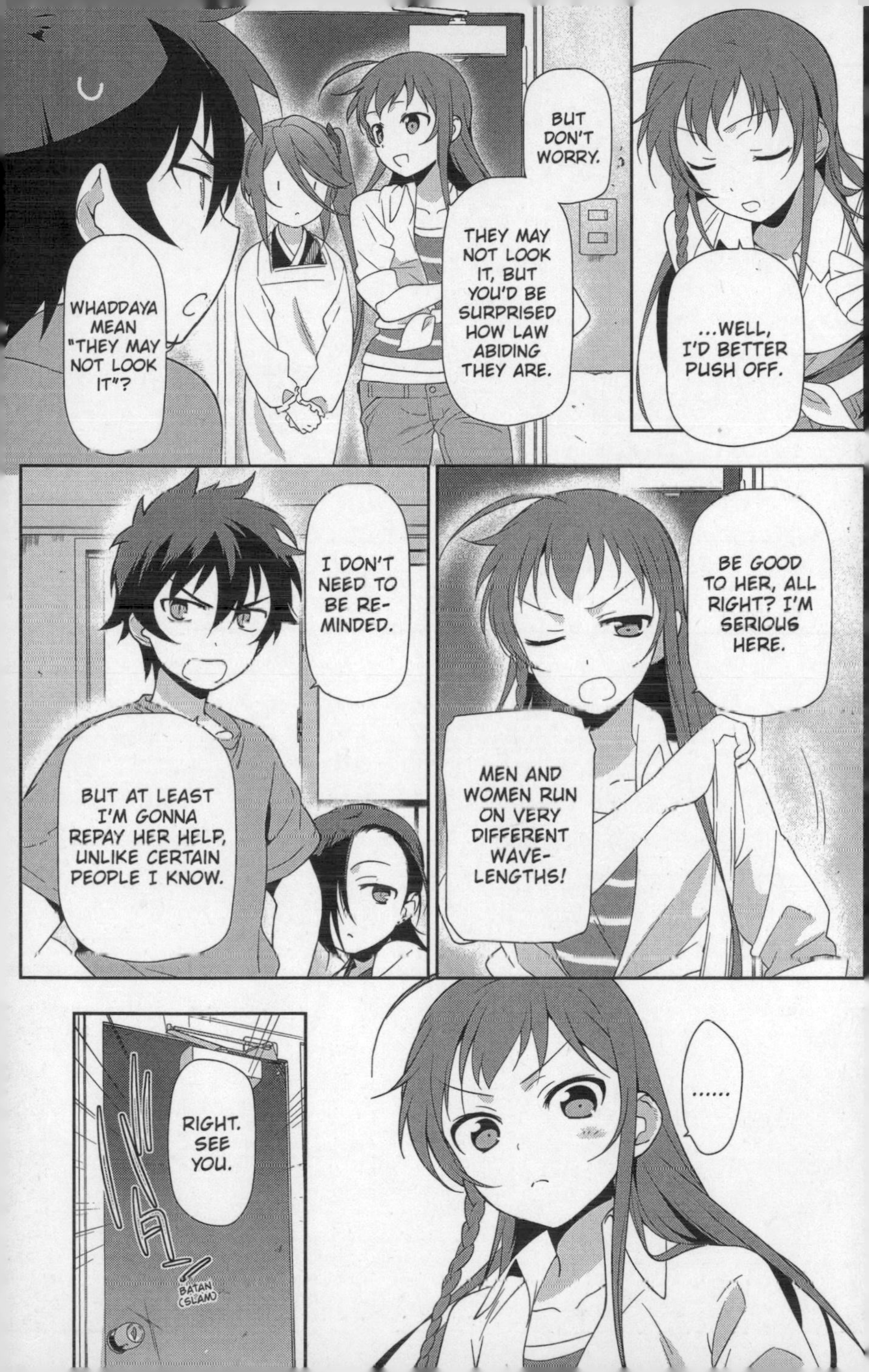
...WELL, I'D BETTER PUSH OFF.
BUT DON'T WORRY.
THEY MAY NOT LOOK IT, BUT YOU'D BE SURPRISED HOW LAW ABIDING THEY ARE.
WHADDAYA MEAN "THEY MAY NOT LOOK IT"?
BE GOOD TO HER, ALL RIGHT? I'M SERIOUS HERE.
MEN AND WOMEN RUN ON VERY DIFFERENT WAVE-LENGTHS!
I DON'T NEED TO BE RE-MINDED.
BUT AT LEAST I'M GONNA REPAY HER HELP, UNLIKE CERTAIN PEOPLE I KNOW.
......
RIGHT. SEE YOU.
BATAN (SLAM)

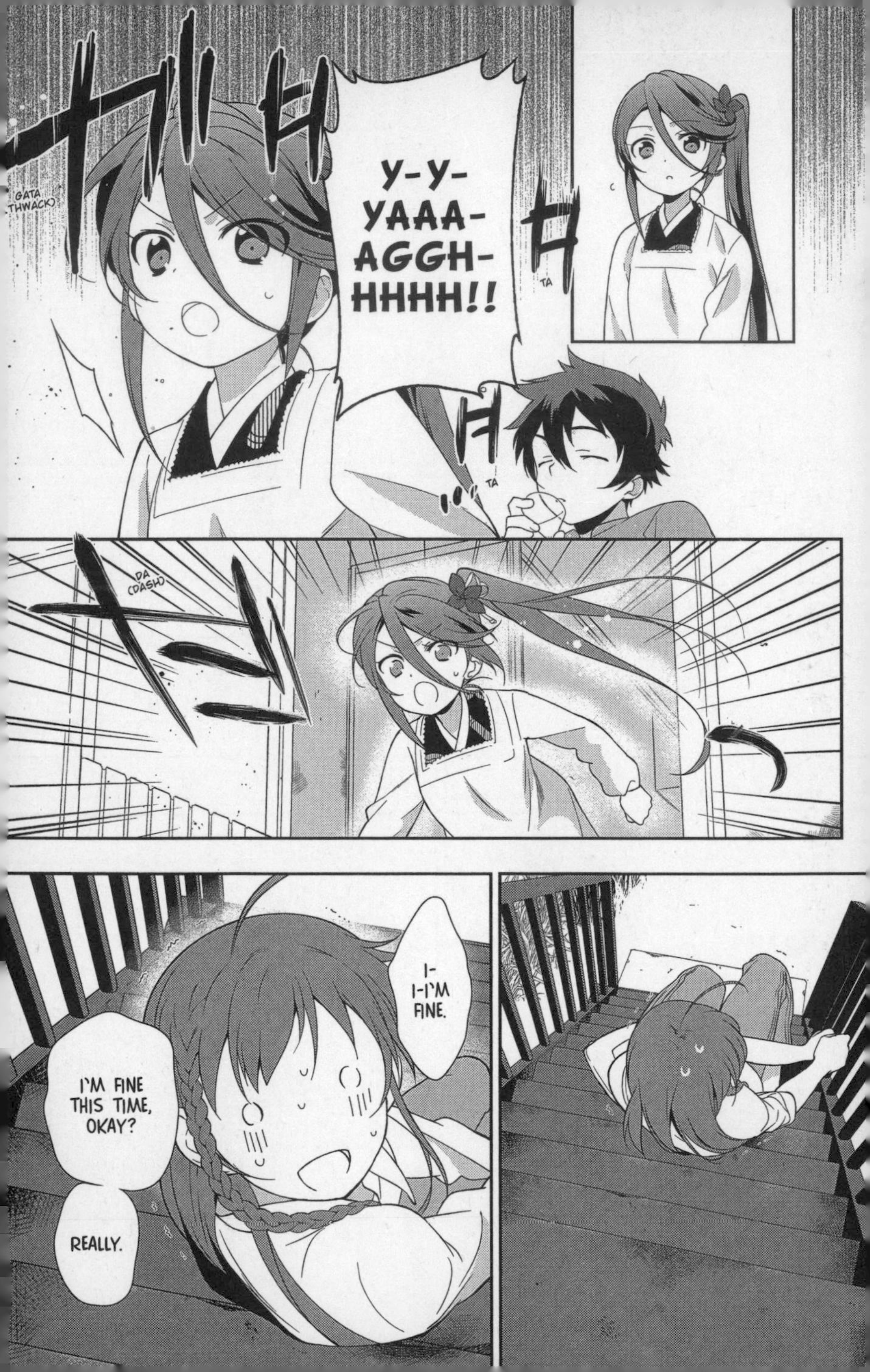
TA
GATA THWACK)
Y-Y-YAAA-AGGH-HHHH!!
TA
DA (DASH)
I- I-I'M FINE.
I'M FINE THIS TIME, OKAY?
REALLY.

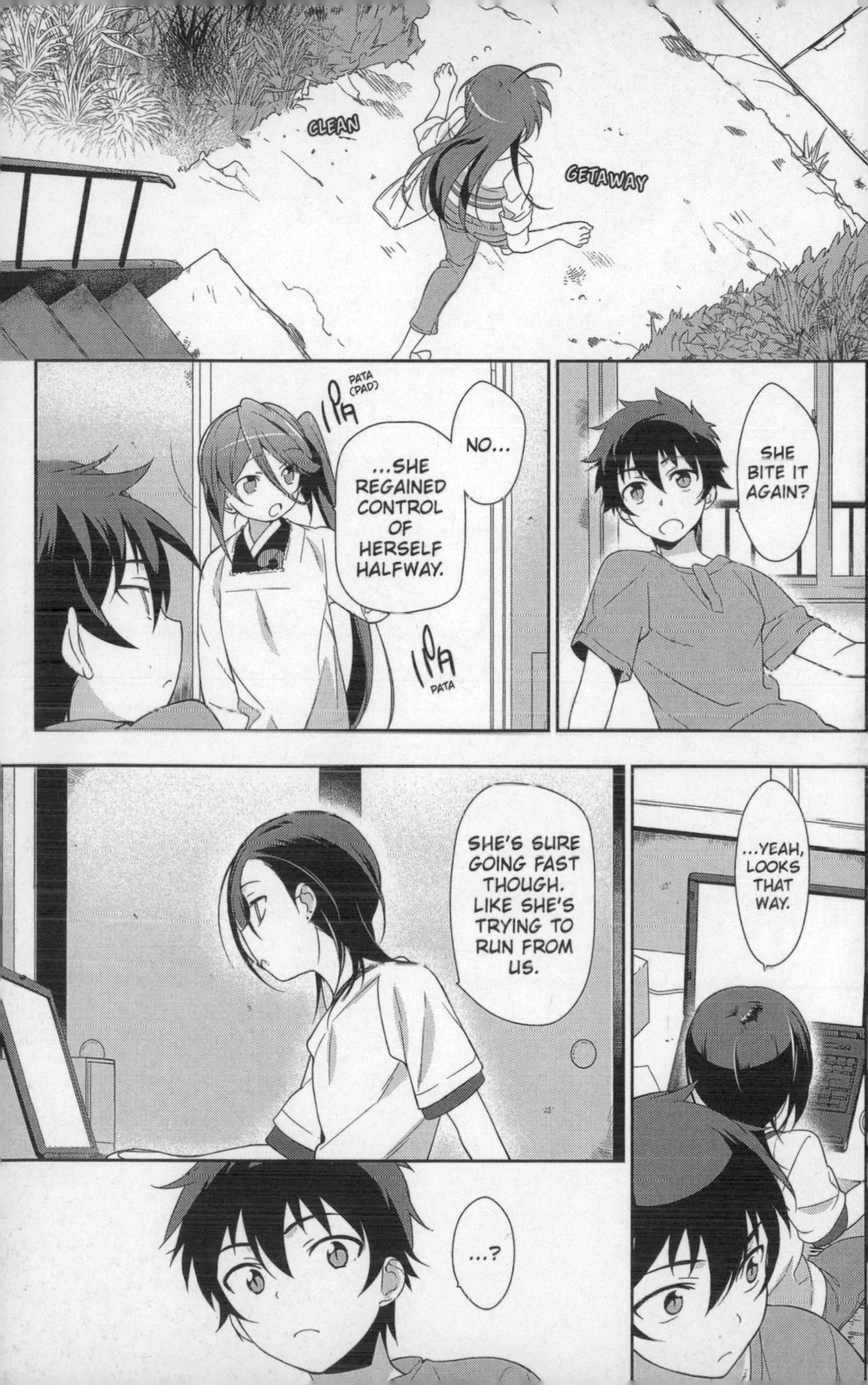
CLEAN
GETAWAY
SHE BITE IT AGAIN?
PATA (PAD)
NO...
...SHE REGAINED CONTROL OF HERSELF HALFWAY.
PATA
...YEAH, LOOKS THAT WAY.
SHE'S SURE GOING FAST THOUGH. LIKE SHE'S TRYING TO RUN FROM US.
...?

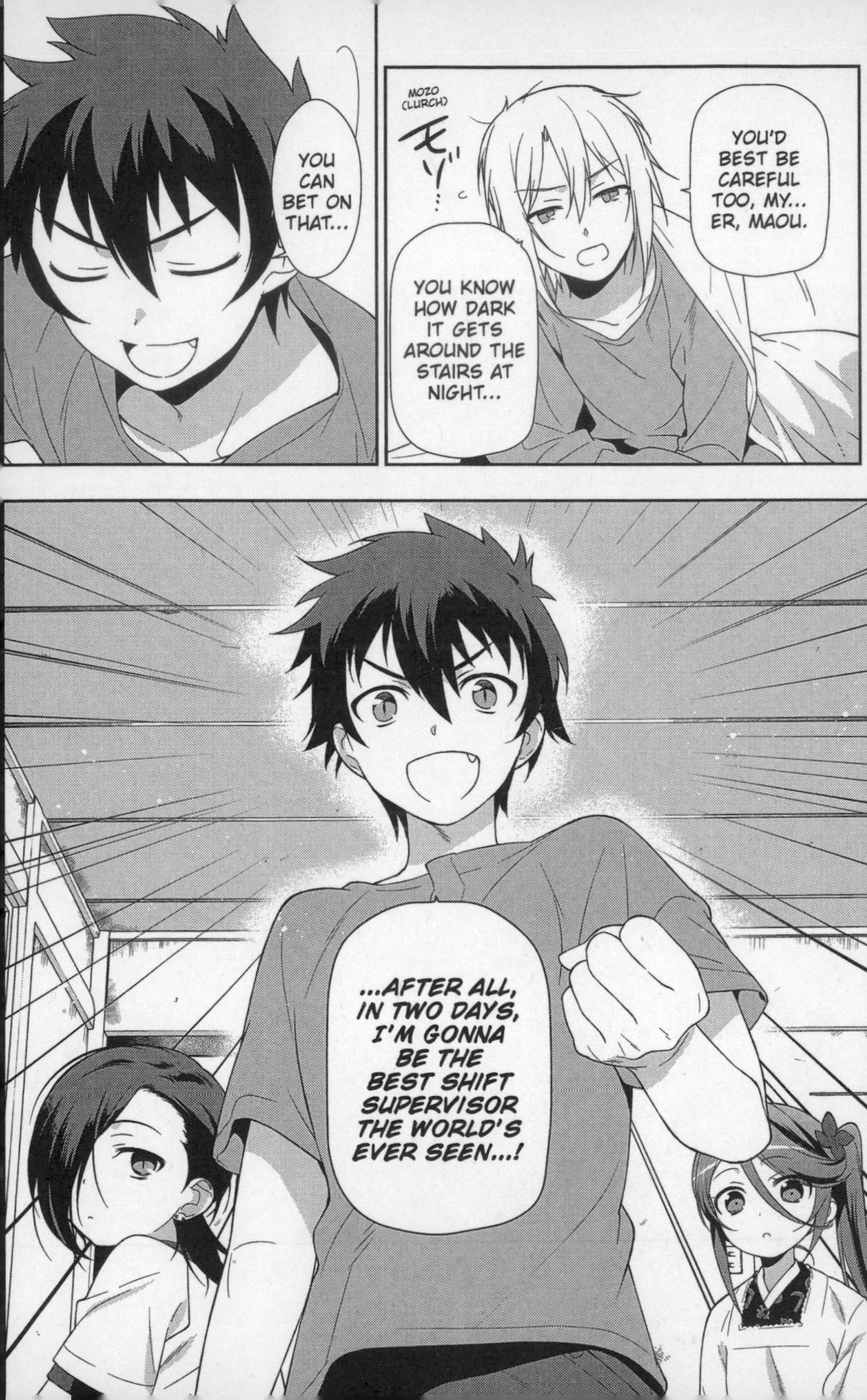
YOU'D BEST BE CAREFUL TOO, MY... ER, MAOU.
MOZO (LURCH)
YOU KNOW HOW DARK IT GETS AROUND THE STAIRS AT NIGHT...
YOU CAN BET ON THAT...
...AFTER ALL, IN TWO DAYS, I'M GONNA BE THE BEST SHIFT SUPERVISOR THE WORLD'S EVER SEEN...!

Emi
Yusa

THE DEVIL IS A PART-TIMER!

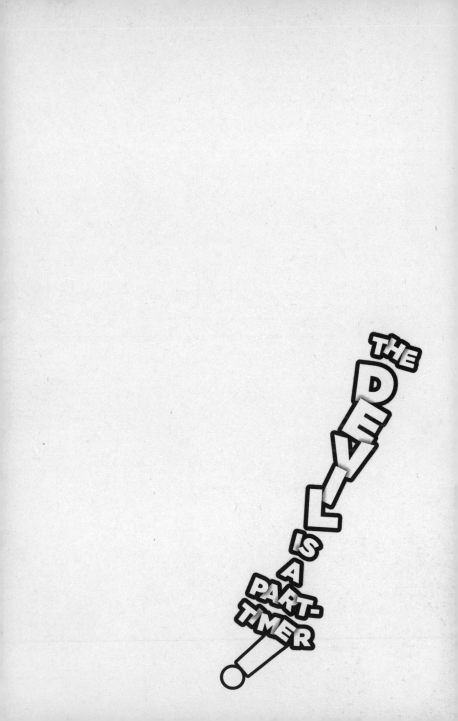

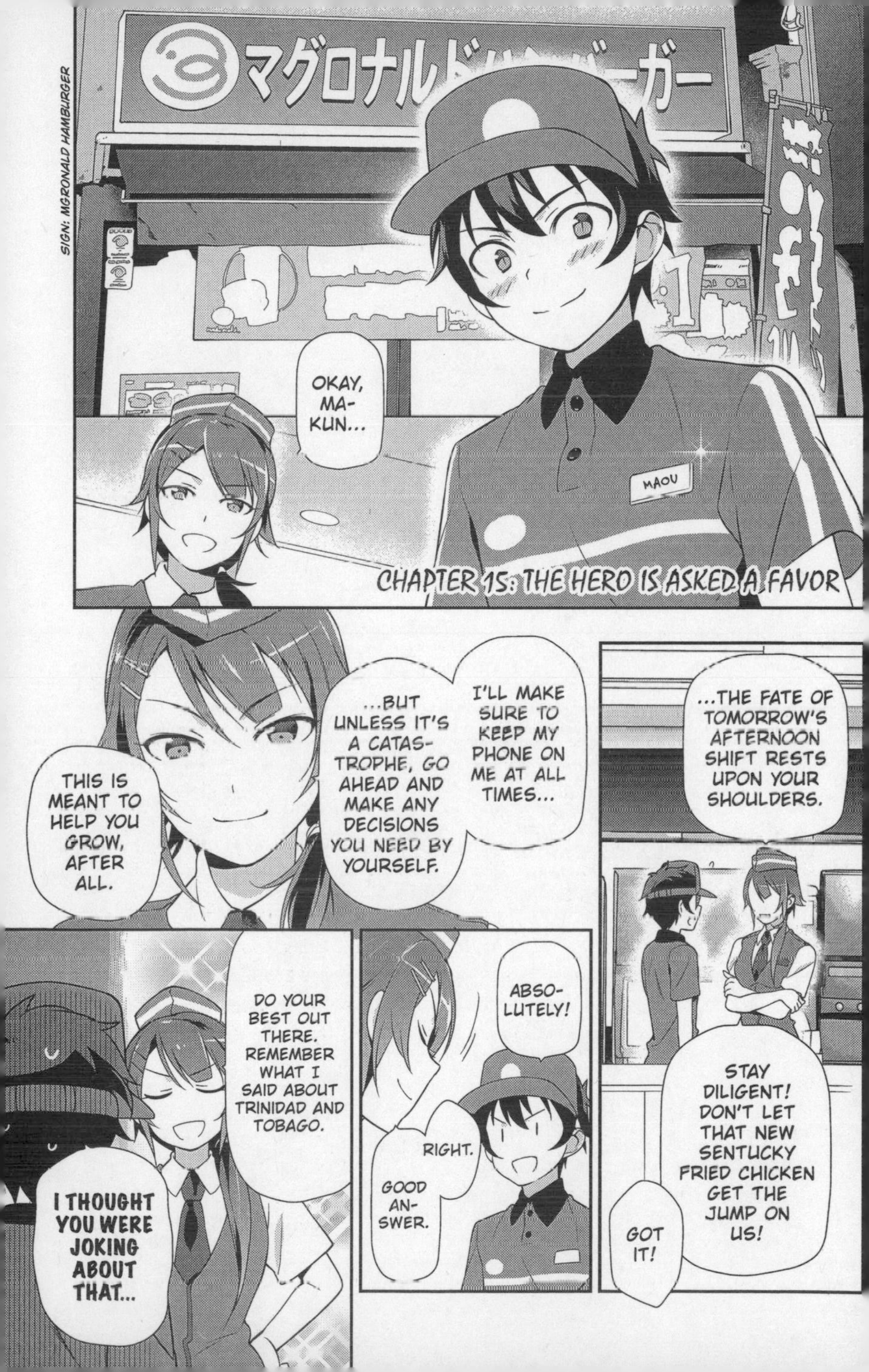
マグロナルドハンバーガー
SIGN: MGRONALD HAMBURGER
OKAY, MA-KUN...
MAOU
CHAPTER 15: THE HERO IS ASKED A FAVOR
...THE FATE OF TOMORROW'S AFTERNOON SHIFT RESTS UPON YOUR SHOULDERS.
STAY DILIGENT! DON'T LET THAT NEW SENTUCKY FRIED CHICKEN GET THE JUMP ON US!
GOT IT!
I'LL MAKE SURE TO KEEP MY PHONE ON ME AT ALL TIMES...
...BUT UNLESS IT'S A CATASTROPHE, GO AHEAD AND MAKE ANY DECISIONS YOU NEED BY YOURSELF.
THIS IS MEANT TO HELP YOU GROW, AFTER ALL.
ABSOLUTELY!
RIGHT.
GOOD ANSWER.
DO YOUR BEST OUT THERE. REMEMBER WHAT I SAID ABOUT TRINIDAD AND TOBAGO.
I THOUGHT YOU WERE JOKING ABOUT THAT...

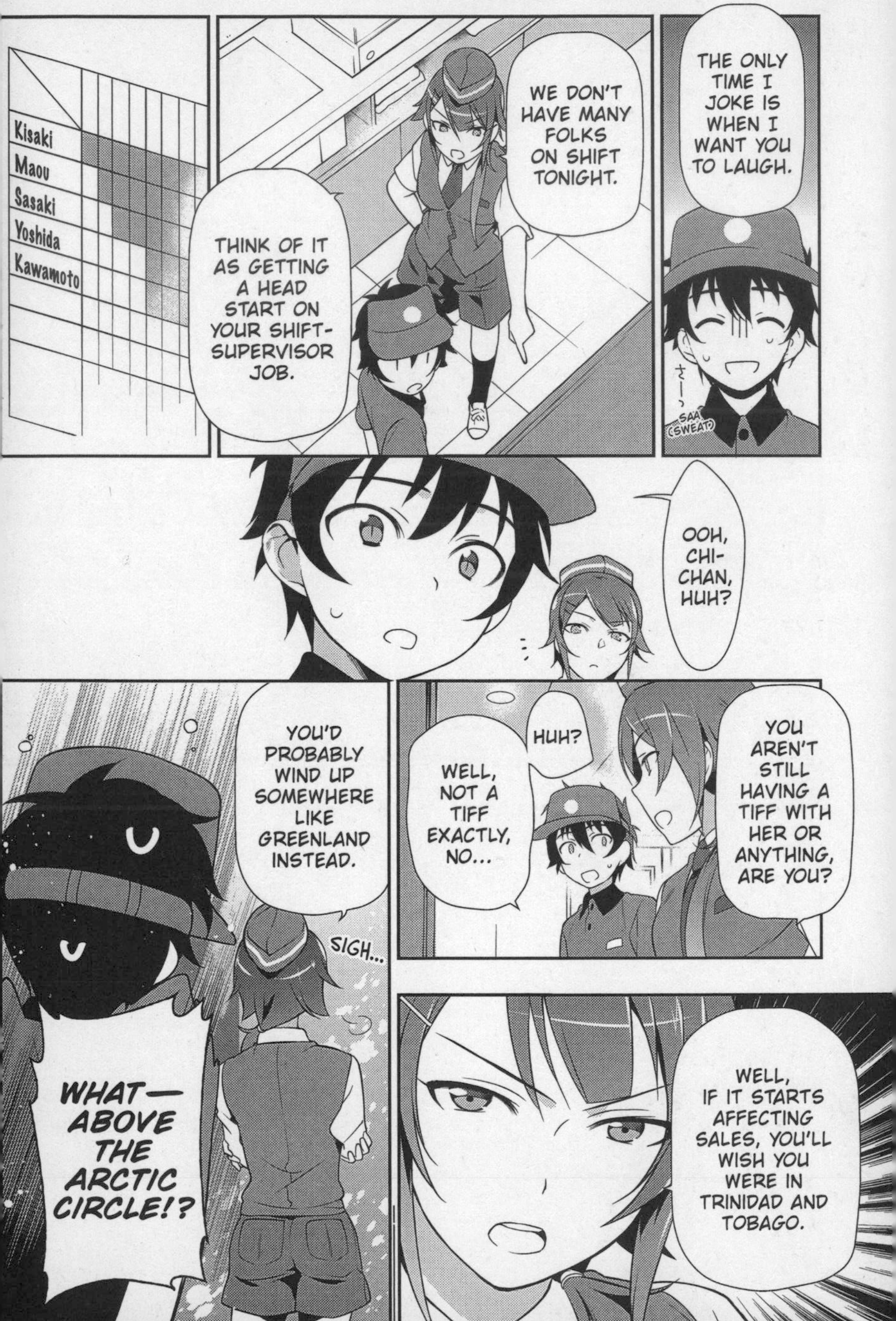
THE ONLY TIME I JOKE IS WHEN I WANT YOU TO LAUGH.
SAA (SWEAT)
WE DON'T HAVE MANY FOLKS ON SHIFT TONIGHT.
THINK OF IT AS GETTING A HEAD START ON YOUR SHIFT-SUPERVISOR JOB.
Kisaki
Maou
Sasaki
Yoshida
Kawamoto
OOH, CHI-CHAN, HUH?
YOU AREN'T STILL HAVING A TIFF WITH HER OR ANYTHING, ARE YOU?
HUH?
WELL, NOT A TIFF EXACTLY, NO...
WELL, IF IT STARTS AFFECTING SALES, YOU'LL WISH YOU WERE IN TRINIDAD AND TOBAGO.
YOU'D PROBABLY WIND UP SOMEWHERE LIKE GREENLAND INSTEAD.
SIGH...
WHAT— ABOVE THE ARCTIC CIRCLE!?

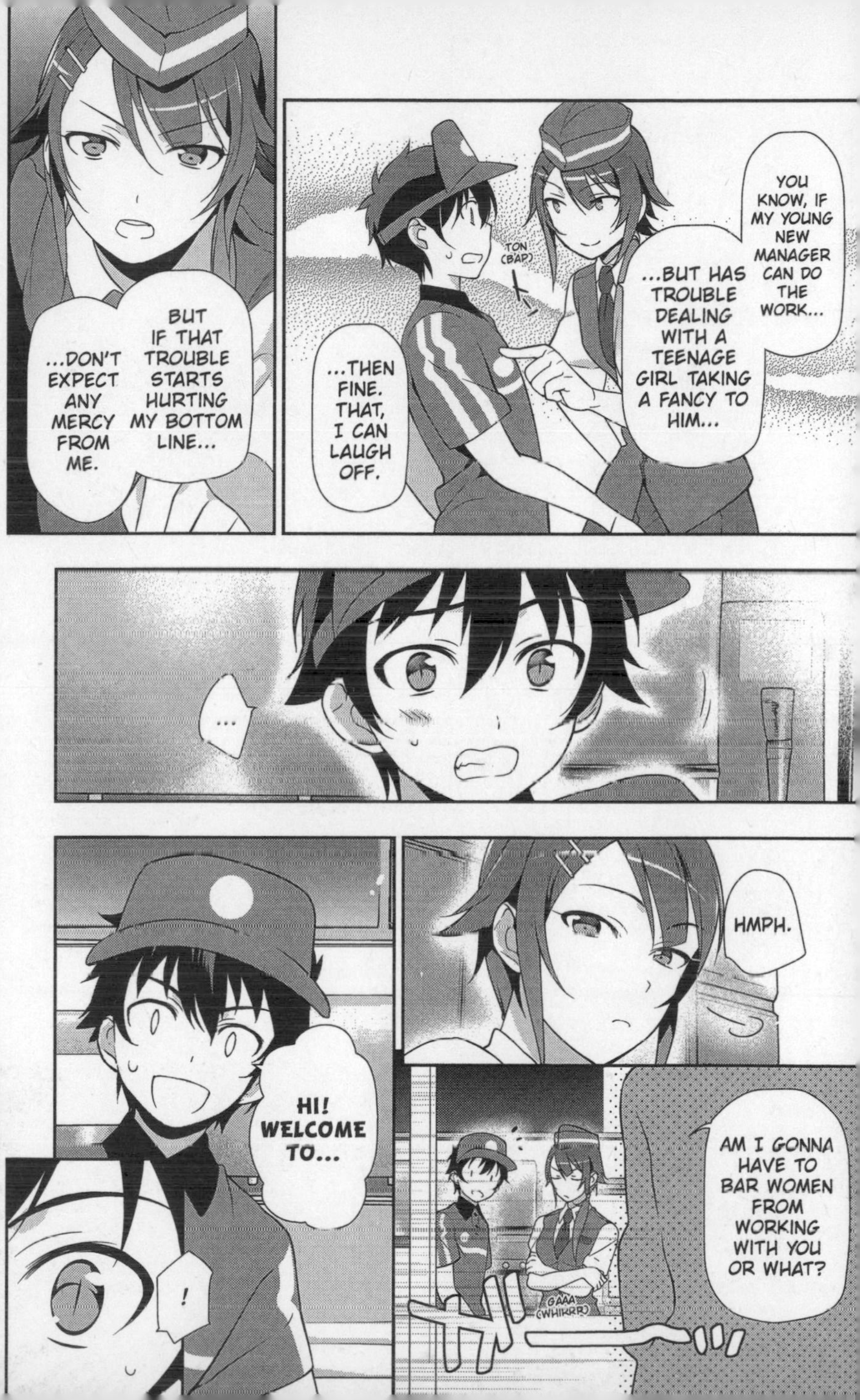
YOU KNOW, IF MY YOUNG NEW MANAGER CAN DO THE WORK...
...BUT HAS TROUBLE DEALING WITH A TEENAGE GIRL TAKING A FANCY TO HIM...
TON (BAP)
...THEN FINE. THAT, I CAN LAUGH OFF.
BUT IF THAT TROUBLE STARTS HURTING MY BOTTOM LINE...
...DON'T EXPECT ANY MERCY FROM ME.
...
HMPH.
AM I GONNA HAVE TO BAR WOMEN FROM WORKING WITH YOU OR WHAT?
GAAA (WHIRR)
HI! WELCOME TO...
!

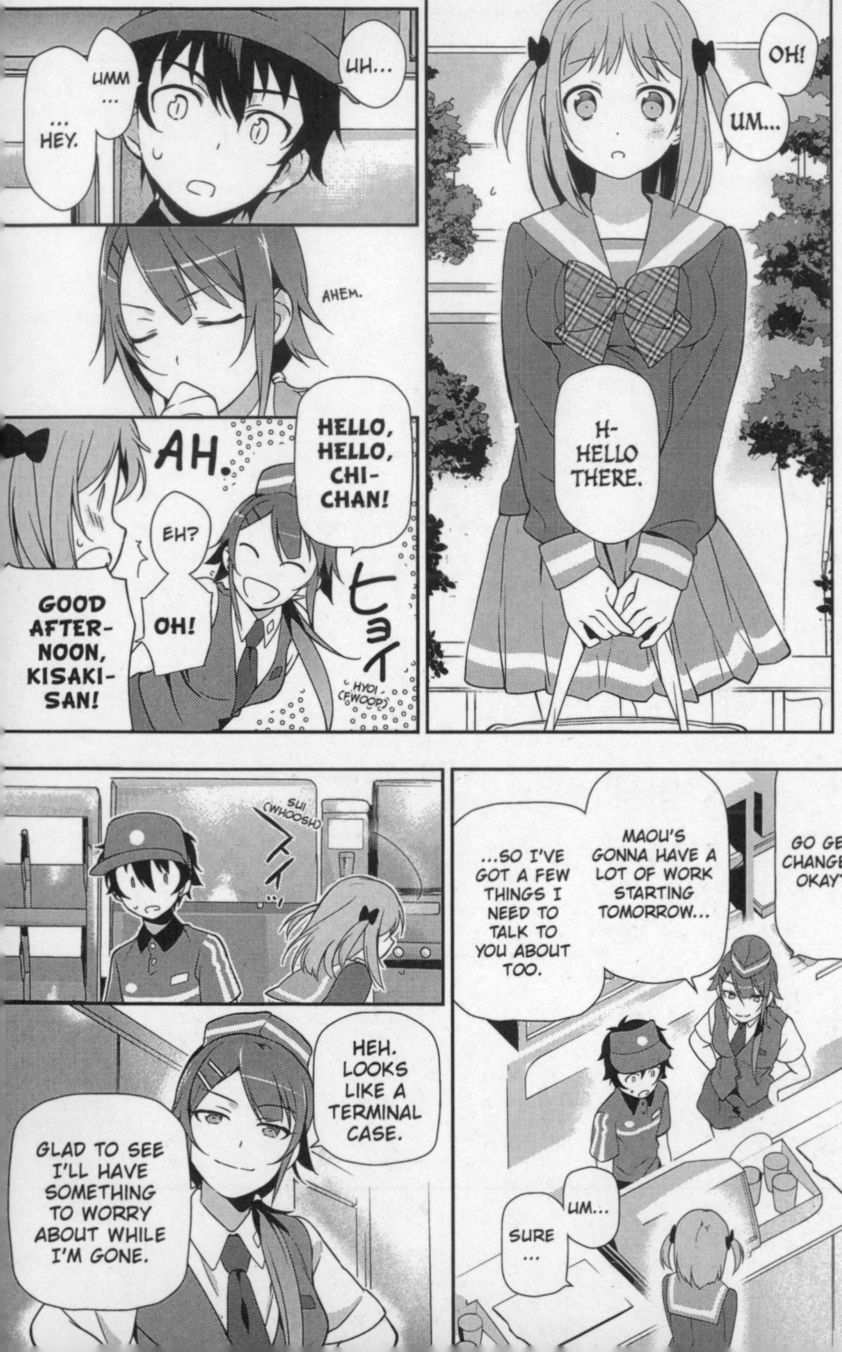
OH!
UM...
H-HELLO THERE.
UH...
UMM...
... HEY.
AHEM.
HELLO, HELLO, CHI-CHAN!
ヒョイ
HYOI (FWOOP)
AH.
EH?
OH!
GOOD AFTERNOON, KISAKI-SAN!
GO GET CHANGED, OKAY?
MAOU'S GONNA HAVE A LOT OF WORK STARTING TOMORROW...
...SO I'VE GOT A FEW THINGS I NEED TO TALK TO YOU ABOUT TOO.
UM...
SURE...
SUI (WHOOSH)
スイ
HEH. LOOKS LIKE A TERMINAL CASE.
GLAD TO SEE I'LL HAVE SOMETHING TO WORRY ABOUT WHILE I'M GONE.

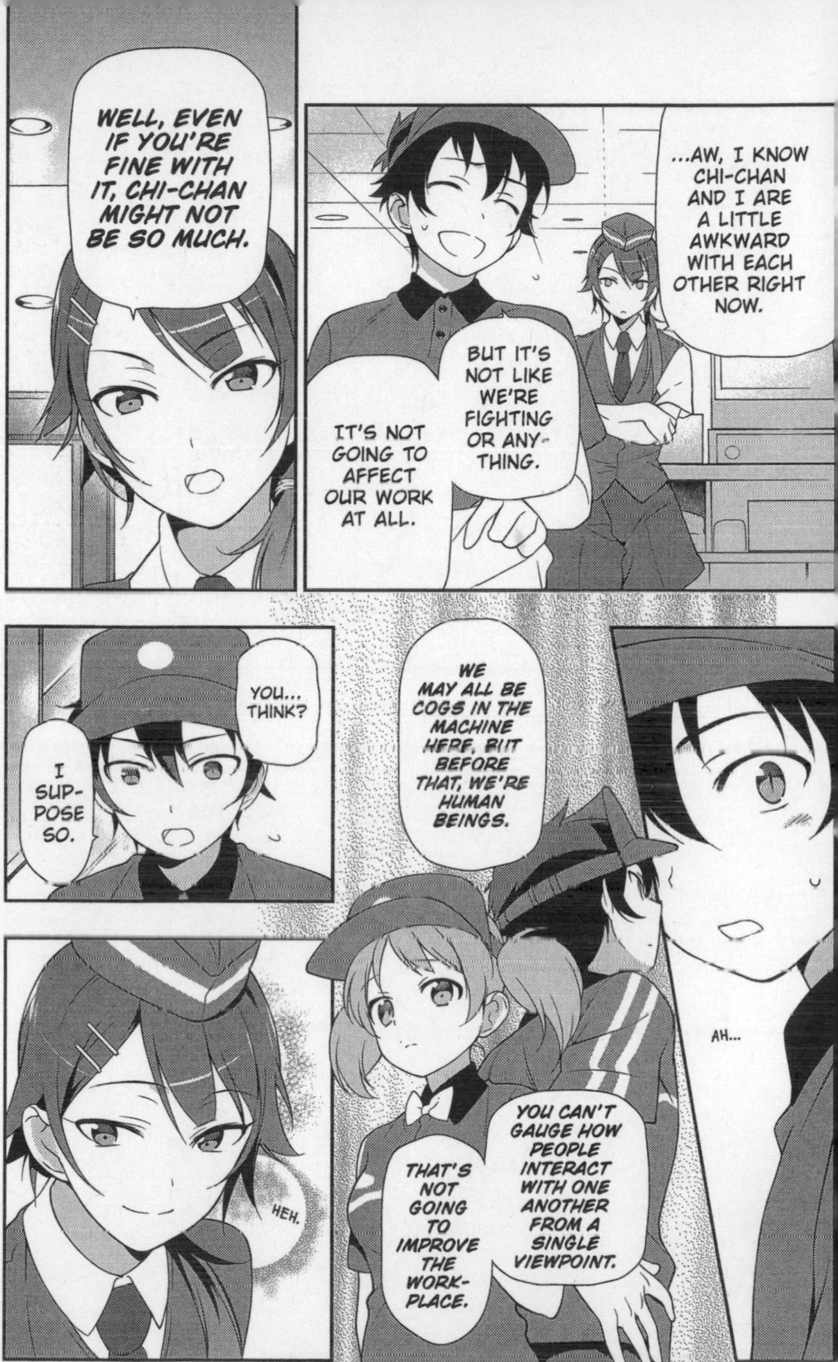
...AW, I KNOW CHI-CHAN AND I ARE A LITTLE AWKWARD WITH EACH OTHER RIGHT NOW.
BUT IT'S NOT LIKE WE'RE FIGHTING OR ANY-THING.
IT'S NOT GOING TO AFFECT OUR WORK AT ALL.
WELL, EVEN IF YOU'RE FINE WITH IT, CHI-CHAN MIGHT NOT BE SO MUCH.
WE MAY ALL BE COGS IN THE MACHINE HERE, BUT BEFORE THAT, WE'RE HUMAN BEINGS.
YOU... THINK?
I SUP-POSE SO.
HEH.
YOU CAN'T GAUGE HOW PEOPLE INTERACT WITH ONE ANOTHER FROM A SINGLE VIEWPOINT.
THAT'S NOT GOING TO IMPROVE THE WORK-PLACE.
AH...

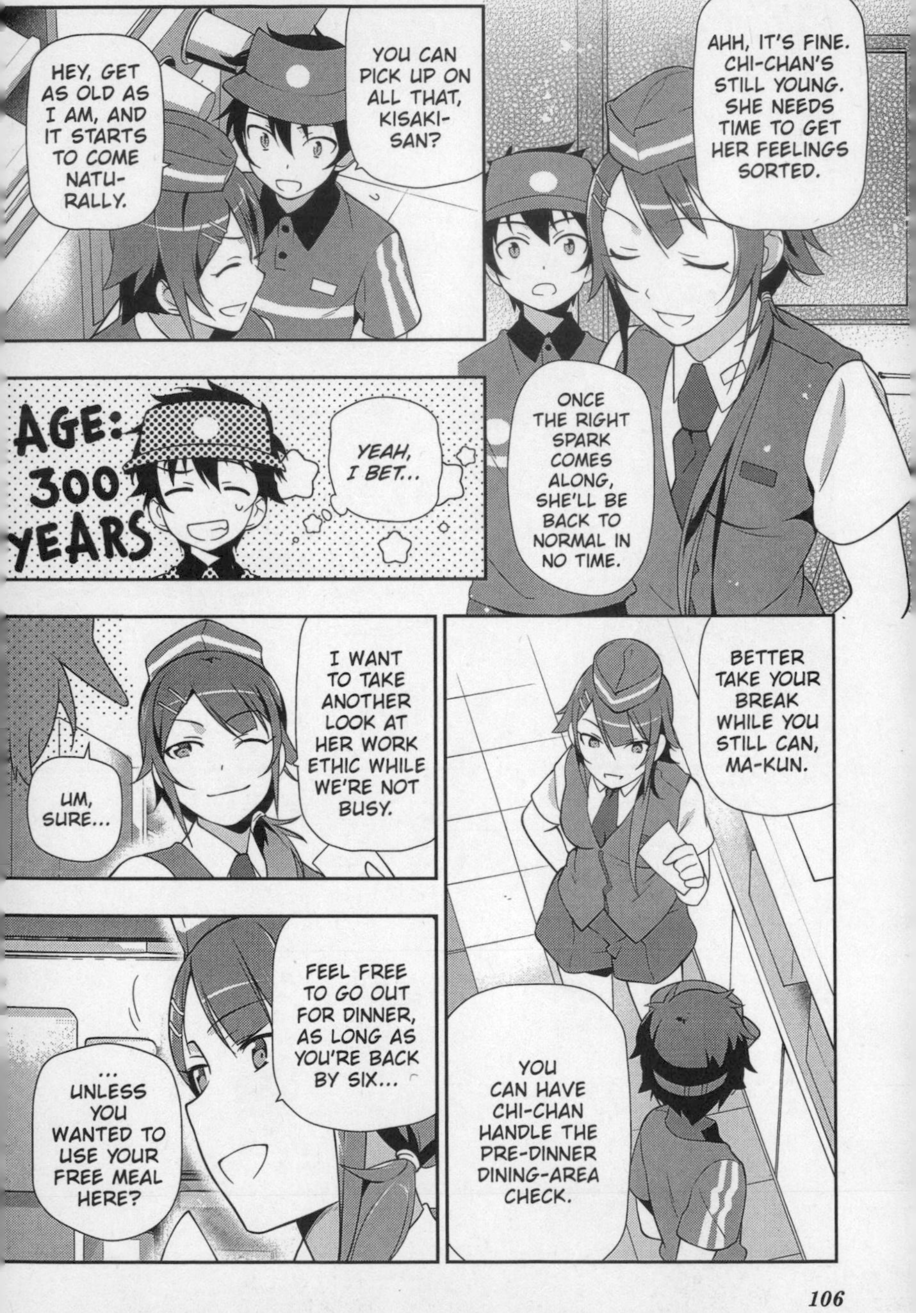
AHH, IT'S FINE. CHI-CHAN'S STILL YOUNG. SHE NEEDS TIME TO GET HER FEELINGS SORTED.
ONCE THE RIGHT SPARK COMES ALONG, SHE'LL BE BACK TO NORMAL IN NO TIME.
YOU CAN PICK UP ON ALL THAT, KISAKI-SAN?
HEY, GET AS OLD AS I AM, AND IT STARTS TO COME NATU-RALLY.
YEAH, I BET...
AGE: 300 YEARS
BETTER TAKE YOUR BREAK WHILE YOU STILL CAN, MA-KUN.
YOU CAN HAVE CHI-CHAN HANDLE THE PRE-DINNER DINING-AREA CHECK.
I WANT TO TAKE ANOTHER LOOK AT HER WORK ETHIC WHILE WE'RE NOT BUSY.
UM, SURE...
FEEL FREE TO GO OUT FOR DINNER, AS LONG AS YOU'RE BACK BY SIX...
... UNLESS YOU WANTED TO USE YOUR FREE MEAL HERE?

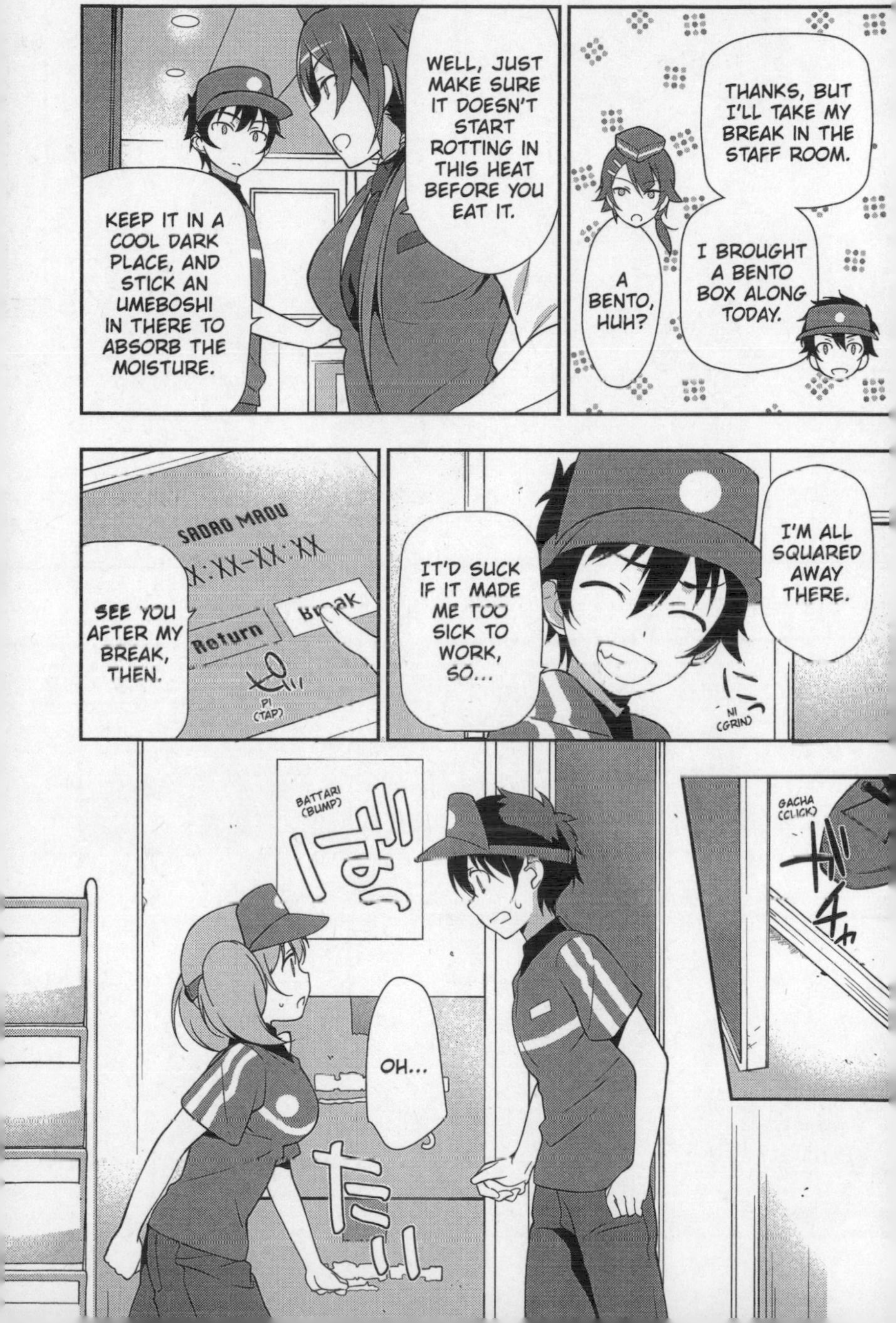
THANKS, BUT I'LL TAKE MY BREAK IN THE STAFF ROOM.
I BROUGHT A BENTO BOX ALONG TODAY.
A BENTO, HUH?
WELL, JUST MAKE SURE IT DOESN'T START ROTTING IN THIS HEAT BEFORE YOU EAT IT.
KEEP IT IN A COOL DARK PLACE, AND STICK AN UMEBOSHI IN THERE TO ABSORB THE MOISTURE.
I'M ALL SQUARED AWAY THERE.
NI (GRIN)
IT'D SUCK IF IT MADE ME TOO SICK TO WORK, SO...
SADAO MAOU
XX:XX-XX:XX
Return
SEE YOU AFTER MY BREAK, THEN.
PI (TAP)
GACHA (CLICK)
BATTARI (BUMP)
OH...

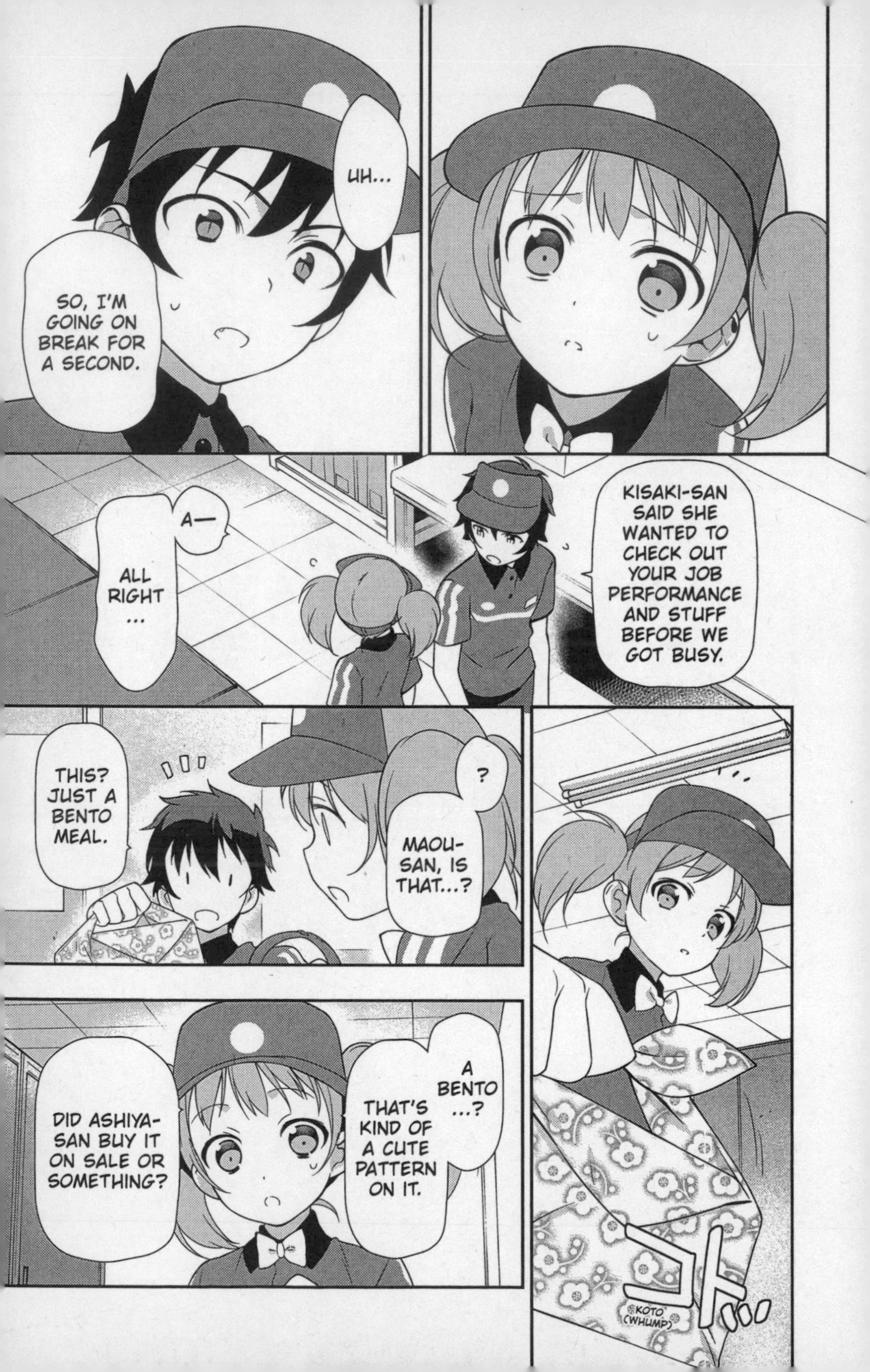
UH...
SO, I'M GOING ON BREAK FOR A SECOND.
KISAKI-SAN SAID SHE WANTED TO CHECK OUT YOUR JOB PERFORMANCE AND STUFF BEFORE WE GOT BUSY.
A—
ALL RIGHT ...
コト
KOTO (WHUMP)
?
MAOU-SAN, IS THAT...?
THIS? JUST A BENTO MEAL.
A BENTO ...?
THAT'S KIND OF A CUTE PATTERN ON IT.
DID ASHIYA-SAN BUY IT ON SALE OR SOMETHING?

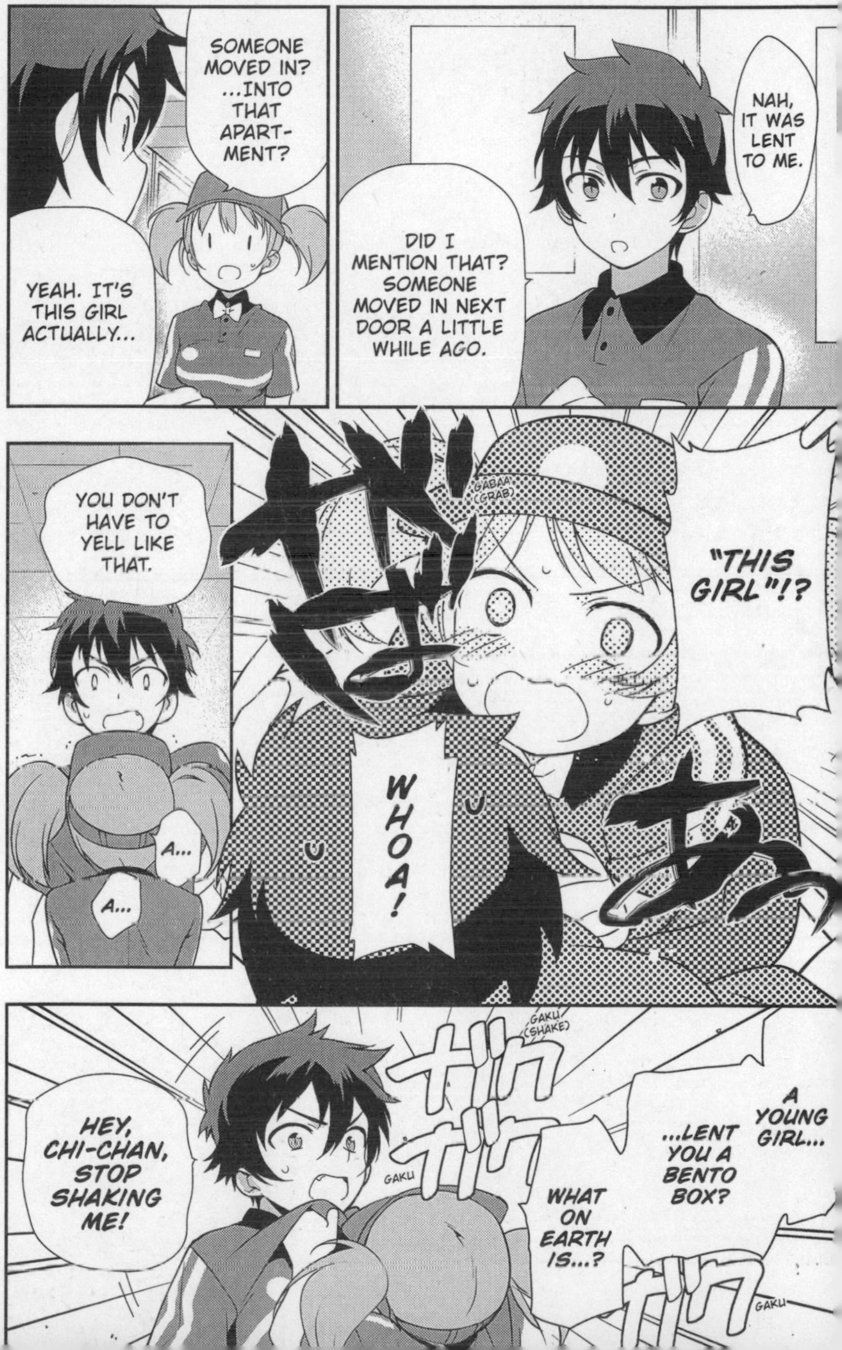
NAH, IT WAS LENT TO ME.
DID I MENTION THAT? SOMEONE MOVED IN NEXT DOOR A LITTLE WHILE AGO.
SOMEONE MOVED IN? ...INTO THAT APART-MENT?
YEAH. IT'S THIS GIRL ACTUALLY...
GABAA (GRAB)
"THIS GIRL"!?
WHOA!
YOU DON'T HAVE TO YELL LIKE THAT.
A...
A...
GAKU (SHAKE)
A YOUNG GIRL...
...LENT YOU A BENTO BOX?
WHAT ON EARTH IS...?
GAKU
HEY, CHI-CHAN, STOP SHAKING ME!
GAKU

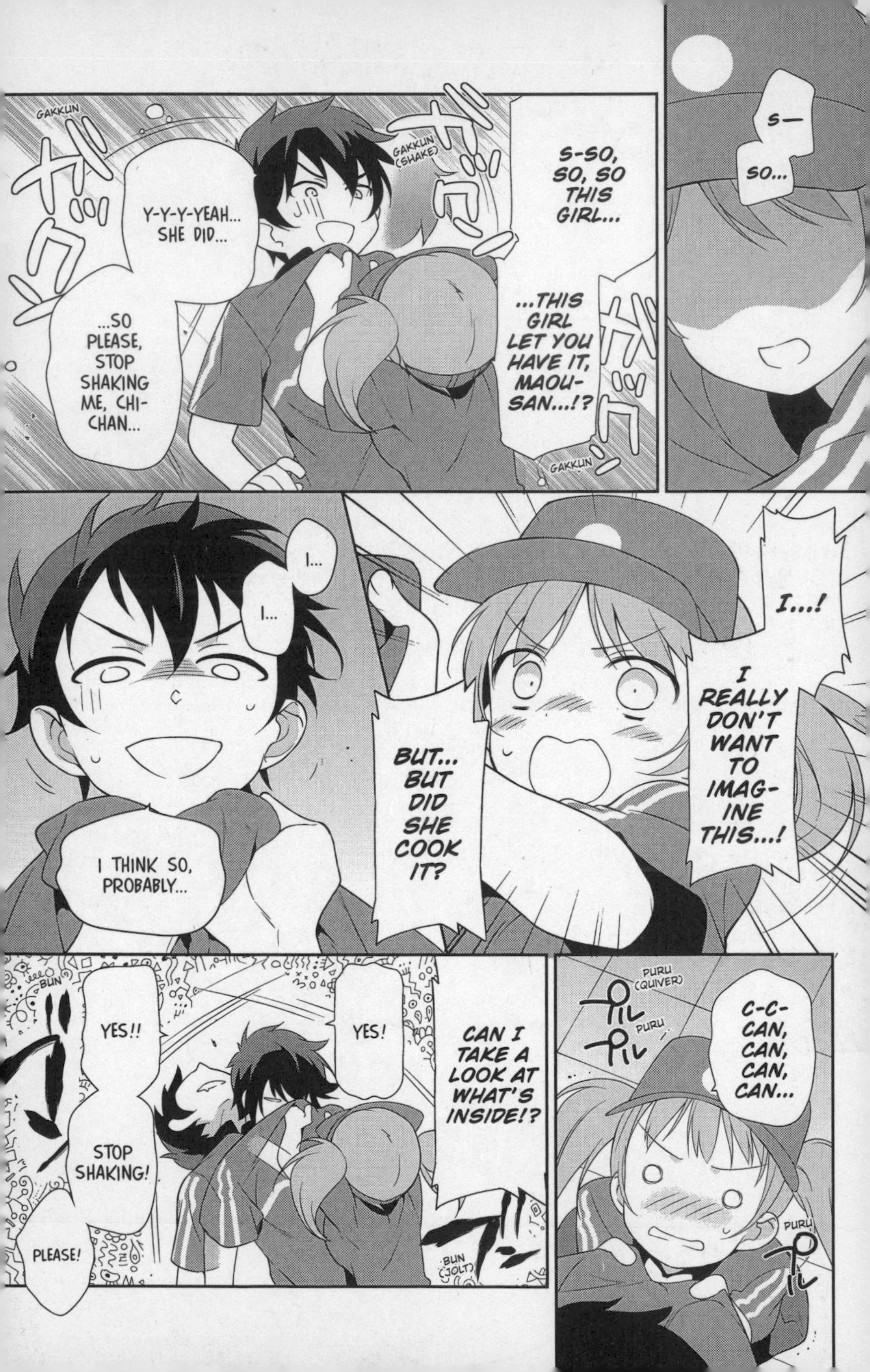
S—
SO...
S-SO, SO, SO THIS GIRL...
...THIS GIRL LET YOU HAVE IT, MAOU-SAN...!?
GAKKUN (SHAKE)
GAKKUN
Y-Y-Y-YEAH... SHE DID...
...SO PLEASE, STOP SHAKING ME, CHI-CHAN...
GAKKUN
I...!
I REALLY DON'T WANT TO IMAGINE THIS...!
BUT... BUT DID SHE COOK IT?
I...
I...
I THINK SO, PROBABLY...
PURU (QUIVER)
PURU
C-C-CAN, CAN, CAN, CAN...
PURU
CAN I TAKE A LOOK AT WHAT'S INSIDE!?
YES!
YES!!
STOP SHAKING!
PLEASE!
BUN
BUN (JOLT)

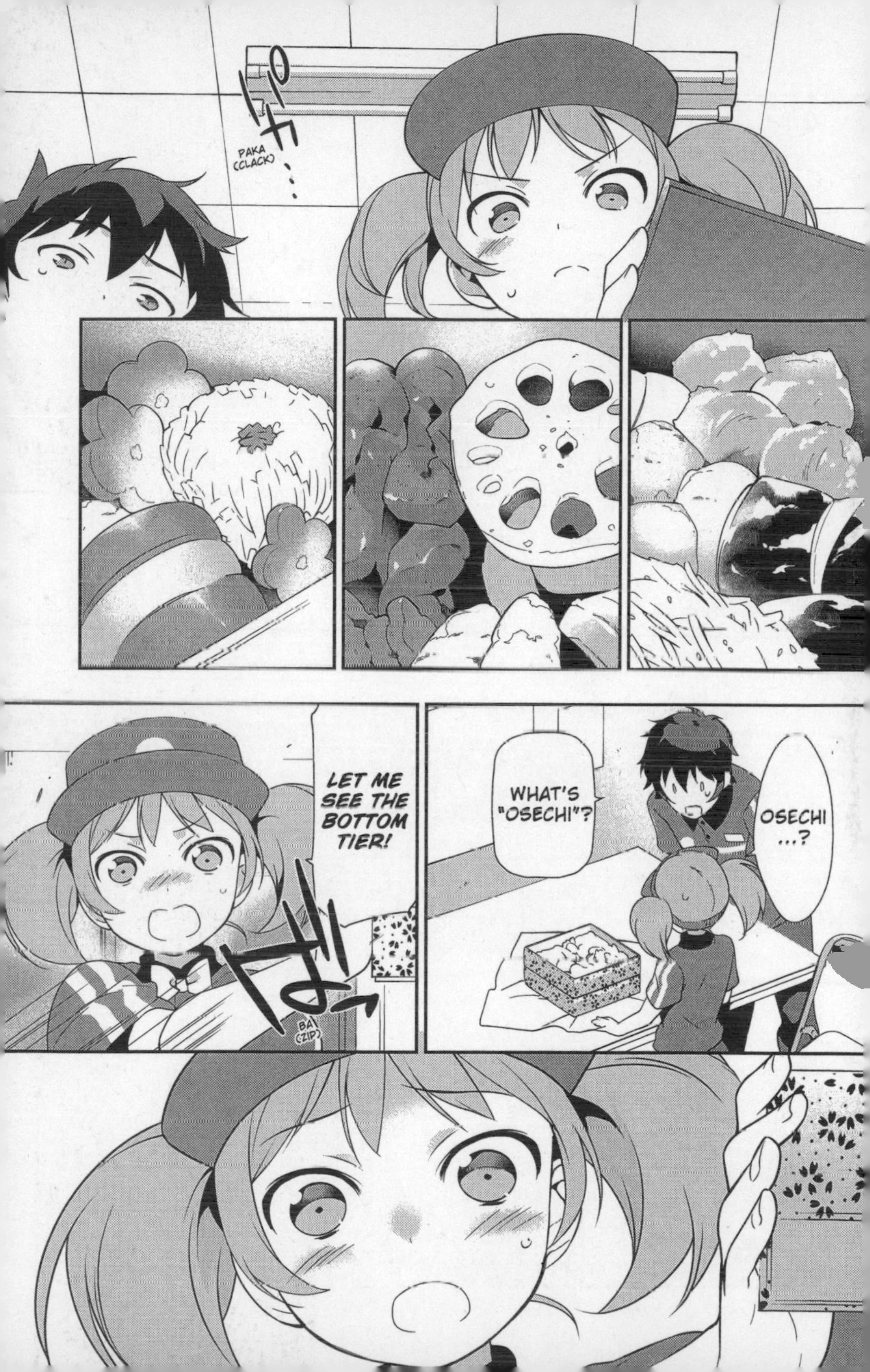
PAKA
(CLACK)
OSECHI ...?
WHAT'S "OSECHI"?
LET ME SEE THE BOTTOM TIER!
BA
(ZIP)

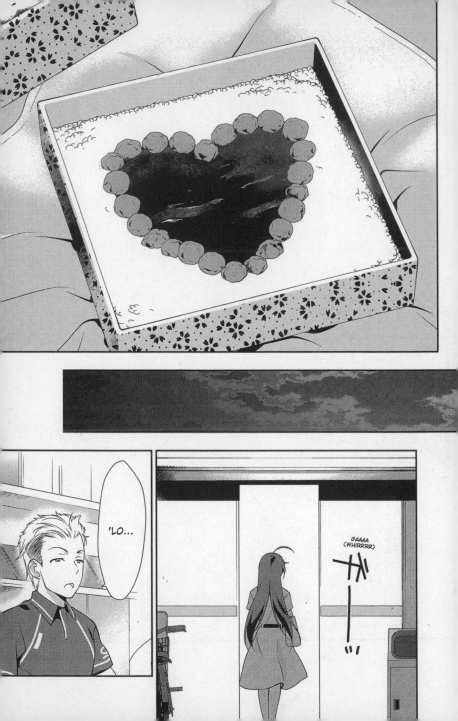

'LO...

GAAAA
(WHIRRRR)

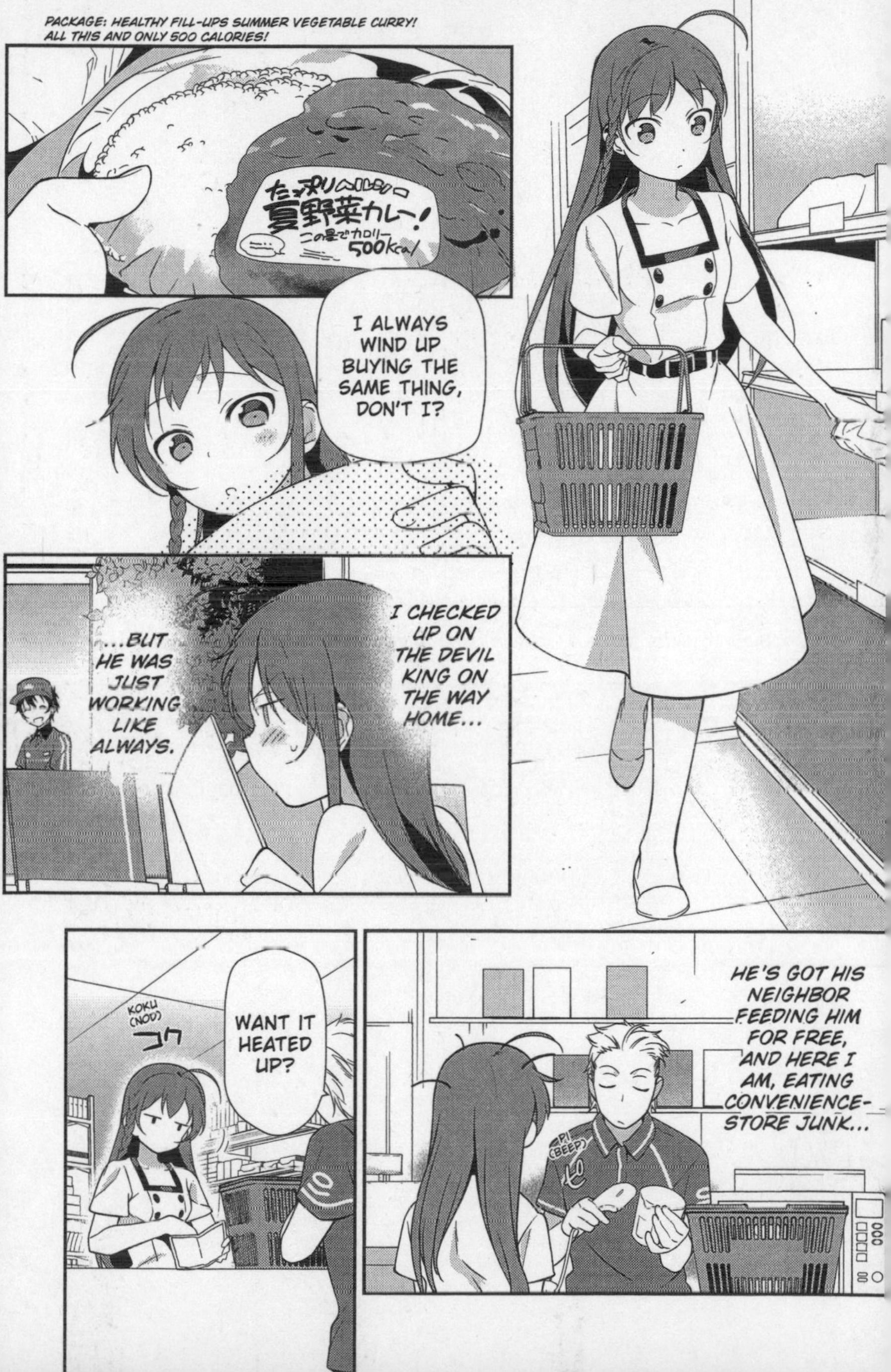
PACKAGE: HEALTHY FILL-UPS SUMMER VEGETABLE CURRY! ALL THIS AND ONLY 500 CALORIES!
たっぷりヘルシー
夏野菜カレー!
この量でカロリー
500kcal
I ALWAYS WIND UP BUYING THE SAME THING, DON'T I?
I CHECKED UP ON THE DEVIL KING ON THE WAY HOME...
...BUT HE WAS JUST WORKING LIKE ALWAYS.
HE'S GOT HIS NEIGHBOR FEEDING HIM FOR FREE, AND HERE I AM, EATING CONVENIENCE-STORE JUNK...
PI (BEEP)
ピ
WANT IT HEATED UP?
KOKU (NOD)
コク

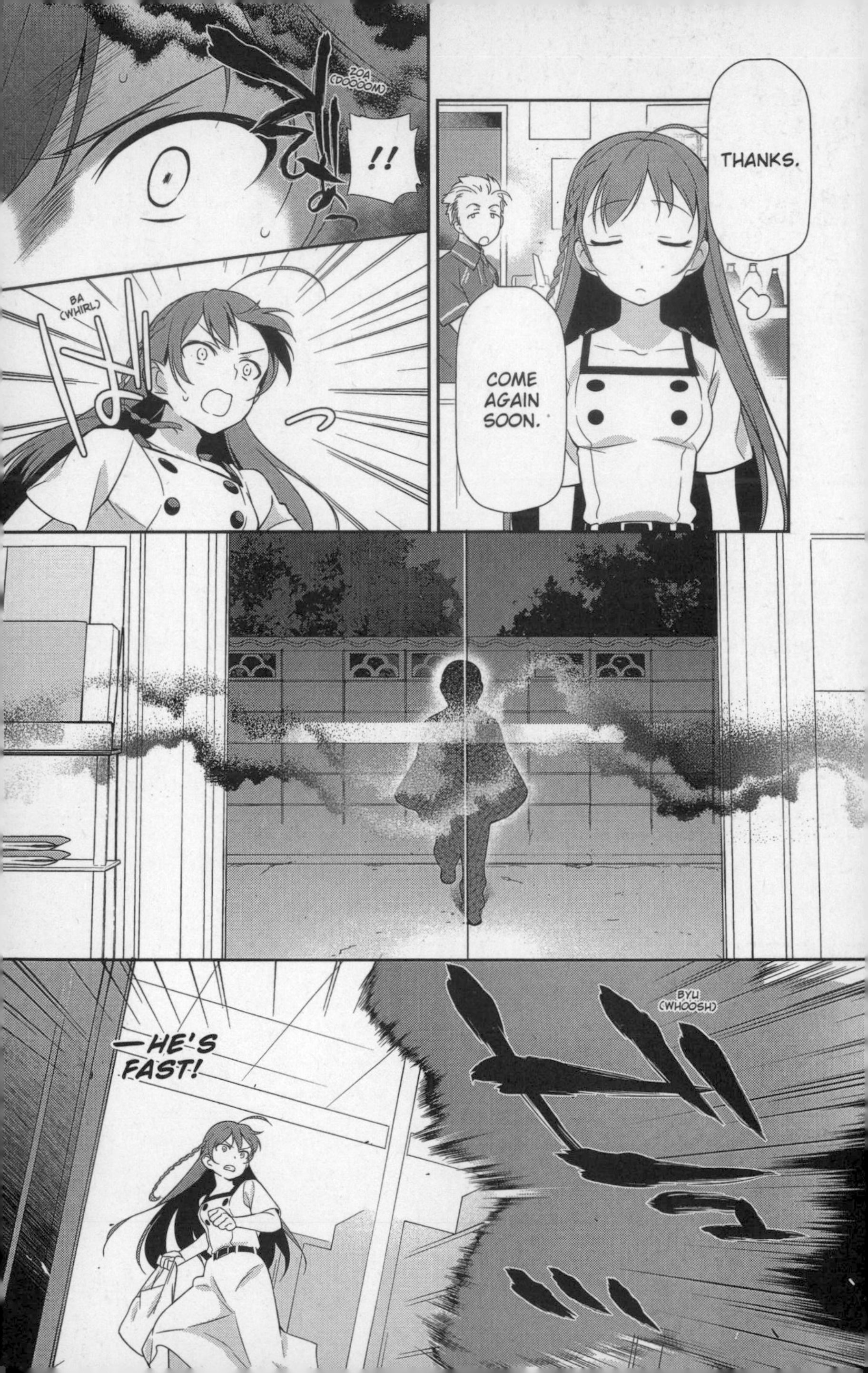
THANKS.
COME AGAIN SOON.
ZOA (DOOOOM)
!!
BA (WHIRL)
BYU (WHOOSH)
—HE'S FAST!

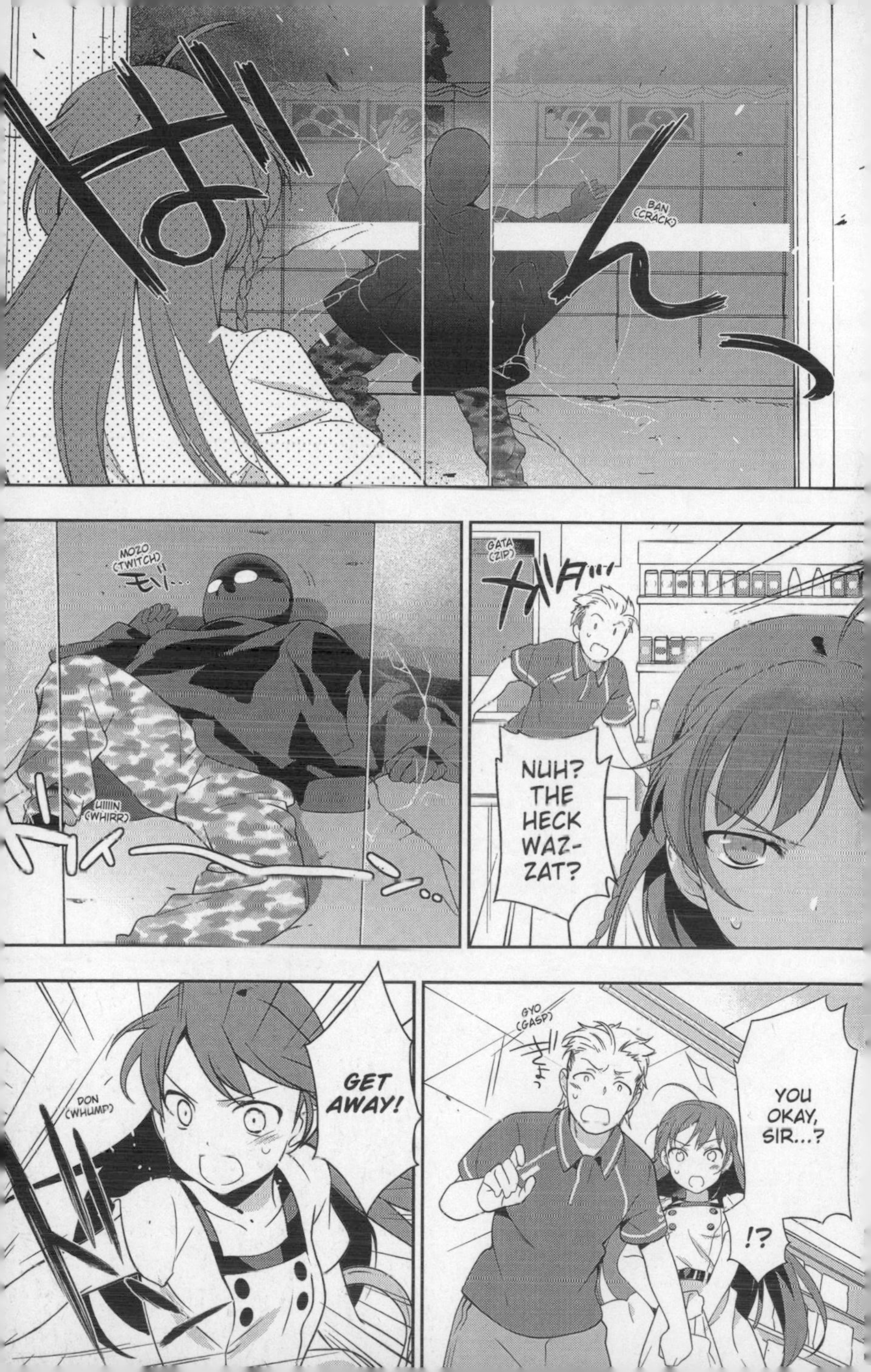
BAN (CRACK)
GATA (ZIP)
NUH? THE HECK WAZ-ZAT?
MOZO (TWITCH)
UIIIN (WHIRR)
YOU OKAY, SIR...?
GYO (GASP)
!?
GET AWAY!
DON (WHUMP)

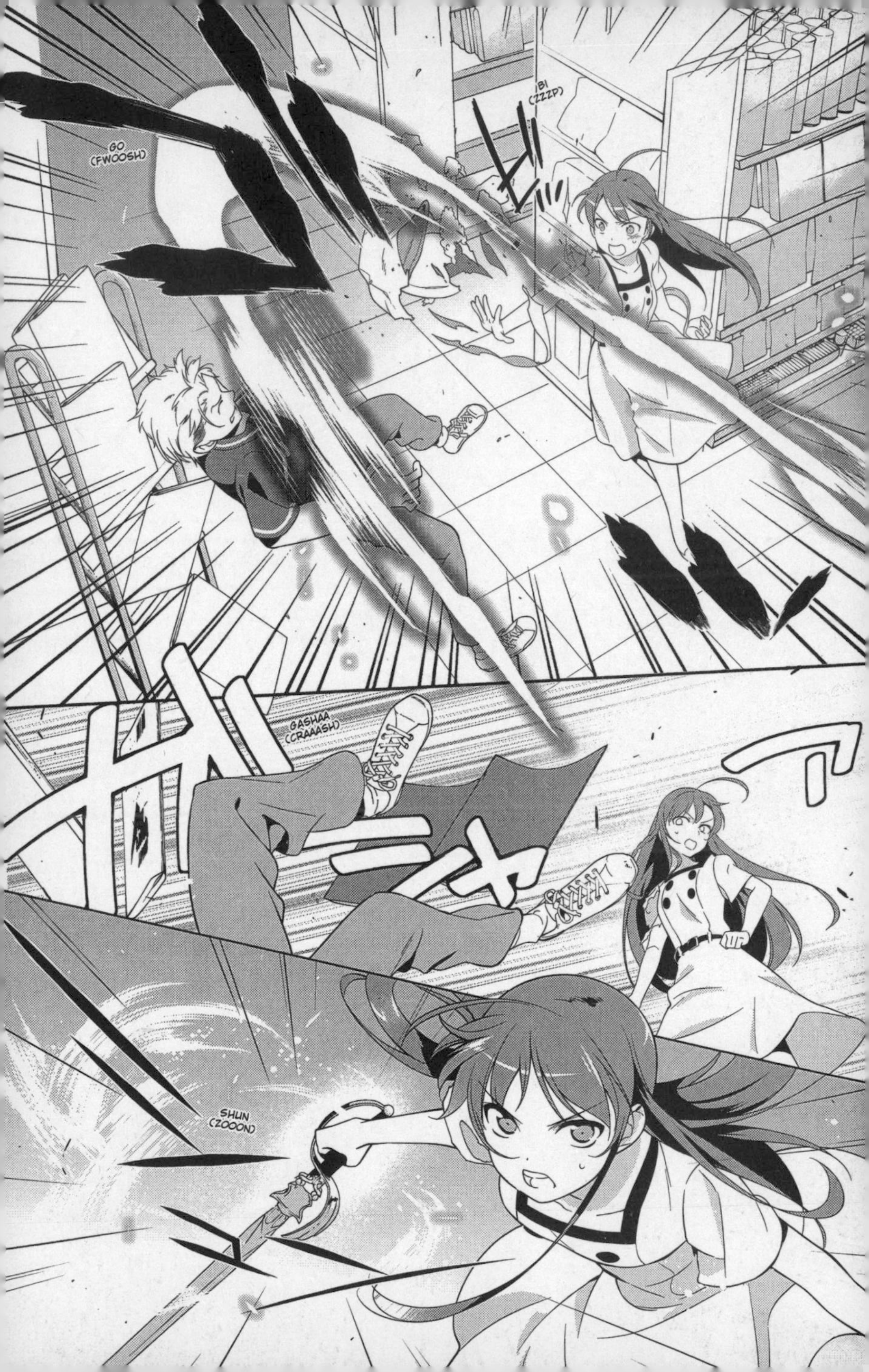
BI
(ZZZP)
GO
(FWOOSH)
GASHAA
(CRAAASH)
SHUN
(ZOOON)

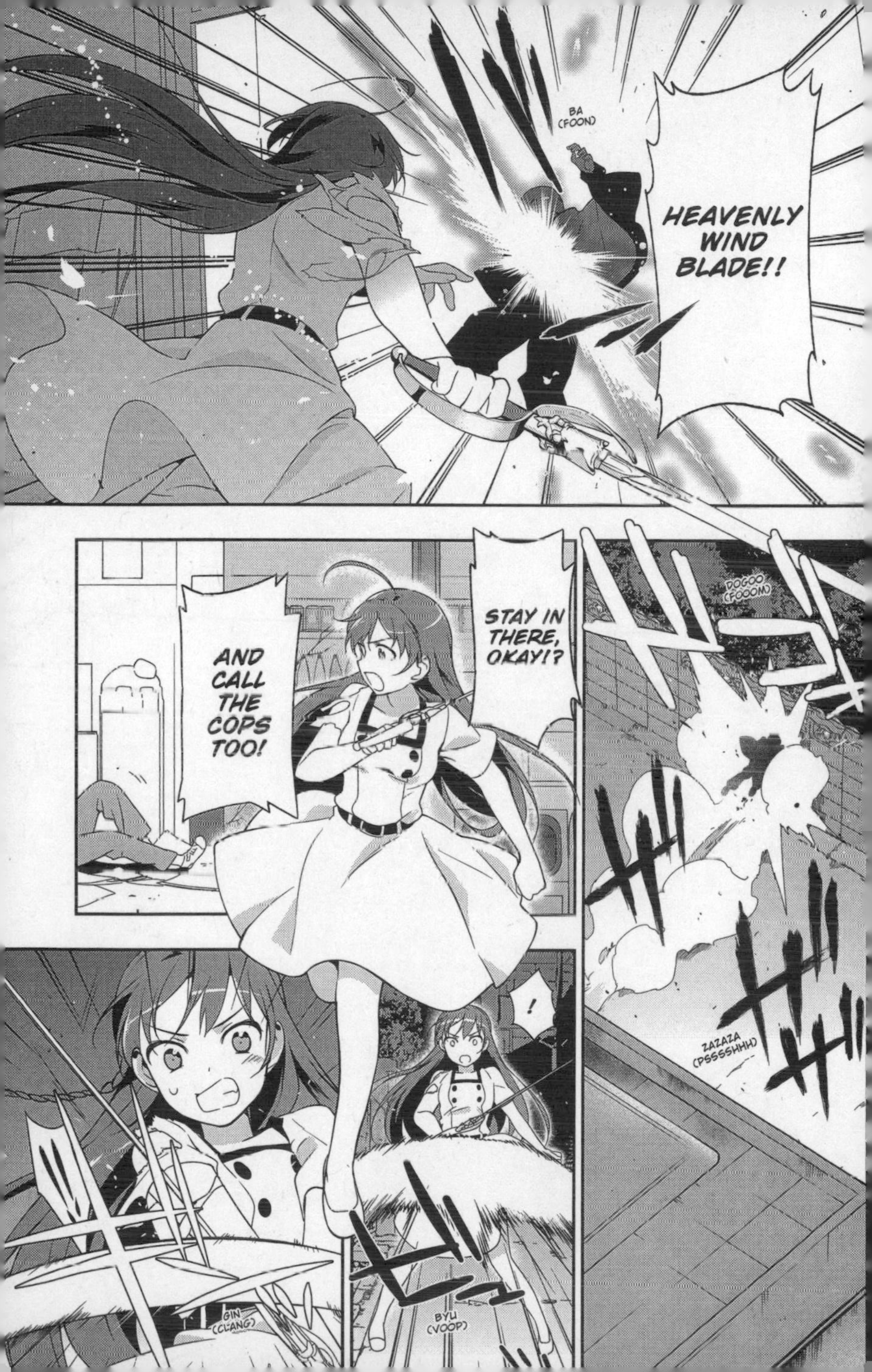
HEAVENLY WIND BLADE!!
BA (FOON)
DOGOO (FOOOM)
ZAZAZA (PSSSSHHH)
STAY IN THERE, OKAY!?
AND CALL THE COPS TOO!
!
BYU (VOOP)
GIN (CLANG)

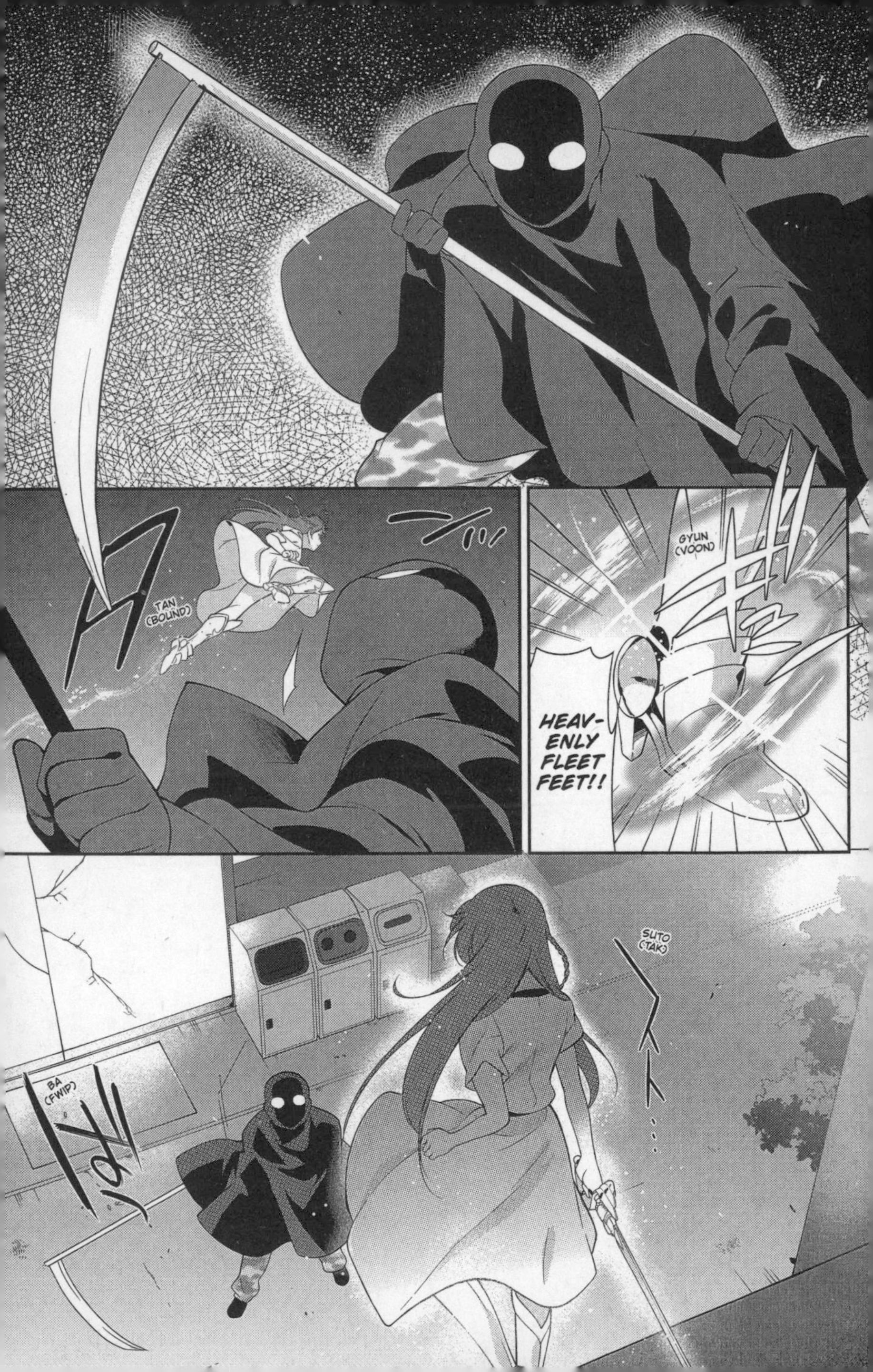
GYUN (VOON)
HEAV-ENLY FLEET FEET!!
TAN (BOUND)
SUTO (TAK)
BA (FWIP)

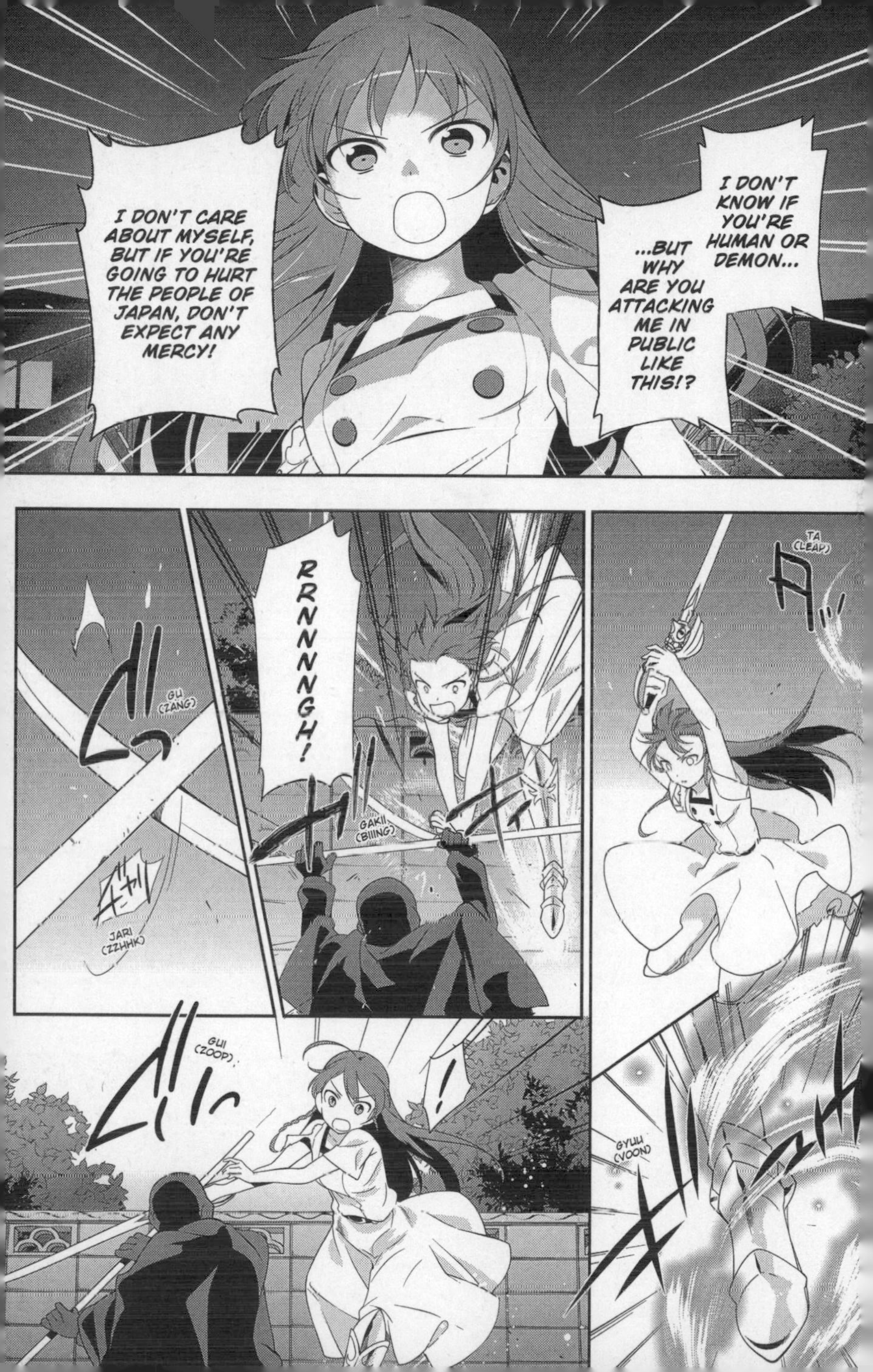
I DON'T KNOW IF YOU'RE HUMAN OR DEMON...
...BUT WHY ARE YOU ATTACKING ME IN PUBLIC LIKE THIS!?
I DON'T CARE ABOUT MYSELF, BUT IF YOU'RE GOING TO HURT THE PEOPLE OF JAPAN, DON'T EXPECT ANY MERCY!
TA (LEAP)
GYUU (VOON)
RRNNNNGH!
GAKII (BIING)
GU (ZANG)
JARI (ZZHHK)
GUI (ZOOP)
!

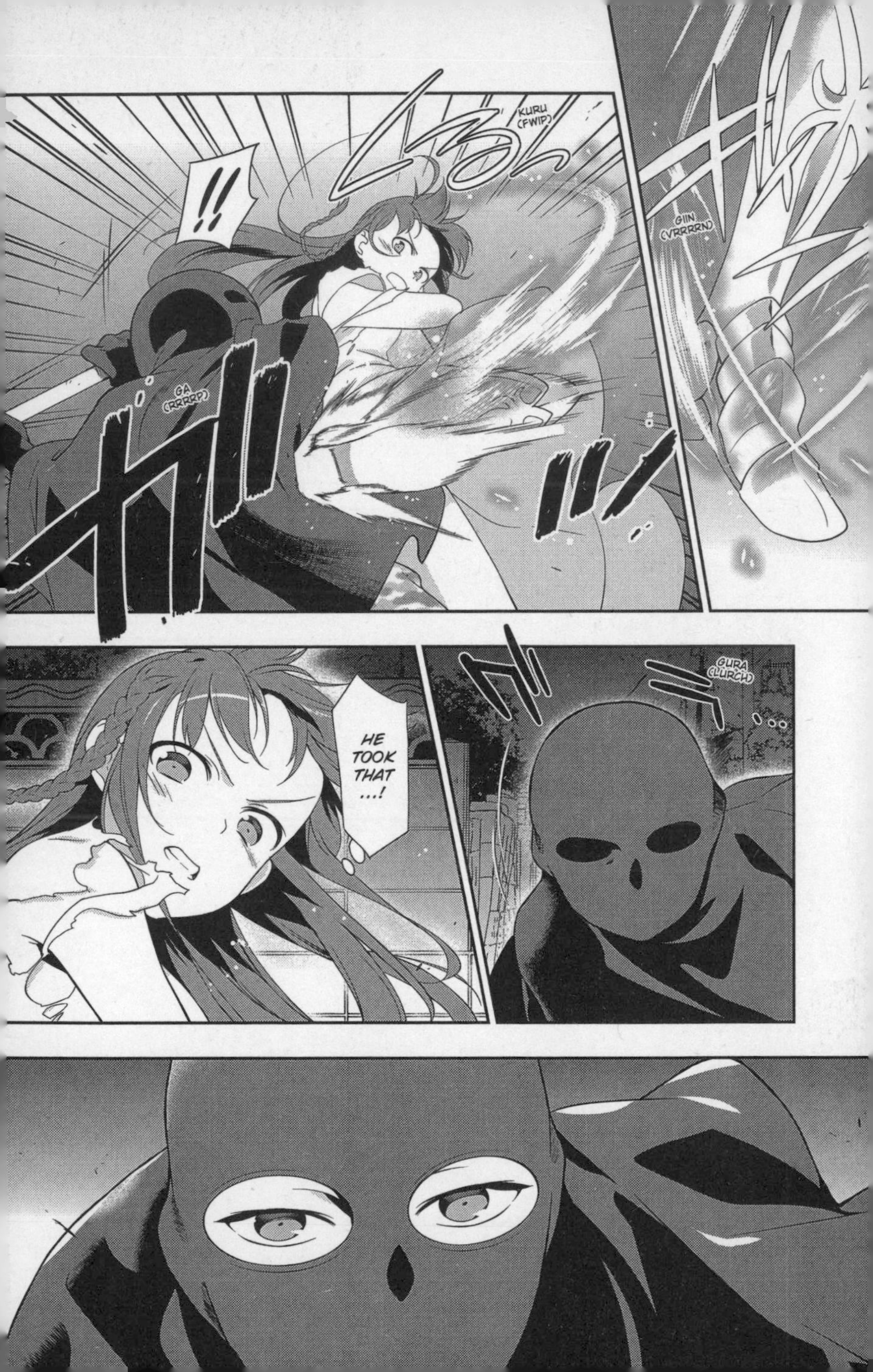
GIIN (VRRRRN)
KURU (FWIP)
!!
GA (RRRRP)
GURA (LURCH)
...
HE TOOK THAT ...!

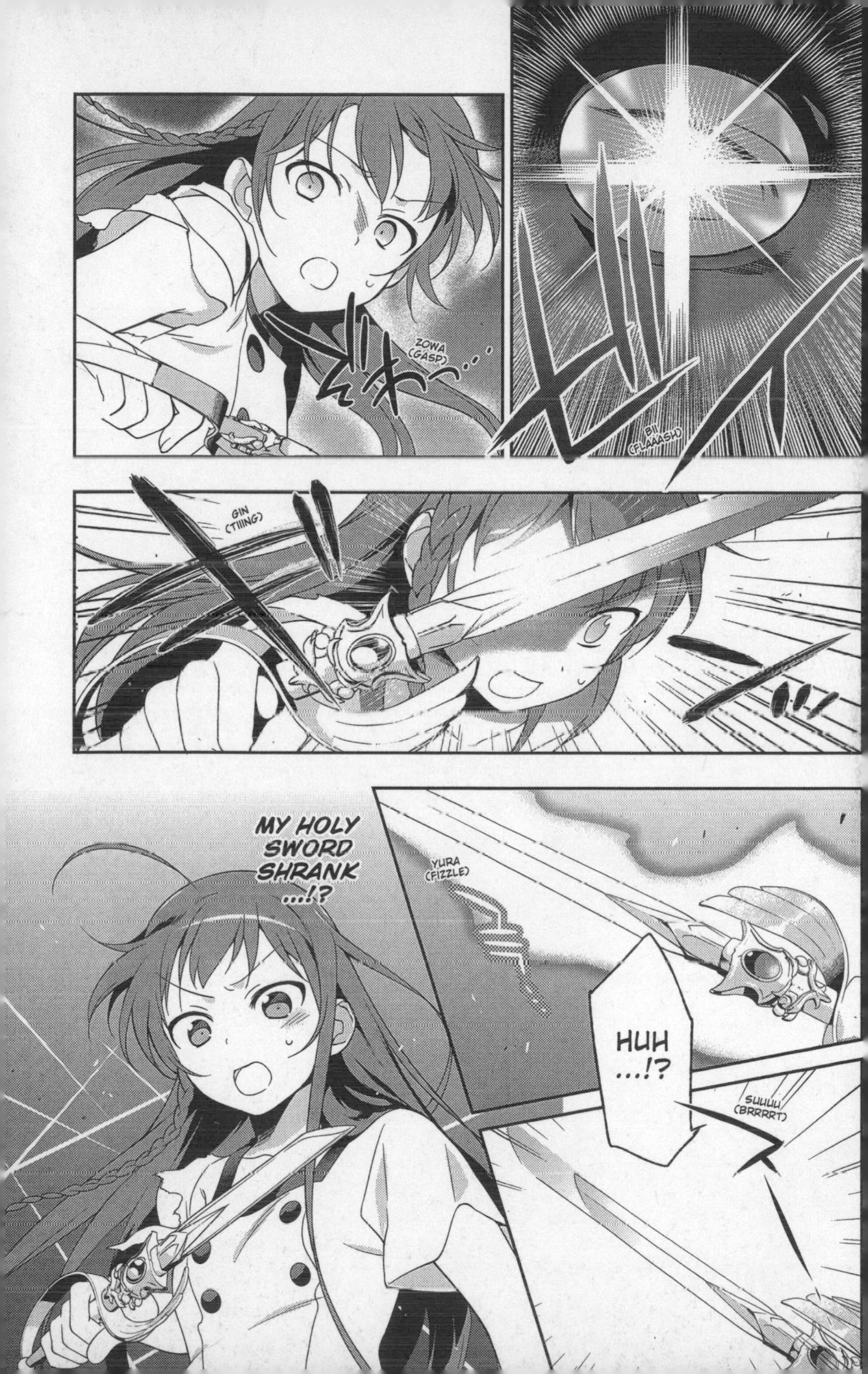
BI
(FLAAASH)
ZOWA
(GASP)
GIN
(TIIING)
YURA
(FIZZLE)
HUH ...!?
SUUUU
(BRRRRT)
MY HOLY SWORD SHRANK ...!?

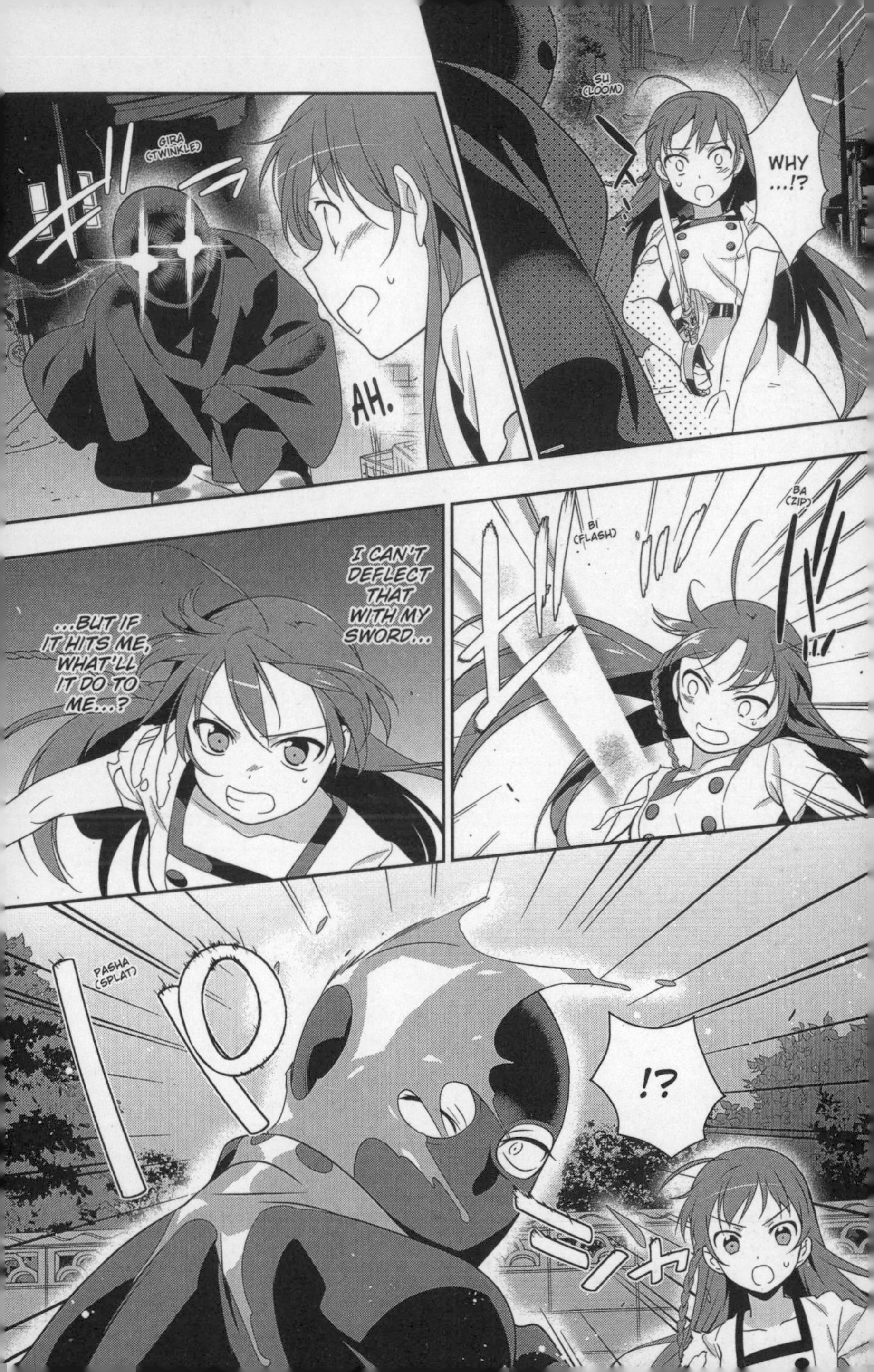
SU (LOOM)
WHY ...!?
GIRA (TWINKLE)
AH.
BA (ZIP)
BI (FLASH)
I CAN'T DEFLECT THAT WITH MY SWORD...
...BUT IF IT HITS ME, WHAT'LL IT DO TO ME...?
PASHA (SPLAT)
!?

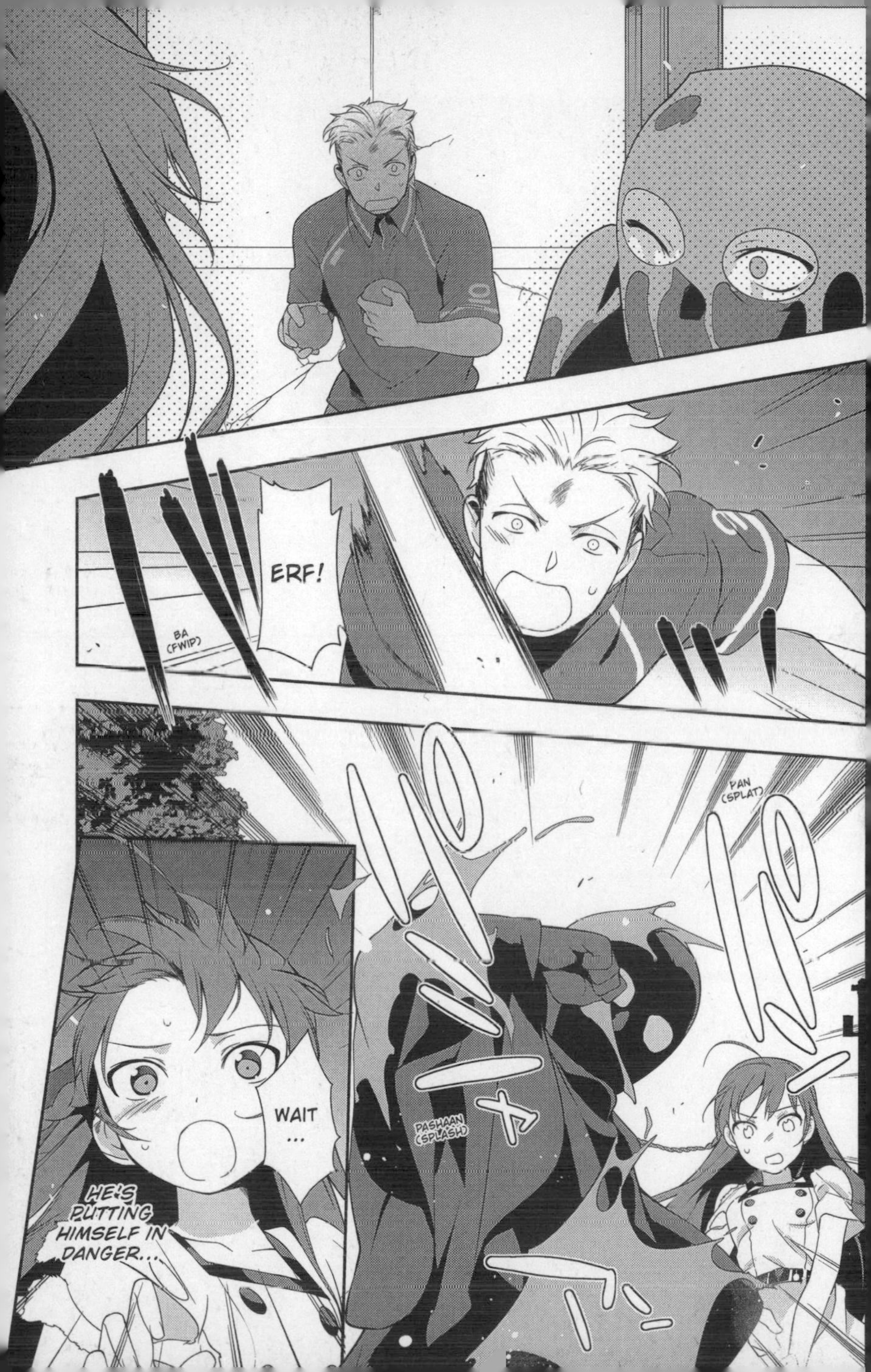
ERF!
BA (FWIP)
PAN (SPLAT)
PASHAAN (SPLASH)
WAIT ...
HE'S PUTTING HIMSELF IN DANGER...

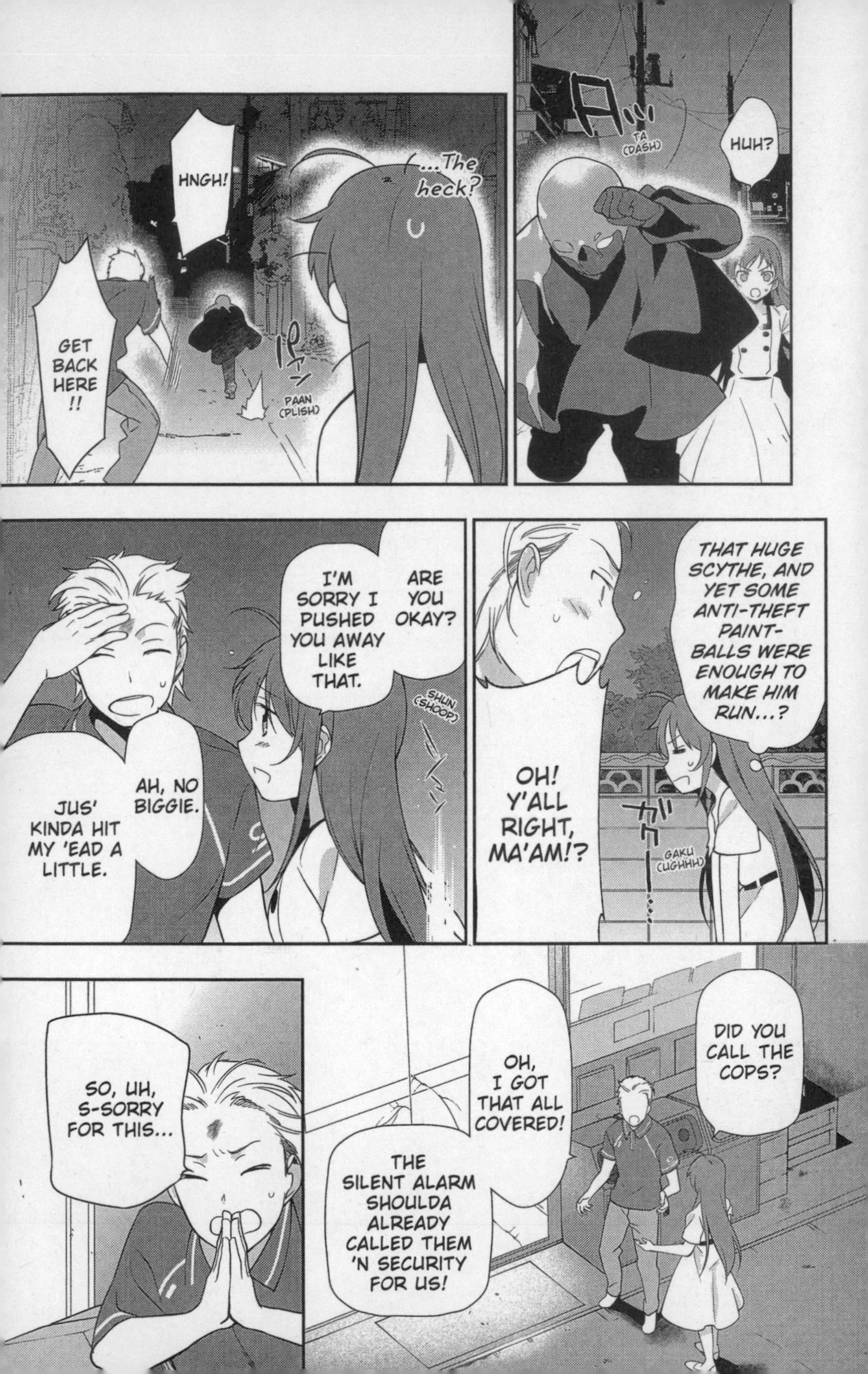
HUH?
TA (DASH)
...The heck?
HNGH!
GET BACK HERE!!
PAAN (PLISH)
THAT HUGE SCYTHE, AND YET SOME ANTI-THEFT PAINT-BALLS WERE ENOUGH TO MAKE HIM RUN...?
OH! Y'ALL RIGHT, MA'AM!?
GAKU (UGHHH)
ARE YOU OKAY?
I'M SORRY I PUSHED YOU AWAY LIKE THAT.
SHUN (SHOOP)
AH, NO BIGGIE.
JUS' KINDA HIT MY 'EAD A LITTLE.
DID YOU CALL THE COPS?
OH, I GOT THAT ALL COVERED!
THE SILENT ALARM SHOULDA ALREADY CALLED THEM 'N SECURITY FOR US!
SO, UH, S-SORRY FOR THIS...

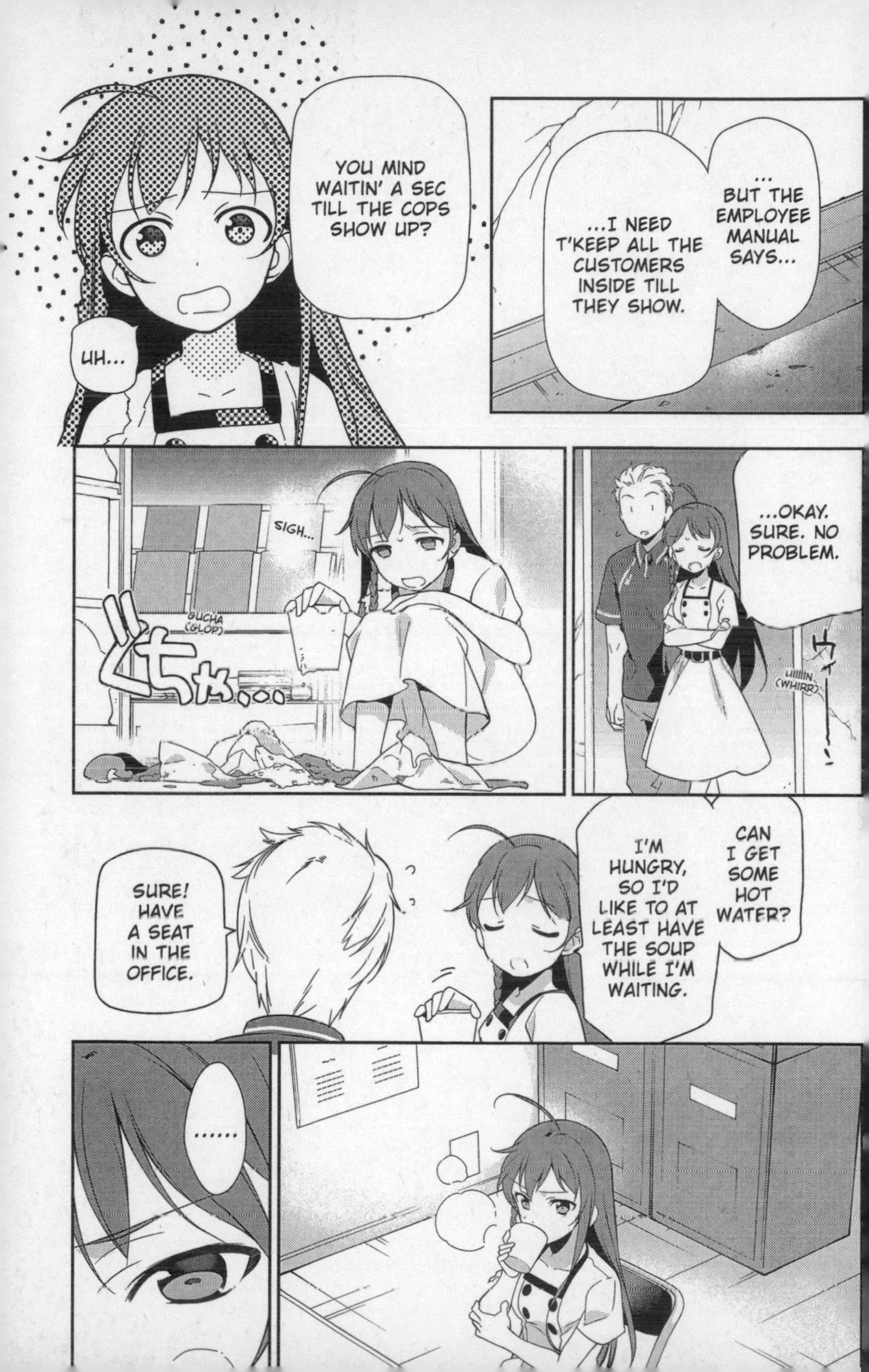
...
BUT THE EMPLOYEE MANUAL SAYS...
...I NEED T'KEEP ALL THE CUSTOMERS INSIDE TILL THEY SHOW.
YOU MIND WAITIN' A SEC TILL THE COPS SHOW UP?
UH...
...OKAY. SURE. NO PROBLEM.
UIIIIIIN (WHIRR)
SIGH...
GUCHA (GLOP)
CAN I GET SOME HOT WATER?
I'M HUNGRY, SO I'D LIKE TO AT LEAST HAVE THE SOUP WHILE I'M WAITING.
SURE! HAVE A SEAT IN THE OFFICE.
......

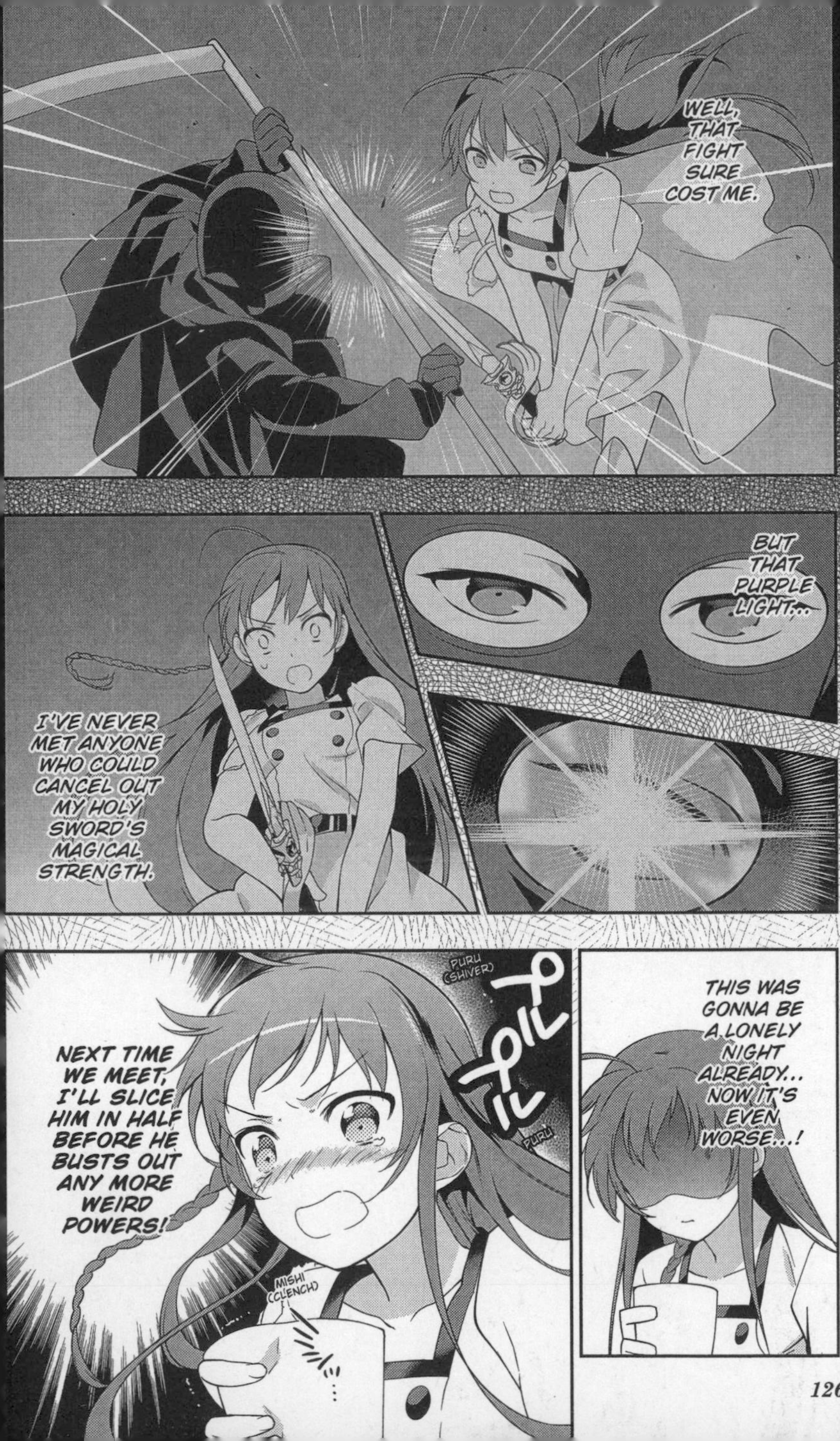
WELL, THAT FIGHT SURE COST ME.
BUT THAT PURPLE LIGHT...
I'VE NEVER MET ANYONE WHO COULD CANCEL OUT MY HOLY SWORD'S MAGICAL STRENGTH.
THIS WAS GONNA BE A LONELY NIGHT ALREADY... NOW IT'S EVEN WORSE...!
PURU (SHIVER)
PURU
NEXT TIME WE MEET, I'LL SLICE HIM IN HALF BEFORE HE BUSTS OUT ANY MORE WEIRD POWERS!
MISHI (CLENCH)
...

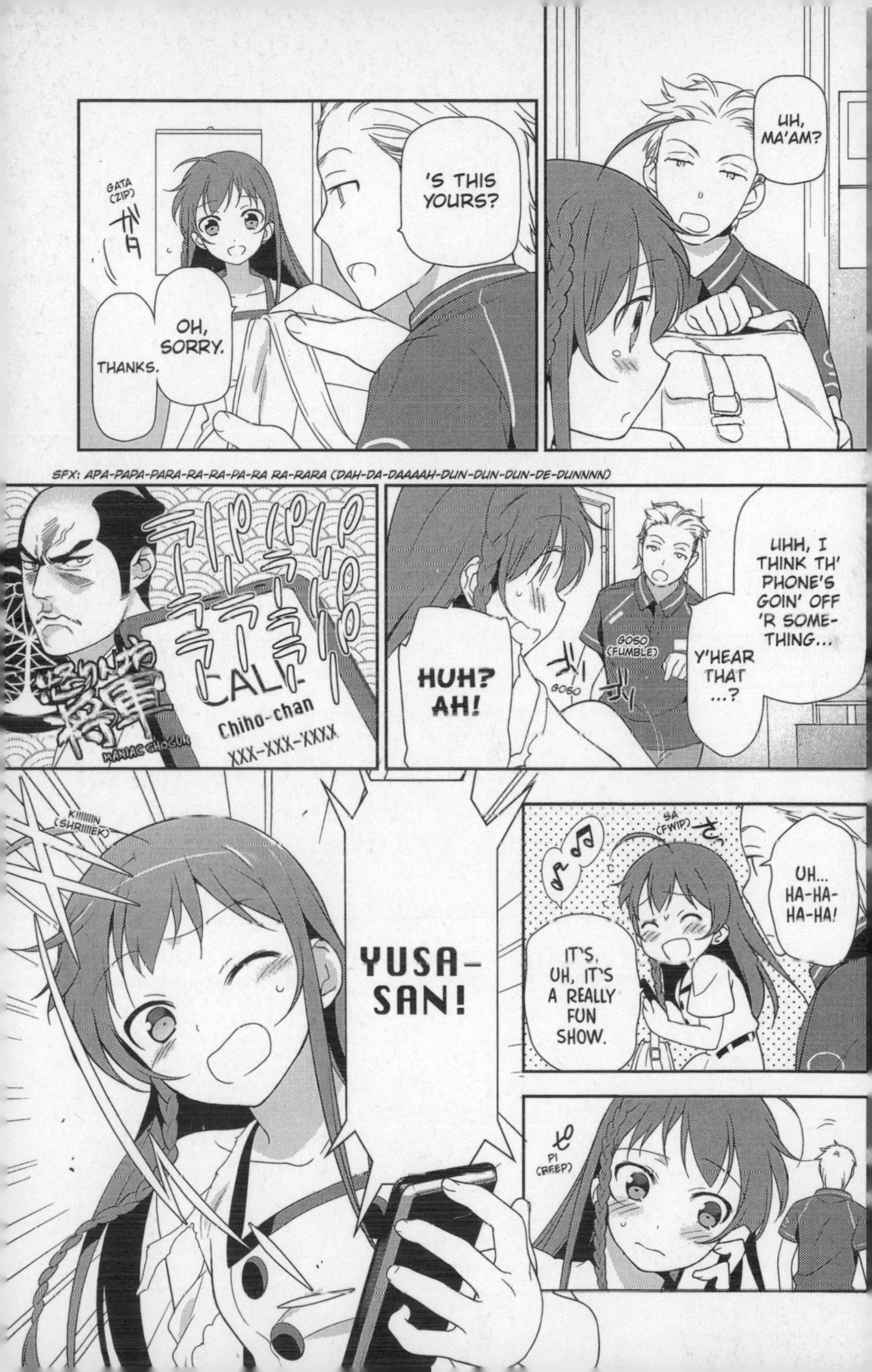
UH, MA'AM?
'S THIS YOURS?
GATA (ZIP)
OH, SORRY.
THANKS.
SFX: APA-PAPA-PARA-RA-RA-PA-RA RA-RARA (DAH-DA-DAAAAH-DUN-DUN-DUN-DE-DUNNNN)
UHH, I THINK TH' PHONE'S GOIN' OFF 'R SOME-THING...
Y'HEAR THAT ...?
GOSO (FUMBLE)
GOSO
HUH? AH!
CALL
Chiho-chan
XXX-XXX-XXXX
MANIAC SHOGUN
SA (FWIP)
UH... HA-HA-HA-HA!
IT'S, UH, IT'S A REALLY FUN SHOW.
PI (BEEP)
KIIIIIIN (SHRIIIIEK)
YUSA-SAN!

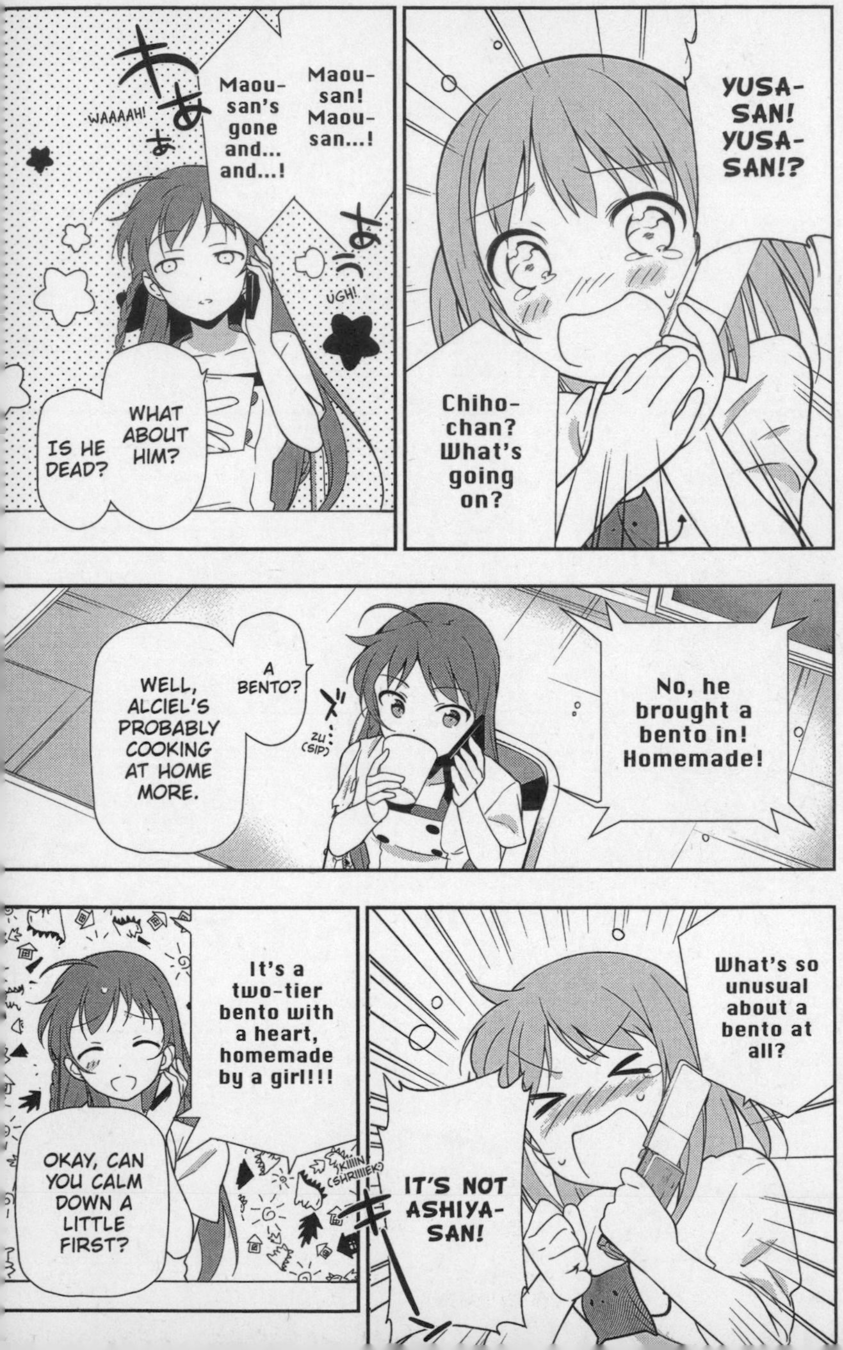
YUSA-SAN! YUSA-SAN!?
Chiho-chan? What's going on?
Maou-san! Maou-san...!
Maou-san's gone and... and...!
WAAAAH!
UGH!
WHAT ABOUT HIM?
IS HE DEAD?
No, he brought a bento in! Homemade!
A BENTO?
ZU (SIP)
WELL, ALCIEL'S PROBABLY COOKING AT HOME MORE.
What's so unusual about a bento at all?
IT'S NOT ASHIYA-SAN!
It's a two-tier bento with a heart, homemade by a girl!!!
KIIIIN (SHRIIIIEK)
OKAY, CAN YOU CALM DOWN A LITTLE FIRST?

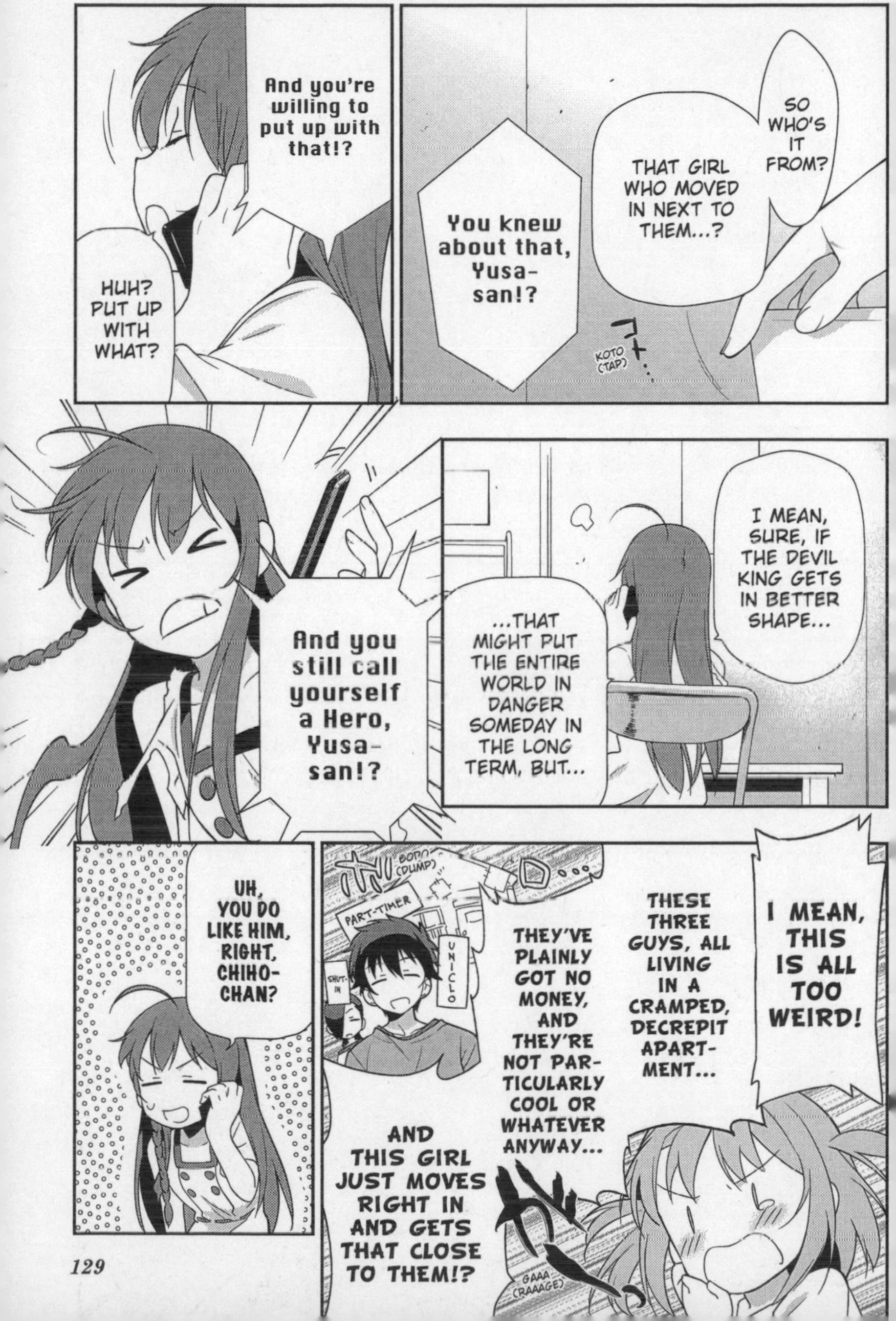
SO WHO'S IT FROM?
THAT GIRL WHO MOVED IN NEXT TO THEM...?
You knew about that, Yusa-san!?
KOTO (TAP)
And you're willing to put up with that!?
HUH? PUT UP WITH WHAT?
I MEAN, SURE, IF THE DEVIL KING GETS IN BETTER SHAPE...
...THAT MIGHT PUT THE ENTIRE WORLD IN DANGER SOMEDAY IN THE LONG TERM, BUT...
And you still call yourself a Hero, Yusa-san!?
I MEAN, THIS IS ALL TOO WEIRD!
THESE THREE GUYS, ALL LIVING IN A CRAMPED, DECREPIT APARTMENT...
BOTO (DUMP)
PART-TIMER
UNICLO
SHUT-IN
THEY'VE PLAINLY GOT NO MONEY, AND THEY'RE NOT PARTICULARLY COOL OR WHATEVER ANYWAY...
AND THIS GIRL JUST MOVES RIGHT IN AND GETS THAT CLOSE TO THEM!?
GAAA (RAAAGE)
UH, YOU DO LIKE HIM, RIGHT, CHIHO-CHAN?

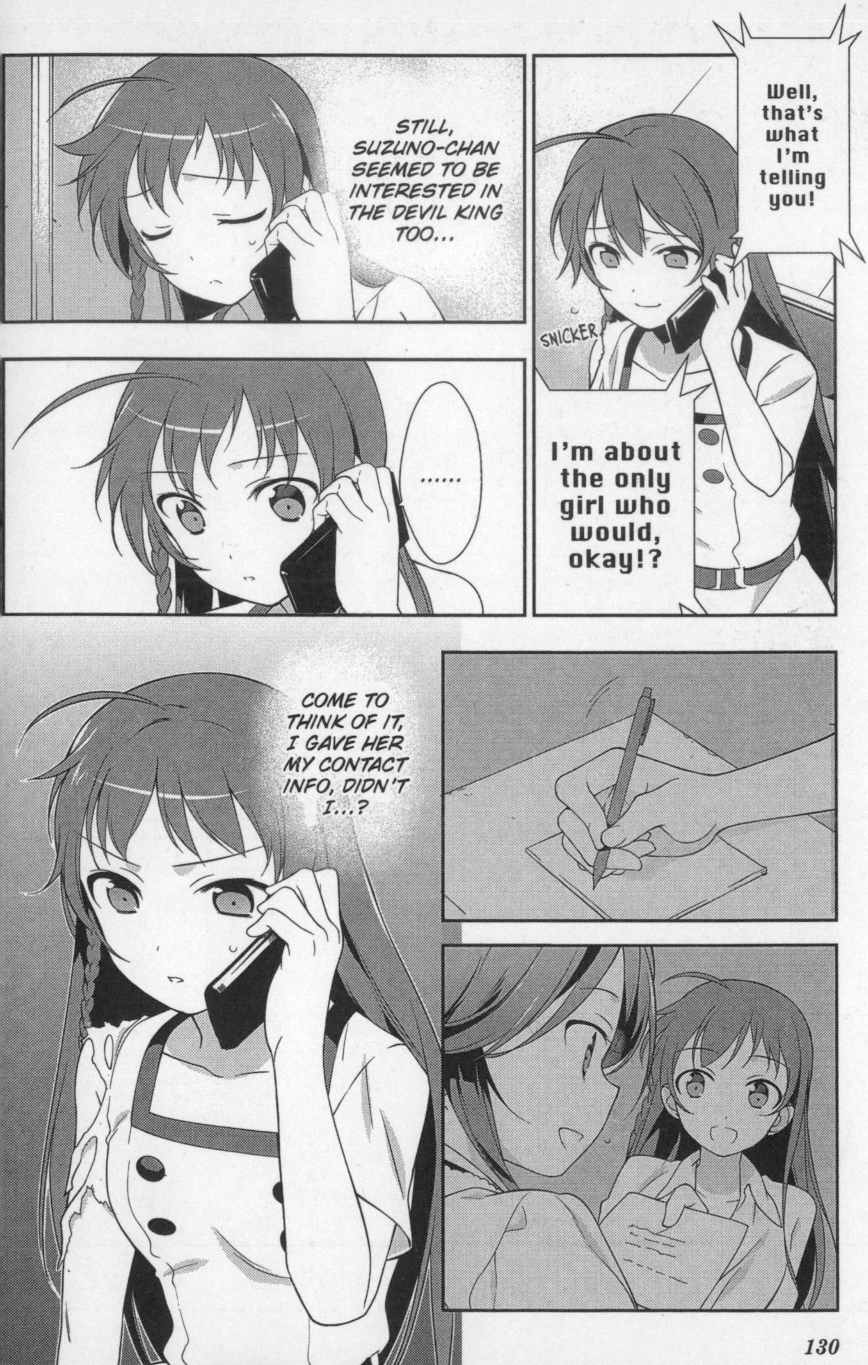
Well, that's what I'm telling you!
SNICKER
I'm about the only girl who would, okay!?
STILL, SUZUNO-CHAN SEEMED TO BE INTERESTED IN THE DEVIL KING TOO...
......
COME TO THINK OF IT, I GAVE HER MY CONTACT INFO, DIDN'T I...?

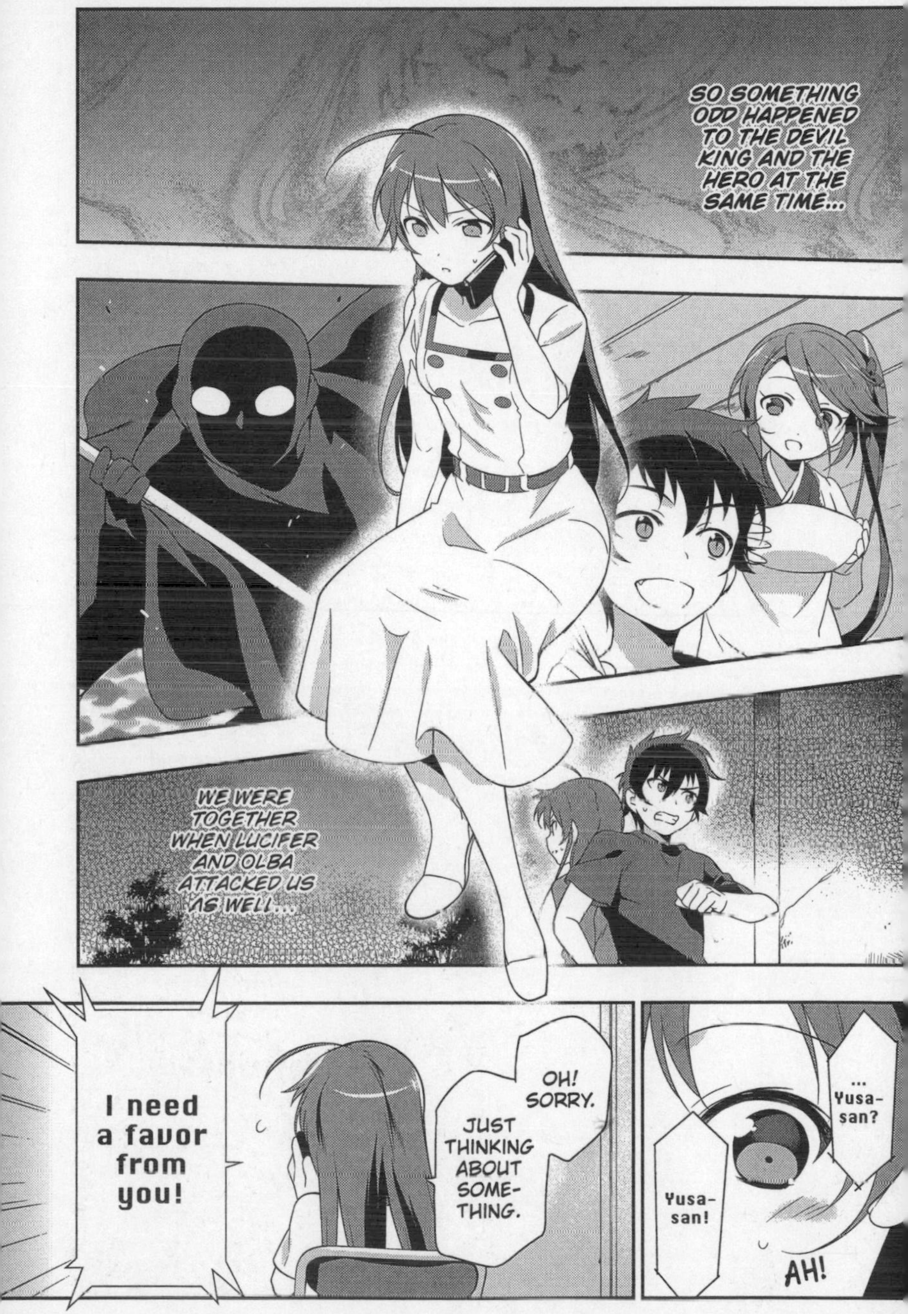
SO SOMETHING ODD HAPPENED TO THE DEVIL KING AND THE HERO AT THE SAME TIME...
WE WERE TOGETHER WHEN LUCIFER AND OLBA ATTACKED US AS WELL...
...Yusa-san?
Yusa-san!
AH!
OH! SORRY.
JUST THINKING ABOUT SOME-THING.
I need a favor from you!

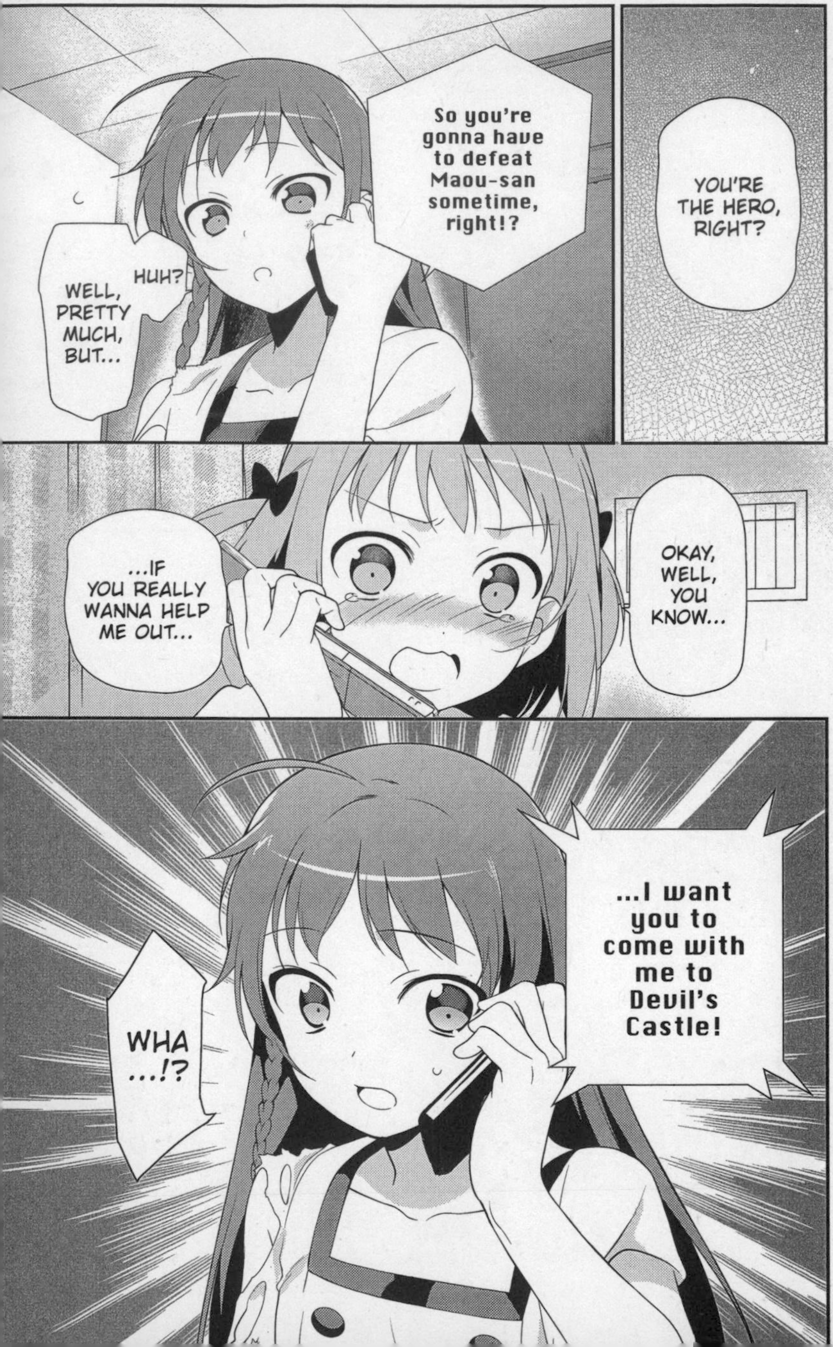
YOU'RE THE HERO, RIGHT?
So you're gonna have to defeat Maou-san sometime, right!?
HUH? WELL, PRETTY MUCH, BUT...
OKAY, WELL, YOU KNOW...
...IF YOU REALLY WANNA HELP ME OUT...
...I want you to come with me to Devil's Castle!
WHA ...!?

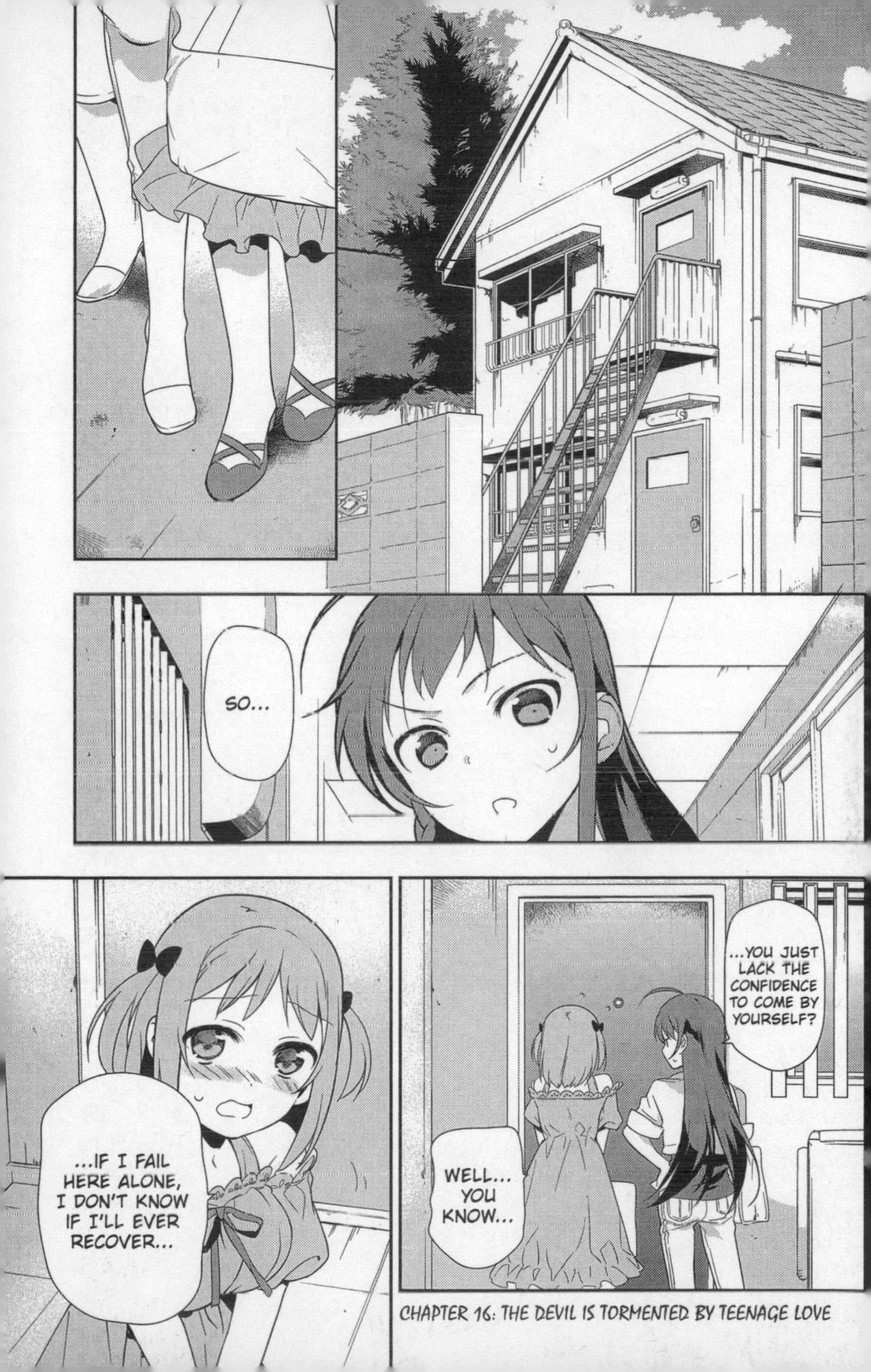
SO...
...YOU JUST LACK THE CONFIDENCE TO COME BY YOURSELF?
WELL... YOU KNOW...
...IF I FAIL HERE ALONE, I DON'T KNOW IF I'LL EVER RECOVER...

CHAPTER 16: THE DEVIL IS TORMENTED BY TEENAGE LOVE

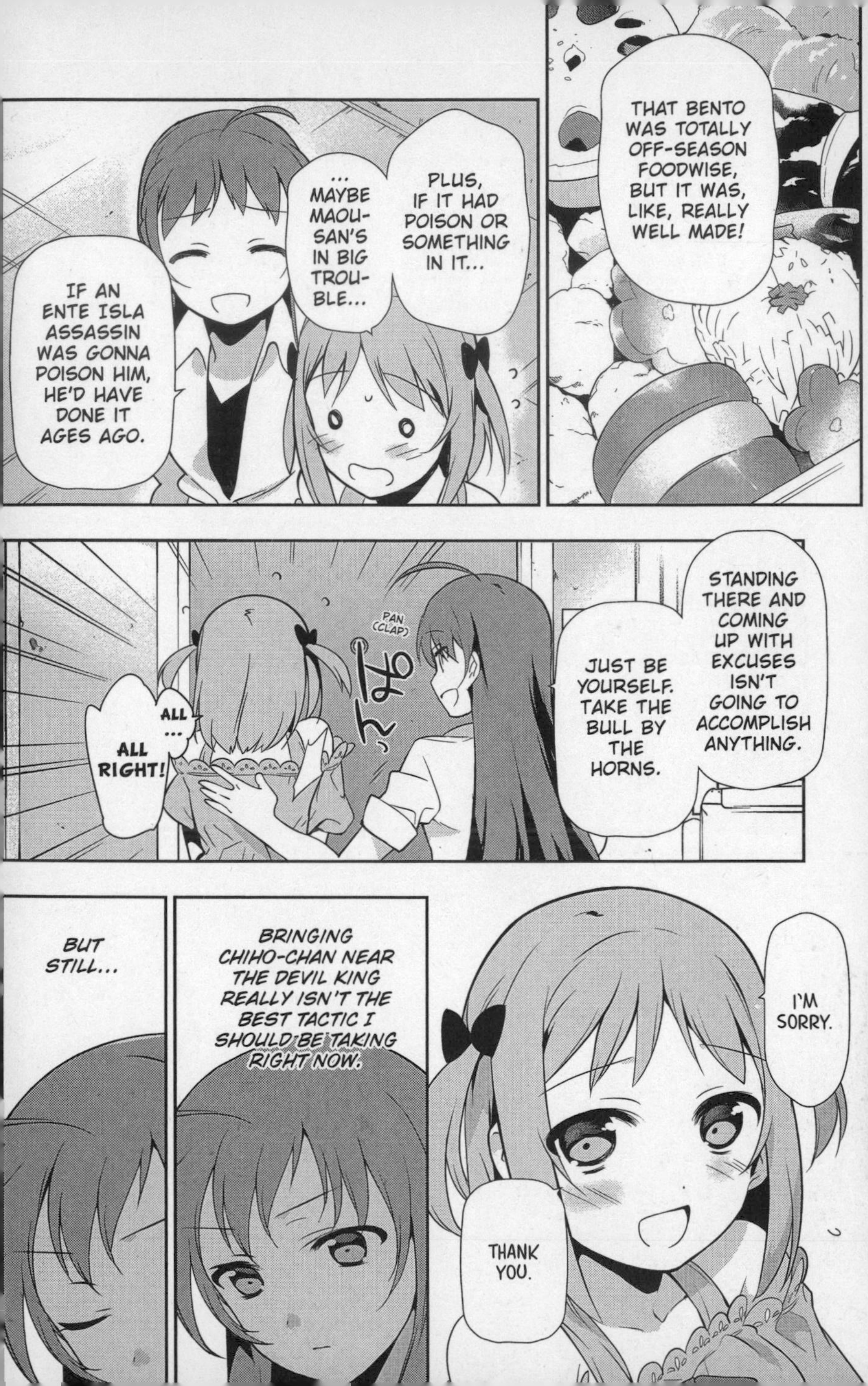
THAT BENTO WAS TOTALLY OFF-SEASON FOODWISE, BUT IT WAS, LIKE, REALLY WELL MADE!
PLUS, IF IT HAD POISON OR SOMETHING IN IT...
...MAYBE MAOU-SAN'S IN BIG TROUBLE...
IF AN ENTE ISLA ASSASSIN WAS GONNA POISON HIM, HE'D HAVE DONE IT AGES AGO.
STANDING THERE AND COMING UP WITH EXCUSES ISN'T GOING TO ACCOMPLISH ANYTHING.
JUST BE YOURSELF. TAKE THE BULL BY THE HORNS.
PAN (CLAP)
ぱん
ALL... ALL RIGHT!
I'M SORRY.
THANK YOU.
BRINGING CHIHO-CHAN NEAR THE DEVIL KING REALLY ISN'T THE BEST TACTIC I SHOULD BE TAKING RIGHT NOW.
BUT STILL...

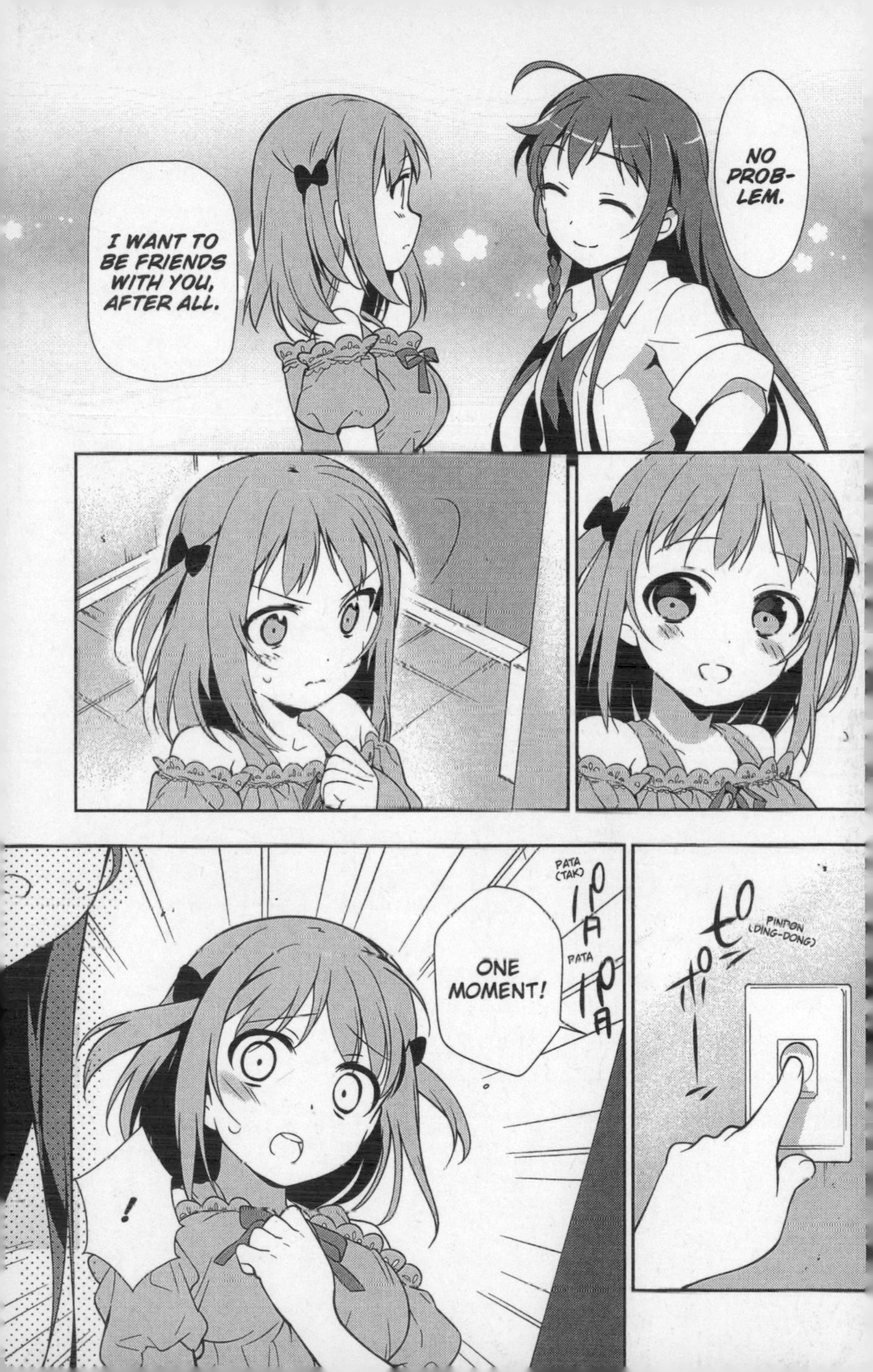
NO PROBLEM.
I WANT TO BE FRIENDS WITH YOU, AFTER ALL.
PINPON (DING-DONG)
PATA (TAK)
PATA
ONE MOMENT!
!

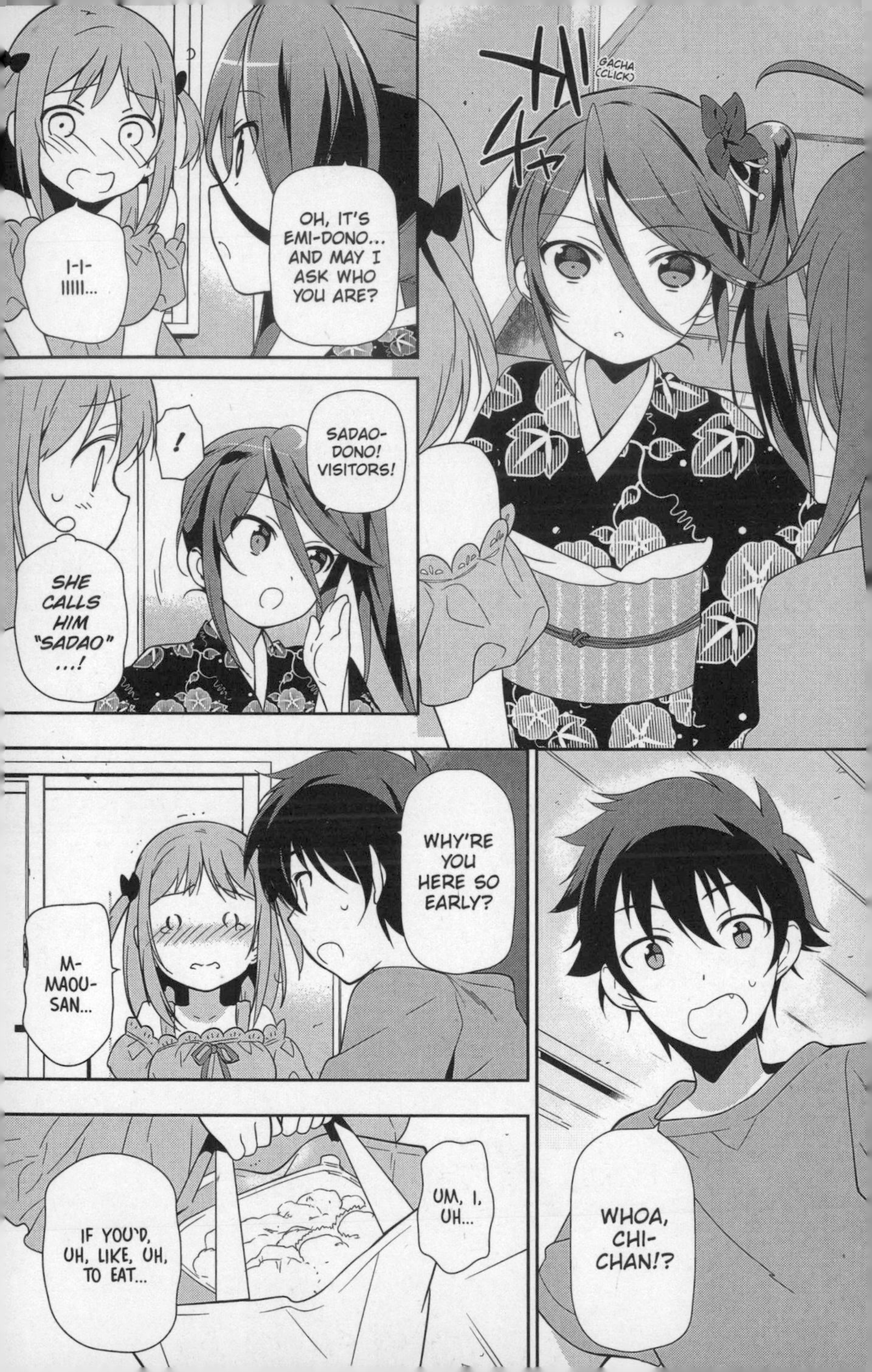
GACHA (CLICK)
OH, IT'S EMI-DONO... AND MAY I ASK WHO YOU ARE?
I-I-IIIII...
!
SADAO-DONO! VISITORS!
SHE CALLS HIM "SADAO"...!
WHOA, CHI-CHAN!?
WHY'RE YOU HERE SO EARLY?
M-MAOU-SAN...
UM, I, UH...
IF YOU'D, UH, LIKE, UH, TO EAT...

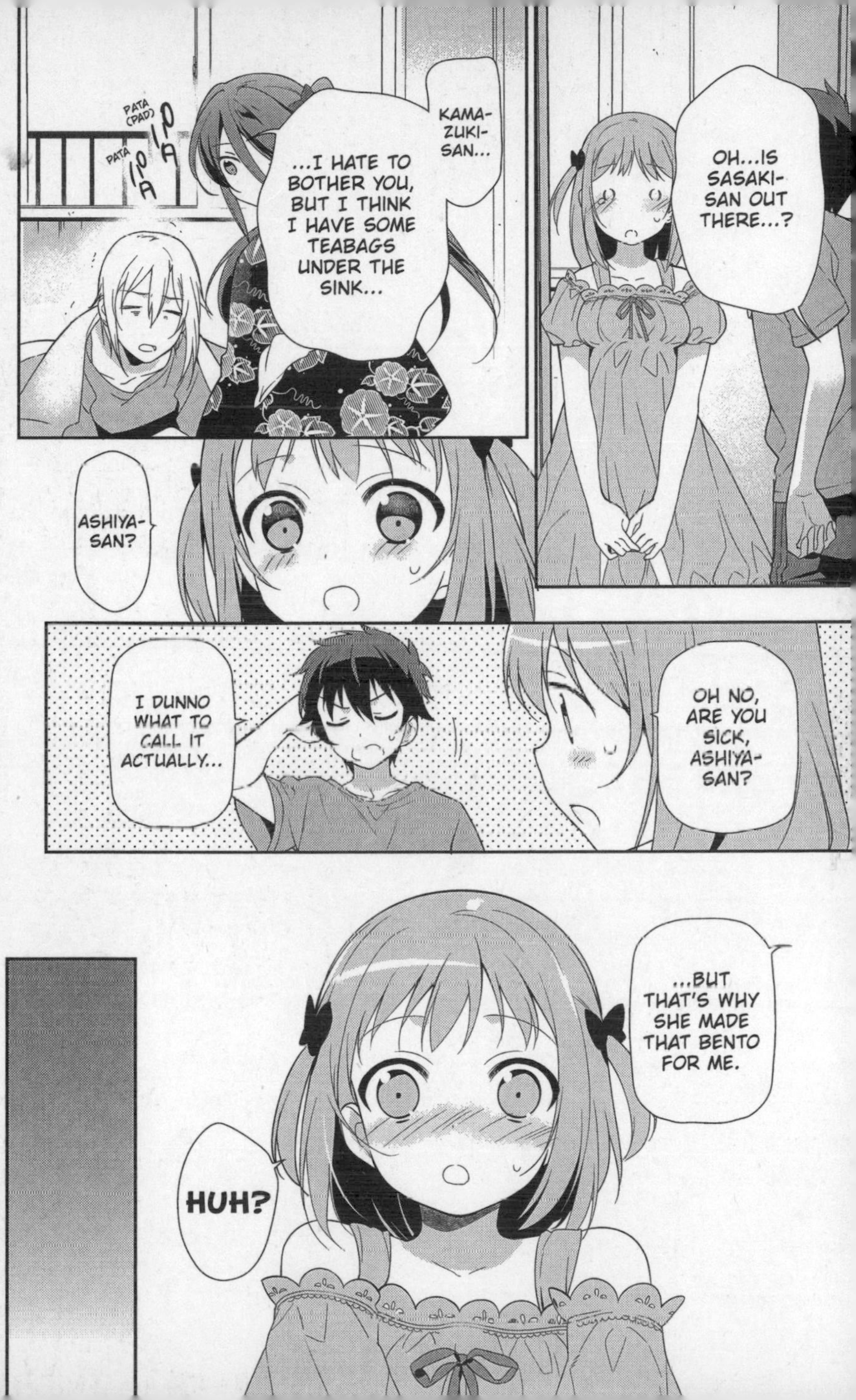
OH...IS SASAKI-SAN OUT THERE...?
KAMA-ZUKI-SAN...
...I HATE TO BOTHER YOU, BUT I THINK I HAVE SOME TEABAGS UNDER THE SINK...
PATA (PAD)
PATA
ASHIYA-SAN?
OH NO, ARE YOU SICK, ASHIYA-SAN?
I DUNNO WHAT TO CALL IT ACTUALLY...
...BUT THAT'S WHY SHE MADE THAT BENTO FOR ME.
HUH?

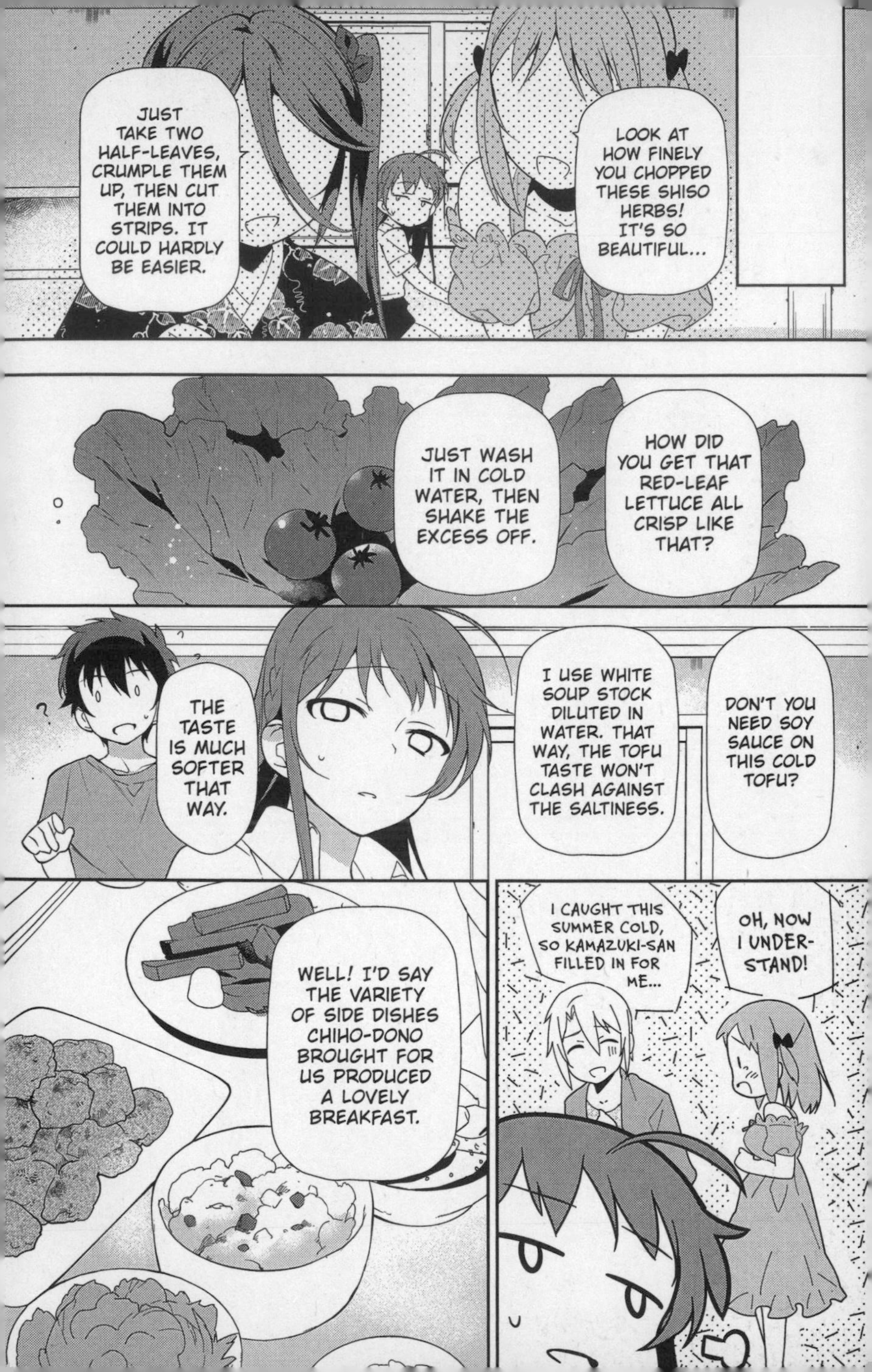
LOOK AT HOW FINELY YOU CHOPPED THESE SHISO HERBS! IT'S SO BEAUTIFUL...
JUST TAKE TWO HALF-LEAVES, CRUMPLE THEM UP, THEN CUT THEM INTO STRIPS. IT COULD HARDLY BE EASIER.
HOW DID YOU GET THAT RED-LEAF LETTUCE ALL CRISP LIKE THAT?
JUST WASH IT IN COLD WATER, THEN SHAKE THE EXCESS OFF.
DON'T YOU NEED SOY SAUCE ON THIS COLD TOFU?
I USE WHITE SOUP STOCK DILUTED IN WATER. THAT WAY, THE TOFU TASTE WON'T CLASH AGAINST THE SALTINESS.
THE TASTE IS MUCH SOFTER THAT WAY.
OH, NOW I UNDERSTAND!
I CAUGHT THIS SUMMER COLD, SO KAMAZUKI-SAN FILLED IN FOR ME...
WELL! I'D SAY THE VARIETY OF SIDE DISHES CHIHO-DONO BROUGHT FOR US PRODUCED A LOVELY BREAKFAST.

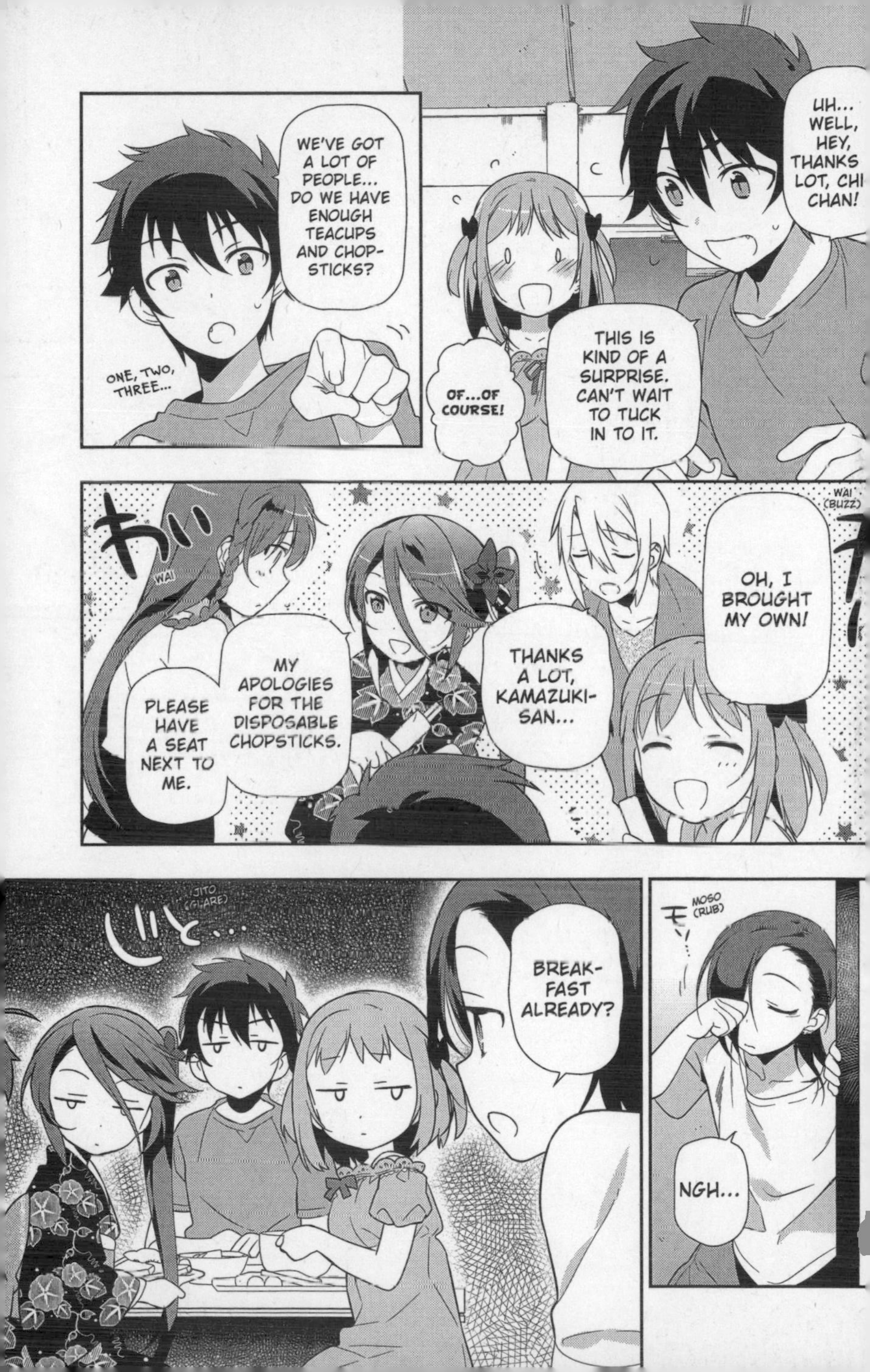
UH... WELL, HEY, THANKS LOT, CHI CHAN!
THIS IS KIND OF A SURPRISE. CAN'T WAIT TO TUCK IN TO IT.
OF...OF COURSE!
WE'VE GOT A LOT OF PEOPLE... DO WE HAVE ENOUGH TEACUPS AND CHOP-STICKS?
ONE, TWO, THREE...
WAI (BUZZ)
OH, I BROUGHT MY OWN!
THANKS A LOT, KAMAZUKI-SAN...
MY APOLOGIES FOR THE DISPOSABLE CHOPSTICKS.
PLEASE HAVE A SEAT NEXT TO ME.
WAI
MOSO (RUB)
NGH...
BREAK-FAST ALREADY?
JITO (GLARE)

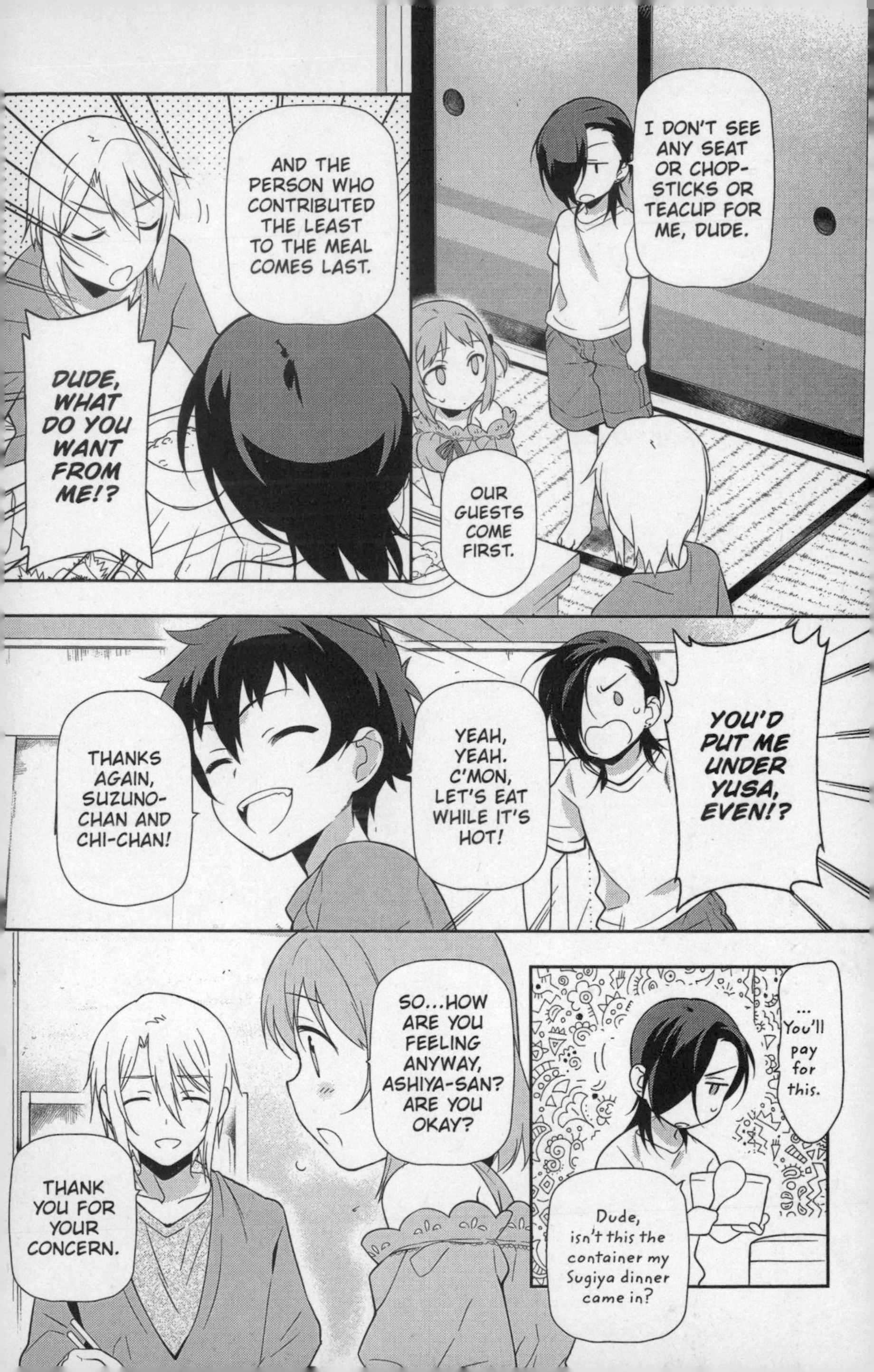
I DON'T SEE ANY SEAT OR CHOP-STICKS OR TEACUP FOR ME, DUDE.
OUR GUESTS COME FIRST.
AND THE PERSON WHO CONTRIBUTED THE LEAST TO THE MEAL COMES LAST.
DUDE, WHAT DO YOU WANT FROM ME!?
YOU'D PUT ME UNDER YUSA, EVEN!?
YEAH, YEAH. C'MON, LET'S EAT WHILE IT'S HOT!
THANKS AGAIN, SUZUNO-CHAN AND CHI-CHAN!
...You'll pay for this.
Dude, isn't this the container my Sugiya dinner came in?
SO...HOW ARE YOU FEELING ANYWAY, ASHIYA-SAN? ARE YOU OKAY?
THANK YOU FOR YOUR CONCERN.

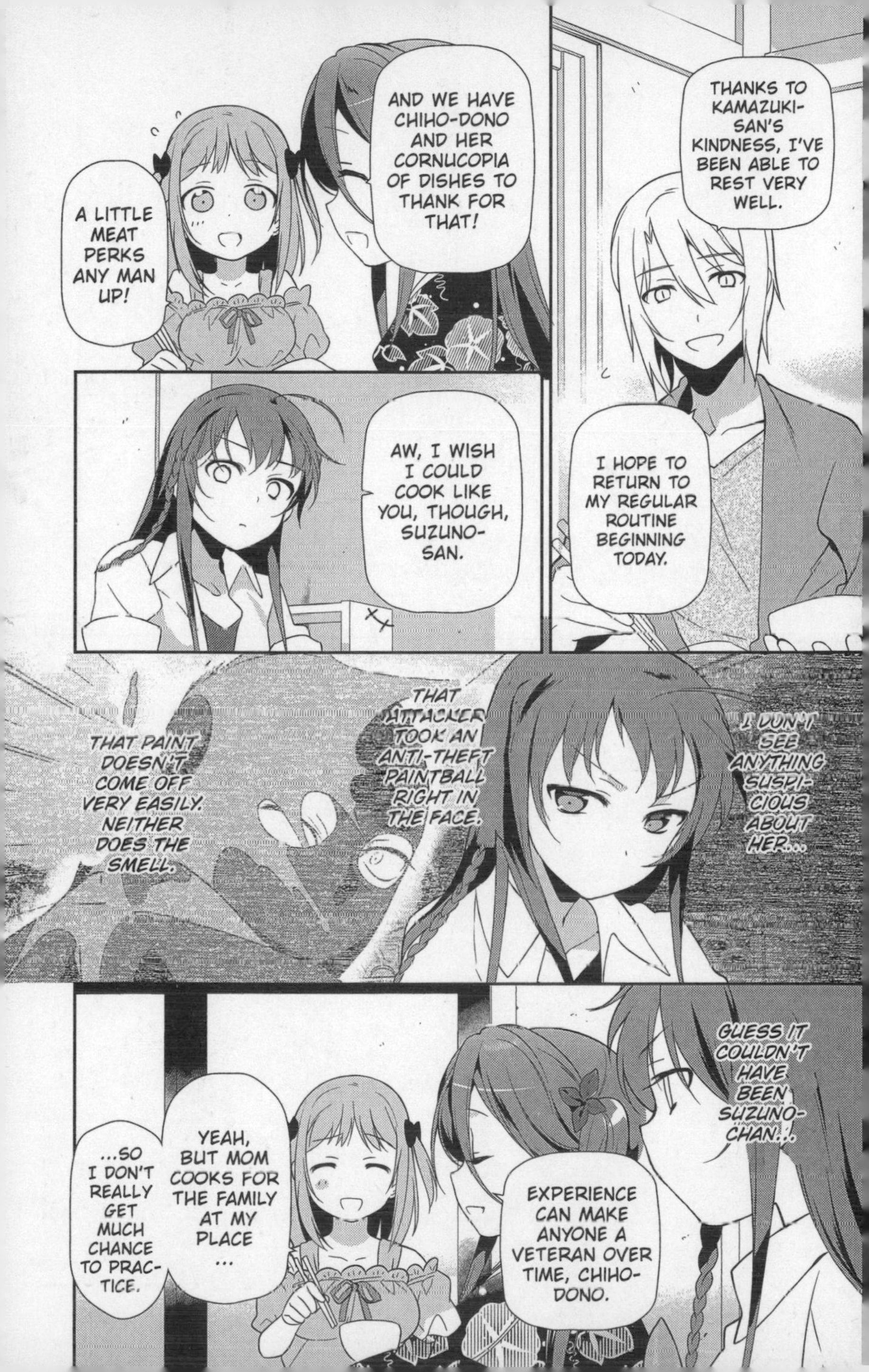
THANKS TO KAMAZUKI-SAN'S KINDNESS, I'VE BEEN ABLE TO REST VERY WELL.
I HOPE TO RETURN TO MY REGULAR ROUTINE BEGINNING TODAY.
AND WE HAVE CHIHO-DONO AND HER CORNUCOPIA OF DISHES TO THANK FOR THAT!
A LITTLE MEAT PERKS ANY MAN UP!
AW, I WISH I COULD COOK LIKE YOU, THOUGH, SUZUNO-SAN.
I DON'T SEE ANYTHING SUSPICIOUS ABOUT HER...
THAT ATTACKER TOOK AN ANTI-THEFT PAINTBALL RIGHT IN THE FACE.
THAT PAINT DOESN'T COME OFF VERY EASILY. NEITHER DOES THE SMELL.
GUESS IT COULDN'T HAVE BEEN SUZUNO-CHAN...
EXPERIENCE CAN MAKE ANYONE A VETERAN OVER TIME, CHIHO-DONO.
YEAH, BUT MOM COOKS FOR THE FAMILY AT MY PLACE...
...SO I DON'T REALLY GET MUCH CHANCE TO PRACTICE.

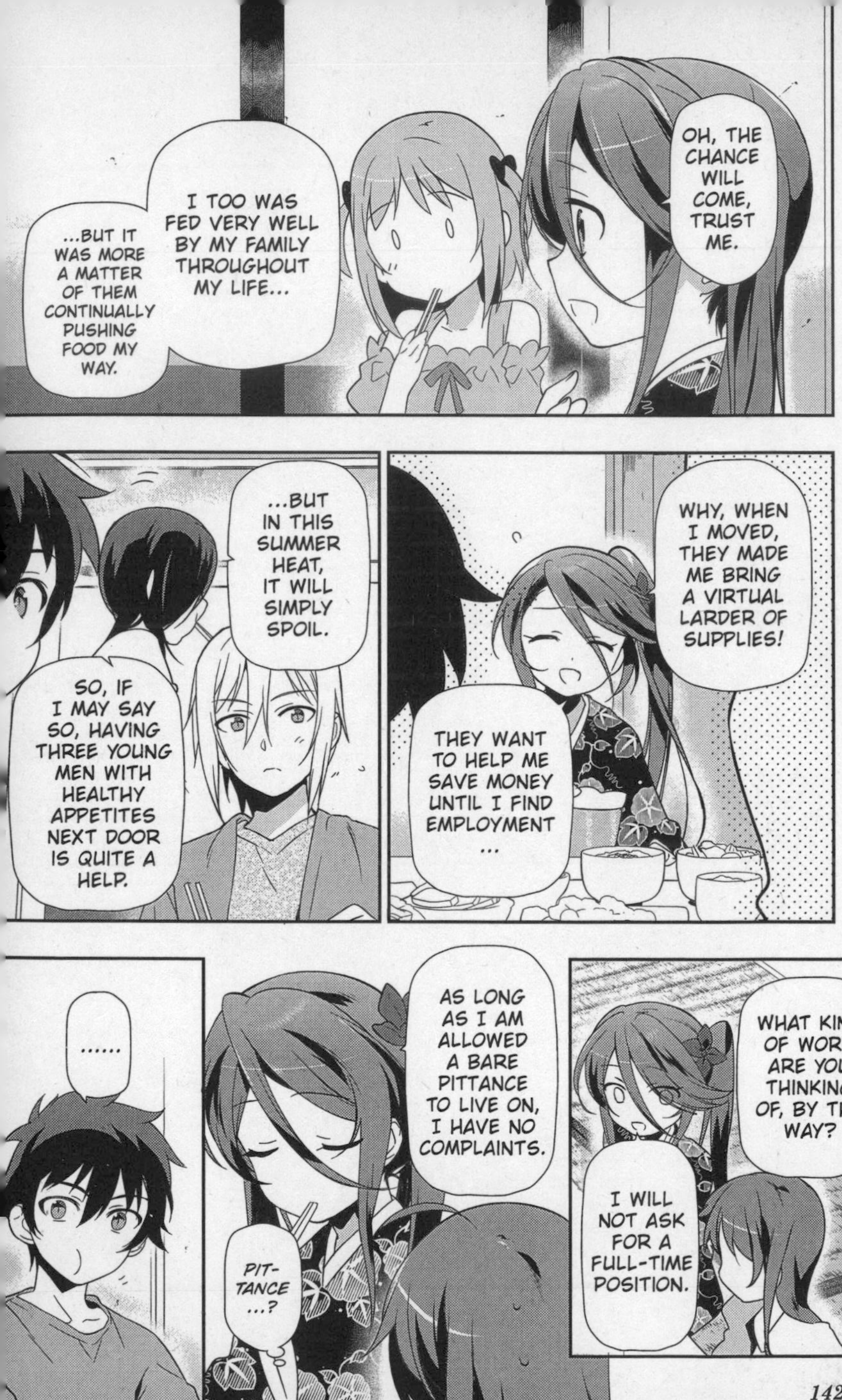

OH, THE CHANCE WILL COME, TRUST ME.
I TOO WAS FED VERY WELL BY MY FAMILY THROUGHOUT MY LIFE...
...BUT IT WAS MORE A MATTER OF THEM CONTINUALLY PUSHING FOOD MY WAY.
WHY, WHEN I MOVED, THEY MADE ME BRING A VIRTUAL LARDER OF SUPPLIES!
THEY WANT TO HELP ME SAVE MONEY UNTIL I FIND EMPLOYMENT ...
...BUT IN THIS SUMMER HEAT, IT WILL SIMPLY SPOIL.
SO, IF I MAY SAY SO, HAVING THREE YOUNG MEN WITH HEALTHY APPETITES NEXT DOOR IS QUITE A HELP.
WHAT KIND OF WORK ARE YOU THINKING OF, BY THE WAY?
I WILL NOT ASK FOR A FULL-TIME POSITION.
AS LONG AS I AM ALLOWED A BARE PITTANCE TO LIVE ON, I HAVE NO COMPLAINTS.
PIT-TANCE ...?
......

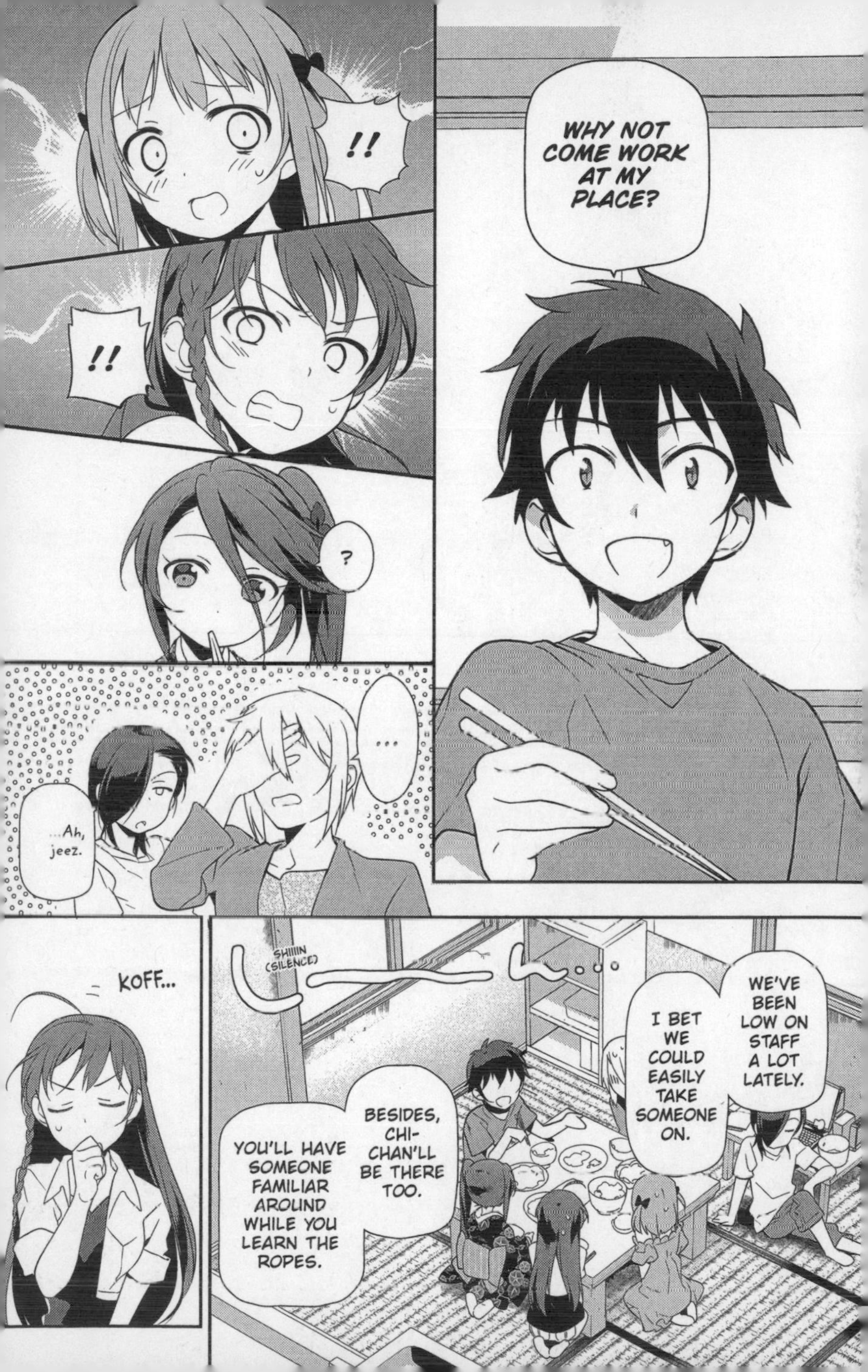
WHY NOT COME WORK AT MY PLACE?
!!
!!
?
...
...Ah, jeez.
SHIIIN (SILENCE)
...
WE'VE BEEN LOW ON STAFF A LOT LATELY.
I BET WE COULD EASILY TAKE SOMEONE ON.
BESIDES, CHI-CHAN'LL BE THERE TOO.
YOU'LL HAVE SOMEONE FAMILIAR AROUND WHILE YOU LEARN THE ROPES.
KOFF...

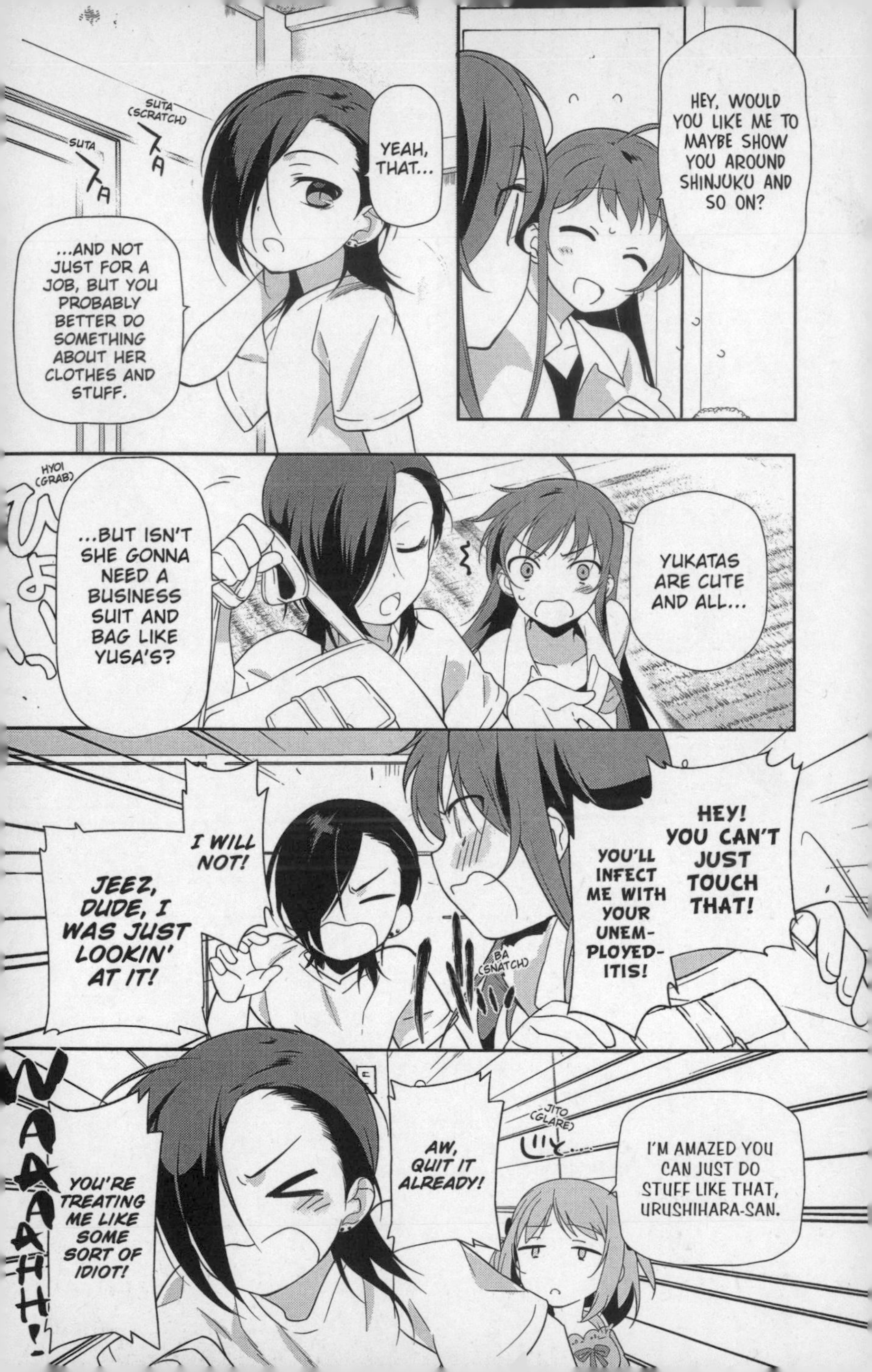

HEY, WOULD YOU LIKE ME TO MAYBE SHOW YOU AROUND SHINJUKU AND SO ON?
YEAH, THAT...
SUTA (SCRATCH)
SUTA
...AND NOT JUST FOR A JOB, BUT YOU PROBABLY BETTER DO SOMETHING ABOUT HER CLOTHES AND STUFF.
YUKATAS ARE CUTE AND ALL...
HYOI (GRAB)
...BUT ISN'T SHE GONNA NEED A BUSINESS SUIT AND BAG LIKE YUSA'S?
HEY! YOU CAN'T JUST TOUCH THAT!
YOU'LL INFECT ME WITH YOUR UNEMPLOYED-ITIS!
BA (SNATCH)
I WILL NOT!
JEEZ, DUDE, I WAS JUST LOOKIN' AT IT!
I'M AMAZED YOU CAN JUST DO STUFF LIKE THAT, URUSHIHARA-SAN.
JITO (GLARE)
AW, QUIT IT ALREADY!
YOU'RE TREATING ME LIKE SOME SORT OF IDIOT!
WAAAAHH!

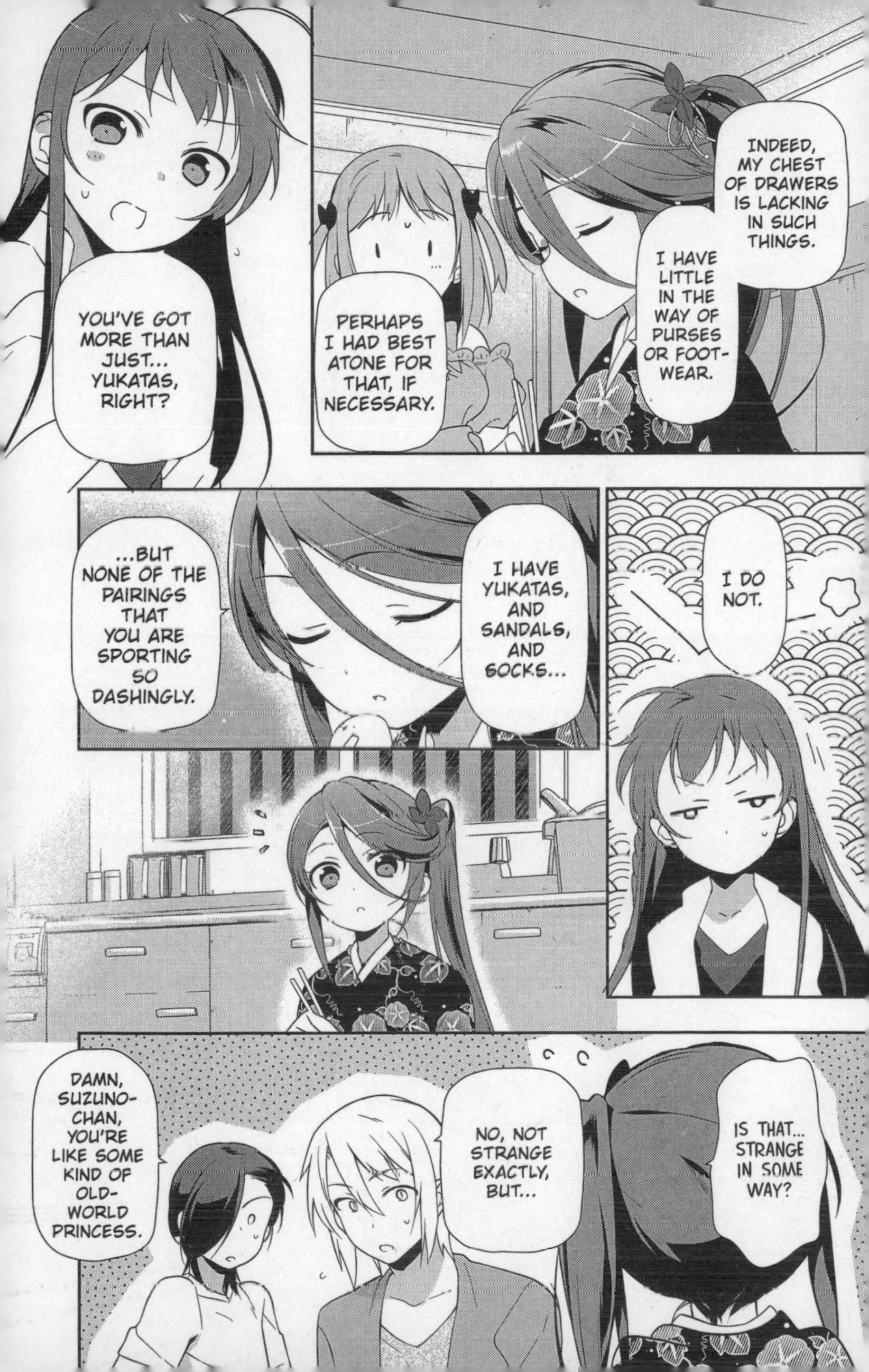
INDEED, MY CHEST OF DRAWERS IS LACKING IN SUCH THINGS.
I HAVE LITTLE IN THE WAY OF PURSES OR FOOT-WEAR.
PERHAPS I HAD BEST ATONE FOR THAT, IF NECESSARY.
...
YOU'VE GOT MORE THAN JUST... YUKATAS, RIGHT?
I DO NOT.
I HAVE YUKATAS, AND SANDALS, AND SOCKS...
...BUT NONE OF THE PAIRINGS THAT YOU ARE SPORTING SO DASHINGLY.
IS THAT... STRANGE IN SOME WAY?
NO, NOT STRANGE EXACTLY, BUT...
DAMN, SUZUNO-CHAN, YOU'RE LIKE SOME KIND OF OLD-WORLD PRINCESS.

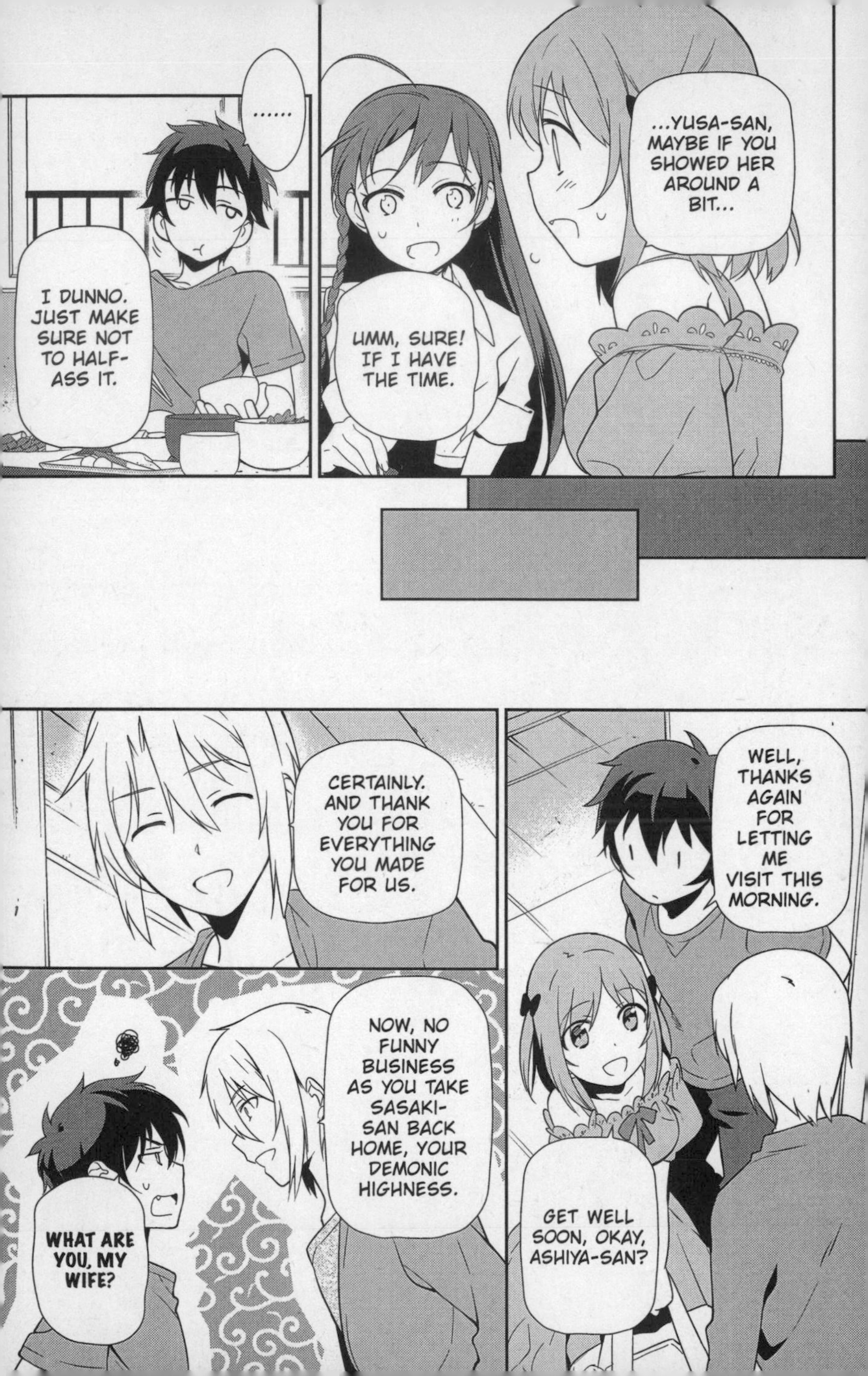
...YUSA-SAN, MAYBE IF YOU SHOWED HER AROUND A BIT...
UMM, SURE! IF I HAVE THE TIME.
......
I DUNNO. JUST MAKE SURE NOT TO HALF-ASS IT.
WELL, THANKS AGAIN FOR LETTING ME VISIT THIS MORNING.
GET WELL SOON, OKAY, ASHIYA-SAN?
CERTAINLY. AND THANK YOU FOR EVERYTHING YOU MADE FOR US.
NOW, NO FUNNY BUSINESS AS YOU TAKE SASAKI-SAN BACK HOME, YOUR DEMONIC HIGHNESS.
WHAT ARE YOU, MY WIFE?

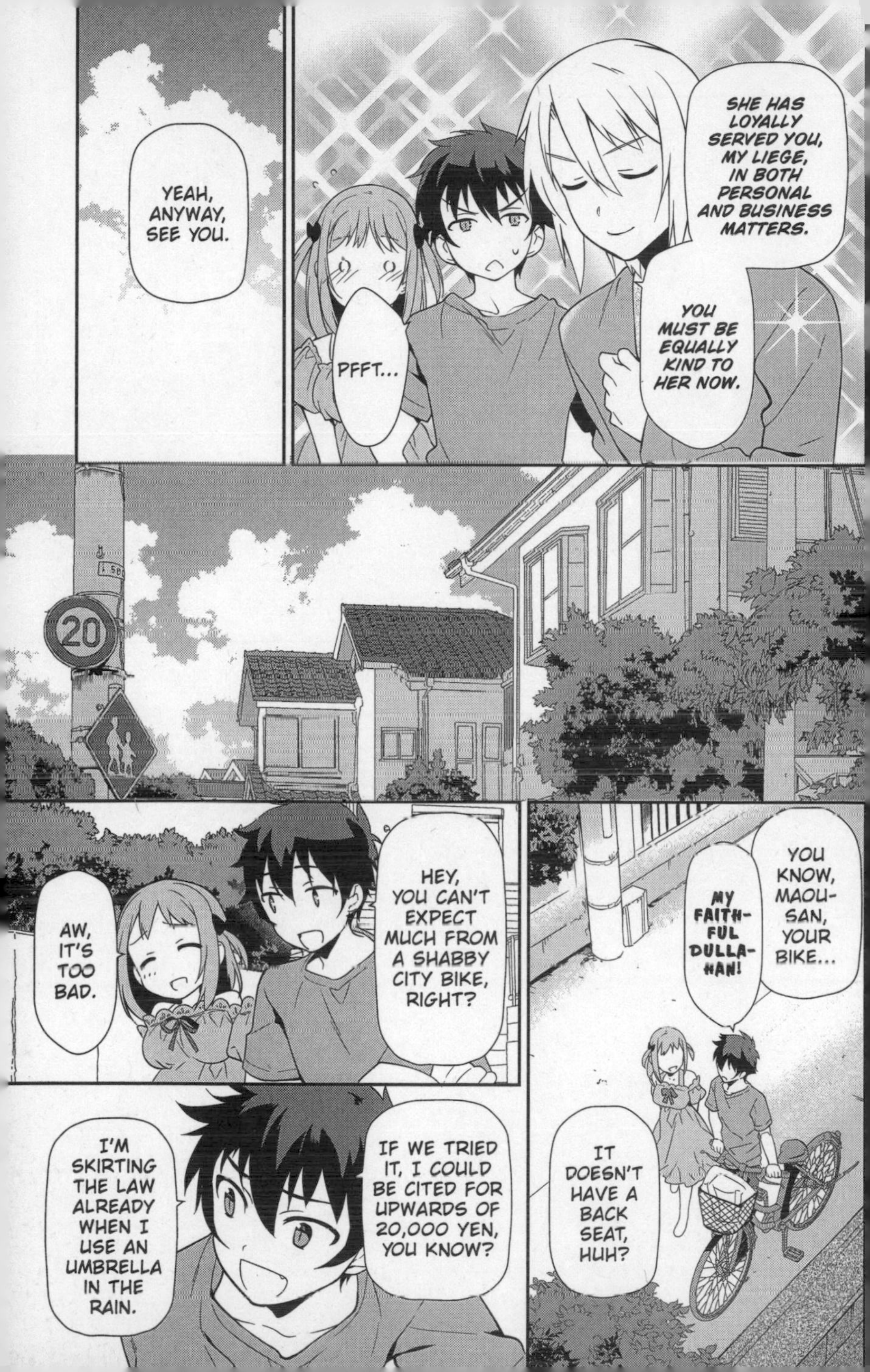
SHE HAS LOYALLY SERVED YOU, MY LIEGE, IN BOTH PERSONAL AND BUSINESS MATTERS.
YOU MUST BE EQUALLY KIND TO HER NOW.
PFFT...
YEAH, ANYWAY, SEE YOU.
20
YOU KNOW, MAOU-SAN, YOUR BIKE...
MY FAITHFUL DULLAHAN!
IT DOESN'T HAVE A BACK SEAT, HUH?
HEY, YOU CAN'T EXPECT MUCH FROM A SHABBY CITY BIKE, RIGHT?
AW, IT'S TOO BAD.
IF WE TRIED IT, I COULD BE CITED FOR UPWARDS OF 20,000 YEN, YOU KNOW?
I'M SKIRTING THE LAW ALREADY WHEN I USE AN UMBRELLA IN THE RAIN.

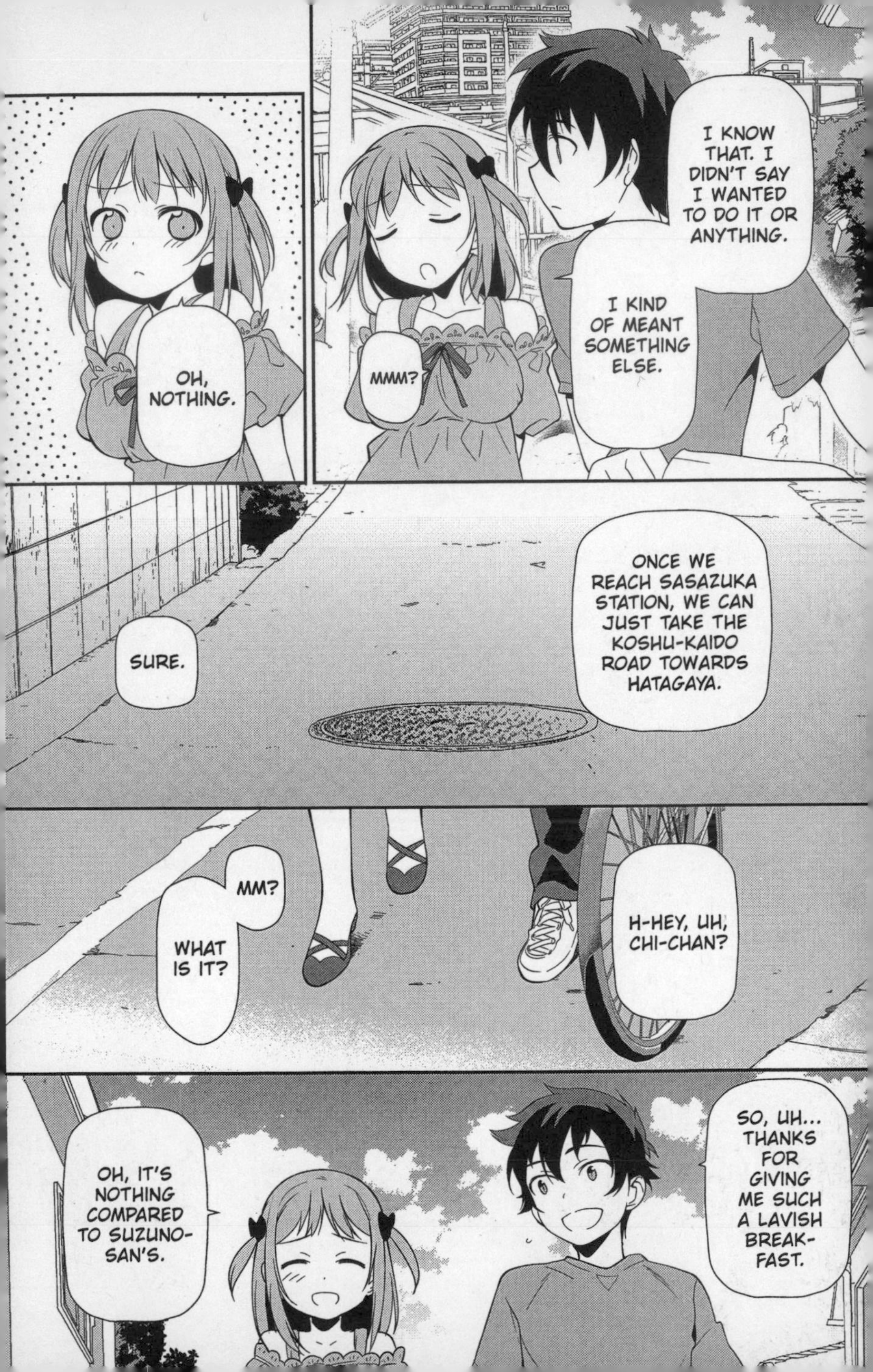
I KNOW THAT. I DIDN'T SAY I WANTED TO DO IT OR ANYTHING.
I KIND OF MEANT SOMETHING ELSE.
MMM?
OH, NOTHING.
ONCE WE REACH SASAZUKA STATION, WE CAN JUST TAKE THE KOSHU-KAIDO ROAD TOWARDS HATAGAYA.
SURE.
H-HEY, UH, CHI-CHAN?
MM?
WHAT IS IT?
SO, UH... THANKS FOR GIVING ME SUCH A LAVISH BREAK-FAST.
OH, IT'S NOTHING COMPARED TO SUZUNO-SAN'S.

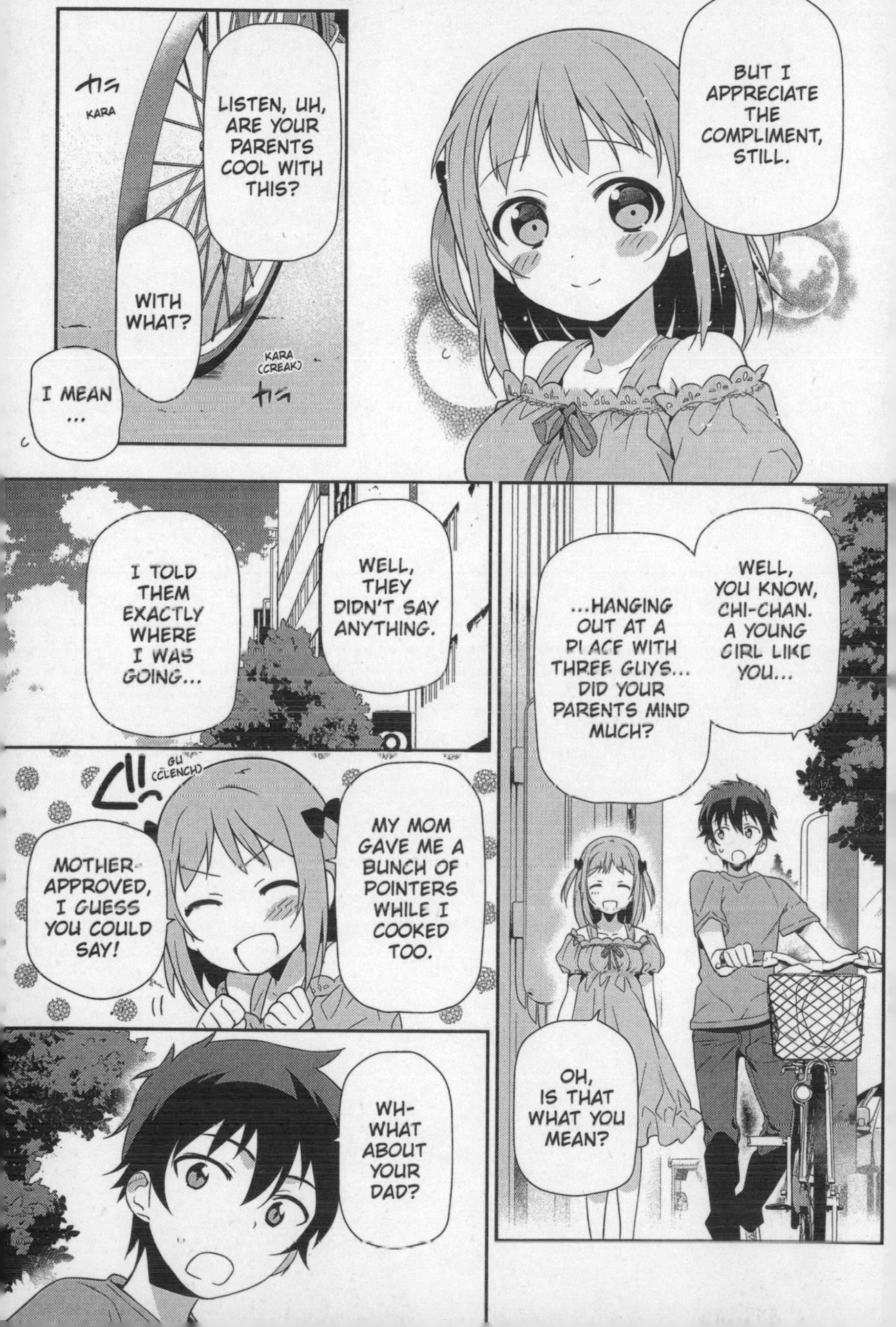

BUT I APPRECIATE THE COMPLIMENT, STILL.
KARA
LISTEN, UH, ARE YOUR PARENTS COOL WITH THIS?
WITH WHAT?
KARA (CREAK)
I MEAN ...
WELL, YOU KNOW, CHI-CHAN. A YOUNG GIRL LIKE YOU...
...HANGING OUT AT A PLACE WITH THREE GUYS... DID YOUR PARENTS MIND MUCH?
OH, IS THAT WHAT YOU MEAN?
WELL, THEY DIDN'T SAY ANYTHING.
I TOLD THEM EXACTLY WHERE I WAS GOING...
GU (CLENCH)
MY MOM GAVE ME A BUNCH OF POINTERS WHILE I COOKED TOO.
MOTHER-APPROVED, I GUESS YOU COULD SAY!
WH-WHAT ABOUT YOUR DAD?

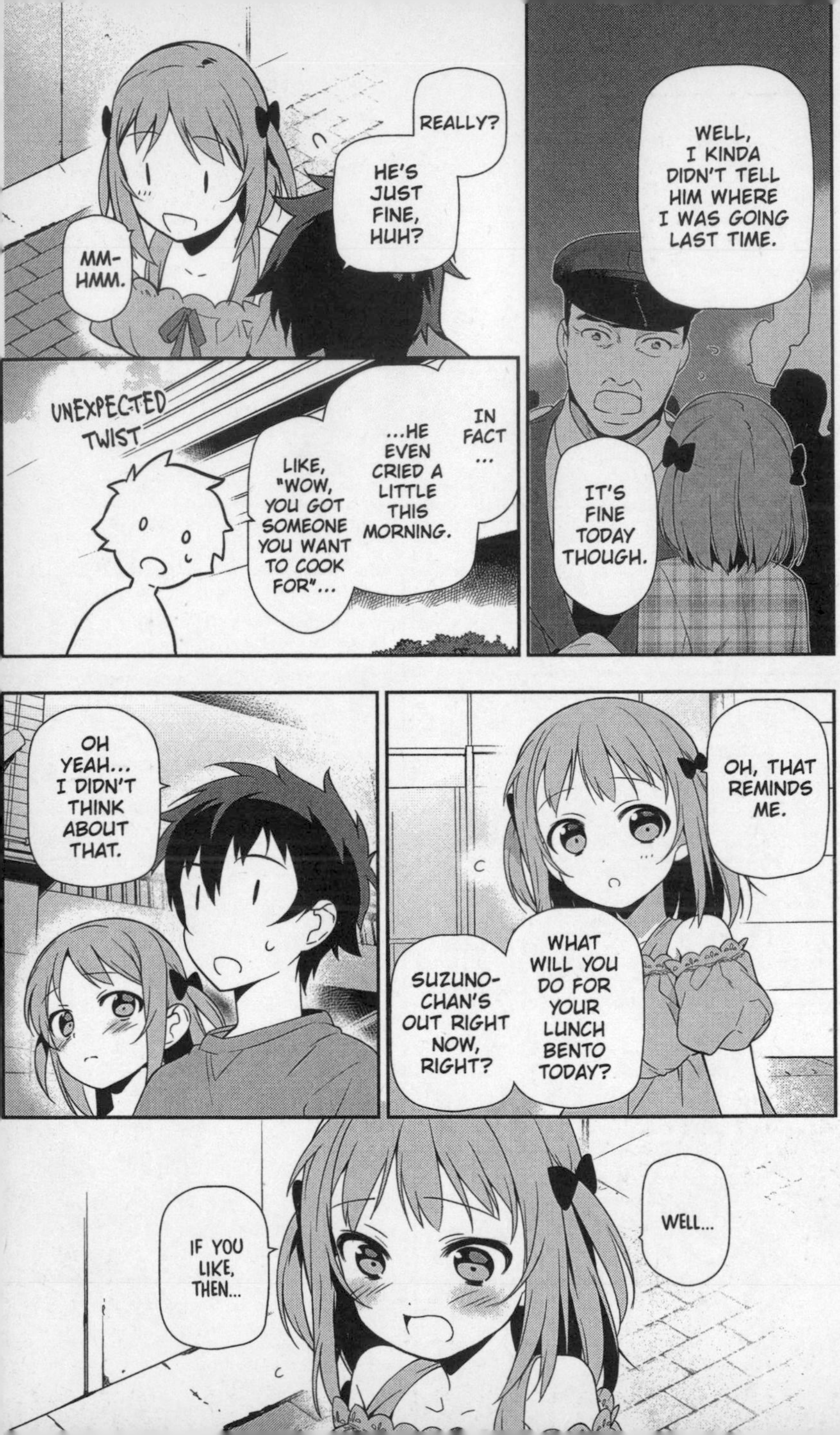
WELL, I KINDA DIDN'T TELL HIM WHERE I WAS GOING LAST TIME.
IT'S FINE TODAY THOUGH.
REALLY?
HE'S JUST FINE, HUH?
MM-HMM.
IN FACT...
...HE EVEN CRIED A LITTLE THIS MORNING.
LIKE, "WOW, YOU GOT SOMEONE YOU WANT TO COOK FOR"...
UNEXPECTED TWIST
OH, THAT REMINDS ME.
WHAT WILL YOU DO FOR YOUR LUNCH BENTO TODAY?
SUZUNO-CHAN'S OUT RIGHT NOW, RIGHT?
OH YEAH... I DIDN'T THINK ABOUT THAT.
WELL...
IF YOU LIKE, THEN...

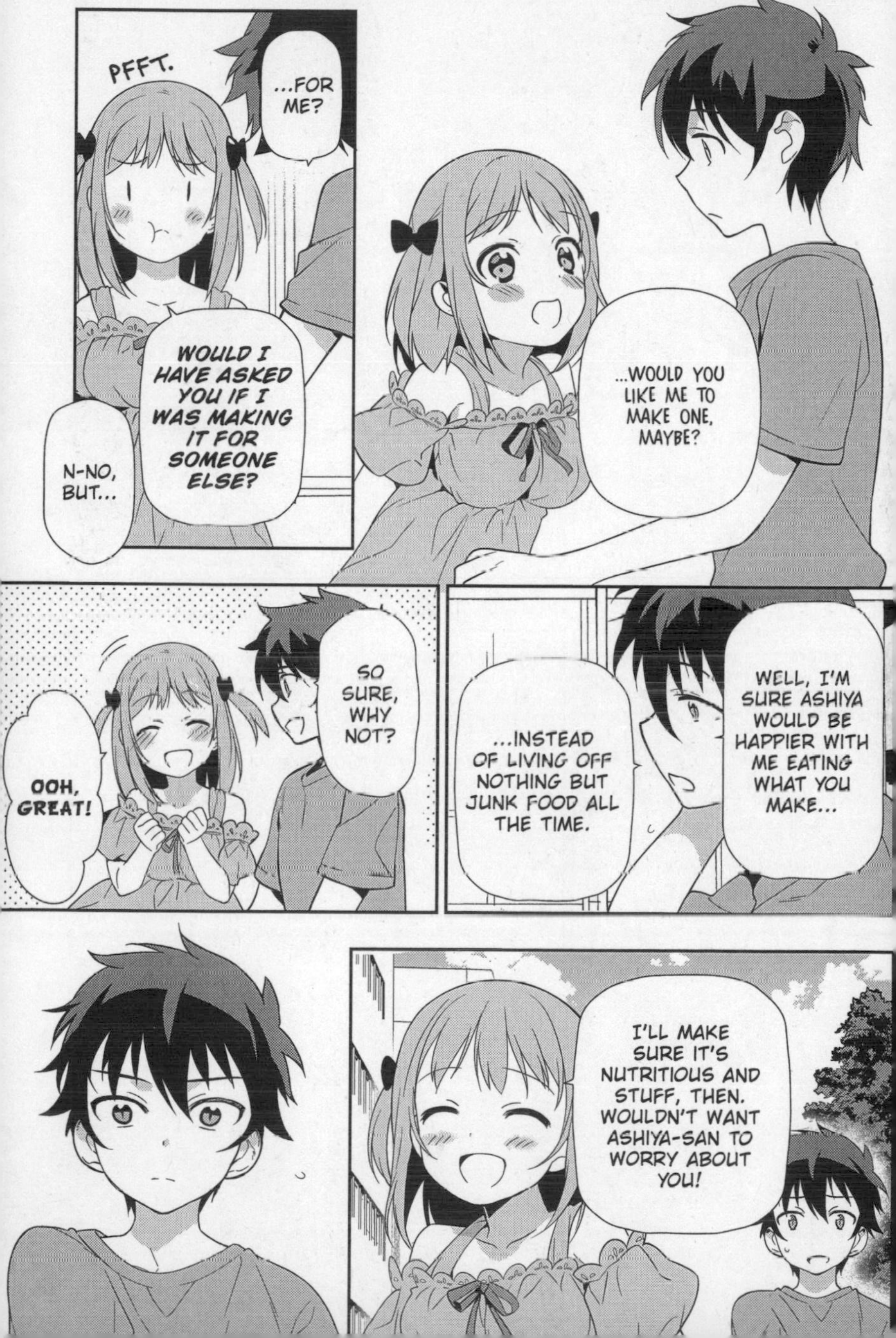
...WOULD YOU LIKE ME TO MAKE ONE, MAYBE?
...FOR ME?
PFFT.
WOULD I HAVE ASKED YOU IF I WAS MAKING IT FOR SOMEONE ELSE?
N-NO, BUT...
WELL, I'M SURE ASHIYA WOULD BE HAPPIER WITH ME EATING WHAT YOU MAKE...
...INSTEAD OF LIVING OFF NOTHING BUT JUNK FOOD ALL THE TIME.
SO SURE, WHY NOT?
OOH, GREAT!
I'LL MAKE SURE IT'S NUTRITIOUS AND STUFF, THEN. WOULDN'T WANT ASHIYA-SAN TO WORRY ABOUT YOU!

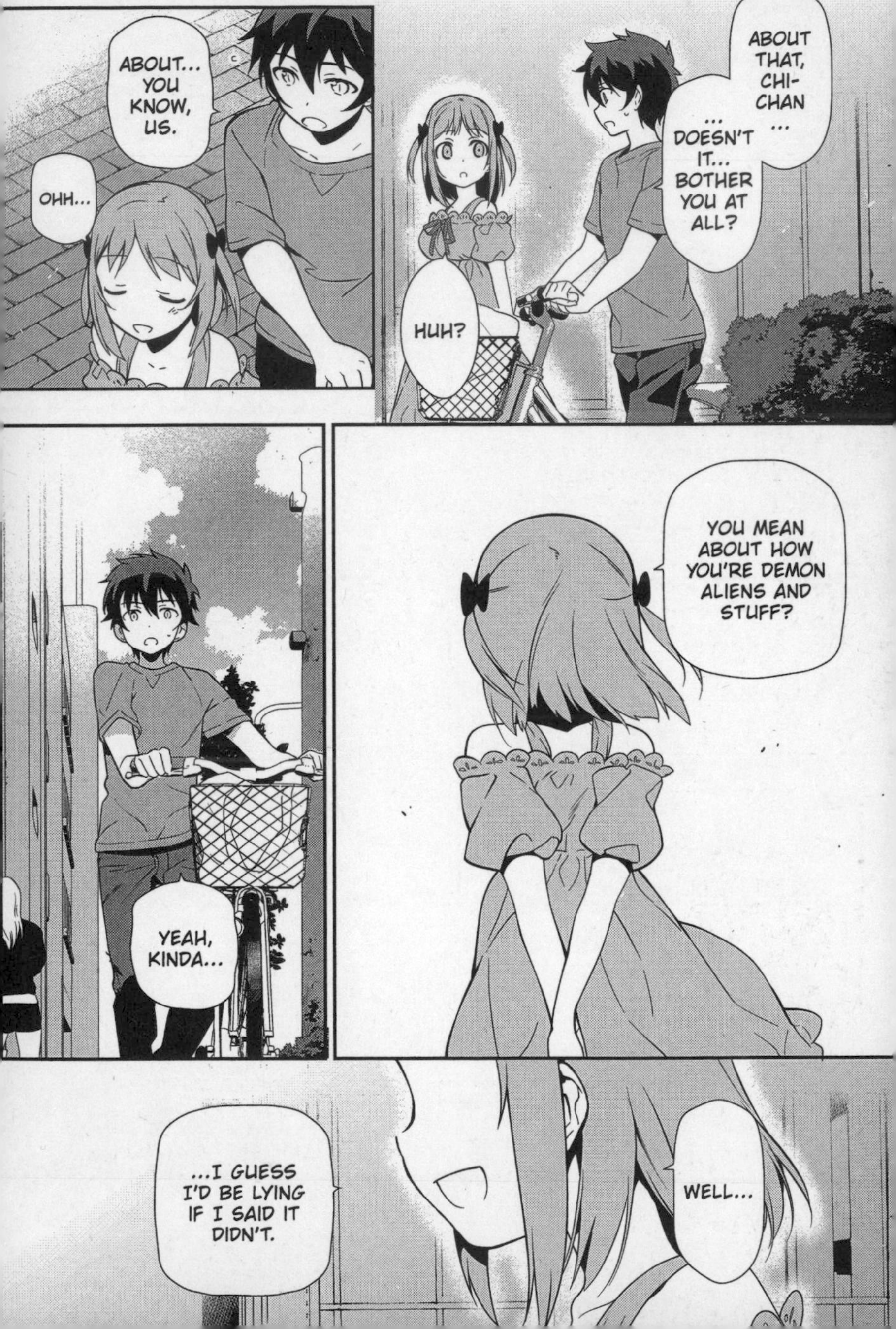
ABOUT THAT, CHI-CHAN...
...DOESN'T IT... BOTHER YOU AT ALL?
HUH?
ABOUT... YOU KNOW, US.
OHH...
YOU MEAN ABOUT HOW YOU'RE DEMON ALIENS AND STUFF?
YEAH, KINDA...
WELL...
...I GUESS I'D BE LYING IF I SAID IT DIDN'T.

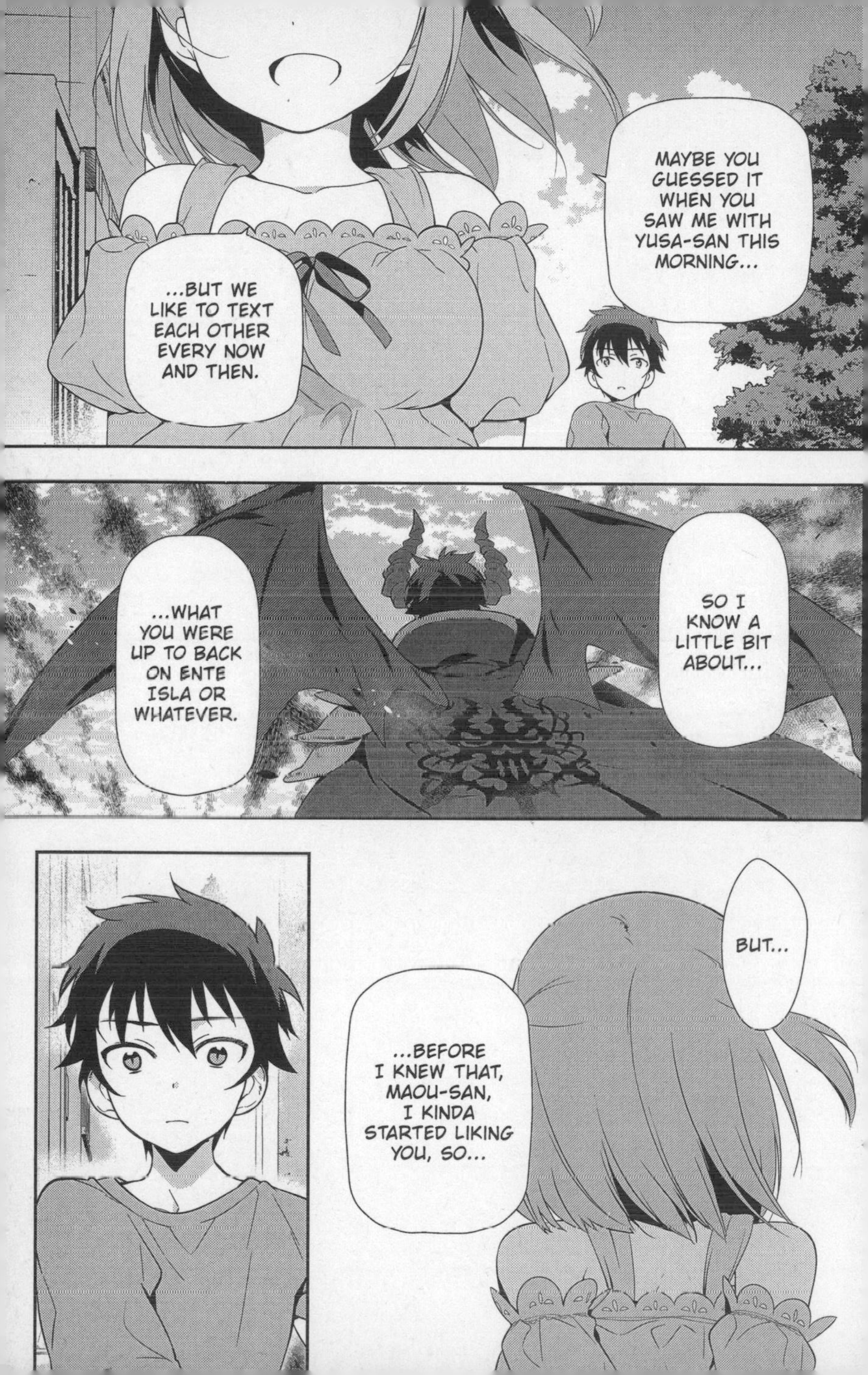
MAYBE YOU GUESSED IT WHEN YOU SAW ME WITH YUSA-SAN THIS MORNING...
...BUT WE LIKE TO TEXT EACH OTHER EVERY NOW AND THEN.
SO I KNOW A LITTLE BIT ABOUT...
...WHAT YOU WERE UP TO BACK ON ENTE ISLA OR WHATEVER.
BUT...
...BEFORE I KNEW THAT, MAOU-SAN, I KINDA STARTED LIKING YOU, SO...

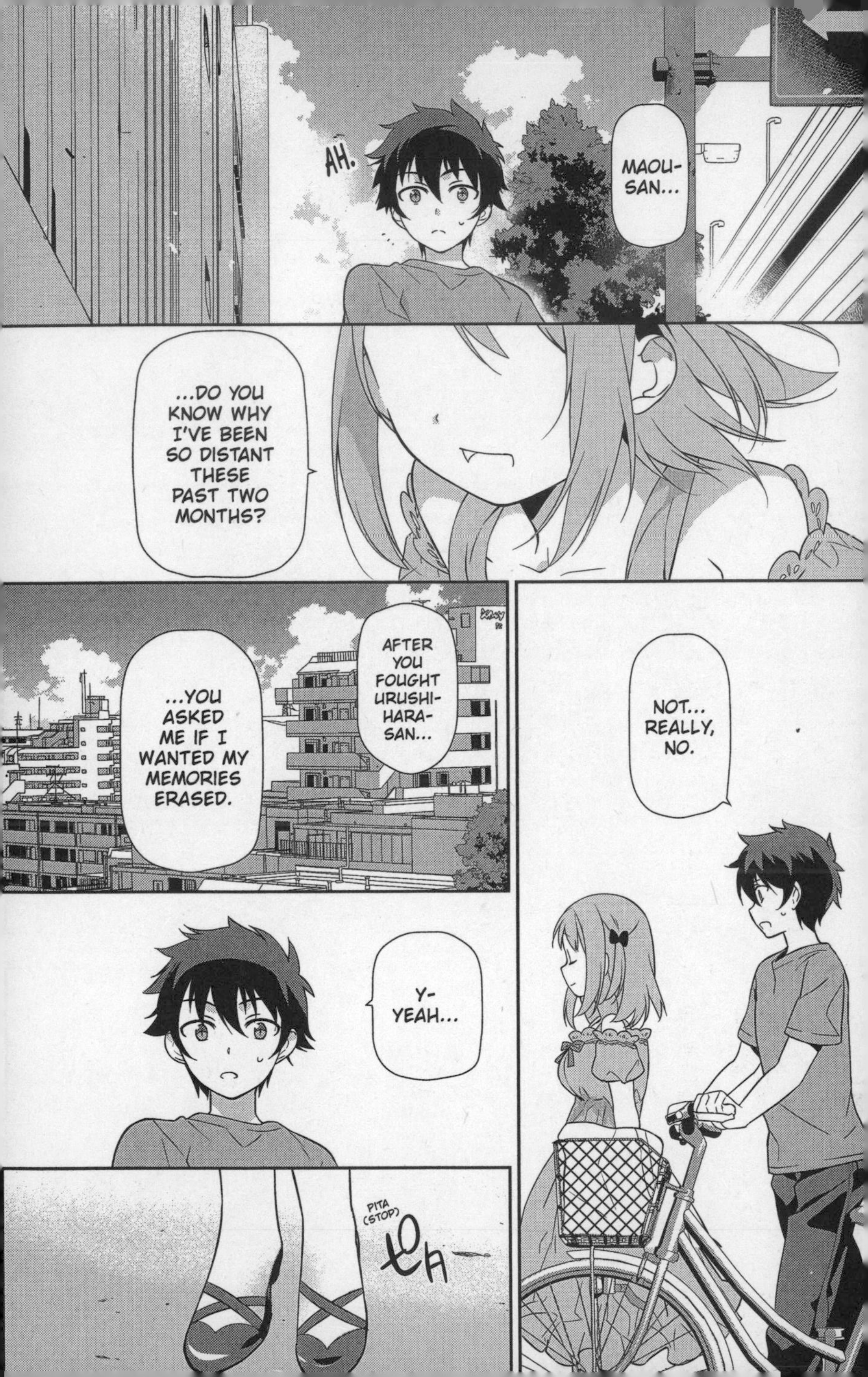
MAOU-SAN...
AH.
...DO YOU KNOW WHY I'VE BEEN SO DISTANT THESE PAST TWO MONTHS?
NOT... REALLY, NO.
AFTER YOU FOUGHT URUSHI-HARA-SAN...
...YOU ASKED ME IF I WANTED MY MEMORIES ERASED.
Y-YEAH...
PITA (STOP)

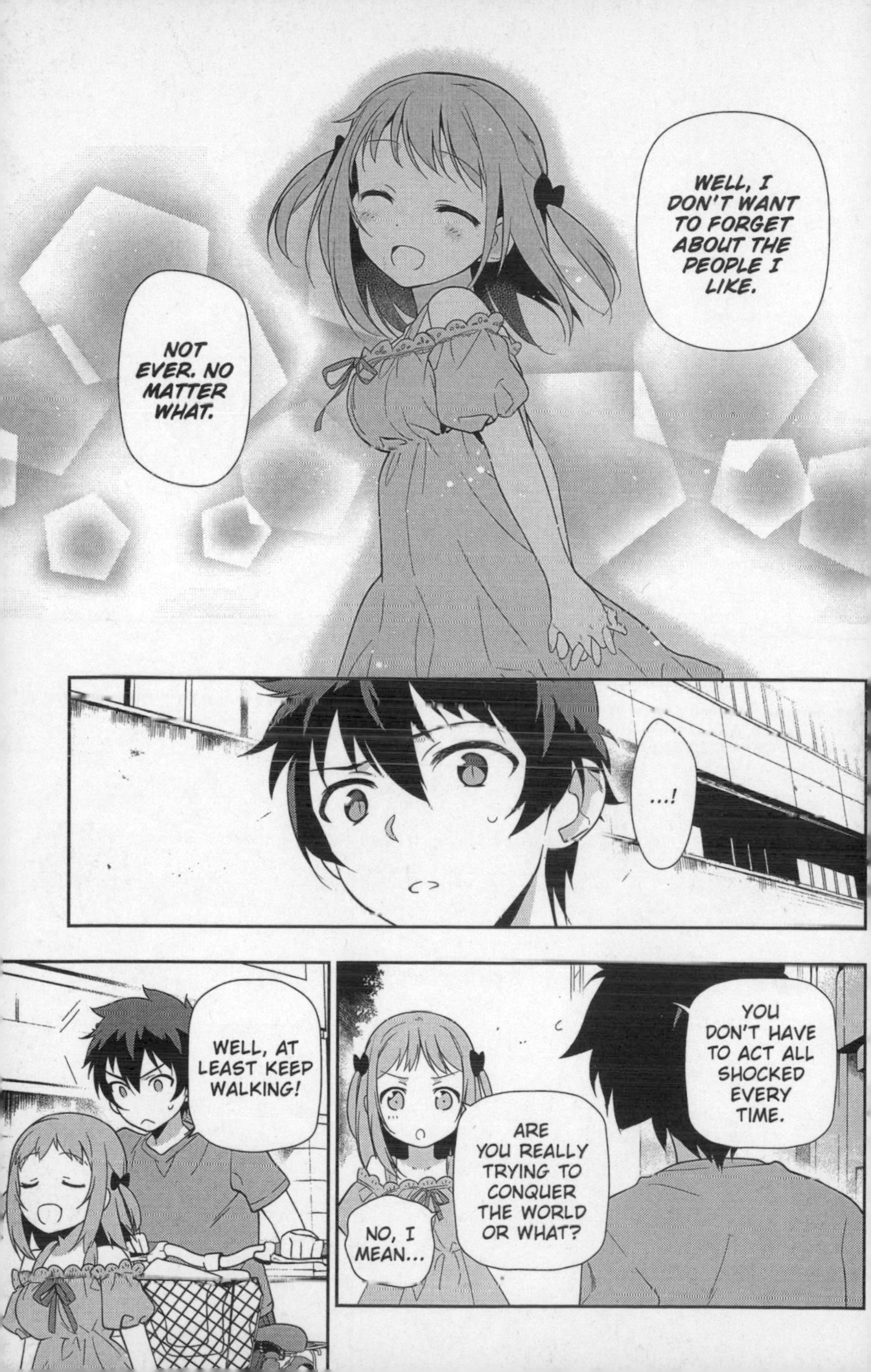
WELL, I DON'T WANT TO FORGET ABOUT THE PEOPLE I LIKE.
NOT EVER. NO MATTER WHAT.
...!
YOU DON'T HAVE TO ACT ALL SHOCKED EVERY TIME.
ARE YOU REALLY TRYING TO CONQUER THE WORLD OR WHAT?
NO, I MEAN...
WELL, AT LEAST KEEP WALKING!

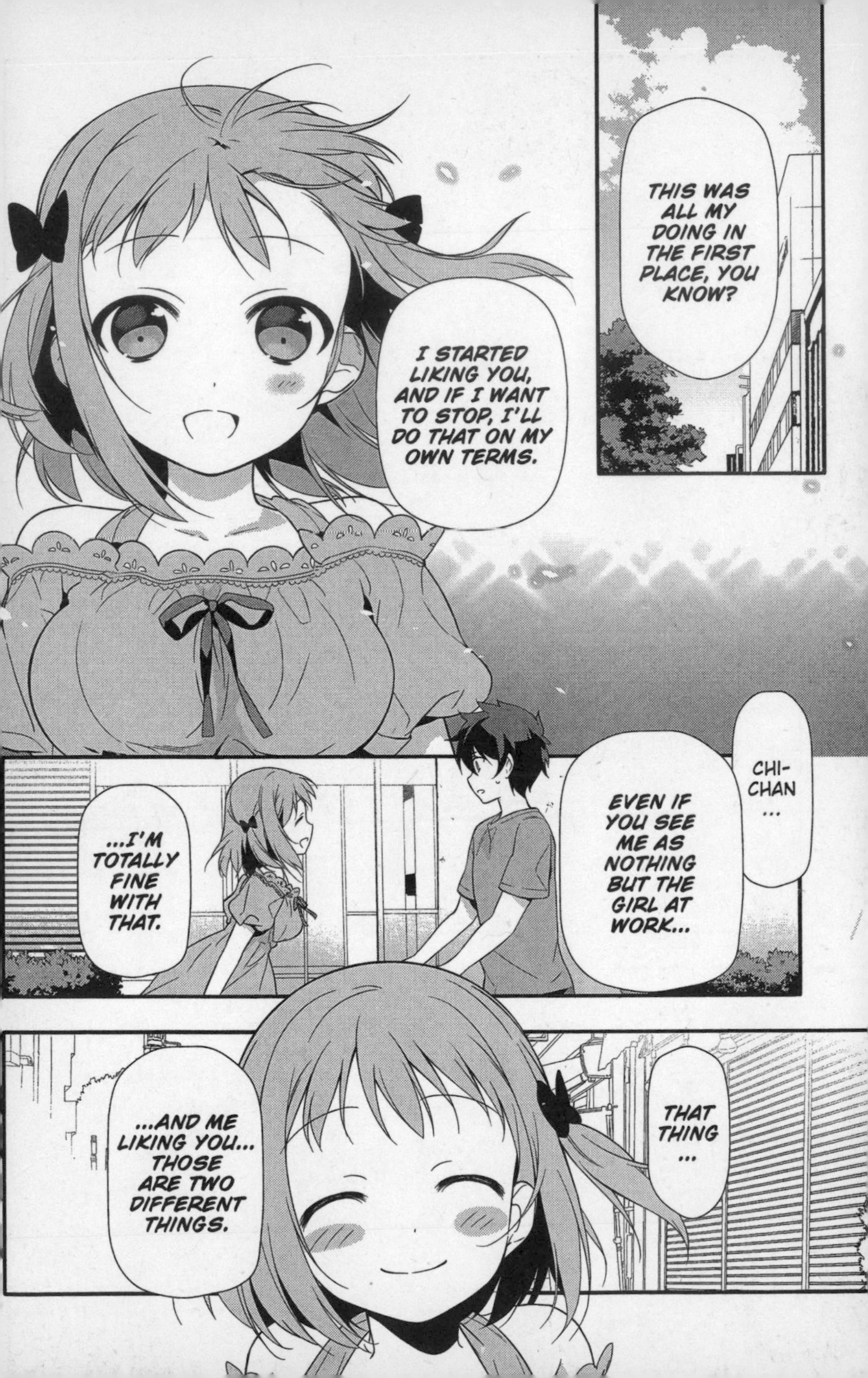
THIS WAS ALL MY DOING IN THE FIRST PLACE, YOU KNOW?
I STARTED LIKING YOU, AND IF I WANT TO STOP, I'LL DO THAT ON MY OWN TERMS.
CHI-CHAN...
EVEN IF YOU SEE ME AS NOTHING BUT THE GIRL AT WORK...
...I'M TOTALLY FINE WITH THAT.
THAT THING...
...AND ME LIKING YOU... THOSE ARE TWO DIFFERENT THINGS.

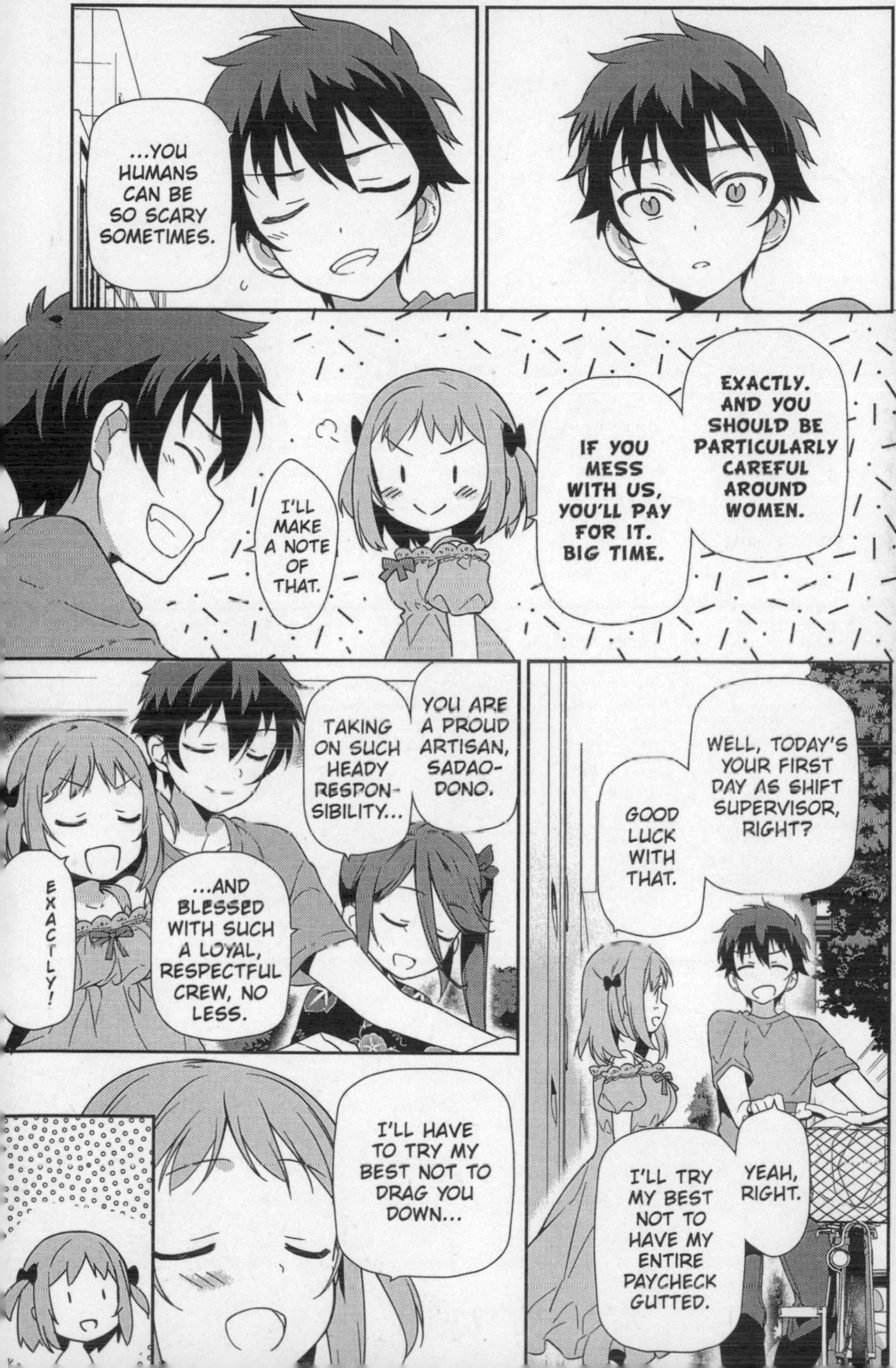
...YOU HUMANS CAN BE SO SCARY SOMETIMES.
EXACTLY. AND YOU SHOULD BE PARTICULARLY CAREFUL AROUND WOMEN.
IF YOU MESS WITH US, YOU'LL PAY FOR IT. BIG TIME.
I'LL MAKE A NOTE OF THAT.
WELL, TODAY'S YOUR FIRST DAY AS SHIFT SUPERVISOR, RIGHT?
GOOD LUCK WITH THAT.
YEAH, RIGHT.
I'LL TRY MY BEST NOT TO HAVE MY ENTIRE PAYCHECK GUTTED.
YOU ARE A PROUD ARTISAN, SADAO-DONO.
TAKING ON SUCH HEADY RESPON-SIBILITY...
...AND BLESSED WITH SUCH A LOYAL, RESPECTFUL CREW, NO LESS.
EXACTLY!
I'LL HAVE TO TRY MY BEST NOT TO DRAG YOU DOWN...

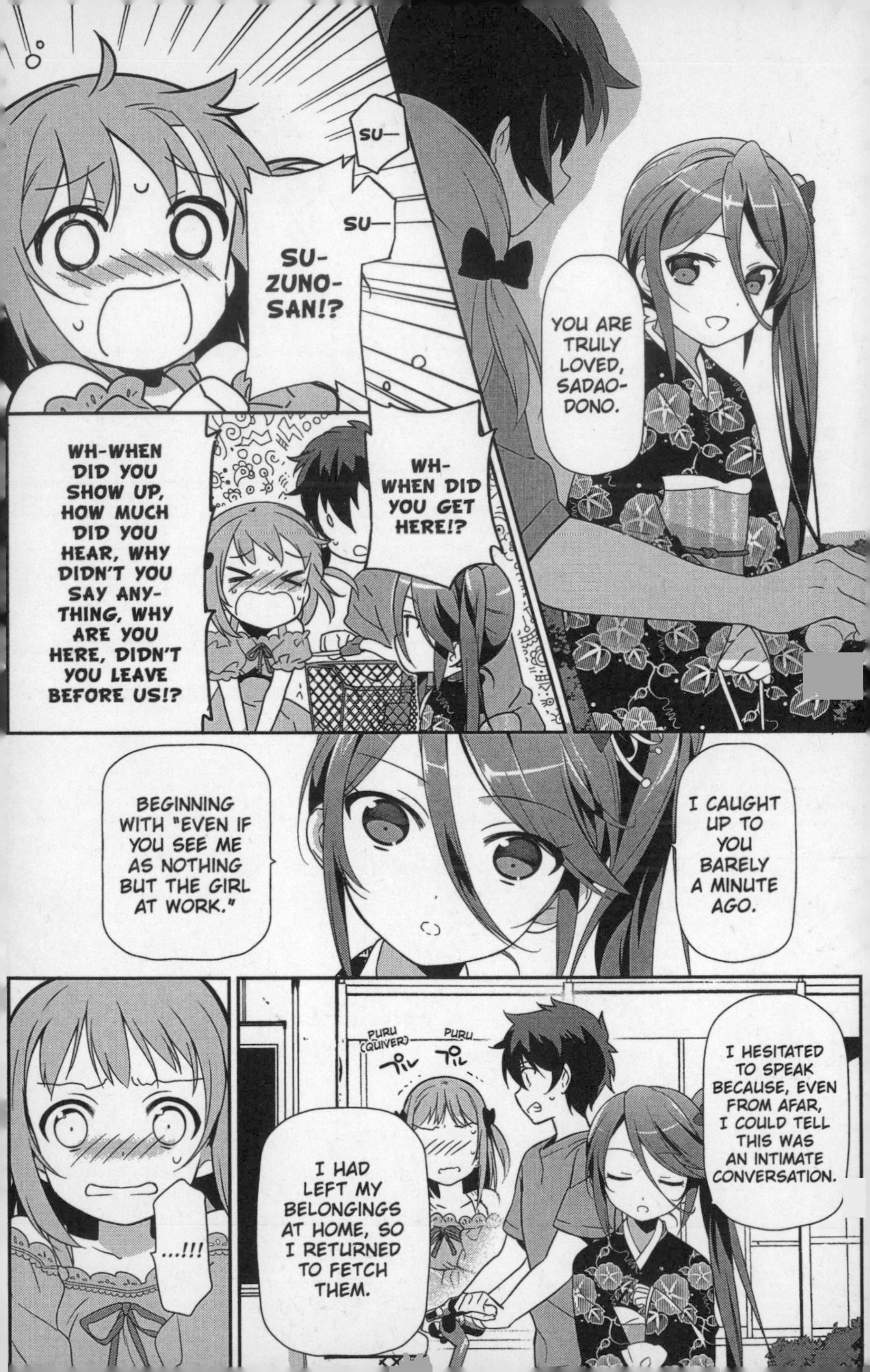
YOU ARE TRULY LOVED, SADAO-DONO.
SU—
SU—
SU-ZUNO-SAN!?
WH-WHEN DID YOU GET HERE!?
WH-WHEN DID YOU SHOW UP, HOW MUCH DID YOU HEAR, WHY DIDN'T YOU SAY ANY-THING, WHY ARE YOU HERE, DIDN'T YOU LEAVE BEFORE US!?
I CAUGHT UP TO YOU BARELY A MINUTE AGO.
BEGINNING WITH "EVEN IF YOU SEE ME AS NOTHING BUT THE GIRL AT WORK."
I HESITATED TO SPEAK BECAUSE, EVEN FROM AFAR, I COULD TELL THIS WAS AN INTIMATE CONVERSATION.
PURU
PURU (QUIVER)
I HAD LEFT MY BELONGINGS AT HOME, SO I RETURNED TO FETCH THEM.
...!!!

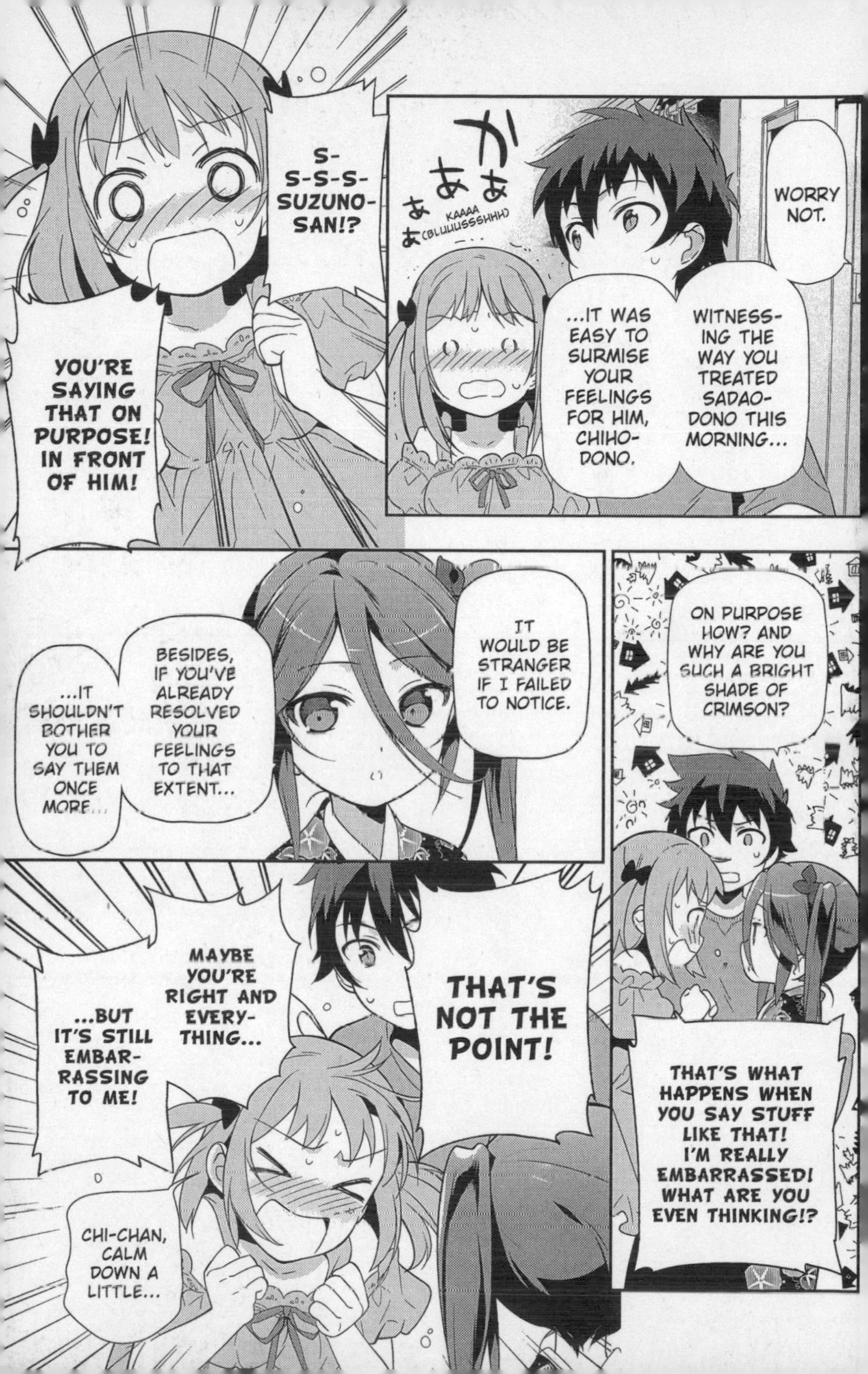

WORRY NOT.
WITNESSING THE WAY YOU TREATED SADAO-DONO THIS MORNING...
...IT WAS EASY TO SURMISE YOUR FEELINGS FOR HIM, CHIHO-DONO.
かぁぁぁ
KAAAA (BLUUUSSSHHH)
S-S-S-S-SUZUNO-SAN!?
YOU'RE SAYING THAT ON PURPOSE! IN FRONT OF HIM!
ON PURPOSE HOW? AND WHY ARE YOU SUCH A BRIGHT SHADE OF CRIMSON?
THAT'S WHAT HAPPENS WHEN YOU SAY STUFF LIKE THAT! I'M REALLY EMBARRASSED! WHAT ARE YOU EVEN THINKING!?
IT WOULD BE STRANGER IF I FAILED TO NOTICE.
BESIDES, IF YOU'VE ALREADY RESOLVED YOUR FEELINGS TO THAT EXTENT...
...IT SHOULDN'T BOTHER YOU TO SAY THEM ONCE MORE...
THAT'S NOT THE POINT!
MAYBE YOU'RE RIGHT AND EVERYTHING...
...BUT IT'S STILL EMBARRASSING TO ME!
CHI-CHAN, CALM DOWN A LITTLE...

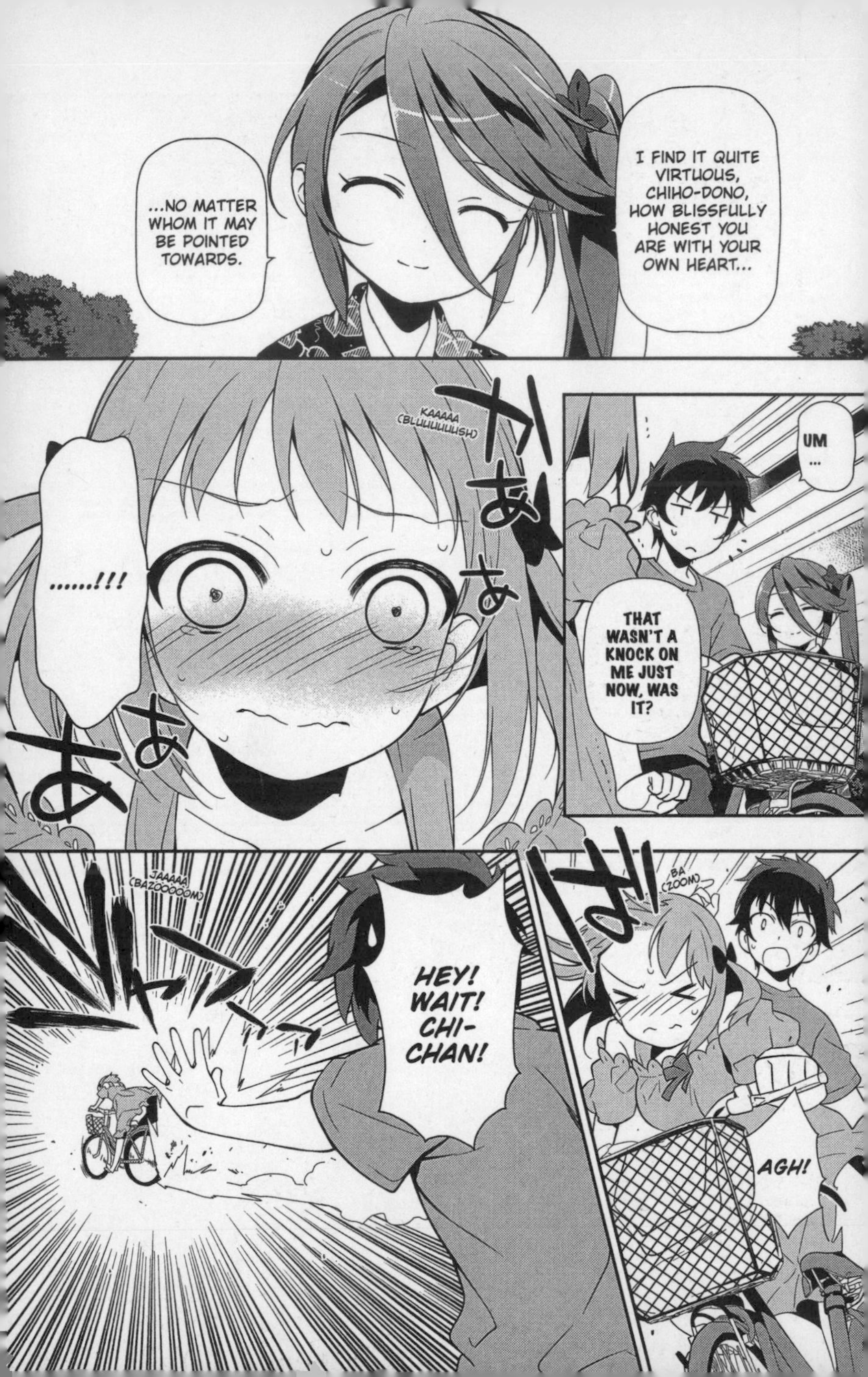
I FIND IT QUITE VIRTUOUS, CHIHO-DONO, HOW BLISSFULLY HONEST YOU ARE WITH YOUR OWN HEART...
...NO MATTER WHOM IT MAY BE POINTED TOWARDS.
UM ...
THAT WASN'T A KNOCK ON ME JUST NOW, WAS IT?
KAAAAA (BLUUUUUUSH)
......!!!
BA (ZOOM)
AGH!
JAAAAA (BAZOOOOOM)
HEY! WAIT! CHI-CHAN!

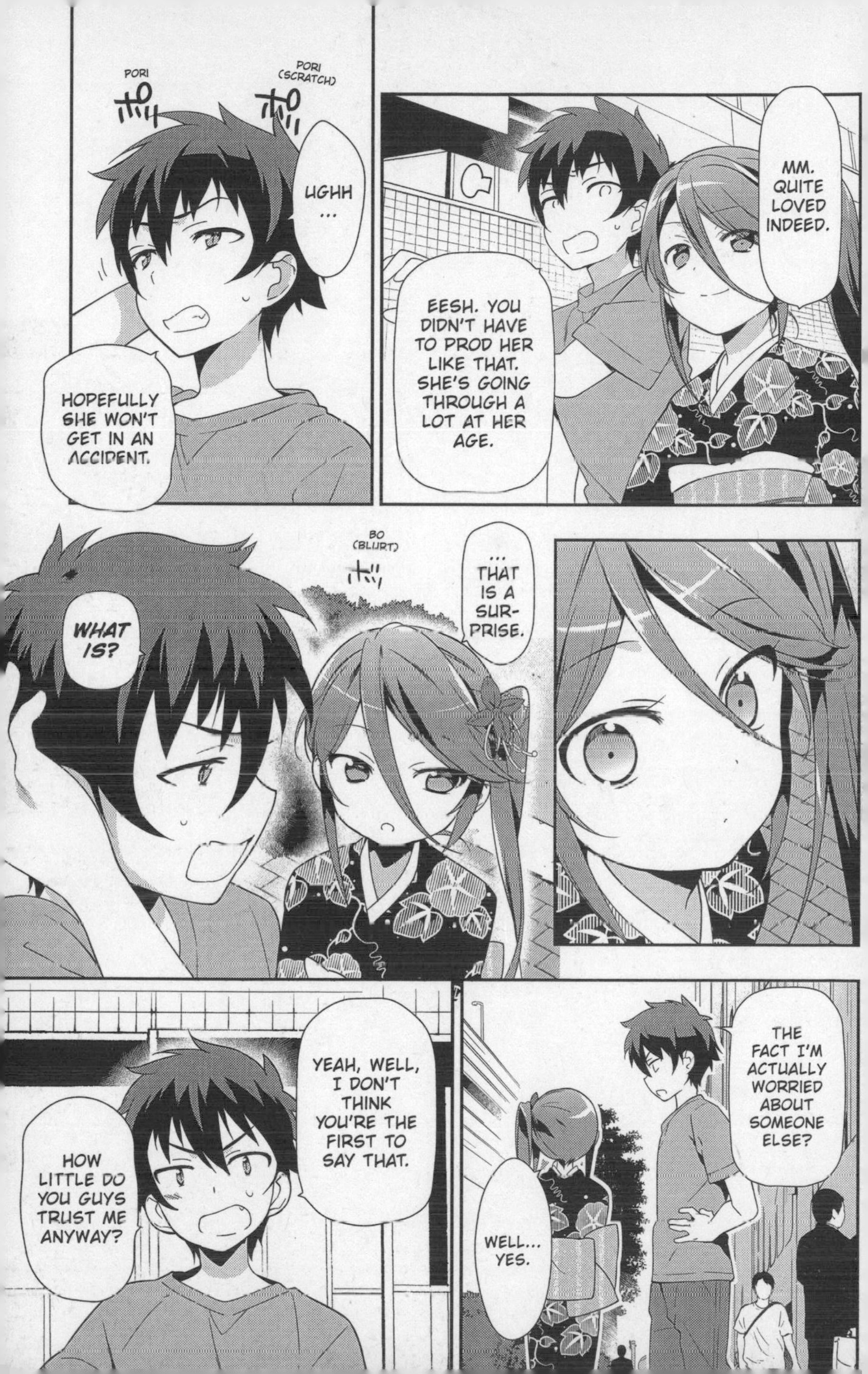
MM. QUITE LOVED INDEED.
EESH. YOU DIDN'T HAVE TO PROD HER LIKE THAT. SHE'S GOING THROUGH A LOT AT HER AGE.
PORI (SCRATCH)
PORI
UGHH ...
HOPEFULLY SHE WON'T GET IN AN ACCIDENT.
... THAT IS A SUR-PRISE.
BO (BLURT)
WHAT IS?
THE FACT I'M ACTUALLY WORRIED ABOUT SOMEONE ELSE?
WELL... YES.
YEAH, WELL, I DON'T THINK YOU'RE THE FIRST TO SAY THAT.
HOW LITTLE DO YOU GUYS TRUST ME ANYWAY?

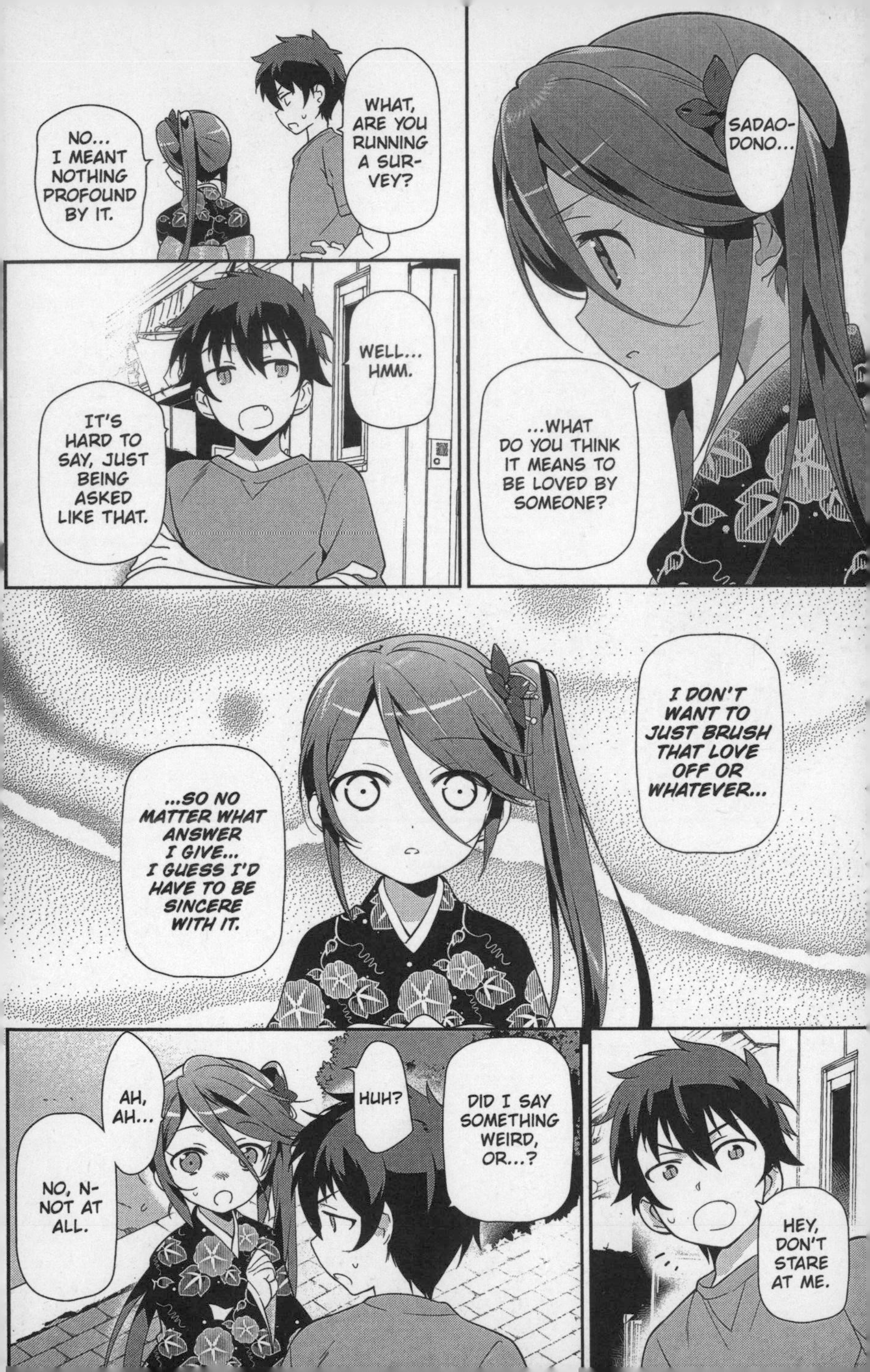
SADAO-DONO...
...WHAT DO YOU THINK IT MEANS TO BE LOVED BY SOMEONE?
WHAT, ARE YOU RUNNING A SUR-VEY?
NO... I MEANT NOTHING PROFOUND BY IT.
WELL... HMM.
IT'S HARD TO SAY, JUST BEING ASKED LIKE THAT.
I DON'T WANT TO JUST BRUSH THAT LOVE OFF OR WHATEVER...
...SO NO MATTER WHAT ANSWER I GIVE... I GUESS I'D HAVE TO BE SINCERE WITH IT.
HEY, DON'T STARE AT ME.
DID I SAY SOMETHING WEIRD, OR...?
HUH?
AH, AH...
NO, N-NOT AT ALL.

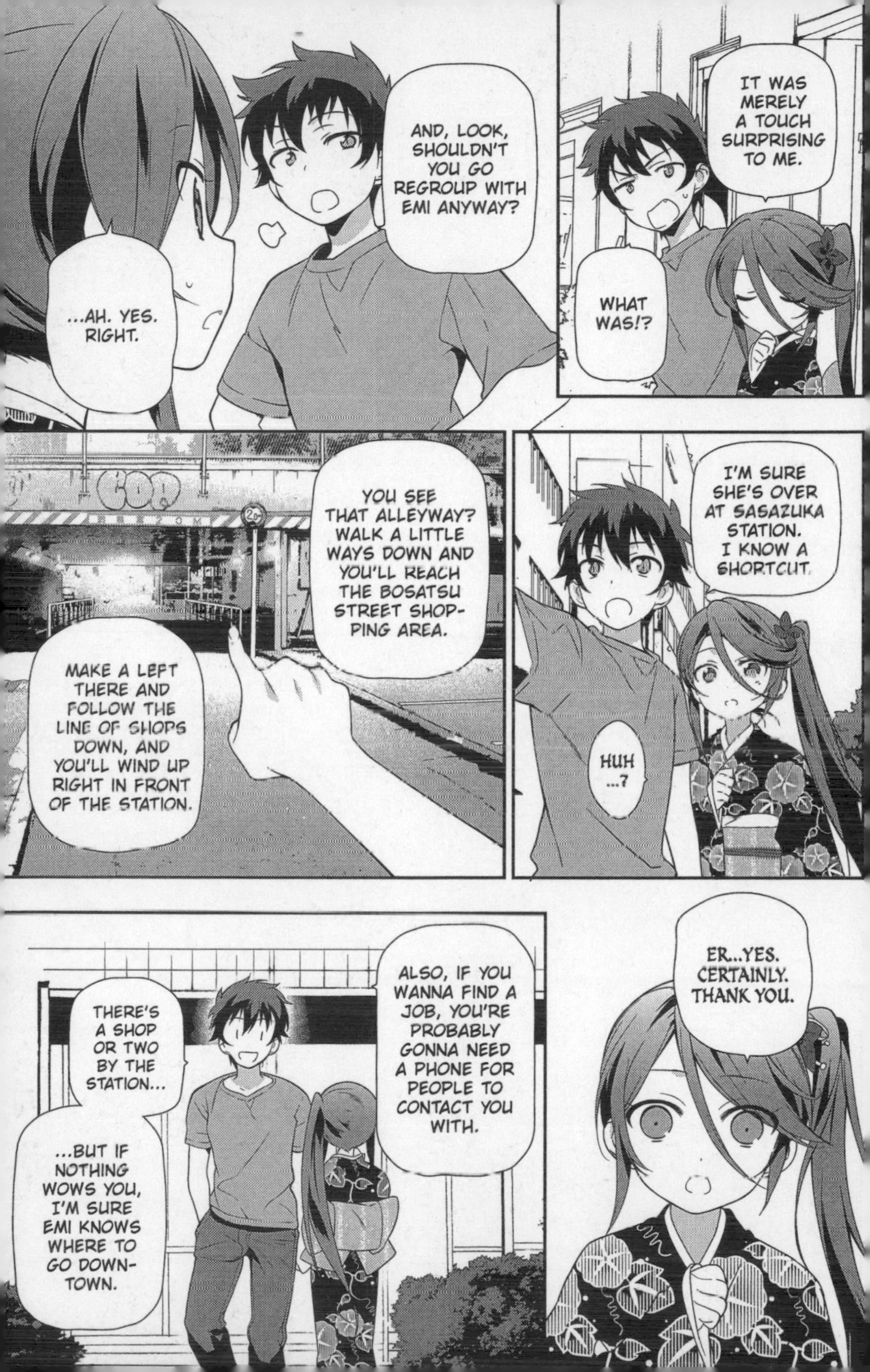
IT WAS MERELY A TOUCH SURPRISING TO ME.
WHAT WAS!?
AND, LOOK, SHOULDN'T YOU GO REGROUP WITH EMI ANYWAY?
...AH. YES. RIGHT.
I'M SURE SHE'S OVER AT SASAZUKA STATION. I KNOW A SHORTCUT.
HUH ...?
YOU SEE THAT ALLEYWAY? WALK A LITTLE WAYS DOWN AND YOU'LL REACH THE BOSATSU STREET SHOP-PING AREA.
MAKE A LEFT THERE AND FOLLOW THE LINE OF SHOPS DOWN, AND YOU'LL WIND UP RIGHT IN FRONT OF THE STATION.
ER...YES. CERTAINLY. THANK YOU.
ALSO, IF YOU WANNA FIND A JOB, YOU'RE PROBABLY GONNA NEED A PHONE FOR PEOPLE TO CONTACT YOU WITH.
THERE'S A SHOP OR TWO BY THE STATION...
...BUT IF NOTHING WOWS YOU, I'M SURE EMI KNOWS WHERE TO GO DOWN-TOWN.

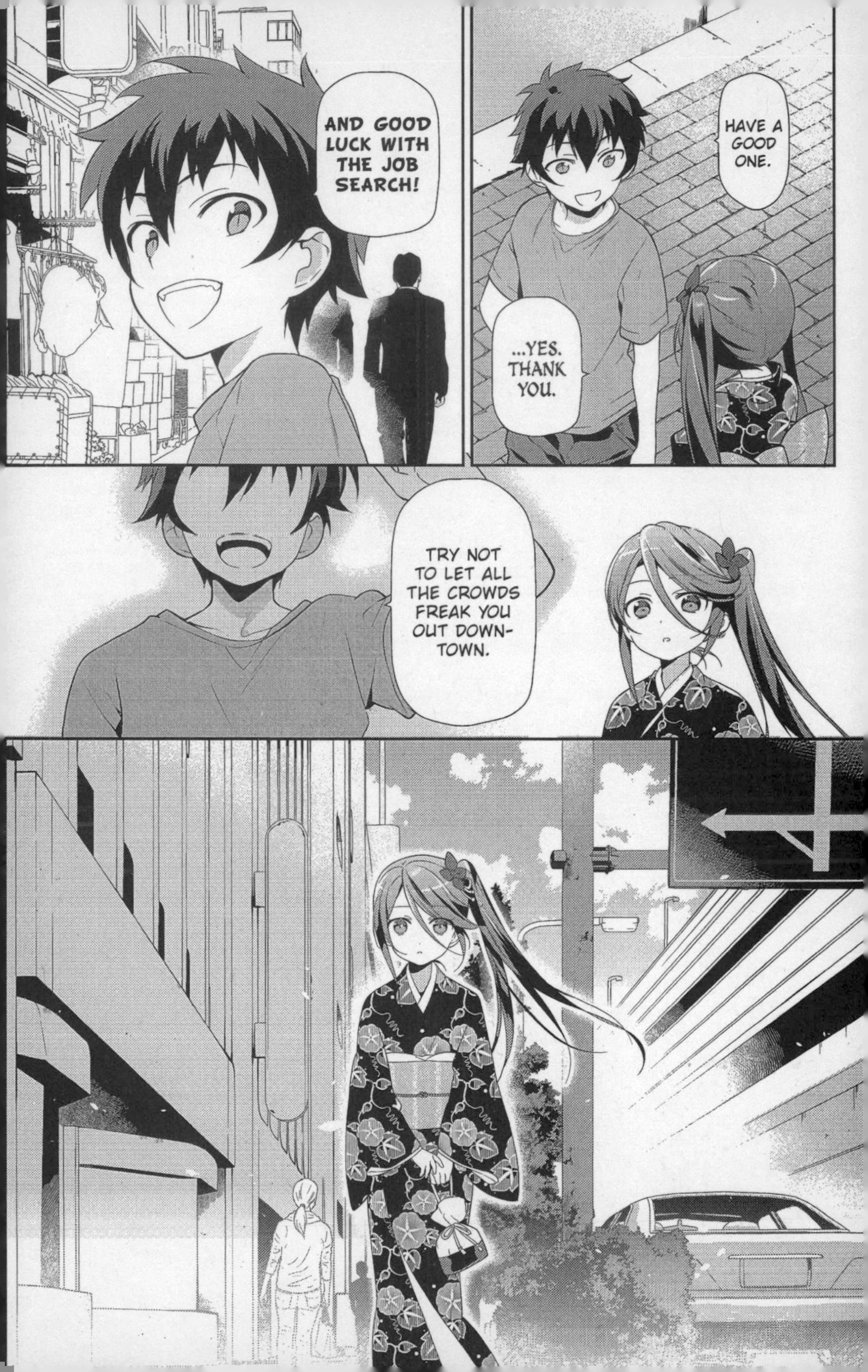
HAVE A GOOD ONE.
...YES. THANK YOU.
AND GOOD LUCK WITH THE JOB SEARCH!
TRY NOT TO LET ALL THE CROWDS FREAK YOU OUT DOWN-TOWN.

Chiho
Sasaki

TRANSLATION NOTES

COMMON HONORIFICS

No honorific: indicates familiarity or closeness; if used without permission or reason, addressing someone in this manner would constitute an insult.
-san: the japanese equivalent of mr./Mrs./Miss. If a situation calls for politeness, this is the fail-safe honorific.
-sama: conveys great respect; may also indicate that the social status of the speaker is lower than that of the addressee.
-kun: used most often when referring to boys, this indicates affection or familiarity. Occasionally used by older men among their peers, but it may also be used by anyone referring to a person of lower standing.
-chan: an affectionate honorific indicating familiarity used mostly in reference to girls; also used in reference to cute persons or animals of either gender.
-dono: indicates respect for the addressee.

PAGE 7
Yakiniku: Grilled meat.
Galbi: Korean-stye marinated grilled meat.
Tontoro: Berkshire pork.

PAGE 15
Horumon: Intestines.

PAGE 107
Umeboshi: Pickled salt plums.

PAGE 111
Osechi: Traditional foods generally eaten at New Year's in Japan.

PAGE 136
"She calls him 'Sadao'...!": In Japan, calling someone by their first name tends to signify a great deal of closeness, hence Chiyo's surprise and anguish.

PAGE 144
Yukata: A more casual form of the traditional kimono, which is usually worn in the summer.

PAGE 174
"Stickers? Like potstickers!?": In Japanese, the original joke is the fact that the word for sticker, "*shiiru,*" sounds very similar to the word for soup, "*shiru,*" hence Suzuno's misunderstanding.

THE DEVIL IS A PART-TIMER!

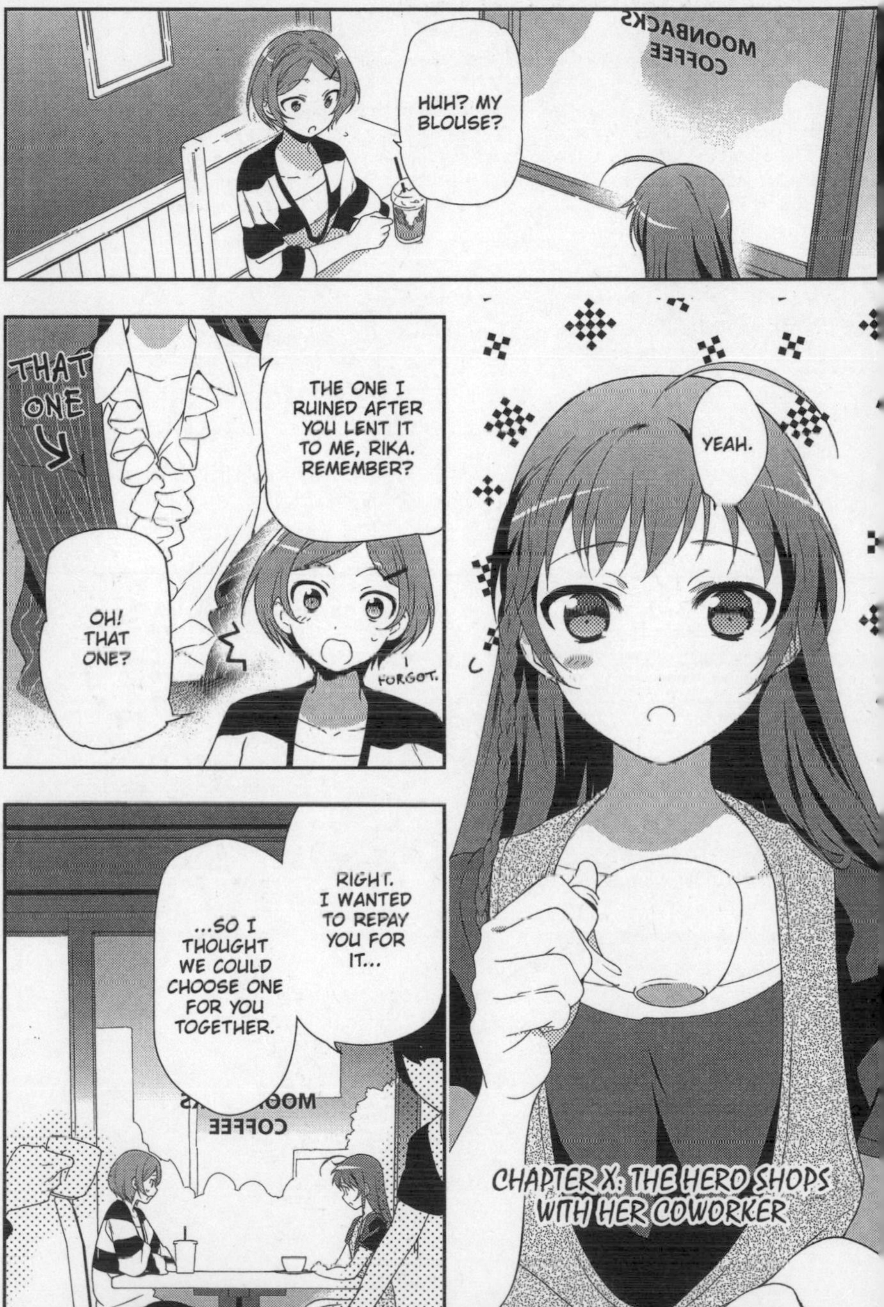
MOONBACKS COFFEE
HUH? MY BLOUSE?
YEAH.
CHAPTER X: THE HERO SHOPS WITH HER COWORKER
THE ONE I RUINED AFTER YOU LENT IT TO ME, RIKA. REMEMBER?
THAT ONE
OH! THAT ONE?
I FORGOT.
RIGHT. I WANTED TO REPAY YOU FOR IT...
...SO I THOUGHT WE COULD CHOOSE ONE FOR YOU TOGETHER.

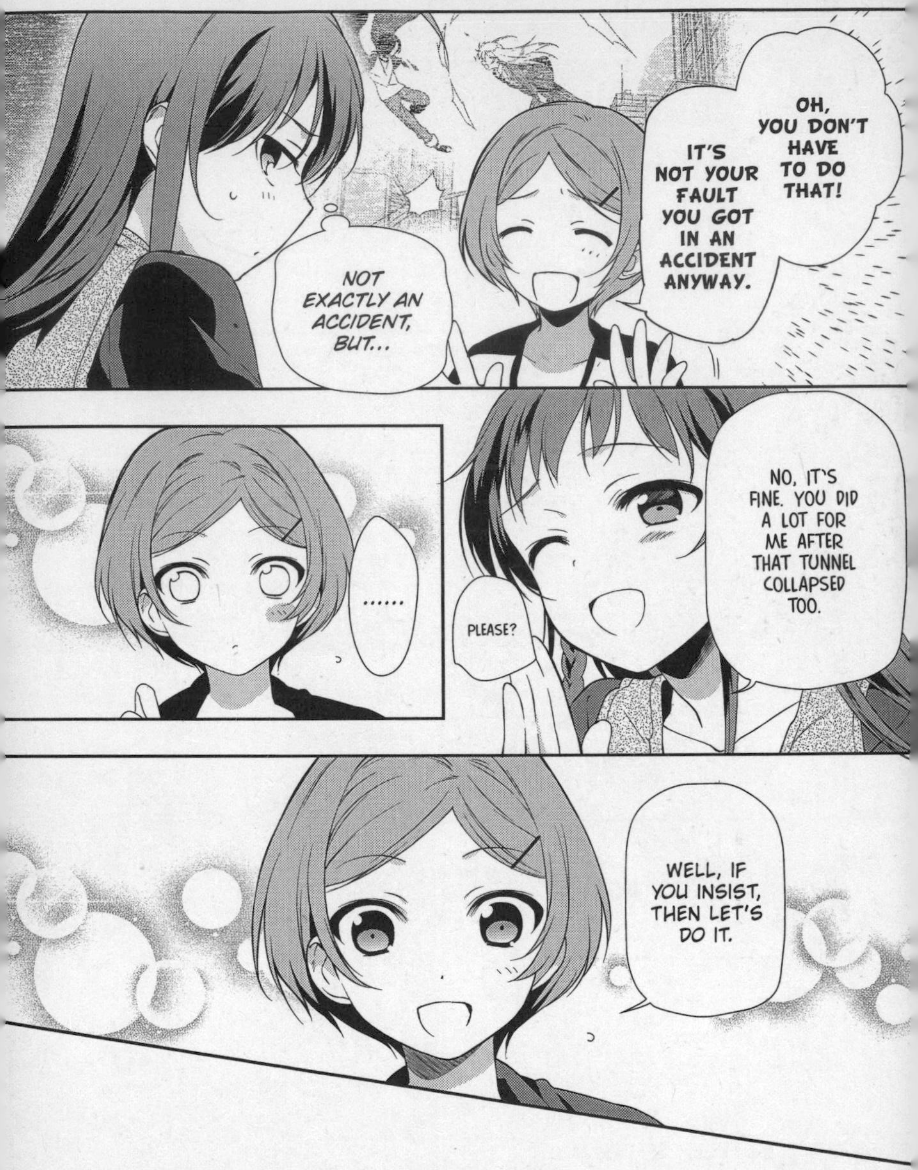
OH, YOU DON'T HAVE TO DO THAT!
IT'S NOT YOUR FAULT YOU GOT IN AN ACCIDENT ANYWAY.
NOT EXACTLY AN ACCIDENT, BUT...
NO, IT'S FINE. YOU DID A LOT FOR ME AFTER THAT TUNNEL COLLAPSED TOO.
PLEASE?
....
WELL, IF YOU INSIST, THEN LET'S DO IT.

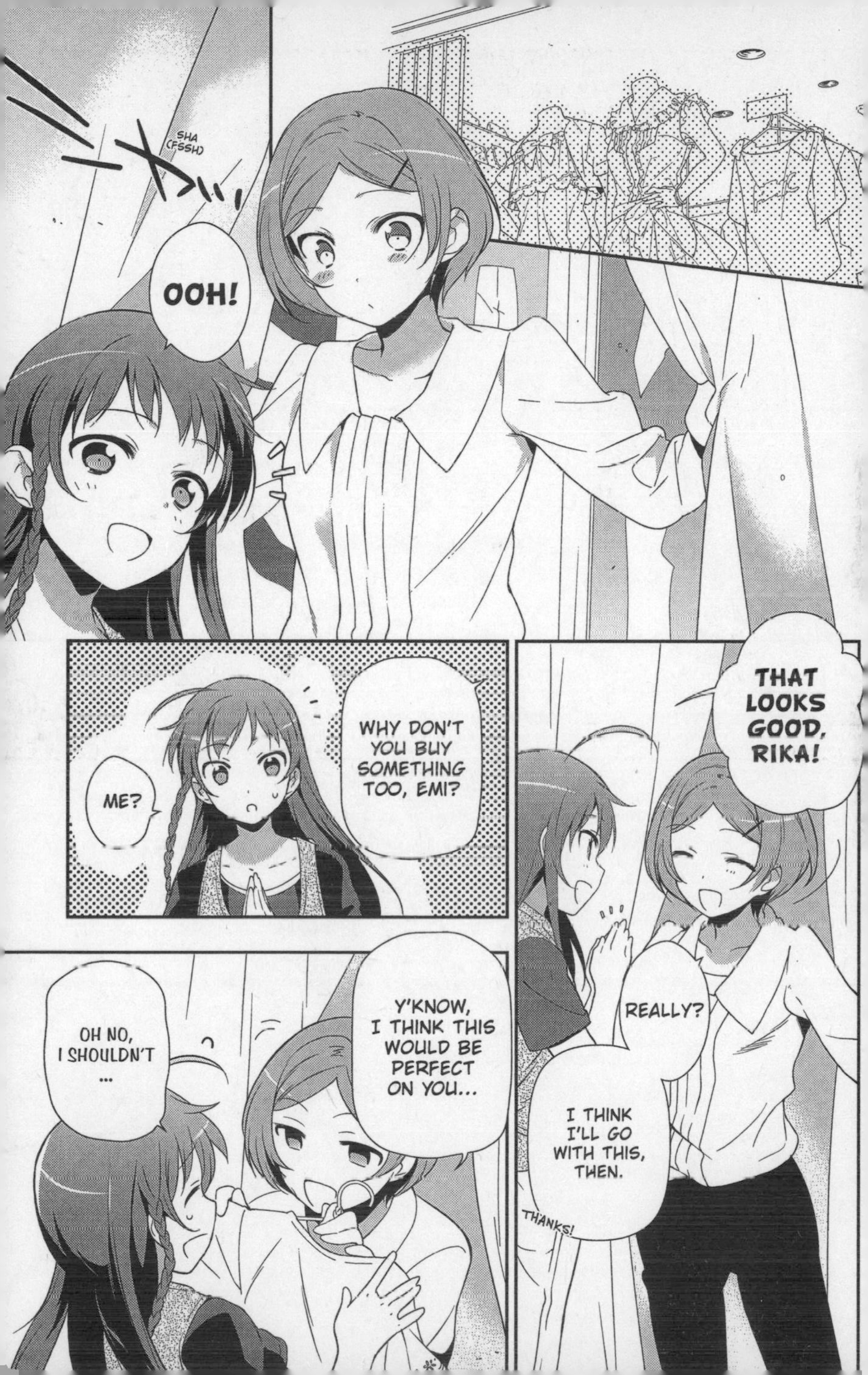
SHA (FSSH)
OOH!
THAT LOOKS GOOD, RIKA!
REALLY?
I THINK I'LL GO WITH THIS, THEN.
THANKS!
WHY DON'T YOU BUY SOMETHING TOO, EMI?
ME?
Y'KNOW, I THINK THIS WOULD BE PERFECT ON YOU...
OH NO, I SHOULDN'T ...

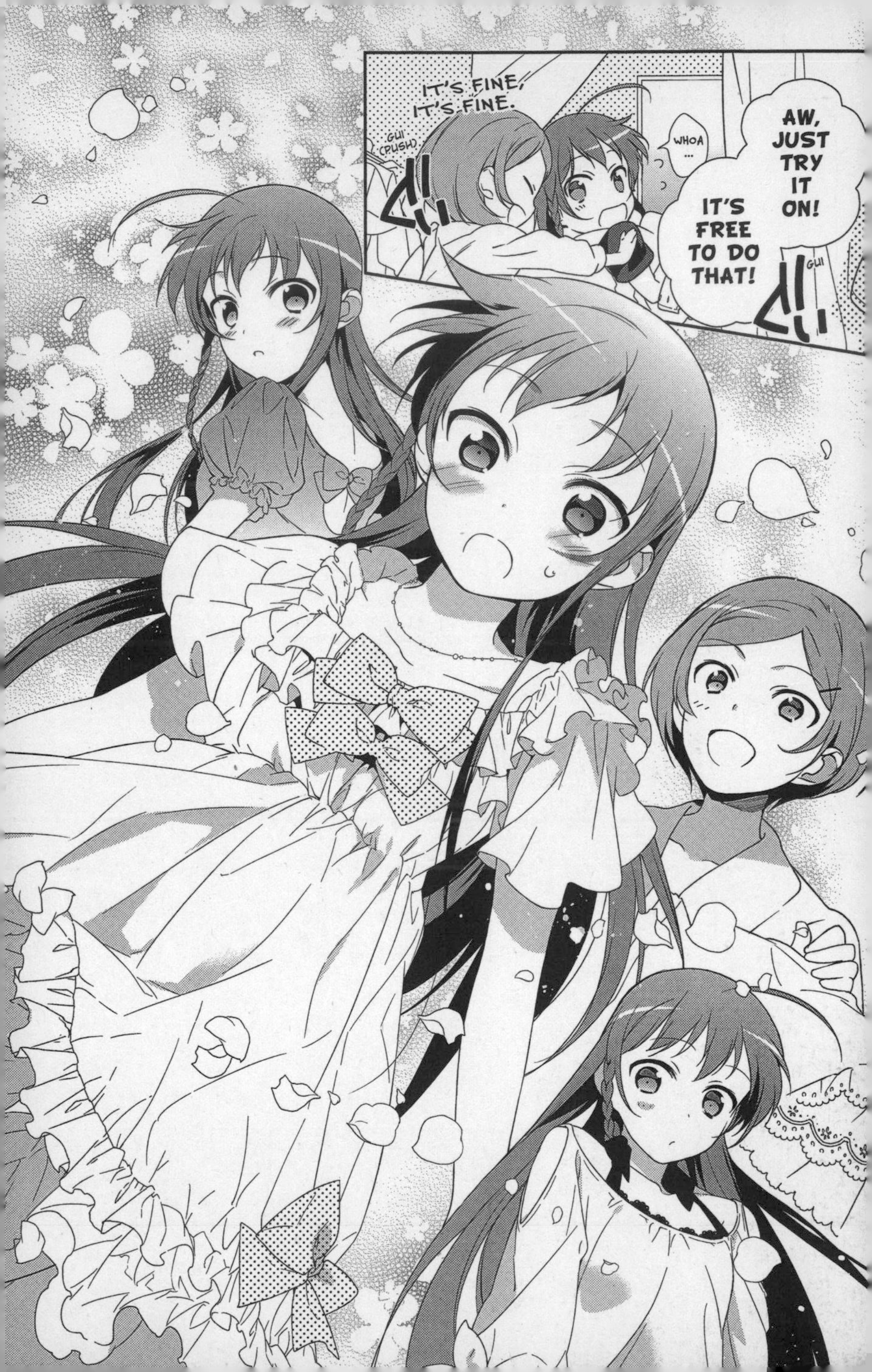
AW, JUST TRY IT ON!
IT'S FREE TO DO THAT!
GUI
WHOA ...
IT'S FINE, IT'S FINE.
GUI (PUSH)

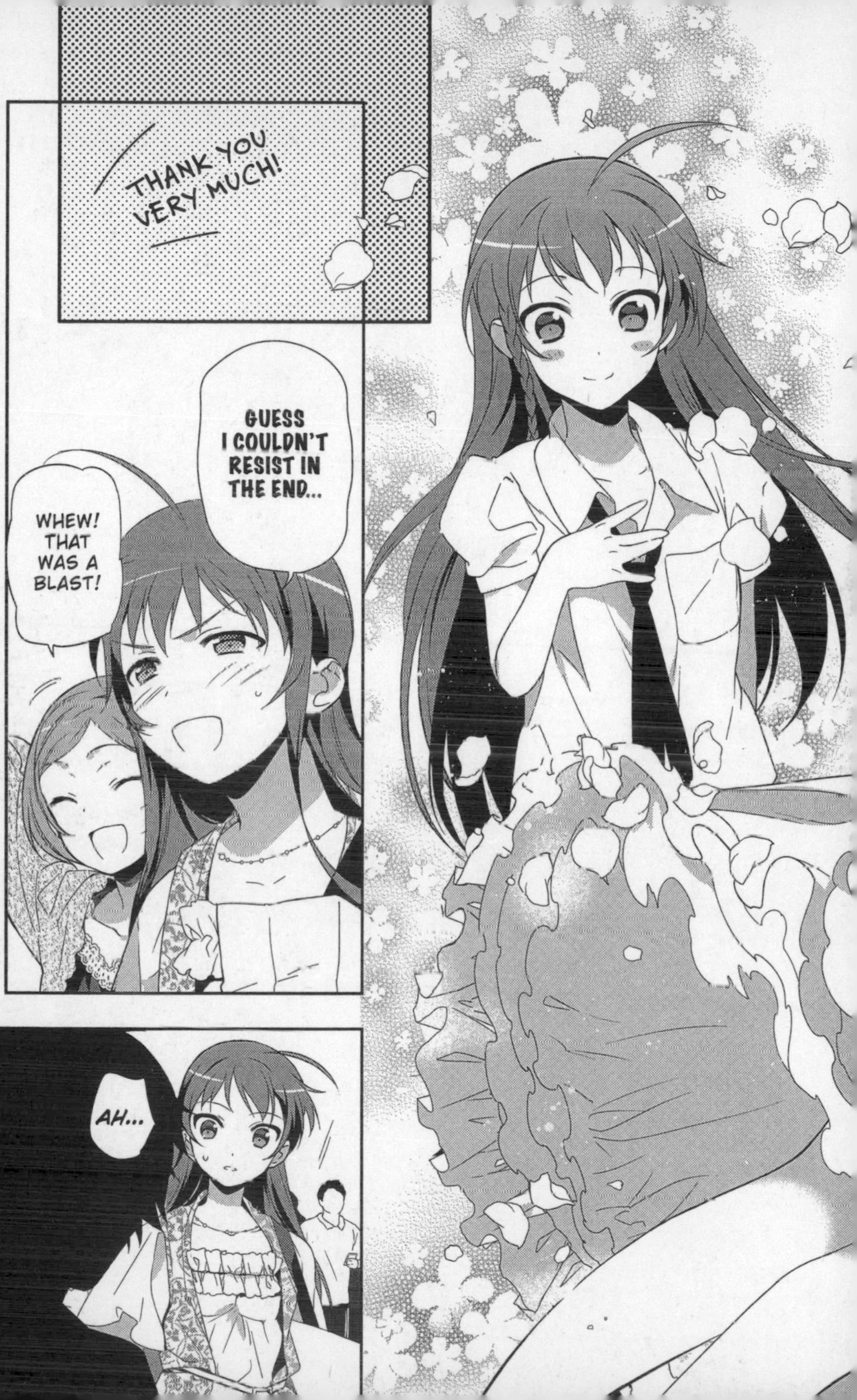
THANK YOU VERY MUCH!
GUESS I COULDN'T RESIST IN THE END...
WHEW! THAT WAS A BLAST!
AH...

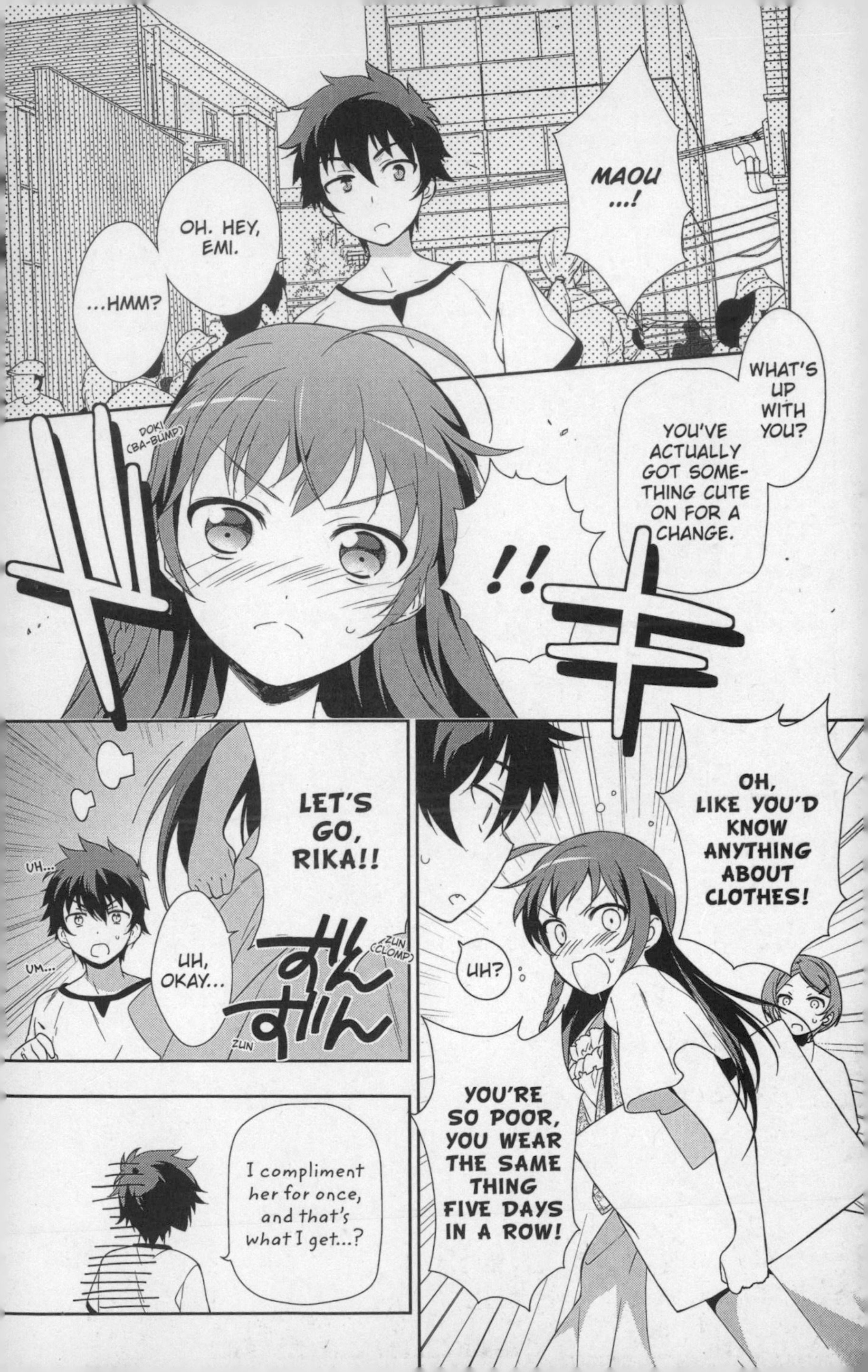
MAOU ...!
OH. HEY, EMI.
...HMM?
WHAT'S UP WITH YOU?
YOU'VE ACTUALLY GOT SOME-THING CUTE ON FOR A CHANGE.
!!
DOKI (BA-BUMP)
OH, LIKE YOU'D KNOW ANYTHING ABOUT CLOTHES!
UH?
YOU'RE SO POOR, YOU WEAR THE SAME THING FIVE DAYS IN A ROW!
LET'S GO, RIKA!!
ZUN (CLOMP)
UH, OKAY...
UH...
UM...
ZUN
I compliment her for once, and that's what I get...?

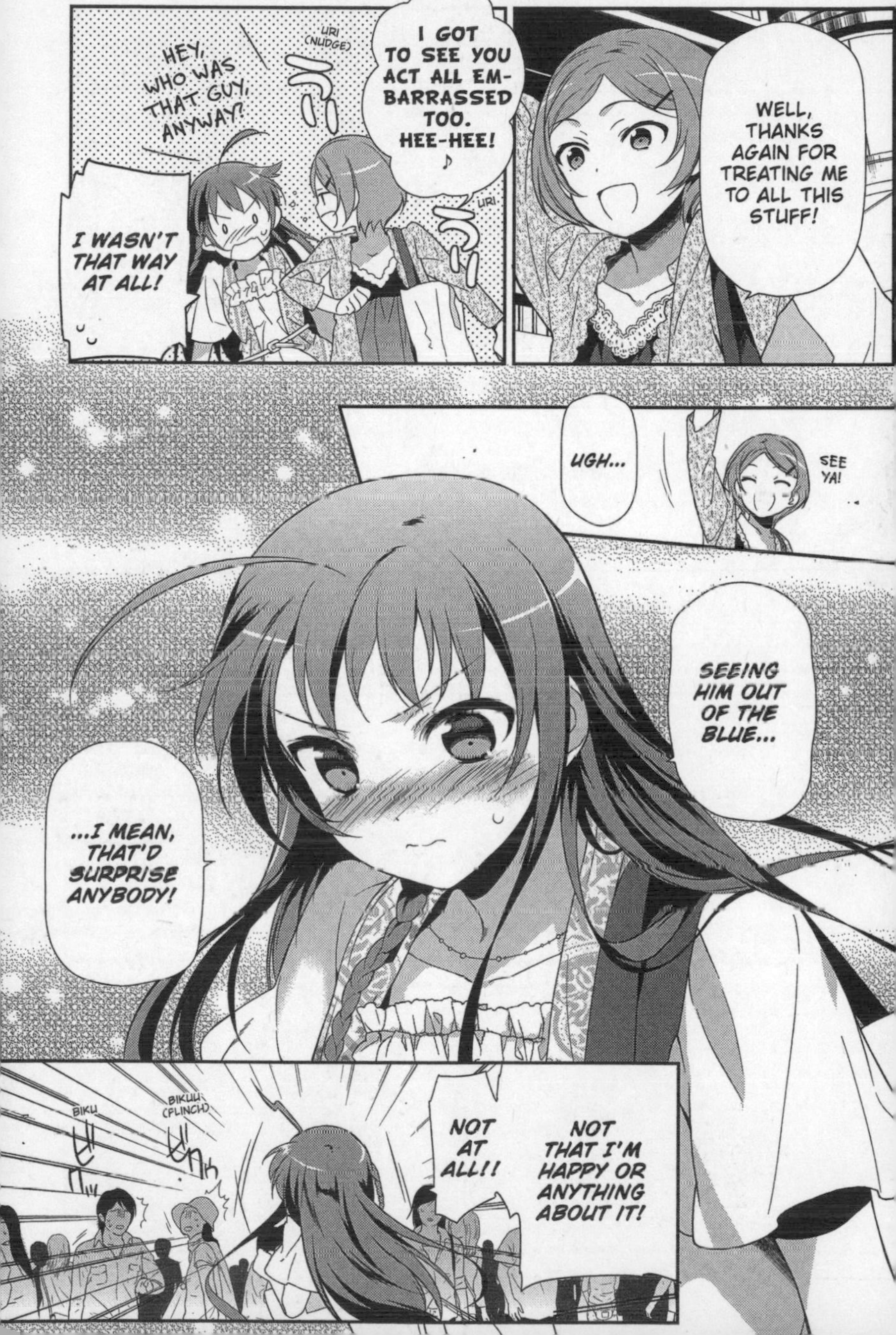
WELL, THANKS AGAIN FOR TREATING ME TO ALL THIS STUFF!
I GOT TO SEE YOU ACT ALL EMBARRASSED TOO. HEE-HEE! ♪
URI (NUDGE)
URI
HEY, WHO WAS THAT GUY, ANYWAY?
I WASN'T THAT WAY AT ALL!
SEE YA!
UGH...
SEEING HIM OUT OF THE BLUE...
...I MEAN, THAT'D SURPRISE ANYBODY!
NOT THAT I'M HAPPY OR ANYTHING ABOUT IT!
NOT AT ALL!!
BIKUU (FLINCH)
BIKU

CHAPTER X: THE HERO USES A PHOTO STICKER BOOTH

TITLE PAGE COLOR ART: BEHIND THE SCENES

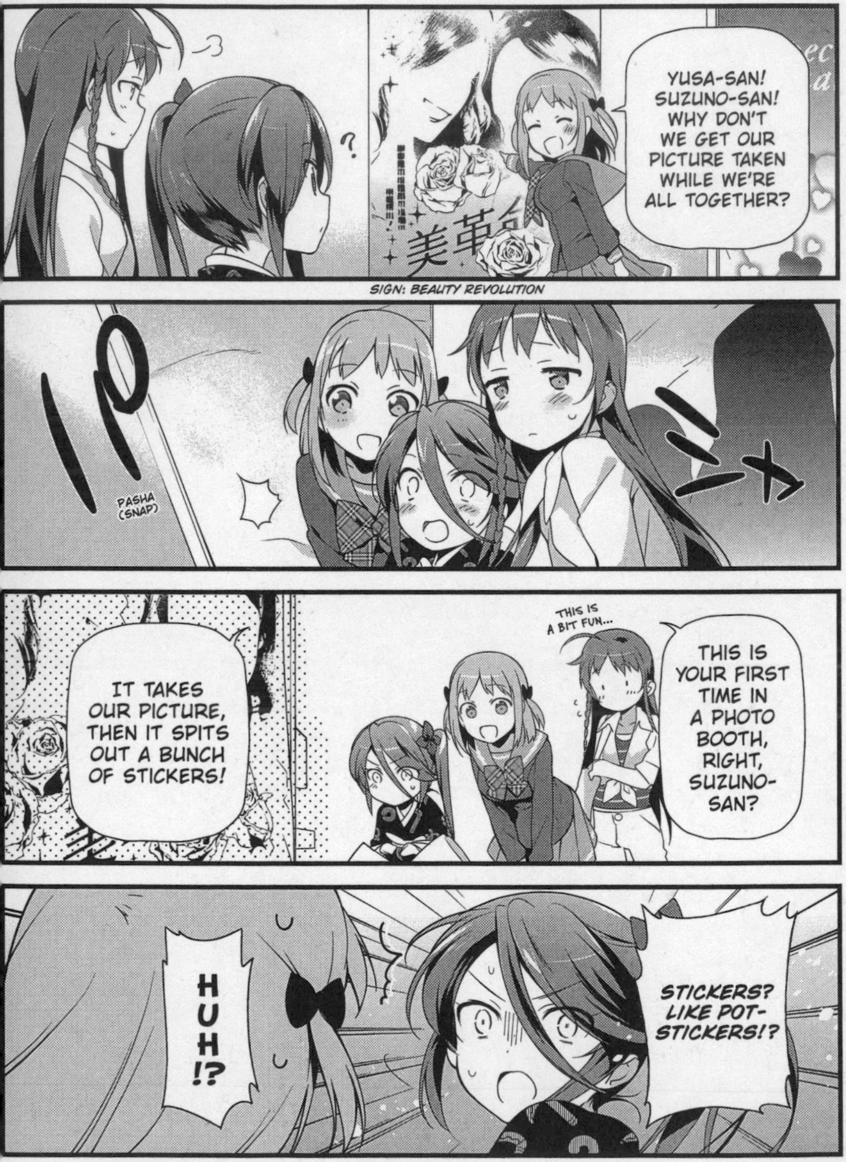
YUSA-SAN! SUZUNO-SAN! WHY DON'T WE GET OUR PICTURE TAKEN WHILE WE'RE ALL TOGETHER?
SIGN: BEAUTY REVOLUTION
PASHA (SNAP)
THIS IS YOUR FIRST TIME IN A PHOTO BOOTH, RIGHT, SUZUNO-SAN?
THIS IS A BIT FUN...
IT TAKES OUR PICTURE, THEN IT SPITS OUT A BUNCH OF STICKERS!
STICKERS? LIKE POT-STICKERS!?
HUH!?

OLD FAMILY PHOTOS

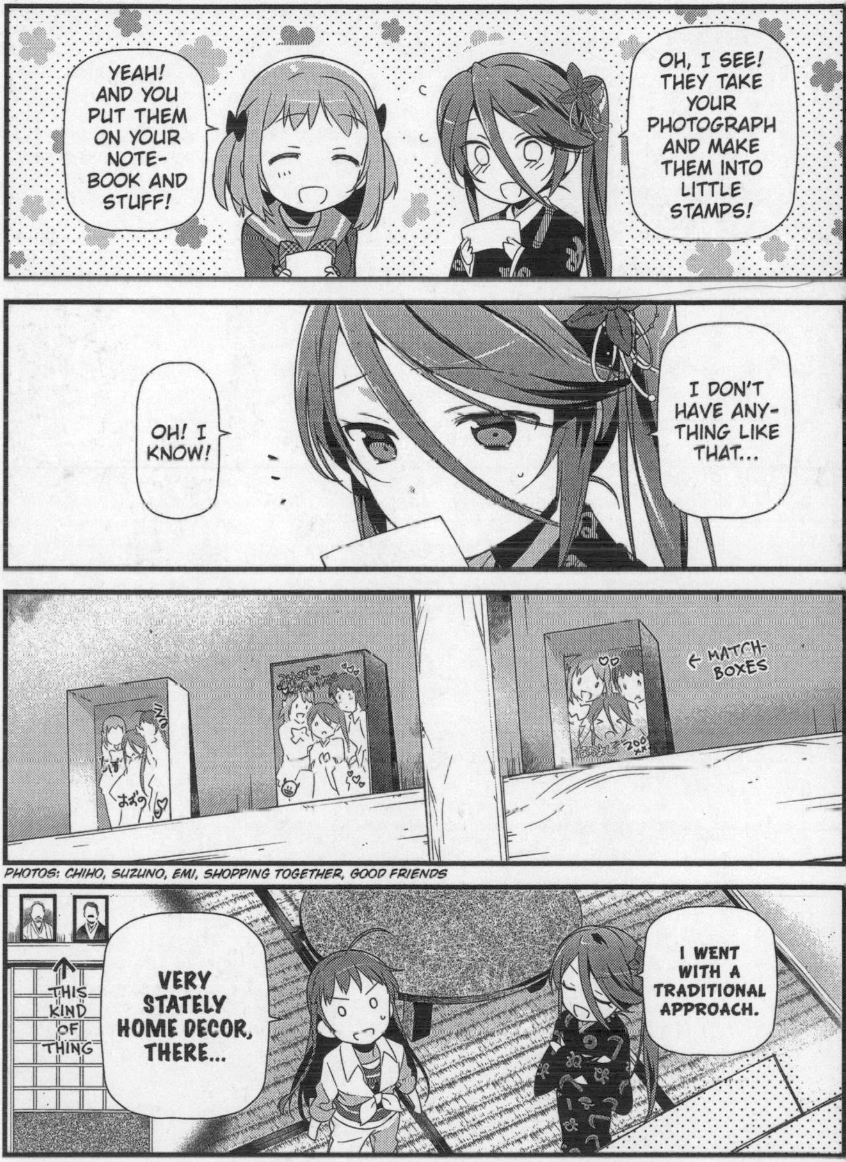
OH, I SEE! THEY TAKE YOUR PHOTOGRAPH AND MAKE THEM INTO LITTLE STAMPS!
YEAH! AND YOU PUT THEM ON YOUR NOTE-BOOK AND STUFF!
I DON'T HAVE ANY-THING LIKE THAT...
OH! I KNOW!
← MATCH-BOXES
PHOTOS: CHIHO, SUZUNO, EMI, SHOPPING TOGETHER, GOOD FRIENDS
I WENT WITH A TRADITIONAL APPROACH.
VERY STATELY HOME DECOR, THERE...
↑ THIS KIND OF THING

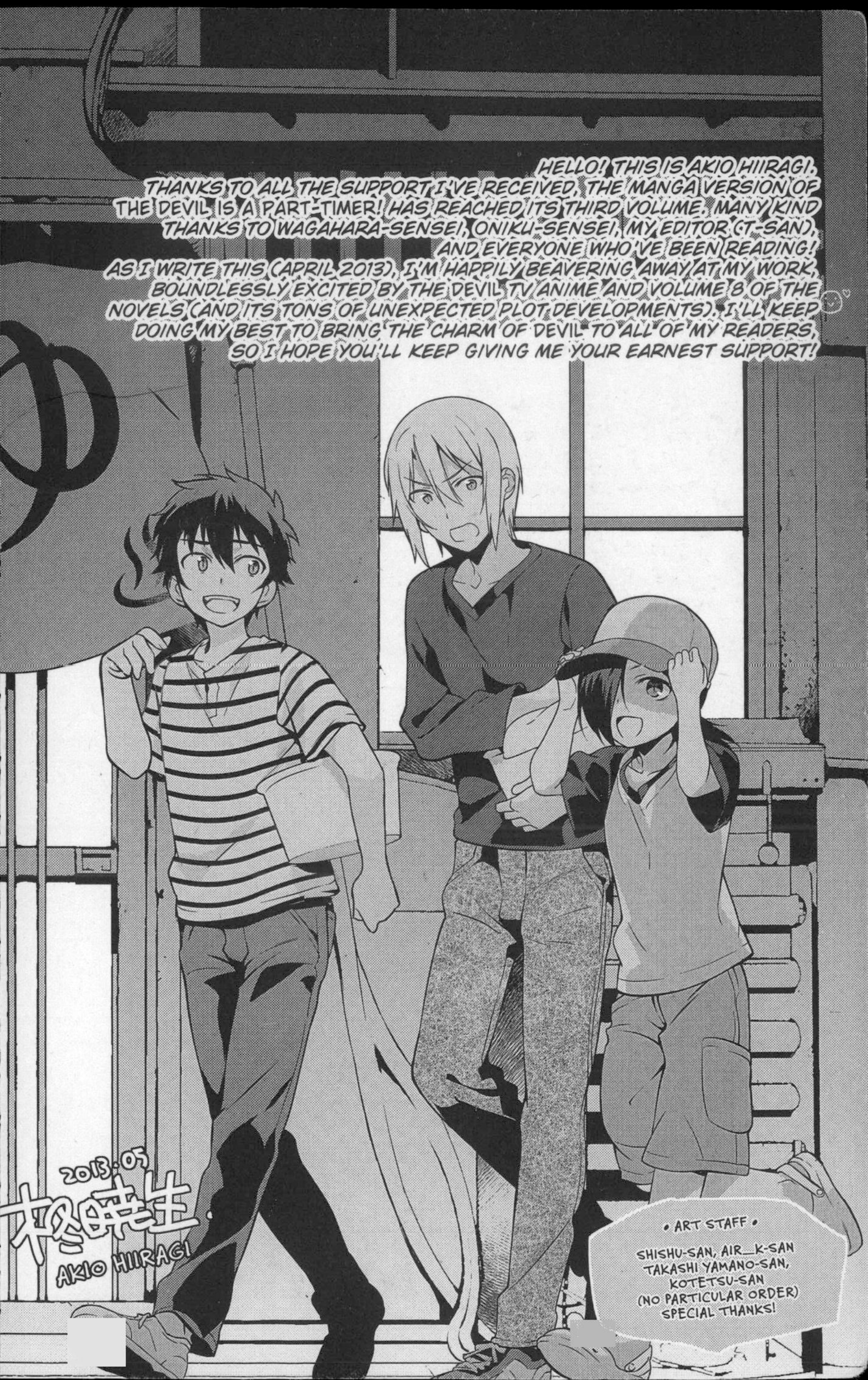
HELLO! THIS IS AKIO HIIRAGI.
THANKS TO ALL THE SUPPORT I'VE RECEIVED, THE MANGA VERSION OF THE DEVIL IS A PART-TIMER! HAS REACHED ITS THIRD VOLUME. MANY KIND THANKS TO WAGAHARA-SENSEI, ONIKU-SENSEI, MY EDITOR (T-SAN), AND EVERYONE WHO'VE BEEN READING!
AS I WRITE THIS (APRIL 2013), I'M HAPPILY BEAVERING AWAY AT MY WORK, BOUNDLESSLY EXCITED BY THE DEVIL TV ANIME AND VOLUME 8 OF THE NOVELS (AND ITS TONS OF UNEXPECTED PLOT DEVELOPMENTS). I'LL KEEP DOING MY BEST TO BRING THE CHARM OF DEVIL TO ALL OF MY READERS, SO I HOPE YOU'LL KEEP GIVING ME YOUR EARNEST SUPPORT!
2013.05
柊暁生
AKIO HIIRAGI
• ART STAFF •
SHISHU-SAN, AIR_K-SAN
TAKASHI YAMANO-SAN,
KOTETSU-SAN
(NO PARTICULAR ORDER)
SPECIAL THANKS!

HELLO TO EVERYONE WHO'VE PICKED UP THE THIRD VOLUME OF *THE DEVIL IS A PART-TIMER!* MANGA IN THEIR HANDS. DID YOU TAKE A GOOD LOOK AT THE COVER AND THE COLOR ART INSIDE? IF YOU ASK ME, THEY SHOULD STICK THAT ART INSIDE DICTIONARIES AND ENCYCLOPEDIAS UNDER THE TERM "TRADITIONAL JAPANESE WOMAN" FOR ILLUSTRATION. DON'T YOU THINK SO? GOOD. BECAUSE I DO.

THIS IS THE FIRST TIME I'VE WRITTEN A MESSAGE FOR THE MANGA VERSION. I'M SATOSHI WAGAHARA, BY THE WAY, WRITER OF THE *DEVIL IS A PART-TIMER!* NOVELS FOR DENGEKI.

ANY SO-CALLED WRITER HAS SOME KIND OF IDEA, WHETHER VAGUE OR WELL DEFINED, OF THE SCENE HE'S PICTURING AS HE ATTEMPTS TO PUT IT INTO WORDS. HOWEVER, SEEING THOSE SCENES MADE INTO REAL-LIFE ART BY THE HAND OF ANOTHER RESULTS IN COMPLETELY NEW DISCOVERIES FOR ME. EVEN THOUGH IT'S THE SAME STORY, IT'S A COMPLETELY DIFFERENT ENTRY POINT TO IT, PROVIDING ITS OWN WEALTH OF NEW ATTRACTIONS AND CHARMS.

THE *DEVIL* WORLD DRAWN BY AKIO HIIRAGI-SAN FEATURES THE SAME STORY AS THE NOVELS, BUT IT'S ALSO A WONDERFUL NEW WORLD, ONE WITH ITS VERY OWN PEOPLE, SETTING, AND TIMEFRAME.

WHETHER YOU'VE BEEN READING THE NOVELS, WATCHING THE ANIME CURRENTLY AIRING IN THE SPRING OF 2013, OR GETTING YOUR FIRST INTRODUCTION TO *DEVIL IS A PART-TIMER!* VIA THIS MANGA, IT IS MY EARNEST HOPE THAT THE COMIC VERSION PROVIDES YOU WITH A WHOLE NEW OUTLOOK INTO THE CHARMS OF THIS WORLD.

AS A CONCRETE EXAMPLE OF THAT, LOOK NO FURTHER THAN THIS VOLUME'S COVER. WHEN I LOOKED AT THE GALLEY COPY, I WAVED THE BOOK AROUND AS I TORE ACROSS THE NEIGHBORHOOD LIKE SOMEONE WHO JUST HIT THE LOTTERY. "LOOK!" I SCREAMED AT EVERYONE. "THIS IS MY BABY, MY OWN DAUGHTER!"

IF YOU SEE A YOUNG, EXCITED, FEVERISH-LOOKING MAN LIKE THAT AROUND THE SASAZUKA AREA, PLEASE CONTACT THE NEAREST POLICE STATION AS SOON AS POSSIBLE. BECAUSE IT'S GOING TO BE ME. GUARANTEED.

SATOSHI WAGAHARA

Every volume of the manga impresses and stimulates me. It's packed with all kinds of famous scenes that never received illustrations in the novel versions, after all.

All the extra illustrations behind the cover are really well made too; I always get a kick out of those as well.

This volume marks Suzuno-san's debut, and I'm naturally going to take advantage!

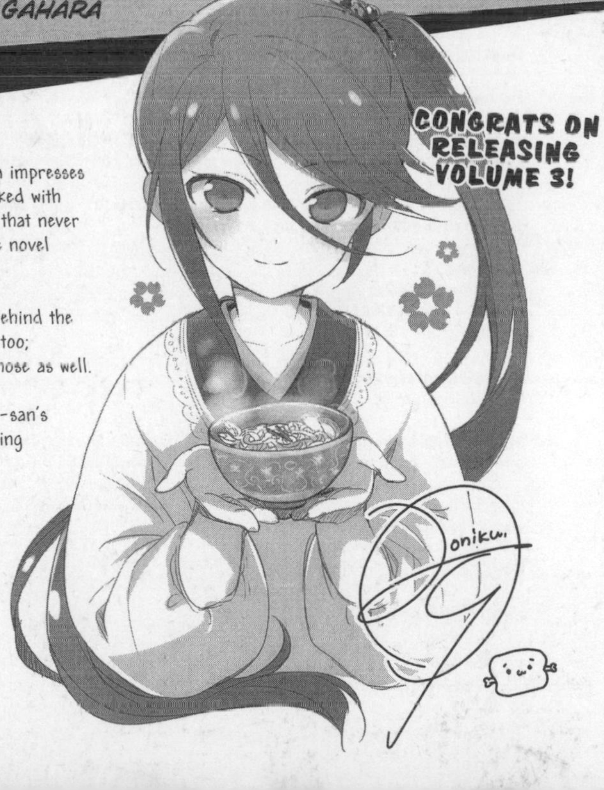
CONGRATS ON RELEASING VOLUME 3!

THE DEVIL IS A PART-TIMER! ③

ART: AKIO HIIRAGI
ORIGINAL STORY: SATOSHI WAGAHARA
CHARACTER DESIGN: 029 (ONIKU)

Translation: Kevin Gifford

Lettering: Brndn Blakeslee & Lys Blakeslee

HATARAKU MAOUSAMA! Vol. 3
© SATOSHI WAGAHARA / AKIO HIIRAGI 2013
All rights reserved.
Edited by ASCII MEDIA WORKS
First published in Japan in 2013 by KADOKAWA CORPORATION, Tokyo.
English translation rights arranged with KADOKAWA CORPORATION, Tokyo, through Tuttle-Mori Agency, Inc., Tokyo.

Translation © 2015 by Hachette Book Group, Inc.

Yen Press
Hachette Book Group
1290 Avenue of the Americas
New York, NY 10104

www.HachetteBookGroup.com
www.YenPress.com

Yen Press is an imprint of Hachette Book Group, Inc. The Yen Press name and logo are trademarks of Hachette Book Group, Inc.

The publisher is not responsible for websites (or their content) that are not owned by the publisher.

First Yen Press Edition: October 2015

ISBN: 978-0-316-38508-4

10 9 8 7 6 5 4 3 2 1

BVG

Printed in the United States of America